D0209646

THE STRUGGLE TO LIMIT GOVERNMENT

A MODERN POLITICAL HISTORY

THE STRUGGLE TO LIMIT GOVERNMENT

JOHN SAMPLES

CATO INSTITUTE
WASHINGTON, D.C.

Library of Congress Cataloging-in-Publication Data

Samples, John Curtis, 1956–
    The struggle to limit government : a modern political history / John
Samples.
      p. cm.
    Includes bibliographical references and index.
    ISBN 978-1-935308-28-7 (hardback: alk. paper)   1. Conservatism—
United States. 2. Federal government—United States. 3. Republican
Party (U.S. : 1954–) 4. Reagan, Ronald—Influence. 5. United States—
Politics and government—1945–1989. 6. United States—Politics and
government—1989– I. Title.

    JC573.2.U6S26 2010
    320.520973—dc22

                                                       2010008728

Printed in the United States of America.

CATO INSTITUTE
1000 Massachusetts Ave., N.W.
Washington, D.C. 20001
www.cato.org

Contents

Preface

This book began at a particular time and place. In December 2005, I attended the conference "The Conservative Movement: Its Past, Present, and Future," sponsored by the James Madison Program in American Ideals and Institutions at Princeton University. I recall a question posed by Larry Bartels, a political scientist at Princeton, to a panel of conservatives who had been active in the 1960s. The panel had been finding fault with the Bush administration. Bartels wondered why conservatism in power had fostered so many complaints from conservatives. His query suggested another question to me. Had the effort to limit government since the election of Ronald Reagan actually accomplished its goals? If not, why not? This book seeks to answer these questions.

This book concerns the political struggle to constrain the activities of the federal government. The federal government undertakes many tasks, not all of which are covered in this book. I have focused on spending and taxing largely because these activities provide our best, if imperfect, measure of the ambit of government. I have largely ignored the foreign policy of the federal government save for the 2003 war in Iraq, which I believe marked a departure in American foreign policy. I took my starting point from Reagan's aspirations in 1980. He did not propose to cut back defense spending or American foreign policy. He did promise to limit government. As it turned out, his foreign policy was restrained. The rest of the book will render my view about his promise to limit government.

I owe thanks to many people for helping with this book. My sincere appreciation goes first to Dan and Paula Cullen and the Opportunity Foundation for their generous support of this work. I appreciate their encouragement and patience, as the work went on longer than planned.

I also owe many debts to the Cato Institute. Studying the history of this era helped me appreciate the unique character of Cato. Ed Crane has managed to keep Cato involved with but not subsumed

1

by the politics of the period treated in this book. He also did a good job of *not* wondering why Samples was taking so long with the book. My other colleagues at Cato also contributed to these pages. They reflect perhaps a thousand conversations with Peter Van Doren, who was generous as always with his time and encyclopedic knowledge of the economics literature. Gene Healy and Justin Logan alerted me to necessary changes late in the writing of the book. My discussions with Bill Niskanen and Jagadeesh Gokhale informed many parts of this book. I also appreciate David Boaz's reading of several chapters.

While each of these people has helped with the book, they are not responsible for its contents or errors. That responsibility lies solely with the author. I also appreciate having access to the holdings of the Sheridan Libraries at Johns Hopkins University.

Finally, I would like to thank my wife for her support and patience. My son Colin also offered some insights into the modern political struggle in Washington. The struggle to sustain individual liberty will soon fall to him and his generation. *In libris libertas.*

1. Building the Old Regime

The politics a president seeks to make must start somewhere. Ronald Reagan sought to limit government. Before his presidency, government had grown in an era dominated by progressive ideas, institutions, and policies. These institutions and policies—what I call here the progressive regime—had persisted for more than two generations before Reagan's coming. That persistence was not a political accident. Master politicians constructed the progressive regime. Their handiwork would challenge and constrain Reagan's effort to limit government. A history of the renewed effort to limit government should begin by understanding how government got too big and why it tended to stay that way.

Progressive Ideas

The story of progressivism does not begin with politicians like Franklin Roosevelt or policies like Social Security. It begins with men and women of ideas moved by a desire to profoundly change the United States. Progressivism goes back to the 1880s. Its advocates included many prominent academics, journalists, and preachers.[1] We need not read them all. In 1909, a leading progressive journalist, Herbert Croly, published *The Promise of American Life*, which summarized the previous two decades of progressive thinking.[2] This book influenced presidents, including Theodore Roosevelt, who plumped for a New Nationalism that reflected Croly's ideas. Progressivism informed what would later be called the "religion of government" espoused by the New Deal.[3] In a word, progressives sought to reconstruct America.

What was Herbert Croly against? The American past: "The bondage from which Americans needed, and still need, emancipation is . . . from the evasions, the incoherence, the impatience, and the easy-going conformity of their own intellectual and moral traditions" (p. 426). Croly identified that tradition with a Jeffersonian aspiration to equal rights and liberty under law. That aspiration implied a political culture. Individuals create government to protect preexisting rights. Government is limited by that delegation of power and by constitutional safeguards for those rights. Government exists to protect liberty so that individuals might pursue the good life as they see fit. Life is not lived for collective ends or collective goods.

Croly recoiled from what he saw as the rampant individualism and purified selfishness fostered by Jeffersonian ideals (p. 49). Jeffersonian liberty did not lead to the correct pattern of economic outcomes: "the traditional American confidence in individual freedom has resulted in a morally and socially undesirable distribution of wealth" (p. 22). The wealthy did not morally deserve their wealth. Businessmen enjoy "economic privilege which enable them to wring profits from the increasing American market disproportionate to the value of their economic services" (p. 115). Society creates profits, and the state taxes citizens "to secure for the whole community those elements in value which are made by the community" (p. 380). More unjust still was the perpetuation of such inequality through inheritance. The son of the rich man did not earn his wealth. Such unearned largesse makes for men of "very inferior intellectual and moral caliber" who contribute little to the economic efficiency of the nation (p. 203). Croly also believed inequalities of wealth loosened the social bond, a bad thing in itself in a democracy (p. 204).

Croly thought America corrupt. The sins of the wealthy and businessmen polluted politics: business tries to corrupt government and sometimes succeeds (pp. 116–17, 130). Business is a symptom of a more general problem: Americans are motivated by self-interest in politics rather than a concern for others or for the national good. Politicians and their party machines run legislatures on the fuel of self-interest while ignoring the public good (p. 330). State legislatures were particularly corrupt (p. 320). Croly called labor unions "powerful and unscrupulous and well-organized special interests" that threaten the national interest (p. 131). The public was also corrupted by tradition and history. Americans remained devoted to Jeffersonian individualism. Public opinion obstructed necessary changes in the United States (pp. 120–21).

Croly wore two masks, the prophet preaching moral decay and the intellectual promising reasoned renewal. Both the prophet and the intellectual went unheard by the people who remained attached to their prejudices received from old Jefferson long ago. Jefferson's shortcomings were the shortcomings of American institutions and political culture. Americans had built their political house on an old and morally unstable foundation. The house needed to be reconstructed. It should become, as Croly's magazine proclaimed, a New Republic.

Americans wanted, according to Croly, "to become a worthier set of men" (p. 12). Such improvement would not happen by itself. Croly thought moral betterment should be planned rather than an outcome of "the chaotic individualism of our political and economic organization." The American state should become responsible "for the subordination of the individual to the demand of a dominant and constructive national purpose" (p. 23). Croly identifies the national purpose as realizing the democratic ideal (p. 6).[4] This nationalism in turn depended on reconstruction: "human nature can be raised to a higher level by an improvement in institutions and laws" (p. 399). The new American would be a person with a "special purpose" in life. Such a purpose would become "exclusive for the individual who adopts it, because of the single-minded and disinterested manner in which it is pursued" (p. 411). The word "disinterested" is crucial here. Quoting a fellow progressive, Croly says democracy ultimately demands that every man "shall think first of the state and next of himself. . . ." This subordination of the self to the collective is described as "the perfection of human nature" (p. 418).

Could humans be improved? Croly called for expanding the powers and activities of the central government (p. 152). The state should "increase the national spirit," and its leaders should consciously "promote the national welfare and those ideas and tendencies whereby it was imperiled" (p. 40). The state should constrain the selfish pursuit of wealth. Taxing inheritances both seizes undeserved gains and improves the character of the heirs (pp. 381–85). Croly says reconstruction permits "the preservation of the institution of private property in some form." The words "in some form" should give us pause, not least because Croly immediately demands "the radical transformation of [private property's] existing nature and influence." The state must assume "many functions now performed by individuals" and improve the distribution of wealth (p. 209). He looked forward to a time when "industry became organized under national control for the public benefit . . ." (pp. 415–16).

Then there was the value of a good war. Croly believed that nationalism and the national spirit might be enhanced in struggle against a foreign enemy; the War of 1812, for example, had increased a sense of national community among Americans (pp. 54–55). Later the Spanish-American War engendered a strong national feeling and "made Americans more sensitive to a national idea and more conscious of their national responsibilities" (p. 169). The war that forged the German nation in the 19th century brought "increased security, happiness, and opportunity of development for the whole German people." Croly concludes, "A war waged for an excellent purpose contributes more to human amelioration than a merely artificial peace . . ." (pp. 255–56). Croly is not an extreme warmonger; he does sense the costs of battle. Yet war had its advantages—"war may be and has been a useful and justifiable engine of national policy"—not least in forging a sense of national purpose (p. 255).

The nation also needed an elite to overcome its past. American political culture had fostered a "cordial distrust of the man of exceptional competence, training, or independence as a public official" (p. 170). These men of special vocation—progressives like Croly—acted from disinterested motives and thus embodied a "higher type of individuality," which itself was "indispensable to the fullness and intensity of American national life" (pp. 64–65). Croly wrote that "in a national state, it is the man of exceptional position, power, responsibility, and training who is most likely to be representative and efficient" (p. 57). "Training, special ability, or long experience" establishes a special claim to public office. The task of reconstruction itself offered such higher types a chance "for all sorts of stirring and responsible work, which would be demanded of individuals under the proposed plan of political and economic reorganization" (p. 406). These efficient and disinterested men would run the state and the economy as a way to build a national democracy. But what of public opinion and its devotion to individualism? Croly called for education: the nation should engage in a hands-on experience of national reconstruction: "its schooling consists chiefly in experimental collective action aimed at the realization of the collective purpose" (p. 407).

Croly hoped these leaders would transform the political culture and institutions of the United States. His new republic would not be a limited government. The national government would have the exclusive responsibility for "the regulation of commerce, the control of corporations, and the still more radical questions connected with the distribution of wealth and the prevention of poverty . . ." (p. 350). More generally, the federal government would be responsible for the national welfare.

Croly believed politics should raise human nature above its normal course by fostering a higher type of person who served the collective from disinterested motives. Such a person reveled in political engagement and government service. In contrast, the lives people live at liberty might turn out to be average, stuck in materialism and selfishness. They too would need to be improved. Government and politics should tend not only to the welfare of citizens but also to their souls. The "higher self" that he hoped would follow the triumph of progressivism showed little respect for the lives chosen by those who did not wish to join his new republic.

It is difficult not to see a religious impulse lurking in Croly's aspirations. The national purpose—the realization of the democratic ideal—was for him a sacred cause that "must be propagated by the Word and by that right arm of the Word, which is the Sword" (p. 21). What is the Sword? The Sword was the American state undertaking "official national action" (p. 24). This talk of the state (the Sword) pursuing a religious task (the Word) may disquiet readers in the 21st century, especially coming from an author who believes the "righteous use of superior force" brings order and peace to domestic politics (p. 312). But Croly was not a sectarian bent on suborning government to Christianity. He was far more interested in a new earth than a new heaven. The transformed nation of his imagination would serve as a substitute for the older biblical religions; philosophers would replace churchmen, and the older creeds would give way to a democratic faith.[5]

Croly assumed his progressive vision could be imposed on the struggle of interests that constitutes politics. He hoped to create a national identity for Americans that would transform their conception of their interests. The means to this transformation would be institutional reform, broadly understood. Croly understood that the progressive turn in American politics would not be merely a reform of this or that abuse. It would be the founding of a new set of institutions and policies, a new American regime, a reconstruction that would change the United States from a nation of individualists under a limited government to a progressive polity inhabited by disinterested citizens devoted to the nation.

Progressives in Power

Historians sometimes say that Franklin Roosevelt followed no guiding ideology in creating the New Deal. He is said to have been a pragmatic problem solver focused on the economic contraction that began in 1929. But Roosevelt worked in a political context informed by the ideas of progressivism, which has been called a foundation of the New Deal.[6] The profound economic problems of the early 1930s provided the atmosphere of crisis needed to turn progressive theories into New Deal practice. Croly had called for transforming the nation through institutional reform. Franklin Roosevelt and his allies sought to make good on that promise. In the 1930s, progressive ideals became a progressive regime.

A New National Purpose

Herbert Croly had admired war as a means to nation-building. In his inaugural address, Franklin Roosevelt compared fighting the economic crisis to "the emergency of war" and asked "the great army of the people" to fight the contraction "with a unity of duty hitherto invoked only in time of armed strife."[7] The appeal to war was more than a metaphor. The New Dealers believed the War Industries Board of 1918 had controlled and rationalized the economy. They "envisioned a much more forceful kind of national planning, rooted in the progressive era's faith in system, process and expertise."[8]

Congress responded by enacting the National Industrial Recovery Act in 1933. The law included a Public Works Administration and a right to organize labor. NIRA sought to imitate government management of the economy along the lines of the War Industries Board through a new agency, the National Recovery Administration. The new agency asserted control over large sectors of the economy by setting prices, wages, and production quotas.[9]

A similar innovation involved agriculture. In 1935, the farm population composed one-quarter of the total population of the nation.[10] The New Dealers undertook to set prices and production levels through the Agricultural Adjustment Act. The AAA did stabilize prices and reduce production, thereby giving benefits to producers at a cost to consumers. Moreover, the AAA had political effects:

farmers became much better organized and more skillful at influencing government.[11]

This expanding government met resistance in the courts. Before the New Deal, the U.S. Supreme Court opposed redistribution, protected liberty of contract, and generally upheld a strong right to private property. In doing so, "they were fulfilling the property-centered vision of society held by the founding generation."[12] This interpretation of the Constitution was incompatible with the New Deal, which claimed broad powers over property and economic activity. The Supreme Court responded in 1935 and 1936 by invalidating several acts of the New Deal, including the NRA. A majority of the Court judged that the NRA lay beyond Congress's power to regulate commerce and constituted an unconstitutional delegation of power from the legislature to the executive.[13] As for the Agricultural Adjustment Act, a Court majority concluded, "It is a statutory plan to regulate and control agricultural production, a matter beyond the powers delegated to the federal government."[14]

FDR responded by proposing to change the Supreme Court's decisions by changing the members of the Court. The defenders of constitutional constraint would quickly come to be outnumbered by the friends of state expansion. The "Court-packing plan" failed on the battlefield of public opinion but won the larger war in the judiciary. By 1941, the Supreme Court openly declared it would not enforce previously recognized constitutional limits on government regulation of business.[15] The New Deal consigned "property to a secondary status with only minimal constitutional protection, a development that allowed a wide sway for economic regulation."[16] The larger question remained—what would the federal government do with its new powers?

The New Dealers had initially focused on reconstruction rather than recovery. They distrusted capitalism and free markets and preferred industrial planning and cooperation of business and labor through cartels managed by the government. The New Dealers believed deflation came from too much competition and production. Consequently, the AAA tried to increase farm prices by cutting output, allowing cooperative marketing, and imposing target prices for commodities. The National Industrial Recovery Act enacted industrial codes that restricted competition and production while imposing labor market reforms. The economist Gene Smiley notes that "the NRA was attuned to discourage recovery, and that is exactly what it did."[17] An economic recovery that began in late 1933 stalled for two years; a more vigorous recovery began in late 1935 and lasted through the election. In 1937, a new depression in some ways more severe than the first commenced. At the end of Roosevelt's second term, the national economy had not recovered fully from the initial contraction of the early 1930s.[18]

Some New Dealers responded to these setbacks by calling for renewed efforts to "tame" and control capitalism through government oversight. These New Dealers developed "a common vision of government—a vision of capable, committed administrators who would seize control of state institutions, invigorate them, expand their powers when necessary, and make them permanent actors in the workings of the marketplace."[19] James Landis, a head of the Securities and Exchange Commission and the dean of Harvard Law School, recommended a rapid and extensive expansion of regulatory agencies to manage the economy. Landis had a deep faith in the "massed expertise of hundreds of administrators" to overcome the alleged shortcomings of markets.[20]

These same New Dealers came to believe that expertise could not conjure lasting solutions to the "conflict and instability" inherent in capitalism. The federal government—now called "the administrative state"—would continually intervene in the economy to solve public problems that could not finally be solved.[21] Croly and earlier progressives had hoped government would create a new and harmonious American republic. The New Dealers certainly shared Croly's desire for a powerful and intrusive national government. They doubted, however, that the state could create lasting solutions to economic problems.

This ambivalent faith in the state reflected the emerging view that the United States was a "mature economy." In the late 1930s, many New Dealers believed that Americans would never again enjoy economic growth similar to the half century of expansion before 1929: "The great age of industrial growth was finally over. The basic industries were built. No new sectors capable of matching railroads, steel, and automobiles as engines of expansion were likely to emerge."[22] A progressive government would be charged with fighting monopolies and ensuring the correct distribution of a limited economic pie. The New Deal apologist Stuart Chase opined that "economic systems are going to be run deliberately and directly for those ends which everybody knows they should be run for. . . . The welfare of the community will be paramount."[23] Progressivism, sans hope for a better future, had become an ideology of permanent planning and muddling through.

FDR had another choice. His advisers (above all, Alvin Hansen) thought government spending could increase consumer demand, which in turn would become the driving force for production and investment.[24] This doctrine—Keynesianism—appealed to progressives (and others) for many reasons. It offered a response to the economic contraction and a way to avoid future recessions. It put the economic expert at the center of government policy and national life. By following the advice of economists, the federal government could select—in theory at least—the correct policies to maximize mass consumption. Continual economic growth and high consumption would become the goals of progressivism.[25]

The experience of World War II belied the aspirations of the administrative state. The enemies of the United States in that war had administered their economies and societies; the experiences in Germany and Italy suggested unhappy possibilities for Americans if their state became too powerful. Advocates of the administrative state implemented some of their ideas during the war years. For example, the War Production Board, the central planning mechanism of the American effort, deeply disappointed liberal hopes. Of course, the war did not displace all articles of the progressive faith. After the war, state management of aggregate demand would be deemed essential to maximizing mass consumption.[26]

A nation's institutions include the rules of its political game.[27] The rules of the American political game changed. The federal government was free of traditional restraints and undertook new responsibilities. The Supreme Court no longer enforced constitutional constraints on government control of economic life. New Dealers had constructed an administrative state. FDR established a new goal (maximized consumption) for the national government. The older public philosophy had understood individual liberty and the pursuit of happiness to be the goal of government, to be achieved through the rule of law. The New Dealers thought the new goal of mass consumption implied activist government, and any weakness in the economy required political attention. In that sense, the goal of maximized consumption seemed biased toward government action. In time, however, theories and evidence might indicate the best means to reach the new goal of prosperity might be less government regulation and control. The successors to both the New Dealers and their opponents would be obligated to attain (or trying to attain) the most consumption possible. Political debate, especially the arguments during a presidential election, would henceforth turn on who could best "fix the economy."

Progressivism in practice changed progressivism in theory. Croly advocated institutional reform to reconstruct Americans morally and politically. The citizens of the New Republic would be devoted to collective good and to overcoming their individualism. The New Deal sought to transform the nation by extending the ambit of the federal government. But larger government did not necessarily translate into more publicly spirited citizens or policies. For example, the NRA benefited incumbent firms by restricting both entry into a sector and price competition.[28] The NRA experience raised the question of whether a government that extensively intervened in the economy would pursue a national good or simply some narrow interest of producers or other interest group. The federal government also appeared to lack the administrative capacity to run the economy.[29]

Keynesianism did not seek to change Americans in any way. It assumed that citizens wanted more of whatever they wanted and that such desires could be best fulfilled if the economy were controlled by experts in the new science of economics. But such control concerned what were called "aggregates," such as total demand. The individual consumer remained the same, even if the economy around him changed. Keynesianism did not seek to foster an individual's devotion to the nation or to some common good. It did not, pace Croly, seek to improve individuals or the nation. Managers of the economy, like businessmen, sought to give consumers what they wanted; it did not seek to improve what they wanted. Progressives would never wholly lose their religious fervor for social betterment, but they had in fact adapted their policies to individualism. This new goal changed politics.

Those who opposed FDR were forced to argue that their policies would bring prosperity. Insofar as consumption became the consensual end of government policies, other ideals—liberty and equality above all—could win debates only by becoming means to the end of prosperity.

Social Security Act of 1935

The Social Security Act of 1935 proved an enduring part of the New Deal. It offered public assistance to categories of people who were deemed incapable of work, among them the blind, the elderly, and dependent children. Over time, Aid to Families with Dependent Children would redistribute billions of dollars and prove to be a political failure. The act also set up two familiar programs: public pensions for the elderly and unemployment compensation. The pensions part—Social Security—would redistribute billions of dollars and remain popular into the 21st century. The design of Social Security would contribute to its public support and its persistence.

The economic problems of the 1930s increased the supply of proposals to redistribute money to the elderly. The programs were considered too expensive even by New Dealers.[30] These plans had a political flaw: they would be funded by general taxation. According to Arthur Altmeyer, an early leader of the Social Security Administration, FDR wanted the program to be "contributory social insurance" rather than a plan funded by general taxation. FDR believed contributions would make the program financially sound and morally acceptable; recipients would feel benefits were "a matter of earned right."[31] Liberals would complain then and now about the regressive nature of Social Security contributions. FDR saw the bigger, political picture: "We put those payroll contributions there so as to give the contributors a legal, moral, and political right to collect their pensions. . . . With those taxes in there, no damn politician can ever scrap my social security program."[32] The "earned rightness" of the program would come from its private character: people worked, paid wages, and received benefits. The design of these programs created the illusion of individual responsibility: you paid into a separate fund and received back the earnings from your investment.[33] The federal government would be "acting as a trustee for those who have built up rights under the system."[34] The "contribution-benefit" appearance also seemed to remove government from the picture. The beneficiary was not receiving government assistance. To be sure, the money came from the government, but its role was incidental in a system of "self-help."[35] Roosevelt's insistence on an appearance of individualism created a problem for the Committee on Economic Security, the group charged with creating Social Security. Its members assumed that the benefits of Social Security would be universal from the start. This conflicted with FDR's direction that the program be funded by contributions. Not everyone had made contributions, but everyone would receive benefits. The committee's staff offered a way out of the dilemma. In the early years of the program, contributions would exceed benefits for the contributors. A part of these "excess" contributions could be used to fund benefits to recipients who had not made any contributions. Eventually, the staff thought benefits would be larger than contributions, thereby creating a deficit in the program that could be covered by general revenues. However, the staff assured the committee that when deficits appeared, they would be offset by declines in federal subsidies to the states for old-age assistance, a redistributive program already in place. Committee members concluded that federal spending on older Americans would remain the same, despite a deficit in Social Security itself.[36] Those who designed Social Security assumed from the start it would *not* be self-financing in the long run. The committee sent a proposal to FDR that foresaw program deficits beginning in 1965.[37] Some later argued for a deficit financed by general revenue raised by a progressive income tax.[38]

Treasury Secretary Henry Morgenthau Jr. had doubts about the committee's work. When the committee's proposal reached FDR's desk early in 1935, Morgenthau apparently directed FDR's attention to the expected deficits of the program. FDR then backed off a bit, telling Secretary of Labor Frances Perkins that the plan should be only one among several Congress might consider. FDR also told Perkins to develop a proposal for a self-sustaining old-age insurance system. The Committee on Economic Security did so, and Morgenthau presented it to the House. The new self-sustaining plan included a higher initial tax rate that rose more sharply in less time. The plan was expected to build a reserve three times the size of the reserve foreseen by the initial proposal.[39] This plan with these terms passed into law.[40]

The plan had a certain political logic. Benefits would start in a few years, whereas the highest combined tax rate would not begin for 14 years.[41] Taxes would support benefits for at least a generation, and some estimates suggested solvency until 1980. And thereafter?

Experts told Congress that "the exact manner of financing the system 40 years hence did not need to be settled at the time."[42] The question of solvency could be left for another day and another generation of politicians and voters.

The future figured into the plan another way. The program would accumulate the reserves necessary to keep taxes and benefits in balance at least for a generation. What would stop members of Congress who were facing election in 2 years from spending the money needed to pay benefits in 20 years? This danger did not occur to the founders, or if it did, they might not have seen it as a risk.[43] They might also have believed younger voters would discipline legislators who spent the money needed for their pension.

The Social Security Board, a part of the executive branch, participated actively in the 1936 election on behalf of its program. The board distributed a pamphlet to labor union members "promising that workers would always get back more than they paid in taxes."[44] Thereafter for decades, Social Security was largely a policy fashioned by its administrators, progressive adepts all. The leadership of the agency consciously hired academics trained in social science. These officials believed—or came to believe, as the leadership sought to inculcate the "religion" of social insurance into its staff—Social Security should be universal, contributory, and ever expanding. One longtime employee would later speak of the staff's "religious zeal" in seeking to expand the program. Scholars studying the program have described the SSA personnel as zealots, "people who believe deeply in the program they are involved with and who feel it is their mission in life to expand it."[45] Yet these zealots also learned to become politicians.

These bureaucrats had the upper hand politically. As experts in recondite matters involving the program, Social Security administrators had a strong advantage over their critics, or indeed over neutral outsiders, including their nominal elected overseers.[46] In practice, this meant incoming administrations had little effective political control over the Social Security bureaucracy. They learned what they knew from the experts already running the show, and inevitably, what they learned was informed by the bureaucrats' commitment to the expansion of Social Security.[47] The experts also provided information and technical assistance to groups interested in expanding Social Security. The administrators were not especially partisan, but

15

they were hardly neutral in the political struggles over Social Security. They offered assistance and information to those who shared their ambition to expand the program incrementally.[48] Those who doubted the sanctity of social insurance received nothing but trouble from the agency. Finally, when Democrats held the presidency, the leaders of the Social Security Administration moved into political jobs to expand their program.[49] The Social Security agency was like an interest group or think tank created by the government, supported by a steady stream of "donations" in the form of taxes, nonpartisan in form but deeply devoted to the preservation and expansion of its part of the welfare state.[50]

The leaders of the SSA also had the advantage of having a long time horizon. They began their careers at the agency quite early.[51] Many of them served for two generations and many administrations. They were able to make compromises and yet continue gradually attaining their larger goals of comprehensive coverage and higher benefits. Their enduring dominance of this policy arena fostered a longer political perspective. They could start cheaply at a low cost and slowly build the program over decades.[52]

The electioneering of 1936 would become lobbying in subsequent years. Wilbur Cohen, a longtime Social Security operative, well understood that rhetoric could determine political choices by making "a lot of things palatable that might be unpalatable to economists."[53] The SSA contacted the public in many ways: laws, official speeches, press conferences, congressional testimony, and public materials. The agency personnel identified Social Security with insurance to foster public acceptance. They also argued that Social Security was a return on work and investment rather than public assistance given at the discretion of the government or a governing majority. Social Security taxes were not taxes but rather "premiums" or "contributions." The agency both encouraged the public to think of Social Security as insurance and believed they did in fact do so, before the agency's prompting. The agency at once defined the program for the public and claimed to be responding to what the public wanted.[54] Insurance also implied the existence of a contract that appeared sound and certain. Benefits were a matter of right, a just return for contributions. To cut benefits was to call into question the integrity of the government, a risky proposition for members of Congress facing reelection.[55]

The leaders of the Social Security Administration did not impose their program on unwilling politicians. Republican presidents sought political credit for the payments arriving monthly to voters. It may even be that governments divided between a Republican president and a Democratic Congress competed for voters, thereby increasing Social Security spending faster than would have happened under a unified government.[56] As for Congress: "Benefits were unambiguously popular, and the general thrust of congressional action was to deliver larger amounts of them, sooner, to more people."[57] For many years, benefits were distributed in a way that made it easy for members of Congress to claim credit. The benefits flowed often, generally in line with biennial elections, and were dispersed widely.[58]

The House Ways and Means Committee, under the domination of Wilbur Mills beginning in 1957, demanded that the program be self-supporting through a tax on payroll. Taxes rose gradually in small increments. They were imposed after an election, an increase in benefits having been delivered before the election.[59] The benefits seemed a natural return from the taxes, though the former probably made a deeper impression on myopic voters.

Yet a puzzle remains. Social Security taxes rose steadily for many years. Current benefits are paid by current workers who then receive benefits of some sort in the future. Why didn't these taxpayers resist such increases? They were a large group that were not organized and probably could not be organized. The institutions that might have organized protests against such taxation—for example, labor unions—supported Social Security.[60]

Taxes did not prove to be a problem for many years. In 1950, Congress amended the Social Security Act to bring 10 million more people into the system, to raise benefits by 77 percent, and to raise the tax rate slowly.[61] The system gradually expanded its coverage, adding more taxpayers than beneficiaries, thereby allowing early entrants to pay low tax rates and to receive relatively high returns in benefits.[62] Martha Derthick summarizes the attraction for members of Congress: "From a political point of view, this bias in favor of early entrants was the most important one in the system. It gave rise to no conflict. Early entrants paid low taxes and realized superb returns while late entrants who were victims of this bias could have no consciousness of it in the program's founding years."[63] If you came along early enough in the history of Social Security, you did indeed get something for nothing. Even those who paid taxes for a lifetime paid only enough to support retirees during their years working. They did not pay enough for their own benefits. The difference between what they paid and what they received defined the something for nothing.

The intergenerational character of Social Security attracted criticism from the start. M. Albert Linton, an insurance executive and adviser to the program, argued that Social Security would create a large and intolerable burden on future generations. He noted that Social Security's experts planned eventually to devote as much as 20 percent of taxable payroll to benefits, a sum that the generation of 1939 had not devoted to the program. Why should the current generation be allowed to commit future generations to a burden it would not impose on itself? Linton's admonition had no effect on Social Security officials. During a presentation about the future of the program, the council's chair, J. Douglas Brown, remarked, "*Aprés nous le deluge*."[64] Future generations could take care of themselves; the experts of 1939, not to mention the politicians running in 1940, had little interest in what happened to people who did not exist.

These arguments were also made in public. A few Republicans in Congress argued that Congress would not tax voters enough to make the program actuarially sound. This political reality meant that early entrants would pay far less into the system than the value of the benefits they received; the public would not understand the true costs on the whole of the program. John W. Byrnes, a Republican House member from Wisconsin, noted on the floor that the benefits granted by the amended law would require a 6.5 percent payroll tax. However, Congress would be taxing the current generation no more than 3 percent. Byrnes recognized the democratic logic behind the bill: "It would be the easiest thing in the world to vote for this bill, because you are giving the beneficiaries who are now on the rolls and who will go on the rolls within the next 20 or 25 years something for nothing; but you are not giving something for nothing to future generations. The future generations will pay for what you are giving away today for nothing. I just do not believe it is honest or sound to burden my children or your children on that basis. Remember we give them no voice whatever in what we are committing them to."[65]

Byrnes had cited two major criticisms of the law. It offered voters something for nothing, and it imposed costs on future generations who had no say about those costs. For most members of Congress, Byrnes's arguments pointed to advantages, not problems, with the new law. Giving people free money was a sure route to reelection, and in any case, if taxes had to rise over time, the changes might be slow and unlikely to motivate voters on election day, or at least not on an election day that would be experienced by any member sitting in Congress in October 1949. The identity between "having no say" and "bearing heavy costs" appealed to Congress.

The financing of Social Security had other advantages. It made the program appear to be self-supporting and thus fiscally responsible. In the short run, voters paid taxes and received benefits they assumed came from past taxes. But the system was not in balance over the long term largely because Congress had decided not to accumulate huge reserves. The long-term costs of the program thus faded from view for the current generation and became a matter of technical debate, of interest perhaps to experts but of little concern to most Americans.[66]

The political design of Social Security contributed to its persistence. In theory, the program could have been largely private in nature. The government could have mandated savings by individuals and families who would remain free to invest their money as they wished. Such plans, however, had one large political disadvantage. The current generation of recipients would not receive any benefits. But the current generation wanted such benefits; they were pushing hard in 1935 for the Townsend Plan, which promised immediate cash.[67] Absent benefits, they would have little reason to support the New Deal in coming elections. On the other hand, the plan that actually passed taxed the current generation to pay for benefits to retirees who had paid nothing or very little into the system. It provided, in other words, a windfall for current beneficiaries, a result that surely would attract their votes.

But those who paid the taxes to fund the system paid a cost and thus had a reason to vote against the New Deal. Of course, current taxpayers would have a moral (though not a legal) claim to benefits in the future, but such spending could not come out of their current taxes. *Their* taxes had gone to the current generation of recipients. The taxpayers of 1935 would thus depend on the taxpayers of, say,

1950 in the same way. Every generation thus has a claim to part of the income of a future generation. Each older cohort would expect, as FDR had surmised, that it deserved a return on the taxes paid earlier in life. The younger generation paying those taxes might wish to be free of such claims on its income, but any effort to end the program would deprive the older generation of its expected return. The cohort of recipients so deprived would thus have ample motivation to organize to protect its expected Social Security benefit. Politicians were not likely to resist such well-organized groups, short of being forced to do so by circumstances. The founders of Social Security left the future to take care of itself, and they had reason to believe the politics fostered by the program's design would ensure its persistence. It is difficult to believe that the master politicians behind the program had not designed Social Security spending to be uncontrollable.[68]

Circumstances required little from Congress for almost two generations. By 1967, almost all recipients had received far more from the program than they had paid in taxes. Among the more extreme winners in this electoral game was Ida Fuller of Brattleboro, Vermont, who paid $22 in taxes before retirement and received $20,000 in benefits.[69] No wonder Social Security had become a sacred cow politically. Who would not exchange his or her vote and modest payments for a tenfold return? Later Martha Derthick would concisely summarize the political appeal of Social Security:

> The program had a powerful appeal to self-interest—the self-interest of the taxpayer-voter, who got back far more in benefits than he paid in taxes, and the self-interests of the politician, who could all at once, provide the current taxpayer-voter with these excess benefits, defer high tax rates to a future generation, and proclaim with a straight face the "fiscal soundness" of the program.[70]

On the other hand, if the early tax rates and cost–benefit ratios had represented long-term costs rather than what would keep the program afloat until the next election, Social Security would have been less popular and less likely to continue.[71]

The men who made Social Security—FDR, Albert Altmeyer, and Wilbur Cohen—were progressives. Yet they were also politicians. They sought to design programs that appealed to self-interest and yet realized what they took to be progressive ideals. But they did not directly undertake the progressive goal of transforming Americans into nationalists devoted to the common good. They sold Social Security to the public as "insurance" that yielded payments justified by earlier contributions. The program thus appealed to a conservative conception of desert. It sought to create a stable and lasting redistribution of wealth in a nation whose citizens largely did not believe in redistributing wealth and might not persistently support a flat pension paid out of general taxes.

The leaders of the Social Security Administration were skillful players of incremental games; they focused on one innovation at a time and spoke often of financial soundness. They were "tireless, ingenious advocates of [Social Security], constantly engaged in an effort to influence public policy."[72] Their patience and skill were rewarded with "substantial change—even radical change" in American politics and society.[73] As Martha Derthick concluded, "The result of the many steps, each small in itself yet in practice irreversible, is a massive shift of resources to the public sector."[74] Social Security was popular and attracted the loyalty of voters.

The program both espoused and undermined the older Jeffersonian ideal of self-sufficiency that had so vexed Herbert Croly and his generation. Social Security fostered political dependence on the federal government. At the start of the program, one question concerned how much of a voter's retirement would be provided by the government. Experts called this ratio between public and private the "replacement rate." It might also have been called the "dependency rate" since it measured how much individuals would depend on government for their retirement income. From the start, program advocates sought a replacement rate of 50 percent. In the 1960s, much higher proportions would be proposed. The advocates for the program—above all, Robert M. Ball—believed Social Security should become the primary source of retirement income for all Americans.[75] From a political point of view, the larger the dependency on Social Security, the better: voters who depend on their elected officials for all retirement income are likely to be grateful on election day or, if not grateful, at least disposed to vote for the candidate most likely to protect their benefits. After all, if Social Security benefits are the only source of a person's retirement income, he or she has strong reason to support the program and whichever party offers the maximum benefits.

The older Jeffersonian tradition had also promised rule by consent of the governed. The politicians and administrators who directed the expansion of Social Security tried to avoid conflict. The early years of Social Security made their job easy. The program gave current voters more than they paid for and postponed any day of reckoning, all the while building an impressive political coalition. Yet the virtual absence of debate about the costs and benefits of the program over the decades provides "grounds for questioning the quality of the general consent to what government is doing."[76] It is difficult to imagine that the quality of the consent to the program mattered much to the architects of the American welfare state. The program was designed to persist and therefore change the nation in subtle and lasting ways, and it did so, by effectively precluding debate and excluding alternatives.

Summary

FDR and his allies failed to sustain systemic efforts at planning and regulating the private economy. They did, however, effectively jettison the older laissez-faire individualism in favor of federal intervention in pursuit of prosperity. Indeed, the New Deal fostered the expectation that the federal government and, above all, the president, should and could "run" the economy for the national welfare. Wealth, not liberty, had become the goal of governing, and progressive experts would maximize the nation's wealth. Another lasting political legacy of the New Deal was the government assuming responsibility for an old age secure from want. In the end, FDR had reconstructed American institutions without wholly creating a new American identity for its citizens. His efforts would be hard to undo, grounded as they were in the self-interest of voters and shaped in ways that favored continuing the status quo. Roosevelt had not reconstructed the nation, but he had laid a foundation on which others might continue building a new republic.

The Second New Deal

In the early days of his administration, Lyndon Johnson stated that John Kennedy had been too conservative. He intended to start his efforts not where Kennedy had left off but rather where FDR had stopped.[77] Like FDR, Johnson wished to remake American society in accord with progressive ideals. His grand scheme was the Great

Society, a reconstruction of the United States by the federal government. This grandiose aspect of his presidency would fail.

Like FDR, Johnson was also a political realist and skilled politician: he worked incrementally and realistically toward expanding the federal government. In his words, his extension of the progressive regime would grow like an individual from a small child into a beautiful woman. Voters would come to "love" the beautiful woman. When that happened, Johnson's regime would become "a permanent part of American life, more permanent even than the New Deal."[78]

Johnson intended to follow the Social Security model of expanding the state, though on a much larger scale. Fanciful metaphors aside, Johnson was convinced that "once programs to aid clientele groups get on the statute books, they survive despite underfunding and delays in implementing them."[79] Benefits would go to specific groups; the costs associated with the benefits would be spread across a much larger population. Johnson's efforts succeeded. From 1960 to 1980, the political scientist Paul Pierson writes, "the American state underwent a great transformation" marked by "a stunning expansion, ushering in a profound set of changes in American politics."[80]

Progressivism Renewed

Johnson first enunciated his vision of the Great Society on May 22, 1964, in a speech at the University of Michigan. The speech reveals LBJ's aspirations and his debt to progressivism.[81] The Declaration of Independence had stated, "Governments are instituted among men" to secure the rights to life, liberty, and the pursuit of happiness. Johnson took a different view: "The purpose of protecting the life of our Nation and preserving the liberty of our citizens is to pursue the happiness of our people. Our success in that pursuit is the test of our success as a Nation." Happiness is a collective good pursued collectively. Johnson saw two means to that collective end: the life of our Nation and the liberty of our citizens. The first is tautological; the second is a means to the collective happiness. Since liberty was secondary to collective happiness, the answer was clear. The subordination of individual liberty to some collective good—the national good for Croly, collective happiness for LBJ—had long defined the progressive project.

The collective happiness he promised would be more spiritual than material: "We have the opportunity to move not only toward the rich society and the powerful society, but upward to the Great Society . . . a place where the city of man serves not only the needs of the body and the demands of commerce but the desire for beauty and the hunger for community." LBJ denounced "soulless wealth," "unbridled growth," and men too concerned with "the quantity of their goods." Economic growth erodes "the precious and time honored values of community with neighbors and communion with nature. The loss of these values breeds loneliness and boredom and indifference."[82]

His speech heralded a new era. To the students and faculty of the University of Michigan, LBJ said: "You have the chance never before afforded to any people in any age. You can help build a society where the demands of morality, and the needs of the spirit, can be realized in the life of the Nation." They have, he concluded, the chance to build a new world. This expansive vision was not an artifact of the campaign trail. After his 1964 landslide, LBJ announced in Detroit, "We stand at the edge of the greatest era in the life of any nation." By then, the fever had spread. His ally, Sen. Joseph Clark of Pennsylvania, thought that LBJ's Great Society would "rid our civilization of the ills that have plagued mankind from the beginning of time."[83]

These men were dreaming, but after defeating Barry Goldwater by 434 electoral votes, Johnson's men possessed untrammeled power to realize their dreams. In 1965, Democrats held two-thirds of the House of Representatives and 68 percent of the U.S. Senate. LBJ seized the moment. During the 89th Congress, he requested 200 major pieces of legislation, and Congress passed 181 of them. As one historian noted, "The president's sweeping proposals sought to remedy almost every ill that was thought to afflict Americans and their nation."[84] Later a sympathetic historian would say 1965 and 1966 were unique, "a liberal interlude unmatched in the twentieth century, except perhaps for the mid-1930s."[85]

The Great Society would be created by Johnson's acumen and progressive experts. LBJ created at least 135 task forces "of the best brains in the country" to concoct the programs that composed his agenda. He believed that once experts had come up with solutions to what he took to be public problems, government need only provide the money to solve the problems.[86] Expertise would not be narrow and technical, content with solving specialized questions. Finally, Croly's "special men" with a higher calling would have a free hand in using state power to remake the nation again.

Reconstruction Again   Johnson sought to transform America by ending racial discrimination and poverty while rebuilding the cities. Each of these efforts quickly lost political support. I turn now to the details of LBJ's efforts and why they failed.

The civil rights movement and the laws it brought about in 1964 and 1965 are part of American history and folklore, and I will not attempt to recall them in any detail.[87] In announcing his War on Poverty, LBJ called students to do "battle to give every citizen the full equality which God enjoins and the law requires, whatever his belief, or race, or the color of his skin."[88] It remained to be seen what "full equality" meant in practice. One answer might have been "equality under law": individuals can expect to have their rights and contractual agreements impartially enforced by the courts. The other traditional answer might have been "equality of opportunity." Each individual has the right to make choices and pursue his or her idea of the good life free from coercion by others, including government officials.

The history of African Americans presented problems for these traditional conceptions of equality. For more than two centuries, laws of the United States had recognized African Americans as property rather than as people. Their status was a systematic departure from equality under law. Following emancipation, African Americans had lived under a system of mandated racial segregation that enacted status differences into law. LBJ appealed to the recognition that the earlier slavery and the more recent segregation profoundly affected the ability of many African Americans to act on opportunities.

Johnson's major civil rights achievements—the Voting Rights Act of 1965 and the Civil Rights Act of 1964—are in part compatible with the limited government philosophy. Both could be seen as constraints on governments, especially in the South. The Voting Rights Act sought to stop government officials from precluding African Americans from voting. The Civil Rights Act banned racial discrimination in any program receiving federal assistance, many of which would be public schools operated by the states. In these respects, both laws sought to give African Americans equal rights to the franchise and to a public good already provided. The law also helped break up discriminatory cartels among private employers, which were ultimately enforced by the threat (or reality) of collective violence.[89]

The civil rights battle did not stop with reforming government, however. Many private owners of restaurants, motels, theaters, and lunch counters refused to serve blacks. The Civil Rights Act of 1964 defined such property as a public accommodation involved in interstate commerce and thus subject to federal regulation. The law guaranteed access to such accommodations regardless of race, religion, or national origin.[90] The law forced some to engage in exchanges they wished to avoid. On the other hand, the law opened the possibility for an individual to stay at a motel or eat at a lunch counter. That possibility conveyed a power (not a liberty) to African Americans, and it did so by increasing the ambit of the state. The Civil Rights Act appeared constrained in aspiration. It did not require that 12 percent of customers at the restaurant in a month be African-American. Indeed, the Civil Rights Act prohibited the use of racial quotas.[91]

Other situations were more complex. Housing was segregated by race, although proving intentional discrimination remained difficult. Such segregation in turn created racial segregation in education since schools related to territory. These facts raised difficult questions for LBJ's administration. How great was the ambit of the federal government? Did it include regulation of private choices if the results of such choices were racially segregated neighborhoods? Or should the government simply forget about determining intent—hardly a plausible project in many cases—and focus on achieving the outcomes that presumably would have resulted if racial discrimination did not inform private choices?

As early as 1965, in a famous speech at Howard University, LBJ answered these questions.[92] Johnson argued that the civil rights movement and his administration needed to change:

> We seek not just freedom but opportunity. We seek not just legal equity but human ability, not just equality as a right and a theory but equality as a fact and equality as a result.

The last phrase "equality as a fact and equality as a result" anticipated affirmative action. But the speech was much more ambitious than that:

To this end equal opportunity is essential, but not enough, not enough. Men and women of all races are born with the same range of abilities. But ability is not just the product of birth. Ability is stretched or stunted by the family that you live with, and the neighborhood you live in—by the school you go to and the poverty or the richness of your surroundings. It is the product of a hundred unseen forces playing upon the little infant, the child, and finally the man.

To achieve equality in fact, government would have to set right (and thus control) the "hundred unseen forces" that resulted in inequality in fact. The federal government, he implied, must have an unconstrained ambit to remake the nation. The same would be true of Johnson's hope to end poverty.

Of all the ills that afflict humanity, poverty is the oldest. In 1964, public officials came to believe that experts could eliminate poverty. After all, the knowledge of natural scientists and engineers funded by Washington had put a man on the moon.[93] On March 16, 1964, LBJ sent a special message to Congress calling for a "national war on poverty."[94] War had been more than a metaphor for progressives for some time. In a war, the state focuses a society steadily on one goal, victory. At the end of the speech, LBJ affirmed the War on Poverty would be "a total commitment by this President, and this Congress, and this nation, to pursue victory over the most ancient of mankind's enemies." He also explicitly drew a parallel between past wars and his current request for a declaration: "On many historic occasions the President has requested from Congress the authority to move against forces which were endangering the well-being of our country. . . . On similar occasions in the past we have often been called upon to wage war against foreign enemies which threatened our freedom. Today we are asked to declare war on a domestic enemy which threatens the strength of our nation and the welfare of our people."

Johnson also appealed to the national hope for "an America in which every citizen shares all the opportunities of his society, in which every man has a chance to advance his welfare to the limit of his capacities." As FDR had done with Social Security, Johnson gestured toward the work ethic and striving for success. But such striving *creates* wealth; wars *destroy* people and property. Of course, war can end poverty in the traditional way by using force to take the property of the affluent and give it to the poor. But Johnson hardly wished to be seen as declaring war on middle-class and wealthy Americans. He hoped to persuade the constituents of Congress that everyone should oppose poverty by appealing to middle-class norms of work and success.

At the same time, Johnson was ambivalent. The abundance Americans enjoyed was not really earned; it was "granted." The word is revealing. Social Security had been based on deserving benefits as a matter of right; working and paying into the system led to a right to the payouts. Public assistance was "granted" by the government. LBJ appealed to work and desert and yet seemed to think the affluence of most Americans had been "granted" by something or someone apart from their work and effort. Near the end of the speech, Johnson remarked in passing that Congress had created the "abundance" that had been granted the American people.[95] The War on Poverty would extend that abundance to the poor. The War on Poverty, like the Great Society itself, honored American norms while implicitly rejecting them.

LBJ's policies reflected that ambivalence. The first attack on poverty would come through the Job Corps and other work-training programs. LBJ spoke of the "enlistment" of Job Corps trainees "whose background, health and education make them least fit for useful work." With the Job Corps, Johnson remained close to American political culture, which values education and self-improvement. The same could not be said of another major part of LBJ's domestic war, Community Action Programs. Each community would draw up "long-range plans for the attack on poverty" in its own locale. LBJ emphasized the local character of these plans; sergeants and privates would compose the plans for attacking poverty. Naturally, the generals would also have some say: 90 percent of the funding would come from the federal government. The rhetoric of local control did not rest easily with the reality of centralized spending (and, inevitably, control). But there was a deeper problem here. LBJ proposed that victory over poverty required a collective, communal response. The War on Poverty would be overseen by its general who oversaw the "national headquarters for the war against poverty," the Office of Economic Opportunity, which was part of the Office of the President.[96] The idea ran counter to individualism and, by implication, to limited government. But even more was needed. Where the poor lived had to be redone through a collective effort.

In the 1950s, urban renewal was thought to be the solution to "urban blight," the spread of slums and attendant decline in a city. Urban renewal thus implied clearing slums to make way for something better. From the enactment of the Housing Acts of 1949 and 1962, more than 146,000 families were displaced by federally assisted urban renewal. The other side of the federal effort was subsidized public housing. By the LBJ era, over 3 million Americans lived in public housing, two-thirds coming from federal efforts. By 1964, the slum clearances, however, were coming to be seen as a government failure.[97] LBJ responded to failure by concocting a grandiose, national plan to reconstruct urban areas and the people who live in them. Introducing his "model cities" bill to Congress, LBJ noted: "At least as vital as the dollar commitment for rebuilding and rehabilitation is the social program commitment. We must link our concern for the total welfare of the person, with our desire to improve the physical city in which he lives." The bill "envisioned a restructuring of the 'total environment' of the residents of 'demonstration' neighborhoods."[98]

This call to a national crusade to reconstruct the cities did not stop in Washington. One of the leaders of urban reconstruction was Richard Lee, mayor of New Haven, Connecticut, who said, "The haphazard growth of our cities and the years of neglect and lack of comprehensive planning have resulted not only in physical ugliness, chaos, and decay, they have also produced the terrible by-product of human waste and suffering." The key terms here are "total welfare of the person," "haphazard," and "comprehensive planning."[99] Critics of the bill correctly saw that it "aims at nothing less than a remaking of our cities according to Federal master plan" as a way to "undermine the American social and political fabric of local government and neighborhood schools." [100] The collective reconstruction of the cities would be planned and led by experts from Washington.[101]

How much would the crusade cost? The mayor of New York, John Lindsay, said, "New York City needed $331 billion [in 2007 dollars] from the Federal Government in the next decade to become 'thoroughly livable.' "[102] Detroit Mayor Jerome B. Cavanagh, a Democrat who served both as president of the National League of Cities and president of the U.S. Conference of Mayors, said his city alone needed $100 billion over the next decade, while cities in general required $3.3 trillion for renewal (both in 2007 dollars).[103]

How would Congress pay for the crusade? Sen. Abraham Ribicoff of Connecticut said, "We can't afford not to raise taxes, then sit back while the cities go up in flames." LBJ had declared war on poverty by proposing a tax cut. Now as his forces massed for the attack, his generals announced that the domestic war would be paid for by higher taxes. Talk had been cheap until the fall of 1966. Reality now began to set in.

Citizens might be willing to pay for a war for the national good, and the poverty warriors no doubt believed their grandiose crusade and concomitant sums would be for the good of the nation in the long run. They sometimes said as much. But they also left the impression that the war would be on behalf of part of the nation. Ribicoff tartly criticized an administration official for "talking about programs that helped suburbia—not the ones that are needed for the cities in the time in which we live." Ribicoff's hearings ostensibly focused on the problems of the cities but were in truth dominated by "the problems of the Negro."[104] Sen. Robert F. Kennedy (D-NY) testified that a program for cities must "attack the fundamental pathology of the ghetto—for unless the deprivation and alienation of the ghetto are eliminated, there is no hope for the city."[105]

Finally, Vietnam. We now think of the war in Vietnam as anything but progressive. The political left opposed the war and in time came to oppose the nation that made that war. The vitriol that accompanied the war in Vietnam has obscured its idealistic origins. Lyndon Johnson, the president most associated with the Vietnam War, saw it both as part of a global power struggle with the Soviet Union and as a crusade to bring the New Deal to Southeast Asia. In April 1965, LBJ laid out the nation's stake in Vietnam. Initially, the United States sought peace through resisting aggression. With peace and the independence of South Vietnam, world order would be affirmed and aggression punished. Johnson was repeating the lessons of Munich, lessons taken for granted by those who made (or aspired to make) foreign policy.

Just as Johnson's War on Poverty served as a means to the Great Society, the war in Vietnam would lead to a greater end. That larger goal was the same as the domestic goal: an end to poverty. "For what do the people of North Viet-Nam want? They want what their neighbors also desire: food for their hunger; health for their bodies; a chance to learn; progress for their country; and an end to the bondage of material misery." The means to that goal would be much the same as the domestic plan: government spending beginning with an initial commitment of $1 billion. Johnson referred twice to the New Deal. The Mekong Delta could produce even more electricity than the Tennessee Valley Authority. Vietnam could then develop as rural Texas had, with electricity provided by its own Rural Electrification Association. Thereafter, hope would replace hunger and so on.[106] In the president's mind, the struggle in Vietnam was informed by the theory and practice of progressivism.[107] Like his War on Poverty, the war in Vietnam sought to remake a society along progressive lines.

Johnson's efforts in civil rights and urban politics should not be judged a complete failure. The War on Poverty created organizations for mobilizing leftist interests. It provided future candidates for office with their first political experience.[108] It created a permanent brand loyalty for the Democratic Party among African Americans. That loyalty was no small matter for Democratic presidential candidates. In an electorate evenly divided, African-American voters provided fully 20 percent of a Democratic candidate's overall vote share.

Yet LBJ's anti-poverty and racial policies rapidly lost support. Unlike FDR, LBJ did little to adapt his vision of the good society to the dominant culture of liberty and individualism. Instead, Johnson called for a frontal assault on the older tradition. He redefined liberty as equality of opportunity and equality of result attained through a social science that would have to control choices that heretofore had been left to individuals, choices that had little to do directly with race. It should also be noted that everyone could expect Social Security benefits. Not everyone could expect benefits from Johnson's various wars of social reconstruction. Those efforts were made on behalf of minorities at a cost to majorities. More importantly, the minorities could expect such benefits, according to the administration, because they had been oppressed by the majority. It is not surprising that by the end of 1966, amid growing disorder, Johnson's vision of a transformed nation dedicated to progressive ends was troubled, though not defeated. He had departed from his own (and FDR's) practical political wisdom. LBJ's real contributions to building the progressive regime would embrace that wisdom.

Pragmatic Progressivism   Like FDR, LBJ believed the federal government should and could manage the macroeconomy toward maximum consumption. His economic advisers were convinced they knew how to end the business cycle.[109] LBJ agreed that his experts could fine-tune the economy leading to sustained high economic growth, which in turn would generate tax revenues that could be used by the state to build his "Great Society."[110] LBJ and his advisers planned to cut taxes by $10 billion in 1965 and 1966; they thought federal revenues would rise by $35 billion by 1970. They were wrong. Federal revenue rose to $150 billion in 1967, up from $94 billion in 1961. The economy was doing well by most measures, with robust growth and increases in disposable income.[111] Voters were happy with the prosperity, and Johnson had money to spend on his more pragmatic efforts to augment the old regime.

By the mid-1960s, Social Security was widely thought to be beyond political reproach. The source of its popularity was obvious. Robert Ball, head of Social Security for many years and its chief defender for many years more, testified in 1967 that beneficiaries and their employers to that point had paid for about 10 percent of the actuarial value of their benefits.[112] LBJ wished to rapidly increase Social Security benefits. He rejected a proposal for a 10 percent annual increase in benefits as too small. The administration proposed a 15 percent increase in benefits, a small increase in the tax rate, a large addition in the wage base, and a big increase in the minimum benefit. The House Ways and Means Committee, however, demurred, forcing a compromise. Congress enacted a 13 percent benefit increase along with an increase in the tax rate. Social Security's taxable base of income also rose by 63 percent between 1965 and 1967. Combined with the increase in the tax rate, this change increased the progressivity of the program.[113] The idea of Social Security also grew to include health care.

Advocates had proposed government provision of health insurance during the New Deal. FDR decided against the proposal, and it made little political headway over the next two decades. President Truman proposed a comprehensive program of health care. The American Medical Association actively opposed the law, and its efforts led in 1950 to the defeat of several members of Congress on the left. Yet the left was making headway. Even a Republican president would say in 1954: "There is nothing to be gained by shutting our eyes to the fact that all of our people are not getting the kind of medical care to which they are entitled. . . . [t]he American people are going to get that medical care in some form or other."[114] The sense of entitlement was growing along with the postwar economy.

Health insurance for the aged attracted significant opposition, not least from physicians who believed the program would compromise their interests in income and professional autonomy. Wilbur Mills, the longtime congressional godfather of social insurance, also opposed health insurance for many years. Mills believed the costs of government health insurance would be less predictable and in any case bore no relation to a voter's wages. The instability might jeopardize the financial foundation of Social Security.[115] Mills did not move on the issue until the Democratic landslide of 1964 added votes in Congress for a leftward turn.[116]

Mills ended up fashioning what became Medicare with his Republican Ways and Means colleague, John W. Byrnes. The Johnson administration proposed a relatively narrow bill that paid the costs of hospitalization and other services. It did not cover physician's fees. Byrnes responded for the GOP by proposing a more comprehensive bill that covered doctor fees, in part through general revenues. Mills then combined the Byrnes proposal with the administration's, producing a more comprehensive (and costly) bill than either Byrnes wanted or the administration expected.[117] Mills also added and expanded an earlier program to subsidize health care for the poor (now know as Medicaid).[118]

Medicare seemed to continue the substance and politics of Social Security. The elderly paid contributions to the federal government, which in turn provided benefits. The benefits of the program would be concentrated on one group, while the costs would largely be spread over the entire population. To contemporary analysts, it seemed likely that Medicare benefits, like Social Security, would automatically increase over time.[119]

The two programs differed in important ways. Social Security did not distinguish poor beneficiaries from the average recipient; Medicare encompassed Medicaid. Social Security taxed the current generation to pay for current benefits. Medicare taxed the current generation to pay for goods and services that in turn were thought to benefit current beneficiaries of the program. With Social Security, the federal government controlled both the raising of revenue (taxes) and the provision of benefits (writing checks). The federal government did not control the producers of the goods and services provided by Medicare.

In 1965, physicians appeared to have lost the battle and the war when Medicare became law. But appearances were deceiving. The law promised to pay physicians' "reasonable" charges largely without indicating exactly what might constitute "reasonable."[120] That determination would be left to politics, and the physicians could be reconciled to a bitter loss over the program if they lived to fight another day about what they would be paid for their services.

Medicare recipients and their health care providers both sought concentrated benefits whose costs were spread over the much larger number of taxpayers. The elderly had proved to be well organized during the history of Social Security. The physicians had proved themselves to be well organized and effective, even in defeat in 1965. Taxpayers were not well organized. Taxpayers seemed fated to perennial defeats at the hands of Medicare recipients and their doctors, druggists, and hospitals. But another possibility existed. What if politics produced "reasonable" charges for providers that, along with the demands of the elderly, pushed costs up enough to attract the notice and opposition of taxpayers?

Johnson had other spending plans. The Constitution did not sanction national authority over education, and the Tenth Amendment stated that powers not granted were retained by the states.[121] Nevertheless, Johnson set about centralizing power over education. The Great Society "witnessed federal intervention on an unprecedented scale into realms of educational policy that hitherto had been almost the exclusive preserve of state and local and private jurisdictions."[122] The Elementary and Secondary Education Act of 1965 established a major new inroad in state and local funding and control over education. All spending in ESEA programs was categorical; the federal government provided the money and stipulated how it should be spent.[123] Federal spending on education increased rapidly.[124]

The ESEA purported to be about providing opportunities to poor children, yet Title I of the act allocated money on the basis of a formula that meant 95 percent of all districts received federal aid.[125]

Almost all members of Congress would have some part of the education pie—enabling them to serve a piece or two at election time. The program sought in this way to foster general public support. A discrete group, the poor, would receive benefits along with the larger majority. Critics might complain that all the aid was not directed to those who needed it most. LBJ might have responded that the real choice was between some aid and none, not between some aid and all.

The ESEA was also an attempt to apply social science to poverty, an effort to fix the "unseen forces" affecting the poor. Title I of the ESEA provided for systematic evaluation of policy outcomes, with a special concern for the effects of spending on the poor. The evaluations were uniformly negative and pessimistic. Evaluations aside, Congress overwhelmingly approved a five-year, $50 billion reauthorization of the ESEA.[126] Whether the law improved the prospects of poor children seemed irrelevant to its political influence and success in Congress. According to historian Hugh Davis Graham, a major goal of the legislation appeared to be providing benefits to organized producer groups that benefit from federal education spending.[127] Once again, narrow groups would benefit while the costs of education spending would be spread across all taxpayers.

Education policy was not unique. Almost all the efforts of the Great Society promoted centralization of power in Washington. This tendency toward centralization was hardly an accident. From Croly onward, progressives had espoused a nationalist outlook that saw in Washington the capacity to solve national (and other) problems. In this regard, LBJ was more of a muchness: the Great Society embodied "the overriding national purpose of promoting the integrative, educational, economic, and redistributive goals of one vast commonwealth."[128]

Data on the period show how far Johnson's administration centralized power. Federal grant-in-aid spending for the states nearly doubled between 1964 and 1968, a 68 percent increase in real dollars. More grant programs (210) were enacted during Johnson's era than in all the years dating back to the first grant in 1879. Almost all these new grants were categorical, which means Washington dictated what would be done with the money. The influence fostered by the new spending reached a wider ambit of governments. The states were often bypassed to directly fund local, urban governments. The cities were not the only targets of largesse: cities, school districts, special districts, and some counties, as well as a range of nonprofit organizations, began receiving grants.[129]

LBJ and Congress used the federal money to control state policies. The Civil Rights Acts of 1964 and 1968, the Architectural Barriers Act of 1968, and the National Historic Preservation Act of 1966 established requirements that applied to all relevant grants. Hence, when a state wished to receive federal largesse under the Highway Beautification Act of 1965, it would have to meet the "crosscutting conditions" set out in these other laws or lose the money for building roads. The Water Quality Act (1965), the Wholesome Meat Act (1967), and the Wholesome Poultry Act (1968) established standards of policies and left the administration to the states, provided they adopted standards equal to those established by Washington.[130] Such coercive grant conditions empowered the national government.[131]

LBJ had created a centralized federalism that had become bigger (in dollars, programs, and jurisdictions involved), broader (in the range of government functions affected), and deeper (in terms of intrusive grant conditions and of the expanding number of recipient local governments and nonprofit organizations).[132] The number and size of federal grants made "the states more dependent on federal financial support."[133] That dependence was clear in the short run: federal money funded new spending for the states. In the long run, states and localities could offer benefits that were paid by taxes raised nationally. Once voters became accustomed to the benefits, state officials who wished to forgo the federal money faced a choice of withdrawing benefits from voters or taxing them to replace the federal spending. Of course, voters in the states were also national taxpayers, but those costs were diffused beyond any particular state while the losses associated with ending a program financed by a federal grant were concentrated. Johnson's progressive nationalism seemed firmly rooted in political reality.

Changing the institutions of the nation would be an important part of the progressive reconstruction of American political culture. But American minds also needed to be changed, and early progressives thought like-minded intellectuals would be able to shape public opinion toward their ends.[134] In that light, LBJ's funding of universities would create support for the regime. Johnson also created and funded a new broadcasting network administered and staffed by progressives.

In the 1960s and early 1970s, the baby boomers hit higher education.[135] Congress began to subsidize higher education with abandon. Between 1965 and 1968, the number of college students receiving federal aid doubled, while related spending tripled.[136] From 1955 through 1974, the absolute number of students rose from 2.5 million to 8.8 million, while the proportion of 18- to 24-year-olds attending college increased from 17.8 percent to 33.5 percent.[137] The proportion of the population older than 25 with bachelor's degrees had doubled from 1960 to 1980; it would rise another 50 percent from 1980 to 2000.[138] The total number of faculty increased by 77 percent from 1960 to 1980 and by 50 percent in the following decade.[139] These new faculty and their new students would become an important part of LBJ's contribution to the progressive regime.

University faculty shape public opinion in many ways. They teach the most capable young people in the nation. They do research and peer review that create bodies of expert knowledge that affects directly or indirectly what elites believe to be true about politics, society, and other matters. Academics write the history of the United States, thereby telling us what the nation has been for good and ill. They also tell us what Americans think about politics by interpreting contemporary public opinion. They serve as experts both in the media and in policymaking circles, recommending some policies and interpreting events for the public.[140] Academics also affect the future. They contrive and advocate visions of a just society, both in the classroom and in the public square.

Did the expansion of universities support Johnson's politics? Many professors believe in what might be called "academic ideology," or the belief that the research, teaching, and political speech of academics are disinterested, neutral, value-free, and hence in the public interest. Faced with charges of political bias, academics refer to the process of peer review, which enforces proper methods and logic on new research. No doubt peer review does constrain some biases, especially in experimental and quasi-experimental disciplines. But many parts of the university are not experimental or quantitative in nature, and peer review in those fields depends more on accepted practices and the judgment of reviewers. If academics generally share a set of political values, research that reflects those values may be less likely to run afoul of peer reviewers. Scholarship that questions progressive values and assumptions may seem strange or poorly done. Questions considered trivial from a progressive point of view may not be asked.

The institutional context of academics does not foster independent or critical thinking about progressivism. About three-quarters of college students go to public universities. Almost 70 percent of faculty work for public institutions and thus are government employees.[141] The material interests of most academics also tend toward expansive government. Tax cutting in the states after 1978 led to drops in relative spending on higher education from 1977 to 2000.[142] Private institutions also receive significant public funding, through both student loan guarantees and direct subsidies for research.

Professors also had other self-interested reasons to support Johnson's regime building. The Great Society rewarded academics with power over policy. In 1965, half the administration's legislative program task forces would be chaired by academics.[143] These appointments were also political: the task force members individually and collectively were expected to contribute to the president's election effort in 1964.[144] By the spring of 1966, LBJ was looking for new ideas to inform his agenda to reconstruct the nation. He sent his most important aides (including Joseph Califano) to ask sympathetic academics three questions: Where should the Great Society go from here? What are the needs still left unmet? What are the new problems we create by our solutions to the old problems? The group ultimately met with 81 professors and experts; their advice led to an "idea book" that went directly to LBJ.[145] Califano would create 11 new task forces composed of 112 members, 51 of whom came from universities.[146] LBJ gave the professors a chance to put their ideas and values into practice. The Johnson administration handed academics the power to formulate policies, which in turn fostered loyalty to the progressive regime. After all, the Johnson administration was "their" government, powerful people handing power to intellectuals.[147]

The rapid hiring of new professors in the 1960s and early 1970s had political consequences. Self-selection was part of the story. People drawn to teaching in universities had been to the left of center politically for some time.[148] But the events of the time changed people. In the 1960s, Vietnam and domestic struggles moved many young people to the left politically. Given the era and the population seeking an academic occupation, a university president choosing assistant professors at random would have moved his or her institution more to the left than it already was.[149]

Time would bring changes to American politics and perhaps even to the commitments of later generations of graduate students. Conservatism would matter more. Those changes, however, would have little effect on the political complexion of the university faculty after 1975, when the growth in new faculty essentially stopped.[150] Instead, as the 1960s' cohort gained tenure, the influence of the Great Society era academics would become permanent. The ratio of Democrats to Republicans in the social sciences would grow from three or four to one in the 1950s and 1960s to eight to one by 2003.[151] In 2003, this partisan difference would correspond to a general progressivism; academic Democrats are more likely to oppose laissez faire and support government activism on 18 political issues.[152] The young academics of 1968 would serve well as a permanent progressive force in American politics and society, a lasting legacy of Lyndon Johnson's skillful building of the progressive regime.

Progressives also controlled the evaluation of government programs. As early as 1901, Robert La Follette, the new governor of Wisconsin, brought together natural and social scientists into what would today be called a think tank. Those intellectuals devoted their research to advancing progressive innovations, including the use of primaries, initiatives, and referendums, as well as advanced measures for conservation.[153] This connection reached its zenith during the Johnson era:

> Through much of the twentieth century, a first generation of largely liberal policy institutes, led by the Brookings Institution and later the Urban Institute, contributed to the formulation of governmental social policy and therewith the creation of the American welfare state. Their role continued the trajectory of the Progressive Era by providing technical expertise to legislators and governmental agencies upon request. Guided by the social engineers of the New Deal and the Great Society, liberal think tanks evolved a style that was distinctly academic, generating quantitative analyses across a range of program activities.[154]

From 1965 to 1980, federal funding for poverty research rose from nearly $3 million to just under $200 million, most designated for the "applied" purposes of measurement, program evaluation, and policy analysis.[155]

The Great Society thus created institutions to evaluate its programs, institutions that would be filled with people that were sympathetic to the cause of progressivism. The employees of such institutions would not necessarily conclude that every progressive program attained its goals. They might be inclined to blame a program's shortcomings on the enemies of progressivism and to suggest alternatives in line with progressive goals. If so, program evaluation would tend to expand program spending even when identifying program failures. The institutions could also serve to criticize non-progressive proposals or analysis of the Johnson-era programs. The evaluation industry provided a more policy-oriented part of the progressive regime. Yet the regime required support from the general public and not just the intellectuals.

In politics, the set of issues talked about may be called the public agenda; the media greatly influence what is on the public agenda.[156] Given this influence on public opinion, it is not surprising that LBJ would include media as part of the progressive regime.

The First Amendment states that Congress shall make "no law" abridging freedom of the press. The private media are independent of the federal government and for current purposes will not be considered here as part of the progressive regime.[157] Unlike the religion clauses in the same amendment, the Constitution does not forbid establishing a national media. Before LBJ, progressives had made some headway on this front.[158] In 1968, Congress established a public corporation to support noncommercial educational television and radio broadcasting.[159] Some in Congress wondered, however, whether the purpose of the new corporation might be to shape public opinion by the federal government.[160] LBJ responded by telling Congress, "Noncommercial television and radio in America, even though supported by federal funds, must be absolutely free from any Federal Government interference over programming."[161] The law's advocates responded by prohibiting public broadcasting stations from supporting or opposing a candidate for office. The law also mandated that the Corporation for Public Broadcasting maintain "strict adherence to objectivity and balance in all programs or series of a controversial nature."[162]

The new network started slowly and did not spend its initial authorization in 1968. By 1969, CPB faced a new, Republican president. It hardly mattered. Over the next decade, CPB funding would rise rapidly.[163] Even if funding slowed, public broadcasting financed by all taxpayers had attained a secure place in the federal budget. At a time when PBS was one of four major networks in the United States, progressives had created a means to shape the public agenda in ways favorable to maintaining their programs and policies. Since this new medium, like the expanded academy, was a part of the government, its work could be counted on to affirm rather than undermine the progressive regime.

Summary   LBJ concluded near the end of his life that "everything I've worked for is ruined," an admission of political failure by a man who sought to permanently expand the progressive regime.[164] His hope to end public and private racial discrimination might be judged a qualified success. His larger, typically progressive vision of transforming the society by controlling social forces, determining equality of outcome, and remaking the cities rapidly lost support. The politics of helping the oppressed by punishing the oppressor did not leave lasting monuments to Johnson's ambitions. Who now runs for office promising an urban policy and equality of outcomes?

Yet LBJ was hardly a failure. He skillfully expanded the ambit of the federal government. Johnson and his allies, people like Wilbur Cohen, who had learned politics by building Social Security, believed the most important moment in the life of a program was its enactment. Even if funding were small, a program once started could build its basis of support in Congress and generate interest groups and executive agencies willing to work for expansion. The spending would matter a great deal to narrow constituencies and would impose hidden or minor costs on taxpayers or consumers. Given this political logic, the spending in question would persist, even if future elections somehow turned against progressives. Self-interest, if not a faith in progressivism, would sustain the federal ambit.

Johnson also created institutions that would shape public opinion in favor of the policies and values of the old regime. Professors, largely progressive in values and interest, would have a chance to convince every person seeking higher education of the virtues of the old regime. The new government media would daily persuade and mobilize its supporters.

LBJ would leave office in all but disgrace. The political regime he augmented would persist long after his passing.

Nixon

The presidential election of 1968 suggested the nation had turned a corner. The Democratic candidate, Hubert Humphrey, received 28 percent less of the vote than LBJ had obtained in 1964.[165] The new president was a Republican and at the time was deemed a conservative. The nation nonetheless continued on the track laid out by Roosevelt and Johnson toward a larger and more intrusive federal government.

Richard Nixon was a shrewd and highly successful politician. He cared little about political philosophy and a lot about winning the political game. Nixon had no particular desire to challenge progressivism and return to the older individualistic ethos.[166] He did hope to create a New Majority to replace the New Deal coalition, thereby altering the history of the nation. His strategy for reaching that goal would be ideologically flexible. The federal government would manage the economy to ensure prosperity. Nixon thought blue-collar Democrats could be turned into Republican voters by continuing to expand the New Deal's welfare state.[167] Nixon also saw that voters wanted more than economic benefits. They wanted a different kind of security that a president could offer in return for a vote: they wanted the security of knowing that their leaders affirmed the traditional moral order.

Economic Policies   Nixon governed domestically as if his administration was filled with progressives (which it was, in part).[168] Almost immediately after taking office, Nixon supported extending a 10 percent tax surcharge that was scheduled to expire. He also refused to cut government spending, contrary to the recommendations of his budget director. To get the tax surcharge through a Democratic Congress, Nixon agreed to repeal an investment tax credit (in effect, to raise some taxes on business). The taxes gleaned from the repeal would be used for revenue sharing with state and local governments, tax credits to stimulate private investment in poverty areas, and a guaranteed income for poor families. Nixon conceded one point after another to liberal Democrats so that he could enact a tax increase on business, which in turn would largely provide funds ostensibly to help the poor.[169] Despite the tax increases, spending outran revenue, and deficits appeared on the fiscal horizon. Nixon's advisers recommended more tax increases, including a value-added tax similar to a European model.[170]

In late 1971 and the election year of 1972, Nixon pumped up the domestic economy while fixing prices and wages. Internationally, he pursued a mercantilist policy that emphasized exports and American jobs. His treasury secretary, John Connally, summarized the new outlook: "My basic approach is that foreigners are out to screw us. Our job is to screw them first."[171] He paid Strom Thurmond for his support in 1968 by backing textile quotas (Thurmond's state, South Carolina, depended heavily on textile manufacturing).[172] Eventually, Connally proposed a package of wage and price controls, tax cuts, and closing the gold window, thereby bringing the Bretton Woods international monetary system to an end. He also proposed doubling a tax on imports. Connally believed the package would both devalue the dollar and give the United States leverage to force other nations to open up their markets in exchange for eliminating the border tax. Exports would rise, the domestic economy would get better, and blue-collar voters would love the harm done to foreigners. His mercantilism served the paramount end of Nixon's reelection.[173]

Nixon also imposed wage and price controls, which initially were quite popular with the public and much of the political class.[174] The popularity of the program engendered a new stage of controls. The administration decided to design and implement a comprehensive system of wage and price controls (Phase II), with authority over each given to separate boards. The wage part, a pay board, included labor and management representatives. The wage board began by approving a large settlement in coal mining while suppressing the price increase requested by the coal companies to match the wage increase. The public approved of the price suppression.[175] The controls also worked for a while and after a fashion. They had little effect on wages but temporarily suppressed prices by squeezing the profits of firms. After the controls were lifted, the businesses sought to restore their profit margins and prices took off again.[176]

Other regulations grew. Congress passed more regulatory programs from 1969 to 1974 than during any other era in American history, including the first five years of the New Deal. More generally, the decade after 1969 saw 130 major regulatory laws come out of Congress.[177] The growth during the 1960s and after came in social regulation, such as consumer protection, workplace health and safety, and the environment. Measured by major legislation enacting regulations, Paul Pierson finds that from 1964 to 1977, the federal government adopted 34 major regulatory laws. From 1947 to 1964, the number was 7; from 1977 to 2002, the number was 11. Hence, the 1964–1977 era saw about twice as many major regulatory laws enacted as the other four decades in what is called the postwar era.[178] Economic regulations, some dating from the New Deal, remained widespread. In 1977, 17 percent of U.S. gross national product was produced by fully regulated industries.[179] The federal government sought through this regulation to create, in Theodore Lowi's words, a "risk-free society."[180]

Much of this growth in regulation, like the more general expansion of government, came during the Nixon years. In 1969, President Richard Nixon created the Cabinet Committee on the Environment. In 1970, he signed separate bills creating a Council on Environmental Quality and an Office of Environmental Quality. Finally, Nixon established the Environmental Protection Agency through an executive reorganization.[181] In setting up the EPA, Nixon said: "We need to know more about the total environment—land, water and air. It also has become increasingly clear that only by reorganizing our Federal efforts can we develop that knowledge, and effectively ensure the protection, development and enhancement of the total environment itself." Creating EPA would organize "rationally and systematically" the environmental regulations of the federal government.[182] A total environment, totally understood, and totally enhanced.

Other regulations also grew quickly during Nixon's tenure, whether measured by the number of pages in the *Federal Register* or the cost of regulations. Theodore Lowi documented 40 new regulatory laws and programs enacted from 1970 to 1976. Republican presidents notwithstanding, the federal government kept "itself involved in every nook and cranny of American society." In the 1970s, both parties added to a "new and positive national state" largely because the federal government had become party to ever more local transactions.[183]

Regulation also became more comprehensive. The Occupational Safety and Health Administration applied to every employer in the country and sought "to provide a safe environment for employment by obliging the new agency to set standards the observance of which would produce the desired state of affairs." The Consumer Products Safety Commission was charged with creating "a safe environment for all consumers by having that agency set standards whose observance will create such an environment." Congress had delegated its authority to make law to these agencies that had the responsibility to achieve some universal end rather than to attack some specific evil.[184] The Environmental Protection Agency would follow the same model. EPA would protect the environment by abating pollution as administrators saw fit. Congress, Lowi notes, "knew nothing in the beginning and admitted it by mandating clean air and water to administrators to pursue entirely as they saw fit." Thereafter, neither the president nor Congress reviewed EPA's work.[185]

Congress and the administration also used tax preferences to manipulate the economy. In 1969, Congress reformed and cut federal taxes. As stated earlier, the new president sought to extend a 10 percent surtax enacted late in the Johnson administration. Congressional liberals balked and sought reform of the tax code among other things as the price for supporting the surtax. The subsequent law would later be described as the most thoroughgoing reform of the tax code in American history. The law gave substantial attention to tax preferences for private foundations and businesses; the oil and gas depletion allowance was cut by one-third. In the end, many preferences survived the changes in the code.[186] Congress did not revisit reforming the tax code during the rest of Nixon's presidency. The 1974 elections empowered liberal Democrats, who renewed the effort to cut back on tax preferences. Just before the 1976 election, Congress passed a tax bill that both increased and decreased the number of preferences.[187] Looking back, both the number and size of tax preferences continued to increase throughout the 1970s.[188]

Social Security Up to 1972, Social Security spending had grown slowly and surely. Increases in benefits followed a buildup in reserves; Congress could only spend, in other words, what the government already possessed. As the economy grew rapidly in the 1960s, Congress had more money to reward elderly voters. In 1972, Congress, led as always by the experts at the SSA, changed its assumptions. It now assumed that wages would rise in the future; the surpluses that would have come about in the future under the older assumption became available for distribution in 1972.[189] Moreover, the future increases convinced Congress that the system would remain financially stable despite the 20 percent increase.[190] Congress was in effect spending a windfall generated by a change in actuarial assumptions, a change pushed by the experts at SSA who had always favored expansion of the program. It also helped, to put it mildly, that the huge increase in benefits in 1972 entailed no increase in tax rates.[191]

The effect on Social Security spending was predictable. In 1969, benefits increased by 15 percent followed by a 10 percent increase in 1971. The binge ended with a 20 percent increase in 1972, which attracted overwhelming support in Congress and in an election year, the signature of a Republican president. Accounting for inflation, benefits rose by 23 percent during the period. The most striking of the lot was the 1972 increase of 20 percent. The U.S. Senate approved the increase by a vote of 82 to 4; the House voted 302 to 35 in its favor. Congress had few qualms about increasing benefits in an election year like 1972, but the 20 percent increase went even beyond expectations.[192] Between 1970 and 1975, Social Security expenditures more than doubled, rising from $32 billion to $67 billion, a rate that far exceeded the increase in the number of recipients and the consumer price index.[193]

The 1972 increase is not hard to understand. Wilbur Mills, the longtime congressional manager of Social Security, decided to run for president in 1972. His campaign began by proposing to increase Social Security benefits by 20 percent. Senator Frank Church of Idaho, working with the senior citizens' lobby, recruited 48 Senate cosponsors for the increase. Richard Nixon decided to catch the Social Security train as it left the station rather than fall beneath its wheels with a futile veto.[194] On election day, the increased benefits must have seemed wise on all sides. But with the new year came a novel problem for the program.

Civil Rights and Beyond   LBJ had promised equality of results to African Americans. His promise suggested his administration would bring about equality in fact rather than equality of opportunity. To accomplish that, the federal government would need both targets and the means to realize them. The administration would have taken control of labor markets, but such interventions would pose political and legal problems. For example, Title VI of the Civil Rights Act of 1964 outlawed racial quotas.

The story of affirmative action begins with the labor unions, specifically the construction trade unions that had long excluded African Americans and others as a way of creating scarcity and high wages for their members.[195] In 1965, Johnson signed Executive Order 11246, which committed the federal government to advancing "equal employment opportunity" in companies receiving federal contracts. The order espoused "affirmative action" but did not set out goals and timetables for allocating jobs to African Americans.[196] The Office of Federal Contract Compliance in the Department of Labor implemented the order and moved quickly toward an emphasis of outcomes. The Office's Philadelphia Plan awarded federal contracts to employers that set targets for hiring minorities. Officials argued that the Philadelphia Plan involved goals rather than quotas, but Elmer Staats, the U.S. comptroller, ruled that the plan imposed quotas, contrary to the will of Congress. The Johnson administration dropped the plan.[197]

The Nixon administration made good on Johnson's promise of equality in fact. Nixon himself endorsed numerical racial goals soon after his inauguration and thereafter a revised version of the Philadelphia Plan. George Schultz, Nixon's secretary of labor, wrote to executive agencies, "The affirmative action concept is indispensable to the President's domestic program."[198] Arthur Fletcher, an assistant secretary of labor, told reporters: "We must set goals, targets and timetables. The way we put a man on the moon in less than ten years was with goals, targets and timetables."[199] Congress disagreed; Staats again decided that the revised plan violated the Civil Rights Act.

The move toward social engineering by the Nixon administration should not have been surprising. Nixon himself had no great commitment to equality of opportunity as a guiding ideal. Campaigning for the presidency, he had said: "You've got to realize that these people in the ghettos have got to have more than an equal chance. They should be given a dividend."[200] Like LBJ, Nixon urged that African Americans be given "an extra start" in the race for jobs and wealth.[201] Some have seen in the Philadelphia Plan a Nixonian bid to split the Democratic Party by pitting the labor unions against the civil rights groups.[202] Yet the timing of support for the plan seems wrong if politics were the primary consideration, and in any case, as Nixon said privately, "With our constituency, we gained little on the [Philadelphia Plan]."[203] Indeed, Nixon would later deemphasize but not disavow affirmative action and the Philadelphia Plan during his bid for reelection in 1972.

By the end of his administration, affirmative action, like other programs, had developed support from Congress, executive agencies, and interest groups. Government and private efforts to promote hiring on the basis of race (along with university admissions) became part of public policy during the Nixon years. LBJ began the policy, but Nixon was "the sire of affirmative action."[204] The program would persist long after Nixon left the White House.

The Question of Order　　Most Americans equate the hope for individual liberty and limited government with conservatism. There is truth in that equation: the founding generation affirmed both liberty and limited government; in the United States, a respect for the past comports well with a love of liberty. More generally, however, those who value liberty above all—classical liberals—diverge from conservatives. Richard Nixon indicates one kind of divergence. He conserved and added to the legacy of Franklin Roosevelt and Lyndon Johnson. Nixon also differed from classical liberalism in another way. He thought government should promise to go beyond protecting rights to protecting against changes in the moral order.

In a society marked by liberty, individuals make choices and are responsible for the consequences of their choices. The relationships between and among individuals are governed by the agreements they make and the rights they have. The rights of others constrain my freedom. No one may legitimately murder others, restrain their liberty, or take their property. Such rights violations constitute crimes. Government exists in part to deter and punish such crimes in the larger context of the rule of law. Government should provide greater security for life, liberty, and property than exists in a state of nature, absent government. When Nixon came to the White House, governments throughout the nation were doing a poor job at that task. By some measures, crime doubled in the United States in the 1960s.[205] Civil order appeared to be losing out to private coercion in the United States.

Many conservatives agree that a society depends on the recognition and enforcement of individuals' rights. They add that the government should also recognize and enforce duties as defined by the moral traditions of a society, or what might be called its moral order. Here the conservative differs from the classical liberal, who would constrain liberty only to protect the rights of others. The conservative believes individuals should not diverge from the obligations of the

traditional moral order for reasons of rights or of social consequences. The conservative would argue that the government should
enforce those moral obligations and limit the liberty of the individual.[206] Before and during the Nixon administration, the traditional
moral order seemed under attack and losing out to what was known
as the counterculture. Individuals tried illegal drugs in pursuit of
pleasure or enlightenment. New sexual relationships reflected individual choices rather than traditional values. The older ways of
living that seemed beyond question had come into doubt. For many
Americans, the security offered by conventional morality seemed to
be slipping away toward moral chaos. The social world seemed
increasingly anomic.

Nixon recognized the political appeal of responding to both kinds
of insecurity. Nixon focused on what he called the social issues,
"race, crime, radical youth, cultural change." This emphasis led the
president to denounce drugs, crime, campus violence, and ghetto
riots.[207] Nixon understood that more was at stake than crime or
public disorder. He was promising to put government on the side
of the authority of traditional morality. He would both recognize
the truth of the traditional moral order and promise to enforce its
obligations.

Nixon the politician understood what classical liberals missed:
many voters considered the federal government a moral guide
whose endorsements or condemnations mattered. A government
that endorses or condemns would also be an active government,
one that provided moral security along with social security. The New
Majority Nixon hoped to build would be an amalgam of progressive
economic security and conservative moral security, the two delivered by a large and active federal government.

In many ways, 1974 was a year of triumph for progressives. They
drove their ancient nemesis, Richard Nixon, from the presidency,
thereby damaging Republican electoral prospects. Democratic candidates picked up 49 House seats and 4 Senate seats in the 1974
congressional elections. Many of these new members were more
progressive than the members they replaced. The 94th Congress
could override any vetoes by President Gerald Ford, assuming
voting along party lines.

Conclusion

From roughly 1935 to 1968, progressives turned their political
philosophy into a political regime, a set of institutions and policies.

The regime was largely constructed in two great bursts of lawmaking in the mid-1930s and the mid-1960s, both in response to a crisis. The New Deal took advantage of the economic collapse of the early 1930s, while the Great Society tried to expand government to deal with civil rights. What aspects of this regime were likely to persist and why?

Extensive government control of the economy and society did not fare well during this period. The National Recovery Administration failed politically and legally. The idea of an administrative state attracted progressive support for a time but failed to thrive. LBJ's plans to make war on poverty, rebuild the cities, and enforce patterns of outcomes by race were not dead by 1975, but each had attracted as much opposition as support. Each of these robust collective endeavors contravened individualism and concomitant limits on the scope of government. Each made government the center of society and the planner of the future. Progressive efforts to directly trans-form America could not overcome the older cultural commitment to individualism and limited government.

Yet progressives also succeeded when they adapted their pro-grams and policies to American political culture. The New Deal's most politically successful innovation—Social Security—offered recipients generous benefits that were "deserved" owing to earlier contributions; public pensions became a kind of reward for individual effort. Medicare followed the Social Security model. Progressives also established the goal of maximizing consumption for government policy. Compared to the NRA or the administrative state, maximizing consumption appealed to the individual: government did not intervene continually to control economic life. Instead, it purported to control the parameters of producing wealth, while individuals and firms actually did so. Future presidents would be expected to maximize consumption.

The progressive regime persisted because it offered benefits to significant numbers of voters. But what of the costs to fund those benefits? A growing postwar economy provided some of the fund-ing. Several programs, as we have seen, provided benefits to narrow constituencies while spreading the costs more broadly. Those constit-uencies have reason to care much more about their benefits than taxpayers or consumers have to resist the costs of any particular program or policy. The politics of concentrated benefits and diffuse costs would tend to conserve any increases in the size of government. Taking benefits away from highly organized constituencies would not garner votes in elections. The larger public of consumers and taxpayers would be unlikely to notice the improvement in their lives.

Did progressives realize their goal of transforming Americans and thereby America? They did not build a nation of citizens devoted to a collective good with no thought of individualism or liberty. Progressives did adapt to American culture as a means to establish and expand the role of government. Americans were changed as a result. They still espoused liberty and limited government, but they also had come to expect government largesse. Those benefits depended in turn on robust economic growth, which voters expected Washington to foster. If the federal government failed to meet that expectation, the old regime could fall into a crisis.

2. The Crisis of the Old Regime

By 1980, progressives had dominated the federal government for over four decades. The scope and spending of government had greatly increased during that time. Until the early 1970s, the progressive regime succeeded politically. Thereafter, it had "become increasingly vulnerable and crisis ridden over time." Its ideals and policy agenda no longer spoke to the problems of the late 1970s. It had become unstable, thereby creating new political prospects.[1] Ronald Reagan wanted to seize those possibilities to limit government and restore individual liberty. However, he faced several challenges to bringing fundamental change. Not least of these challenges was sheer inertia. Over 40 years, progressive leaders had designed their regime to persist politically. This chapter will examine the factors that both undermined and preserved the old regime as a way to gain perspective on Reagan's possibilities and limitations. I begin by considering the failures that brought the progressive regime to its crisis in the 1970s.

Two Wars Lost

Public support for the Vietnam War rapidly eroded in the late 1960s. By 1967, a slight majority doubted the wisdom of administration policy.[2] The political left had led the opposition to Vietnam, but the war's failure harmed progressivism. Until Vietnam, Americans believed in their government. The federal government was credited with saving the nation from the Great Depression and for protecting Americans from Hitler and communism.[3] Thereafter, public confidence in government dropped steadily for almost a generation. Vietnam and its aftermath, the Watergate scandal, taught Americans to distrust government and public officials. The government could not achieve the goals set by elected leaders, but progressivism at home and abroad required public faith in collective action.

Lyndon Johnson's other war quickly lost political support. The War on Poverty turned quickly against the older ethos of individualism and self-reliance. Welfare roles began rising rapidly as the poor organized to demand redistribution.[4] Legal aid to the poor provided by taxpayers sought to increase welfare benefits and loosen eligibility. In the same period, race riots broke out in many American cities, effectively ending the integrationist phase of the civil rights movement. Edward Berkowitz describes the political atmosphere of 1967: "Having engaged in an idealistic effort to end poverty and rehabilitate ghetto residents, the nation now found itself abused, tormented and threatened by the very people it has sought to help."[5]

The poor sought to overturn rather than participate in the political system. The Community Action Programs fostered the emerging black power movement, which continually challenged local officials.[6] These challenges angered urban mayors, the backbone of the Democratic Party, who demanded constraint on anti-poverty efforts.[7] Johnson mollified them for a while, but CAP proved politically implausible. In 1967, Congress tried to control public assistance and to cap welfare benefits.[8]

The War on Poverty had also failed as a policy. Even sympathetic analysts drew dire conclusions:

> Unprecedented generosity . . . had not made much of a dent in the poverty, dependency, delinquency, or despair against which the 1964 war had been declared. . . . few would disagree with the contention that the poverty gap remained wide and that if it had been narrowed at all, the narrowing was not commensurate to the decade's expenditure of effort and money. Indeed, there would probably be universal agreement that the impact of the War on Poverty had fallen far short of the claims of its designers.[9]

The War on Poverty had experienced its Tet Offensive.

The war in Vietnam did not persist beyond the Nixon administration. Although it benefited some interests—for example, defense producers—the costs of the war were not hidden. The War on Poverty lost momentum in the early 1970s, but this failure to reconstruct America or to ameliorate poverty more generally did not mean the programs themselves failed politically. The War on Poverty, afterall, funded good jobs in patronage machines for Washington representatives.[10] Had the poverty bureaucracy, failures notwithstanding, become entrenched?

Economic Decline

Progressivism meant the rule of experts, not least the rule of the macroeconomist. Keynesian experts advised a tax cut in 1964 to revive a stagnant economy. When rising employment and stable prices followed the tax cut, many decreed the end of the business cycle. In the 1960s, experts agreed the Phillips curve, specifying the tradeoff between inflation and unemployment, offered an important tool in managing the economy. A policymaker could in theory predict the price level if he decided to pump up the economy to lower unemployment.[11] The economy seemed to be a machine run by those who understood its workings and thus knew which dials to turn and buttons to press. Experience, however, slowly belied this optimistic assumption.

In the 1970s, the U.S. economy performed worse than it had in the 1960s and worse than other nations did in the 1970s. Per capita economic growth declined and unemployment rose. The rate of growth of labor productivity declined, a troubling development since increases in wealth came from productivity growth.[12] The United States experienced its only peacetime burst of inflation in the 1970s. The era saw three inflation cycles, each larger than the one before. The first peaked in 1969, the second in 1973 and 1974, and the third in 1980. Unemployment rose after each burst of inflation, and here too the unemployment rate was higher after each cycle. J. Bradford De Long recounted the economic harms associated with inflation and concluded that the inflation of the 1970s "may have been very expensive to the United States in terms of the associated reduction in human welfare."[13] In the late 1970s, both unemployment and inflation rose, a result that eluded the older Keynesian consensus. The simultaneous rise in prices and unemployment—stagflation—had deleterious effects on the legitimacy of the progressive regime. The experts who had been supremely confident in 1964 were completely stumped by 1978.

Paying for Spending

From 1954 to 1975, federal nondefense spending almost tripled as a share of gross domestic product. Federal spending also shifted from defense to domestic programs after 1965. State and local outlays nearly doubled from 1955 to 1975.[14] Spending on entitlements rapidly took up most federal outlays. Defense spending fell.[15] Congress essentially redirected spending from national defense to entitlements.[16] The shift toward entitlements complicated controlling spending. Entitlements were not subject to yearly appropriations by Congress. Such spending could therefore be reduced only by new authorizing legislation, a difficult task.[17] Annual appropriations governed less than half the budget by 1974, and 75 percent of federal spending was considered uncontrollable.[18]

The minders of Social Security in Congress and the Social Security Administration had long assured the public of the soundness of the program. In 1972, as Congress considered a 20 percent increase in Social Security, Wilbur Mills said, "I can assure the membership of this House that we will over the next 75 years take in each year more money than we will be paying out."[19] Robert M. Ball, the leading champion of Social Security, said in 1973 that its current tax rate would suffice into the next century. That same year, the Social Security account showed a deficit for the first time.[20] Beginning in 1975, Social Security began paying out more to recipients than government collected in taxes. Government actuaries foresaw persistent deficits that would deplete trust fund reserves in a few years. Congress responded by enacting the largest peacetime tax increase ever. Over the next 10 years, the tax increase more than tripled the maximum tax payment for middle- and upper-income taxpayers. Four years after Ball's assurance of soundness, Congress raised Social Security taxes by an additional $227 billion over the next decade.[21]

The history of Social Security may be divided into two eras. The first runs from 1935 to 1972 and is marked by relentless expansion in benefits, taxes, and covered groups of taxpayers. The program appeared to have a logic and momentum of its own: "If social security is a representative case . . ., aggrandizement is inherent in the modern welfare state, or at least inexorable."[22] The second era begins in 1973 with the appearance of deficits. During the first era, advocates of the program completely controlled its political agenda and outcomes. During the second, critics began to have some influence over public understanding of the program, if not over policy outcomes. The program was no longer beyond question. The core of the progressive regime was troubled, if not in trouble.

In 1960, taxpayers financed about 25 percent of health care spending; by 1970, the public funded 38 percent of health care spending. Ten years later, the public paid for 43 percent of all health care.[23] Both Medicare and Medicaid were passed in 1965. Five years later, the federal government was spending $13.8 billion on Medicare (in 2005 dollars). By Reagan's first year in office, Medicare spending had risen to $84.7 billion and was expected to rise to $181.2 by 1990. All in all, Medicare spending rose by 500 percent from 1970 to 1980.[24] During the first seven years of the program, physicians' incomes rose about 11 percent annually. Hospitals billed on a cost basis without any controls on the services provided.

Medicaid was even more open-ended in paying for health care[25] and also grew quickly. By 1971, annual spending had reached $6.5 billion with over 16 million enrollees. Spending increased on average by more than 50 percent each year during Medicaid's first five years, while enrollment grew at an average annual rate of nearly 33 percent. The number of covered services also grew so much so that per-enrollee growth exceeded general inflation by nearly 11 percentage points. The number of people receiving Medicaid benefits increased nearly 17 percent each year from 1967 to 1973, as welfare rolls also climbed.[26] In 1972, Congress amended the Social Security Act and expanded Medicaid eligibility. The amendments contributed to total spending growth, averaging 18 percent per year from 1972 to 1976. During the next five years, annual spending on the program grew by an average of 15 percent.[27]

During this period, the public and policymakers still expected to balance the federal budget. Transitory deficits might appear, but politicians and budget planners expected (and believed voters expected) government accounts would tend toward balance in a year or two. Taxes had to be raised more or less to keep up with the rapid increase in spending.

Before World War II, individual income taxes were about 1 percent of GDP, while corporate taxes averaged about 1.5 percent of GDP. The war changed all that: income taxes rose to 8 percent of GDP, and corporate taxes took up 7 percent of national wealth. When peace returned, taxes did not go down: income taxes remained at least 5.9 percent of GDP. From the Korean War until the late 1970s, income taxes equaled about 8 percent of GDP. State and local taxes grew during the 1960s and afterward, as did payroll for entitlements.[28]

As early as 1965, LBJ proposed a surtax to pay for the Great Society. The Democrats lost a large number of congressional seats in 1966, in part because of the higher taxes.[29] The resistance to taxes continued. In 1967, LBJ said in private to the researchers at the Urban Institute: "Here's the number one problem for anyone that wants to help their country and the people in it. You've got to figure out how to raise the taxes to pay for these social programs our people need and to rebuild our cities and educate our children. . . . What we need is someone smart enough to tell us how to convince the American people that they should ante up."[30] Even in the heyday of American progressivism, paying for the welfare state was not politically popular.[31]

Inflation provided part of the answer to LBJ's plea for more revenue. The inflation that plagued the United States during the 1970s was bad for the economy but good for government. Rising prices and wages pushed taxpayers into ever-higher tax brackets, thereby increasing government revenue without explicit tax increases. The budget deficit remained low relative to GDP, and experts could believe that surpluses would appear after three years. Members of Congress could propose new spending or lower taxes while assuming the resulting deficit would be short-lived.[32]

For all the subterfuge, most voters were paying higher taxes. Eugene Steuerle examined the average and marginal increases in taxes from 1960 to 1980 for the poor, the middle class, and the affluent. The average tax rate of those at twice the median income rose from 12 to 18 percent (a 50 percent increase), while their marginal rate about doubled (from 21 to 40 percent). Average rates for middle-income earners rose from 7 to just over 10 percent even though their marginal rate dropped from 20 to about 18 percent. For the poor, those at one-half the median income, average taxes rose from 1 to 5 percent, while their marginal rate rose from almost zero to 18 percent in 1980.[33] State income taxes and local property taxes also doubled during this period.[34] Exemptions from taxation declined in value. The growing burden of taxes was not confined to demonized groups like the affluent. Voters near the median and well below the median income were also paying higher taxes.[35] Relative to the nation's wealth, federal taxes grew especially quickly from 1976 to 1980.[36]

Eventually taxes did provoke resistance, most famously in California, where voters by a two to one margin used the initiative process to write Proposition 13 into the state's constitution. It reduced property taxes by almost 60 percent and decreased annual property tax revenues from about $12 billion to $5 billion. In November 1978, 12 other states constrained taxes or spending through direct democracy.[37]

Congress heard protests against ever-higher taxes and did little. An increase in Social Security taxes in 1977 caused an outcry, and the House Democratic Caucus voted overwhelmingly to instruct the Ways and Means Committee to substitute general revenues for the revenue from the planned tax increase. Ways and Means decided against the change, but Congress reduced individual income taxes to offset some of the rise in Social Security taxes and the effects of inflation on tax obligations. The law also cut corporate tax rates, especially for smaller businesses, and expanded investment tax credits to encourage purchase of new plants and equipment. The federal tax take continued to rise for most Americans.[38]

At the same time, the tax system was losing its legitimacy. Progressivism had promised policies pursuing "the common good" and similar goals. Government often gave some groups exemptions from taxes in exchange for specified conduct. The logic of tax provisions meant the benefits went to small, highly organized groups; indeed, the logic indicated that the general public would end up being the "someone else" that paid the taxes forgone. Often the provisions went to businesses, ostensibly to promote investment or to add jobs. Those who disliked commercial interests thus complained of "special interest" influence. The progressive tax code was not or understood to be a means by which the people pursued a common good. Rather, it was a corrupt plaything of narrow interests. To be sure, many people benefited from the corruption, but they noticed the special interests and ignored their own corruption.

In 1980, a plurality of respondents thought the federal income tax was the least fair tax, and the proportion of the public holding this view had doubled since 1972. This loss of faith went beyond affluent households. The federal income tax was losing support in the lower middle class, where almost one-half of the respondents named it as the least fair tax. Blue-collar employees were also more likely than the average American in 1980 to name the federal income tax as the least fair tax. Publicity about tax preferences (or loopholes) contributed to these declines in public support.[39] Big government required big revenues. By 1980, the federal government was losing support for its system of revenue collection.

The growth in spending and taxing forced reform of Congress. President Nixon argued that Congress "not only does not consider the total financial picture when it votes on a particular spending bill, it does not even contain a mechanism to do so if it wished." In his view, Congress simply appropriated money on various programs as if they were "unrelated and independent actions."[40] Nixon claimed the president could refuse to spend funds appropriated by Congress. Specifically, he sought discretion from Congress to curtail or eliminate programs if total federal spending exceeded \$250 billion in the 1973 budget. Denied such discretion, the administration began impounding appropriated money for federal programs. Nixon's impoundment provoked Congress to constrain executive authority over the budget.[41]

Until Nixon, few progressives had worried about the centralization of unchecked power in the presidency. FDR and LBJ had shown how a strong executive could enact progressive changes. In contrast, Congress seemed little more than an atavistic drag on needed change.[42] Nixon provoked second thoughts by suggesting a president might hamper, if not stop, the growth in federal spending and the scope of government. Congress responded to the Nixon crisis by reclaiming its power relative to the executive.

In 1974, Congress reformed its budget process to unify decisions about revenues and spending. Many members and much of the public hoped the new process would bring spending under control: "Republicans hoped that 'spenders,' forced into the glare of public scrutiny, would retreat from their nefarious schemes. Democrats hoped that the conservative priests of budget balance . . . would no longer be able to deceive the public with platitudes. Each believed that God, which in a democracy means the public, was on its side. The public . . . was on both sides and neither side."[43]

The 1974 budget reform reflected the recommendations of a Joint Study Committee on Budget Control appointed by Congress. This committee had recommended "restrictive rules if spending increases were proposed without compensatory revenues or spending reductions in other areas." Any action that violated these rules could be subject to a point of order; the rules could only be waived by a two-thirds vote of Congress. This rule did not become law.[44] The final reform of the process imposed few rules or restraints. Budget expert Aaron Wildavsky wrote of the 1974 act: "It created rules for Congress, but any majority can change such procedures. Legislation in the House and Senate often is considered under rules tailored for the occasion; amendment of those rules on the floor is common enough. Congressmen would follow the budget act's rules only if they wanted to do so; they would want to do so only if they valued the process itself more than they valued what they would lose if they obeyed the act."[45]

Regulatory Failure

A 1979 Economic Survey by the Organization for Economic and Cultural Development set out the emerging consensus among economists that "productivity growth has probably been slowed somewhat due to increased government regulations concerning industrial safety, health and environmental protection . . . as well as government regulation of specific industries." Research on economic regulation also indicated that deregulation and more competition would lower prices, an abiding concern given high inflation. Moreover, traditional justifications for economic regulation seemed wrong.[46]

Some experts concluded that regulations were often perverse. For generations, experts and the lay public alike had assumed that regulations served the public interest. By the late 1970s, many economists had concluded that regulations bestow privileges on private interests at some cost to the public. Barriers to entry and controlled prices—two common methods of economic regulation—appeared to stifle competition, raise prices to consumers, and increase profits and wages in regulated industries.[47]

Some regulatory failures mattered more than others. The price of oil rose rapidly in both 1973–74 and 1978–81. The earlier increase followed war in the Middle East and marked the apparent success of an embargo by major oil-producing nations, the Organization of Petroleum Exporting Countries. The second rise reflected the psychology of producers and consumers in the context of revolution and war involving Iran.[48] The federal government appeared helpless to mitigate the economic disruptions that followed the price increases. In fact, government policies made cyclical increases in energy costs worse through poor and inconsistent policies.[49]

Regulations created serious political problems. As early as 1969, the political scientist Theodore Lowi noted that Congress tended to write laws that identified general goals and delegated a broad authority to realize them to federal agencies. A struggle of interests followed the delegation of authority, leading to rules or regulations chosen by agency officials. Lowi saw in the 1960s and after the growth of an administrative state freed of congressional control. By allowing "policy without law," Congress created a federal regulatory authority that lacked democratic accountability or legitimacy.[50]

Writing as Reagan rose to the presidency, Lowi imagined a revised Constitution for this Second Republic of the United States. Its first article would state the purpose of government was "to provide domestic tranquility by reducing risk. . . . In order to fulfill this sacred obligation, the national government shall be deemed to have sufficient power to eliminate threats from the environment through regulation . . . ." Its preamble would say: "There ought to be a national presence in every aspect of the lives of American citizens. National power is no longer a necessary evil; it is a positive virtue."[51] In a later article, Lowi described how trying to create a risk-free society expanded the ambit of government:

> The delegation of power from the legislature is not merely a straightforward grant of authority to an agency. . . . The language of these broad statutes is a systems language, a language that attempts to incorporate all of the variables that characterize the problem and might tend to explain the existence of the problem and provide a lead toward a solution of the problem. . . . Embracing the system as the universe of analysis led policy makers to think of regulation as embracing that entire system. This imposed upon the perspective of the lawmaker and the administrator a complexity beyond human capacity— to incorporate for the purpose of empirical causal analysis and to control the totality of interdependent causes and effects.[52]

The ambit of regulation thus grew steadily and just as surely failed to achieve its grandiose promises.

Congress and some states began to deregulate several industries in the late 1970s. These changes were surprising. If industries benefited from regulation, deregulation would impose losses on the regulated, who in turn would fight to keep the regulation and related privileges. Since deregulation and competition would benefit a large, diffuse group—consumers—it seemed unlikely that regulations would ever be repealed. And yet some were.[53] Even Democrats, the party responsible for the old regime, had begun to have doubts about the value of regulation.[54]

The moral and practical decline of economic regulations undermined the theory and practice of the progressive regime. But those regulations had been imposed for four decades, providing benefits to the regulated if not to the public. Given that, how far could any president deregulate the American economy?

Civil and Social Rights

The federal government rapidly moved to enforce civil rights in the 1965 to 1975 era. Affirmative action, as discussed earlier, became a national policy under Nixon. The federal courts were charged with deciding what to do about de facto segregation. Judges ordered busing of students to achieve the desired racial compositions in schools throughout the nation.[55]

The ambitions of public officials seemed even larger than controlling outcomes in employment and schooling. Left to themselves, progressives argued, Americans were hopelessly racist and inegalitarian. Just as progressive governments had intervened in economic choices for decades, public officials now sought to use state power to change what people believed and said.[56]

Beyond race, the regime recognized and enforced new views of civil liberties. Here, the courts sometimes limited the power of governments. It prevented state governments from banning birth control and abortion, state and local law enforcement from nonphysically coercing criminal defendants, and state courts from convicting defendants without an attorney. But constraining state and local governments came at a price: "the nationalization of political authority and policy in the United States." The place of the federal government in daily life greatly expanded.[57]

The judiciary, or course, was not elected and, at best, could claim only limited democratic legitimacy. Of course, judges could claim to be enforcing constitutional rights against majorities or public officials. The new rights recognized by the Warren and Burger Courts seemed to be implications of the Constitution and its design for limited government; *Roe v. Wade*, for example, removed state authority from decisions about reproduction. Protections for defendants constrained collective coercion.

This appearance was misleading. The decisions reflected more a preference for equality than a concern about expansive government. *Roe* freed women's bodies from the power of their oppressor, men. Strengthening protections for criminal defendants could be seen as helping the poor against an oppressive society. These egalitarian efforts limited the power of the federal government, but only by accident.

The struggles to enforce the new social and civil rights added to the problems of progressivism in the 1970s. Busing of public school students fostered resistance, not all of it in the South. Affirmative action taught voters that progress for African Americans imposed losses on those from a European background. The protections for defendants often put progressives on the side of criminals just as crime was escalating nationwide. The right to choose an abortion divided the nation. It slowly became clear that "the oppressed" were not a majority, and their "oppressors" included much of the middle class.

After 1965, progressives defined oppression as the problem and government as the solution. The oppressors composed much of society, and, hence, the solution to oppression would be controlling and transforming society to end oppression. The federal government would have to reconstruct society and inevitably the people who made up the society. It would do so on behalf of the oppressed, a minority, and against the presumed oppressor, a majority. The political appeal of proposing policies intended to harm most of the society would prove to be limited.

Federalism

In the 1970s, the aggrandizement of the national government over the states continued. Daniel Elazar stated that "increasing federal preemption of state and local powers in the mid-1970s led to the notion that the federal government was the policymaker by right, while the states and localities were merely convenient administrative arms to be subjected to all kinds of federal regulations, whether authorized by Congress or not." By 1980, "the states were increasingly being excluded by federal preemption from fields that until relatively recently were considered their exclusive prerogative." In such matters, Elazar continued, Congress "has acted with no restraint," and the Supreme Court made little or no effort to restore some balance in the federal system.[58]

In federalism, as elsewhere, the public saw problems rather than promise. In the late 1970s, the Advisory Commission on Intergovernmental Relations surveyed political leaders and federalism experts of all political views and found four serious and systematic problems: (a) administrative failures, red tape, and tension between the levels of government; (b) poor performance and inadequate results; (c) excessive cost and waste; and (d) lack of adequate control and responsiveness through the political process.[59] As the ACIR authors observed, these shortcomings were not merely expert conclusions. The public was losing faith in the competence of the federal government to realize its promises.[60]

Legitimacy Problems

Progressivism in power had also lost its way morally. The call to national goals and collective effort lost its rationale:

> By 1976, the liberalism of Roosevelt had become a grab bag of special interest services all too vulnerable to political charges of burdening a troubled economy with bureaucratic overhead. Expedience eclipsed enthusiasm in the bond between the regime and the nation. Supporters of orthodoxy were placed on the defensive. The energies that once came from advancing great national purposes had dissipated. A rule of myopic sects defied the very notion of governmental authority.[61]

Much of the electorate had concluded: "Democrats lost both their rationale and their argument as to how spending programs, which served their constituents, were good for the whole nation."[62] In particular, African Americans and the poor had become interest groups that, like other such groups, would soon acquire the adjective "special" and thereby lose their previous moral authority.[63]

Progressives had long admired expertise in action to improve life through government. Critics now saw in the new generation of progressive experts a "New Class" of managers and intellectuals whose ambitions and ideals drove the expansion of the state ever deeper into the private sphere and civil society. The progressive regime had encouraged the public to see experts as the friend of the common man who would stand up for the "little guy" against the dangers posed by "big business" and "the robber barons." This view of the world neatly reconciled progressivism's admiration for expertise and "special men" with its democracy and the interests of ordinary people.

The New Class argument redefined these terms. The author Kevin Phillips, who had become famous by publishing *The Emerging Republican Majority* in 1969, criticized this emerging elite who had "a vested interest in change—in the unmooring of convention, in socioeconomic experiments, in the ongoing consumption of new ideas."[64] The managers of the War on Poverty were "upper-middle class graduates of elite universities who had been dazzled by trendy sociological theories" in the words of Irving Kristol, a leading neoconservative critic. The experts who wished to help ordinary people, according to the critics, were actually a privileged and moralistic elite who had little in common with most Americans.[65] By 1980, these critics were making headway in defining progressives as an elite hostile to the interests of most Americans.

Public opinion also turned on the regime. Progressive politicians promised that once in power they would provide security to voters and, in the long run, reconstruct American society on new foundations. For a time, the promises seemed to be fulfilled; wars were won and pensions grew well beyond contributions. By 1980, wars abroad had been lost, war had erupted inside American cities, and the economy was both unstable and beyond the ken of experts.

Public opinion began to doubt the capabilities of the federal government. At the pinnacle of progressivism, 76 percent of Americans said they trusted the federal government to do what is right "most of the time" or "just about always." Thereafter, the number declined steadily until 1980, when it fell to 25 percent.[66] Other measures of legitimacy fell also.[67] The older generation had grown up believing the end of the Great Depression and the victory in World War II were triumphs of the federal government. The postwar, younger cohort had a rather different experience of failed leaders and failing government.[68] By 1980, few people believed the federal government was either competent or righteous.

Behind the failure of trust in government lay a larger, more important failure of progressivism on its own terms. From Croly onward, progressives had hoped to transform the political culture of the United States away from the older individualism and toward a new unified nation. Americans would become less concerned with their liberty and their rights and instead become devoted to a larger collective good.

That change of mind did not happen; Americans had not been reconstructed. By 1975, citizens were no longer willing to "bear any burden" to win the Vietnam War or the War on Poverty. The public had not embraced redistribution of wealth as a means to equality of condition.[69] Support for an expansive state weakened. The number of people who wished to decrease government services and lower taxes rose, fell in the early Carter years, and then rose again in the second half of Carter's term. No more than 6 percent of the population wished to increase services and taxes in this era.[70]

Yet the regime had not completely lost public support. Survey researchers found that support for government services (and thus spending) had not changed much. Fewer people wished to pay for the services or believed their share of such costs were fair and thus legitimate. In late 1978, four scholars of public opinion concluded:

> Public attitudes vis-à-vis the contemporary state generally, and particularly toward its taxing and spending, are splendidly ambivalent. Specifically, there is real resistance to taxation and real support for the services which taxation provides.[71]

At the same time, many Americans believed that government wasted so many resources that current services could be provided with much smaller budgets, presumably with outlays consistent with their desire for lower taxes.[72]

As the 1970s ended, an increasing number of Americans wanted the same or perhaps increased services from government, wanted to pay less for such services, and believed the government was both incompetent in providing the services and unfair in raising revenue to pay for them. Many analysts noted this ambivalence; fewer asked whether the average American really wanted government services if he or she was unwilling to pay for them.

Lost Votes

In 1976, Jimmy Carter ran as an outsider who would take on "Washington." He was running against Watergate, but the progressive regime was located in Washington, D.C. Carter appeared to be a conservative to many in his party. He stood against the "interest group liberalism" that comprised the constituency groups of the Democratic Party, all of which wanted something from the federal government.[73] The electoral problems of the New Deal coalition, however, ran deeper than Carter's apparent heresies.

The New Deal coalition depended on reliable support from union members, urban dwellers, southerners, and others. The coalition ruptured from 1968 onward. A much larger proportion of African Americans began voting for Democrats after 1964. As late as 1960, both Kennedy and Nixon could strongly contest and hope to win the black vote. By 1980, that bloc went solidly to the Democrats, and blacks had "become a key component of the Democratic coalition." About the same time, Democratic support among southern whites declined sharply. Scholars discovered that the probability of Democratic identification for native southern whites declined from .77 in 1952 to .41 in 1988. On the other hand, the average probability of Republican identification for the same group rose from .09 in 1952 to .22 in 1988. Southern whites stopped giving majorities to Democratic presidential candidates after 1964.

This decline in Democratic identification among southern whites related to ideology, since the decline could be found almost exclusively among political conservatives. In 1972, 50 percent of southern conservatives still identified with the Democratic Party. By 1984, only 29 percent of white conservatives in the South were Democratic, while 61 percent were Republican.[74] Other scholars have found that the appeal of New Deal issues, programs, and groups declined during the 1970s.[75]

The Democratic coalition changed in other ways. In the 1960s, "a large proportion of the Democratic coalition was made up of white mainline and evangelical Protestants, and the Democratic coalition had a higher overall level of religious orthodoxy than did the Republican coalition."[76] As late as 1966, a majority of people who regularly attended a Protestant evangelical church identified with the Democratic Party. That proportion had declined steadily by 1980. The number of Roman Catholics who attended church regularly and identified as Democrats also declined during this period, though not as steeply. The Republicans began to have realistic hopes of winning the Catholic vote.[77]

Those who professed no religion or atheism—called seculars by scholars—became less Democratic in the early 1960s and maintained their level of commitment thereafter until 1980.[78] It should be noted that the Democratic loss of evangelical Protestants and Roman Catholics did not translate into gains among such voters for the GOP during the pre-Reagan era. Support among churchgoing evangelicals, for example, remained steady during this era, apart from a sharp drop from 1976 to 1978.[79] The same could be said of Roman Catholics.[80] The Republican coalition of 1980 remained about as religiously orthodox as it had been during the previous two decades. The Democrats, in contrast, had lost Evangelical support.

Challenges to Change

On July 15, 1979, President Carter gave a nationally televised address that would become known as the "malaise speech."[81] Carter said that the nation suffered a "crisis of confidence" manifested in "the growing doubt about the meaning of our own lives and in the loss of a unity of purpose for our Nation." Carter blamed materialism and consumption for the crisis he discerned: "We've discovered that owning things and consuming things does not satisfy our longing for meaning." The complaint was standard among critics of capitalism in the later 1970s. But the New Deal had given the federal government the job of maximizing consumption. Now Carter was saying a major purpose of progressives in power deprived life of meaning. What then could be the goal of progressive governance?

Carter's complaint about the loss of unity—"Why have we not been able to get together as a nation to resolve our serious energy problem?"—reveals much about the crisis of the old regime. Herbert Croly had defined national unity of purpose as the prime task of a rising progressive movement, a task taken up by FDR. Lyndon Johnson had called for the nation to unify as for war to create his Great Society. Carter had described the energy challenge as the "moral equivalent of war." But the nation had not unified for domestic battle. Progressives had failed at their most important task.

In July 1979, Jimmy Carter, the heir to FDR and LBJ, admitted that after 40 years of expanding government, progressives had brought neither progress nor unity. Carter's speech was candid about the failures of the old regime: the lost wars, the abuse of power by presidents, the damage done by inflation, and the weakness of the economy. Yet the crisis could not be dealt with by the federal government. Washington was isolated from Americans; leaders were offered "false claims and politics as usual", and the political system appeared "incapable of action." Congress was "twisted and pulled in every direction by hundreds of well-financed and powerful special interests." In the words of one scholar, Carter "all but declared the bankruptcy of the federal government as he found it."[82]

A moment of truth seemed to have arrived. The progressive regime appeared to be near its end, but appearances may have been deceiving. The economy was contracting. Nonetheless, the regime had not collapsed. The entitlement programs at its core were troubled and troubling, but they were not bankrupt. The economy was bad, but the question remained open whether things were bad enough to foster fundamental changes. Perhaps the solution to the ills of the age could be limited to a new set of managers that knew better than Carter how to guide the economy back to long-term growth. The obstacles to an alternative post-progressive government were formidable.

The American Constitution itself posed the greatest obstacle to fundamental changes in policy and institutions. In the United States, the status quo need only find the support of 40 votes in the Senate to block change.[83] If a president sympathized with progressives, a majority of two-thirds in both chambers of Congress would be required to overcome his veto. Support from the judiciary might also be required. Even state elected officials might matter to success depending on the issue. The American Founders intended to prevent rapid change, an institutional choice that might ironically frustrate reforms to revive their hope to limit the federal government.

The Democratic majority in Congress appeared entrenched whatever Carter's problems. The House had become resistant to electoral tides. Before the Civil War, the average length of service for an incumbent was two terms. Before the New Deal, the average was twice that. By 1976, the average incumbent had served for five terms.[84] To be sure, around 40 House seats had changed parties in 1964, 1966, and 1974. But most elections saw movements of 10 seats or fewer. In any case, a Republican majority in the House would require a swing of 60 seats in the 1980 election, a number unseen after World War II.

An entrenched Congress would not limit government, and the U.S. House of Representatives could constrain any leader wishing to cut back the national government.[85] The House had the constitutional obligation to begin all bills "raising revenue" and had to agree to any cuts in spending. The election following Watergate had brought to Congress many liberal Democrats. From the start, they preferred to spend more and expand government. They changed Congress by vitiating the power of committee chairs and congressional leaders. These new members wished to win reelection, which required delivering benefits to their constituents. The needs of the Watergate class added to the existing pressures for more spending.[86]

Even if Republicans somehow came to control Congress, a question remained, considering the Nixon and Eisenhower experiences, whether a new GOP majority would be willing to take apart the progressive regime and create something new.[87] Limiting government would be a real change for Americans, and the conservative temperament of Republicans tended to preserve the status quo.[88] In practice, Republicans had also favored expansions in government, not the least of which were Nixon's wage and price controls. Republicans wished to spend more on defense. Defense spending had declined throughout the 1970s; the Carter administration reversed that trend in its last two years.[89] The Republican preference for a more assertive foreign policy would require even larger defense budgets and thus more spending by the federal government.

The Democrats had been the party of more spending, and they had dominated politics for four decades.[90] The Democrats had used their long stay in power to entrench their programs and policies. As noted earlier, LBJ had passed as many laws as possible, assuming that programs once started would never cease to exist. The programs would develop support in society (interest groups), in executive agencies, and in congressional committees. Whether or not the programs achieved their goals or whether the nation as a whole wished to continue paying for the programs did not necessarily challenge Johnson's political logic. After all, those who benefited from the programs had more of a stake in their survival than voters at large had in saving a small sum of money by eliminating each program.[91] President Carter had tried to restrain federal spending in 1978 and failed.[92] Could a liberalizing president overcome the logic of special-interest politics?

A reformer's task might be even more daunting. Progressives had presented themselves as champions of the poor, but programs like Social Security and Medicare provided benefits to everyone, not just the poor. The progressive regime might be an example of Director's law. If most people are middle-class and policy is made by majority rule, most spending by government—transfers and subsidies—would go to the middle class.[93] Director's law implied that the poor would receive little from government (contrary to the progressive model), and the rich would provide the revenue for middle-class transfers and subsidies. The law might also explain other increases in the ambit of government: regulation might promise to protect the middle class from risks.

Director's law raised the uncomfortable possibility that the expansion of government might not be the work of special interests and welfare cheats. It might reflect the interests of the American middle class, long praised as part of the nation's uniqueness and assumed to be enamored with limited government. On this account, the federal government would be an instrument of a majority that that was neither progressive nor libertarian but rather relentlessly democratic. A government elected by a majority would have trouble denying the middle class its subsidies and security. The question of middle-class commitments suggested a deeper question about American political culture.

Conclusion

Progressivism had not fully reconstructed America. But that failure did not necessarily mean Americans would support dismantling the entire legacy of progressivism and embrace a revived world of liberty and risk. Progressive policies might have changed Americans enough to ensure the survival of the regime. Americans might have come to expect that the government should protect them from some risks associated with freedom. A president who restored liberty would ask voters to take on risks and renounce benefits, but did the voters care enough about liberty to endorse that tradeoff?

3. Revival and Reform

Jimmy Carter had a terrible 1980. The first week in February, a solid majority approved of his presidency. By early May, his approval rating stood at 43 percent. By the second half of July, he had lost half of those who had approved of his presidency early in the year. He bottomed out at 21 percent public approval. Not surprisingly, 52 percent of Democrats in one August survey wished the party would nominate someone else for the presidency. But Carter would be the nominee, problems notwithstanding.[1]

Oddly, given his approval rating, Carter did not seem certain to lose his reelection bid until late October. Six weeks before the election, a leading survey showed Carter slightly ahead of Reagan, 41 percent to 37 percent. The final preelection polls from Gallup and CBS News/*New York Times* showed Reagan barely in the lead and well within the margins of error. The Harris Poll found a clear Reagan advantage of 5 percentage points, slightly more than half his actual margin of victory. Many voters apparently made up their minds at the last minute to the benefit of candidate Reagan.[2]

Reagan won going away. In a race with a significant third-party candidate, Reagan won more than half the popular vote cast (50.7 percent), while Carter won only two out of five votes (41.0 percent). Reagan dominated the Electoral College. Carter carried only six states and carried only three—the District of Columbia, Georgia, and Rhode Island—by more than 10 percentage points. His other four wins were within 5 points. Reagan carried 24 states by more than 10 points and 14 states by more than 20 points.[3] Since the Civil War only two presidents—Taft in 1912 and Hoover in 1932—lost their reelection bids by larger popular votes than Carter. Even Hoover won more popular votes, relatively speaking, than Carter.[4]

Reagan's victory was remarkable in another way. He had long criticized the scope and activities of the federal government. As late as 1976, he was considered too conservative to be elected president. Reagan did not renounce his opposition to the old regime to legitimize his candidacy. He spoke of government being the problem and of the value of liberty. His victory suggested the progressive regime might give way to something at once new and old. As we shall see, Reagan had another side, more reformist, and adapted to the status quo. I turn now to what Reagan made of his 1980 victory. Did he change the old regime? Or did Reagan ultimately leave things as they were? Our story in this chapter will end with the 1982 elections, the first chance a national electorate had to pass on the Reagan performance.

The Mandate

What did Reagan's victory mean? Looking back, contemporary surveys provide some insights. In 1980, voters faced a choice between continuing the Carter administration and trying out an alternative. They rejected Carter.[5] Did they reject the old regime? Exit polls indicated that most people were thinking about economic issues when they voted in 1980: jobs, inflation, and a balanced budget. A majority disagreed that tax cuts were more important than a balanced budget. The "Needs of the Cities," a name for Great Society liberalism, was mentioned by 2 percent.[6]

During the campaign of 1980, the number of people who thought the nation should decrease spending rose, while support for more spending dropped by half. More Americans came to believe that the government regulated business too much.[7] Other surveys found support for reducing the level of government services and spending for those services. In October, those who favored "some decrease" or a "large decrease" in such spending composed 49 percent of the population. One-third of the nation favored increases.[8] The two parties as well as liberals and conservatives were divided about spending in predictable ways. Yet Republicans and conservatives became more convinced of the need for cuts as 1980 passed; their desire for reduction peaked in October.[9]

Polls also showed that Reagan had successfully presented himself as the candidate to constrain government. In September, a poll showed that 49 percent of the electorate believed Reagan wanted to cut government spending; 14 percent thought he wished to raise it.[10]

Reagan did wish to raise some government spending, in particular, spending on defense. The public shared this desire.[11] The number of people desiring an increase in defense spending in 1980 outnumbered those hoping for reductions by at least three to one.[12] Some analysis indicates Reagan's support for higher defense spending contributed more than any other factor to his victory.[13]

The general mood of the public helped Reagan. A political scientist, James Stimson, has measured the public's mood toward government over several decades. This index provides an answer to the question, "What does the public want government to do?" The higher the index, the more the public wants from government and vice versa. Stimson's mood index then fell steadily from 1964 to 1980, indicating declining support for more public spending.[14]

Looking back, the mood of public opinion also raised questions for Reagan. The trend in public opinion was moving toward Reagan. If we exclude those who wanted government spending to remain the same, the number of Americans who wanted more spending still slightly outnumbered those who did not in 1980. Many of the people who wanted more spending identified themselves as conservatives.[15] The public wanted less government than in the recent past. The question remained, how much less.

Public opinion about taxes shows a different picture. In general, about 45 percent of the electorate called for some tax reduction, and about half that group supported what would become the new administration's proposal.[16] Three-quarters of those who had an opinion about taxation wanted some relief. They did not constitute a majority of the population, but the same could be said of the much smaller proportion of voters who wanted government to do more. In both cases, a "third party" favored the status quo.

Later, Reagan would allude to a mandate: "The simple truth is that Congress heard the voice of the people, and they acted to carry out the will of the people."[17] Politicians generally claim to hear (and act on) the voice of the people. The truth is somewhat more complicated. An electoral mandate does not stand above political struggle's guiding outcomes; it is an outcome of struggle and deliberation, an effort to assign public meaning to an election. Reagan began to win that struggle for a mandate on election day; he finished his victory in the spring and summer of 1981. The economic difficulties of the 1970s, the tax revolt, and the loss of the U.S. Senate convinced members of Congress, not least the House Democratic leadership, that Reagan had won a mandate to reduce social spending in November 1980.[18] That conclusion would matter a great deal over the next year.

On election night 1980, Jeff Greenfield, a former aide to Robert Kennedy, said the election's results marked "the end of an idea whose time has passed. Liberalism has come unstuck. Now, compassion has to be separated from dependence on government programs."[19] Voters clearly wanted a conservative change in direction in policy.[20] But Reagan's victory did not imply a return to limited government. Conservatism might turn out to mean nothing more than more spending on different constituencies. It was also far from certain that a new coalition favoring limited government would replace the faltering New Deal alignment. The opportunity existed to create such a coalition, nothing more.[21] Much depended on the convictions and skills of Ronald Reagan.

Corruption and Reform

Ronald Reagan favored the individual over government.[22] On behalf of the individual, he wished to reduce the scope of government and to encourage profit making and commerce. Reagan's individualism recognized the importance of internal constraints for fostering and preserving individual liberty. Reagan appealed to the Protestant Ethic, which joined moral constraint to economic liberty. That ethic promised that if a person behaves well, strives hard, and saves, success will come. Capitalism and markets are not indifferent to those personal virtues; indeed, they depend on them.

When he announced his intention to run for president in 1979, Reagan said that the nation hoped "to see government once again the protector of our liberties, not the distributor of gifts and privilege."[23] Reagan believed government should ignore those who seek favors from government. He thought the decline of personal responsibility fostered both government spending and attendant deficits. Spending reflected waste and demands to live at the expense of others. Deficits, a consequence of spending, undermined self-reliance.[24] Reagan's individualism implied a moral conservatism; he reconciled constraint and liberty. Indeed, personal constraint was essential for political liberty. His views implied the progressive era had fostered moral decline in the nation.[25]

During the 1960s and after, another view of social mores took hold: to be truly free, the individual must be liberated from traditions of conduct endorsed by society or local communities, mores often backed by revelation. In contrast, the new morality assumed that neither society nor the government should control the truly free individual, who would act authentically according to his or her true self. This new conception of freedom denied that individual liberty consisted of freedom from coercion by public officials. If the government did nothing, the individual might still be a slave to tradition or religion. In this view, government should not leave people alone. Instead, it should actively liberate the individual from these local customs and superstition. The new freedom implied active, not limited, government.

Conservatives rejected this liberating vision of positive freedom. They did so because they were conservative; the 1960s' ideal rejected custom as an illegitimate constraint on the true self. Beyond that, conservatives offered different paths away from the 1960s' corruption.

Neoconservatives believed that the 1960s' ideal had corrupted Americans who had come to accept hedonism as a philosophy of life. Hedonism was not compatible with the work ethic, the foundation of American wealth.[26] If the people were corrupt, America needed a moral revival that would stave off decline.

But how could such a revival come about? A government that simply left people alone to pursue their interests and ideals would reflect, not overcome, the corruption of the nation. Perhaps government could foster the needed revival in bourgeois virtue. But a government fostering such virtue might not be a limited government. At the same time, a government whose citizens lacked such virtues could not be limited, for limited government demanded bourgeois constraints among the people.

Religious conservatives thought secularism was the problem. The 1960s embodied an aggressive attack on religious orthodoxy. The self, not the deity, should guide individual conduct. The individual freed from God rejected orthodoxy in favor of individual choice, that new order included both a right to choose abortion and open homosexuality.

Religious conservatives saw a revival of faith as part of the solution to secularism. But they also believed more was needed: government had advanced the cause of secularism; perhaps it could also cure the malady it had caused. At a minimum, as Nixon had shown, government might recognize the superiority of religious virtue over secular hedonism, a recognition that might foster respect for faith even from skeptics. A conservative government would not leave people alone; it would take sides in the enduring struggle between faith and doubt.

Reagan's first inaugural address stated that "government is not the solution to our problem." He juxtaposed progressivism in power founded on the belief that "government by an elite group is superior to government for, by, and of the people" with a government based on the consent of the governed. This criticism suggested a path that was both conservative and radical: "It is time to check and reverse the growth of government, which shows signs of having grown beyond the consent of the governed." The problems of the moment— Reagan spoke of a crisis—are "parallel and are proportionate to the intervention and intrusion in our lives that result from unnecessary and excessive growth of government." His address implied that cutting back government would solve the nation's problems. Corruption would perhaps heal itself.[27]

The issues that dominated later conservative politics—abortion and homosexual rights—had little practical meaning for the Reagan years. Reagan talked about ending abortion but spent little political capital on that task; the rights of gays were hardly an issue for Washington. He did not seek to use government to enforce disputed moral truths ultimately grounded in religious revelation.[28]

This skepticism toward government did include a concept of corruption, one that differed from other conservatives. The best articulation of this notion of corruption may be found in David Stockman. No one understood Reagan's promise and prospects better than Stockman, who had been a member of Congress from Michigan during the decade-long crisis of the old regime and won appointment as Reagan's director of the Office of Management and Budget. In that job, Stockman planned and guided through Congress Reagan's first and most important budget in 1981. Stockman later wrote a flawed but insightful book, *The Triumph of Politics*, which remains essential for understanding the first Reagan term.

A decisive moment in Stockman's political education came with a rereading of Theodore Lowi's *The End of Liberalism*. Stockman recalled:

> Here indeed was the conceptual formulation that revealed the true scheme of things. . . . Public policy was not a high-minded

nor even an ideological endeavor, but simply a potpourri of parochial claims proffered by private interests parading in governmental dress. Much of the vast enterprise of American government was invalid, suspect, malodorous. Its projects and ministrations were not spawned from higher principles, broad idealism, or even humanitarian sentimentality; they were simply the flotsam and jetsam of a flagrantly promiscuous politics, the booty and spoils of the organized thievery conducted within the desecrated halls of government.[29]

This indictment suggested both the moral force of the Reagan effort and its sober prospects. The progressive regime had corrupted the government, and perhaps the nation. Government put force behind private plunder. For Stockman, the central problem was not a loss of bourgeois virtue or religious faith. Government had become too big and thereby corrupt.

This analysis had some political advantages. It did not require government to foster virtue or faith. It required only that government do less. But those who benefited from "organized thievery" would resist a reduction in their spoils. Their resistance might not matter if most Americans supported limiting state power. Stockman's political experience fostered a faith in the people. He had run to represent Michigan's Fourth Congressional District with "absolute fidelity to a free-market, anti-statist position."[30] He won election with 60 percent of the vote.[31]

Stockman also took from his Michigan experience a faith in strong leadership. The voters would respond to a clear and principled call to revive limited government. Weak politicians had constructed and sustained the welfare state.[32] Reagan thus seemed to offer a way around a corrupt system. He appealed to broad moral themes—liberty and individualism—that were rarely disputed by Americans.[33] Reagan as leader could fashion a majority ready to affirm liberty by cutting back government, a majority not unlike Stockman's constituents in Michigan. The people were basically healthy in their mores. Once government was pared back, the virtues of the American people would reassert themselves, leading to a renewal of the nation's promise. Everything depended on the average American. But the old regime had been built on the votes of Americans for many years? What if the people too had become corrupt?

Reagan's Program

Beyond Reagan the man, there was Reagan the politician and leader. Presumably, his 1980 campaign program reflects his convictions as a public matter. In August 1979, Martin Anderson wrote Policy Memorandum No. 1, which laid out the economic agenda of the Reagan for President campaign.[34] This memo set out the "basic economic strategy" for the Reagan presidency. As we shall see, the memo provided a blueprint for most of the major initiatives of the Reagan administration over the next eight years. The hopes of the Reagan presidency can be found in this document. The document was both reformist and radical: it accepted and tried to undermine the old regime.

The memo identified inflation as the main domestic problem facing the United States, a problem caused mainly by the federal government's budget deficit. Anderson argued that the deficit might be dealt with by reducing the rate of growth of federal expenditures while stimulating the economy so that the private sector grew proportionately more than the public sector. Anderson was proposing a relative, not absolute, reduction in the size of government as measured by federal spending.[35] Over time, if the private sector grew, government would control less of the society and individual liberty would increase.[36] Anderson did not mention liberty as the reason for reducing the relative size of government. In fact, liberty did not appear to be the goal of the Reagan program.

Anderson set out several policies to increase economic growth. Tax rates that "are too high destroy incentives to earn, cripple productivity, lead to deficit financing and inflation, and create unemployment." He proposed reducing federal tax rates over three years. From the start, the Reagan campaign did not intend to actually reduce federal spending: "It is not necessary to cut federal spending from its current levels, but it is necessary to reduce the rate of increase in federal spending." Anderson believed this more limited target could be met by eliminating "waste and extravagance" in the federal budget, by establishing effective controls on federal spending, by giving the president line-item veto power over the budget, and by transferring some federal programs back to the states.

Policy Memorandum No. 1 did not suggest that cutting taxes would foster so much additional revenue for the government that spending need not be cut. The first two parts of the plan are cutting taxes and spending, which lead to the third part, a balanced budget. The memo associates cutting taxes with renewed economic growth and makes no mention of increased tax revenues.[37]

The Reagan administration should also foster growth by eliminating "counterproductive federal regulation." Deregulation can lead to "better products and services for consumers, lower prices, more jobs, more profits for business, and more tax revenues for government." Anderson estimated the costs of regulation to be $75 billion annually, which was passed on to consumers and hence contributed to inflation. But the memo also notes that "this does not mean we should eliminate all regulation now."

Anderson's memo did offer radical ways to constrain government: (a) a two-thirds majority to approve every major appropriations bill, (b) a constitutional limitation on the percentage of the people's earnings taken by the federal government, (c) devolution of spending and taxing, (d) a prohibition on wage and price controls, and (e) a constitutional requirement of a balanced budget. If these proposals were enacted, federal spending and taxing would face serious constraints.

Memorandum No. 1 denies the benevolence of government and seeks to reduce its ambit, thereby increasing liberty. But increasing liberty was not the goal of Reagan's economic program. It was a means to restart economic growth, to produce higher standards of living, and generally to overcome the pessimism of the time. Memorandum No. 1 set out a strategy to attain the goal that had long defined the old regime: maximizing consumption. The means to that end differed deeply from the policies of the previous years, but the goal of "rapidly rising standards of living" had apparently become beyond dispute, at least during an election campaign.[38]

Before Reagan, candidates and groups had resisted progressivism in the name of liberty and limited government. Their efforts had failed.[39] Reagan probably agreed with the earlier efforts, and all things being equal might have run on a platform of restoring liberty, quite apart from its economic benefits. But all things were not equal. The campaign apparently believed that a candidate devoted to liberty could only win the presidency by linking limiting government to increases in economic well-being. The economic disorders of the 1970s and previous years created an opportunity. Liberty might be restored not because voters wanted to be free of government but rather because they wanted to be richer, and the federal government had turned out to be an obstacle to that desire.

Ronald Reagan sought to reduce the scope of government largely as a means to promote prosperity and thereby win elections. He did not primarily seek to undo the old regime and establish a renewal of liberty or virtue. Reagan believed what most Americans believed by 1980: the government had gotten too big and thus incompetent to foster economic growth. His most radical changes were secondary hopes rather than initial proposals. Reagan from the start was primarily a reformer of the old regime. He believed, not without reason, that the electorate would not tolerate anything more.

The First Seven Months

The American Constitution, designed to constrain political threats to liberty, threatened Reagan's reforms. Both chambers of Congress must approve a president's proposals, not least in matters of spending and taxing. Members of the two chambers represent different constituencies. When Reagan came to office, the Senate had just come under Republican control, but the House remained in Democratic hands and was ably led by Tip O'Neill, a resourceful poll from Massachusetts and exemplar of the old regime's mantra of "tax and tax, spend and spend, elect and elect." Moreover, Reagan could not count on a unified GOP. Many Republicans had found success under the old regime; they were unlikely to support reducing the size of government. Failure seemed to await Reagan.

The New Congress

From the start, David Stockman realized that the initial Reagan budget proposal "depended on the willingness of the politicians to turn against their own handiwork." Why would they do so? Perhaps they might accept that Reagan had a mandate to reduce federal spending. If in fact they did accept that mandate, more would be needed to actually restrain spending. Reagan's initial proposal showed a federal deficit of $110 billion, or about 13 percent of spending. He assumed members would conclude that such a deficit would cause them trouble on election day. Hence, spending would have to be cut because members would face two unpleasant choices, and cutting programs would be the best of the worst.[40]

The 1980 election gave Stockman something to work with on Capitol Hill. Republicans did well in congressional elections, though not as well as Reagan did. The GOP picked up 12 seats from the Democrats in the Senate, thereby taking control with a 53-seat majority. Democrats had 24 Senate seats at stake and lost half of them; the 10 GOP seats remained with that party.[41] In the House, the Democrats retained control by 26 seats but nonetheless lost 33 seats in the election, leaving the Democrats with a majority of 51 votes. A unified Republican majority needed to attract only 26 Democrats to pass a bill.[42]

Congressional elections, like the Reagan-Carter contest, continued some familiar trends. The percentage of southern seats in the House held by Democrats declined from 94 percent in 1953 to 64 percent in 1981. In 1953, the Democrats held all the Senate seats from the South, but in 1981 they controlled only 55 percent. The South was no longer a Democratic stronghold for presidential or congressional candidates.[43] Republicans were still some distance from taking Congress, but the foundations of the long Democratic hegemony over that institution were eroding.

The 1980 election shifted Congress to the right philosophically. The lost Democratic House seats were filled in almost all cases by more conservative Republicans. Southern Democrats who retained their place in Congress were generally more conservative than those who departed, a shift that moved the entire Democratic delegation to the right in the House.[44] The Republicans did not take over the House in 1980, but it appeared that a conservative majority might have. After the election, assuming that the members of the new Congress voted as they had in the past, it appeared that a conservative majority might win budget fights by 20 votes.[45] In the Senate, departing Democrats were generally more liberal than those who remained, and the proportional replacement of Democrats by Republicans was greater than in the House. The Senate outcomes thus hurt liberal Democrats in three ways: their party lost control, their party became noticeably more conservative, and Republican conservatives were strengthened.[46]

The Spending Struggle

Near the end of his first speech on the budget, Reagan said "that spending by Government must be limited to those functions which are the proper province of Government."[47] The speech indicated the proper functions of government. National defense required more money. The social safety net that supports "those who through no fault of their own must depend on the rest of us, the poverty stricken, the disabled, the elderly, all those with true need" was exempt from cuts. Other programs apparently were also within the proper functions of government: Medicare; Social Security; veterans' pensions; free school lunches for the poor; supplemental income for the blind, aged, and disabled; Project Head Start; and summer youth jobs. Spending on these would not be restrained. As Reagan himself noted, the proper province of government included $216 billion in social welfare programs.

What then lay outside the legitimate powers of government? "Individuals or particular business interests where real need cannot be demonstrated."[48] As David Stockman would later say, the administration targeted weak claims, not weak clients.[49] Those who had built the old regime howled.[50] Yet Reagan was largely correct. He had not proposed deep cuts to the welfare state. That difference between abstract desire and concrete reality evinced the political strength of government spending.

Reagan also believed that a major part of current taxation was not legitimate, including the current 70 percent marginal tax rate. Following Memorandum No. 1, Reagan proposed that marginal tax rates be reduced by 10 percent for the next three years. These reductions would later be praised and decried. They were hardly radical. The proposal implied that government could legitimately take one-third of an individual's income.[51] The proposal indexed tax rates to inflation and lowered business taxes through faster depreciation schedules.[52]

Reagan linked the budget to renewed prosperity. His program "can help America create 13 million new jobs, nearly 3 million more than we would have without these measures. It will also help us gain control of inflation."[53] He predicted the tax cuts would lead to more wealth for average workers.[54]

The budget did fulfill Reagan's campaign promise by cutting the growth rate of government spending.[55] Federal spending would be higher in the coming year than in 1981.[56] Perhaps that would be a starting point for the withering away of the federal government. But even Reagan's modest agenda still had to get through Congress.

Reagan's task was clear and daunting: hold the Republicans in both chambers together in support of his budget proposals while attracting enough House Democrats to pass the resolutions and the budget law. The challenge to holding the Republicans together came from the "Gypsy Moths," a coalition of 20 to 30 eastern and midwestern Republican representatives in the House. Many of them represented urban areas or university towns, places where voters might vote for a Democratic challenger if Reagan's economic proposals became too painful.[57] In 1981, they were willing to vote with Reagan and their party so long as transportation, fuel assistance, or education was not cut in ways that clearly harmed their districts.[58]

"Boll Weevils" was the informal name given to a group of mostly southern conservative House Democrats. They set up the Conservative Democratic Forum with more than 40 members.[59] These conservative Democrats might support tax and spending cuts. If House Republicans held and the Boll Weevils voted for his program, Reagan would have a working majority of 232 members.

The Reagan administration won the budget battle of 1981 by skillful control over procedures. Stockman had won election to Congress shortly after the new budget process went to work. He proposed to use the new procedures to solve the problem of "interest group liberalism" identified by Lowi. The process begins with Congress's adopting a concurrent budget resolution that sets out spending and revenues for several years and allocates spending among 20 functional categories. The details are then filled in by authorizing, appropriating, and taxing committees in Congress after much negotiating. Crucially for Reagan, budget resolutions cannot be filibustered in the U.S. Senate; both chambers required a simple majority to pass the resolution. Reagan had that majority in the Senate, and he was close to it in the House.[60]

Congress then reconciles revenues and spending to the totals in the budget resolution. Reconciliation comprises two steps. First, Congress tells its committees and members how to reconcile spending and taxes in the budget resolution itself. These instructions, however, are not binding. Second, Congress passes a reconciliation bill that changes revenue and spending laws to bring them in line with the resolution.[61] Typically, the reconciliation bill comes late in the process. Overall, the process usually involves much back-and-forth between the budget committees and other committees in Congress. Normally, the budget committees do not dominate outcomes. Committees generally wish to spend more on their programs. Lacking a controlling authority, the fragmented budget process tends toward spending more on government activities.[62]

Stockman realized that cutting spending required imposing a plan on Congress; the usual process of negotiation and consultation would lead to the usual increasing growth in spending. Congress would act as the agent of a national majority—Reagan's majority—rather than as representatives of discrete interests.[63] The reconciliation process provided the means to this end. Stockman put his proposed cuts into an omnibus reconciliation bill that the Senate would vote up or down in March. By putting their spending reductions in one bill and forcing the House and Senate to vote on a single measure, Republicans hoped to prevent congressional committees and interest groups from chipping away at the president's budget plan.

The reconciliation process marked two kinds of changes in American politics. It transferred power from the authorizing and appropriations committees to the budget committees. The president, not Congress, was the moving force behind the first budget, and it was the Senate, not the House, that ultimately drove the cuts and the final product.[64] The authorizing and appropriations committees—usually supporters of spending—were forced "to meet stringent budget requirements they had had little role in developing."[65]

Stockman thus proposed to take the "interest group" out of interest-group liberalism: "My aim in this tactic was to take the Hill by storm before the interest group opposition to spending cuts congealed."[66] The corruption in the American system would simply be bypassed. The tactic worked. Its novelty had the additional advantage of introducing confusion among political professionals in the capital. It was not clear who had to make the cuts. With time short, "the public and special interest groups were denied their usual participation in the congressional decision-making process because of the scope and constrained time frame."[67] Excluded from the process, they had less chance to influence its outcomes.

The strategy worked. House Democrats wanted separate votes on all cuts through reconciliation. The Reagan administration wanted one vote on the entire bill. The question came to a vote over the rule governing debate about the bill on the House floor. The Boll Weevils voted for Reagan and eventually for Gramm-Latta II, a substitute that reconciled committee spending to the first budget resolution.[68]

Reagan won in the traditional way: he held onto GOP votes and garnered enough Democrats to pass the budget. All but one House Republican supported the president on both reconciliation spending reductions. Eighty-eight percent of House Democrats opposed the reconciliation bill. The Boll Weevil Democrats were ideologically as conservative as the average Republican and much more conservative than their Democratic colleagues.[69] The same was true of their voters. The constituents of the Boll Weevil Democrats were about as likely to have voted for Reagan as the constituents of other members supporting the Reagan program.[70]

All in all, 196 members of the House supported Reagan on almost all votes taken on his economic reforms. Of those, 115 were continuing members whose previous voting records would lead one to predict support for Reagan's program. Another 28 members voted consistently for Reagan even though their previous voting records would not have suggested such support was likely. These members, most of whom were southern Democrats, could be seen as "converted" by Reagan's mandate. The remaining 53 members of Reagan's coalition were elected in 1980. Two-thirds of these new members replaced a Democrat.[71] The election thus mattered a lot to policy outcomes in 1981.

In 1981, a survey asked legislators why they supported the Reagan economic program. Many wanted to stimulate the economy. Others believed their constituents wanted the bill and that it would help the middle class. These are overall results. The crucial swing constituency, however, were conservative House Democrats. The Boll Weevils believed the bill would stimulate the economy and wished to follow opinion in their districts.[72] The scholar conducting the survey concluded that "supporters were more likely to have cited policy motivations, district pressures, and a Reagan mandate."[73]

These perceptions were rooted in reality. Constituent mail to members overwhelmingly supported both the tax plan and the spending cuts.[74] Reagan's initial success owed much to what is often called grassroots organizing. The political scientist Darrell West argued that the views of these activists differed from general public opinion in the congressional districts whose representatives supported Reagan. The activists strongly favored Reagan's economic proposals, whereas the broader public was less supportive.[75] The Reagan success might seem to lack democratic legitimacy.

But members always rely on district mail and phone calls as one gauge of constituent opinion. Mail and calls measure the intensity of constituent opinion, while polls capture the views of more people, even though many of them may attach little importance to their response or may not have considered the issue in question at all. For members, activist opinion matters to their reelection prospects. It is part of the American method of keeping representatives accountable to their districts.[76]

We should not forget how chance shaped this outcome. The Democrats had begun to rally their supporters to oppose the Reagan proposals in late March 1981. The Speaker of the House was set to attack the Reagan budget at a meeting of the Building and Construction Trades Council of the American Federation of Labor and Congress of Industrial Organizations. Reagan addressed them first and was shot by John Hinckley immediately afterward. Reagan's recovery and his response to the shooting powerfully affected public opinion: "His pollster concluded that that event made a permanent impression on the public, creating a reservoir of good will that would go on protecting him even when his policies were controversial."[77] When Democratic House members went back to their districts for Easter recess, they found that Reagan had overwhelming support.[78]

Many Americans thought Reagan had changed the course of history with his 1981 budget victory.[79] Had he really reduced the size of government? David Stockman had his doubts. He thought the cuts were only "promises and paper savings." In fact, Gramm-Latta II had cut only $16 billion over three years, more than the alternatives posed by the committees. In Stockman's reckoning, Congress needed $256 billion in reductions over three years to balance the budget.[80] Other analysts support Stockman's skepticism. More prosaically, Reagan's "historic" turnaround had cut the *projected* spending of the federal government by 4.7 percent for the next fiscal year. In retrospect, Reagan's "cuts" seem small indeed and hardly the "draconian" changes complained of then and now. Taking inflation into account, the Reagan cuts were real, though small (about 5 percent of the total cost of government).[81] Sen. Pete V. Domenici's was correct to call the law "the most dramatic reduction in the ongoing programs in the history of the country" because the spending of the federal government had risen relentlessly for three decades, both absolutely and relative to the nation's wealth.[82] Any cuts at all would have been dramatic against that history.

The Omnibus Budget Reconciliation Act of 1981 "defined the boundaries of what Congress was willing to cut from domestic government." The Boll Weevils were willing to cut government spending as long as agriculture and water projects, impact aid, and the military were protected. The Gypsy Moths were willing to support the GOP so long as their spending priorities (transportation, fuel assistance, and education) were not cut in ways that clearly harmed their districts.[83] But even those willing to support cuts were not willing to cut some programs. Most programs had defenders. The few that did not were the ones that ended up with real cuts over the two Reagan terms. Let's consider some programs that were cut and why.

The Comprehensive Employment Training Act of 1974 offered job training and public-sector employment. The program had grown rapidly under Carter.[84] The program did give people jobs but failed to make them employable outside of government.[85] It was also flawed politically. As a block grant, CETA gave money to local officials to spend on hiring people. The local officials got the political credit for the jobs while Congress had to impose the taxes that funded the program.[86] Given that flaw, CETA was a prime target for members. It was the *only* program totally eliminated in 1981.[87]

Some of Lyndon Johnson's handiwork attracted budget restraint. The Community Development Block Grant program was a successor to LBJ's urban policies. Most of this money had gone to cities with many poor people or older cities.[88] The party representing those voters had lost the 1980 election and seemed likely to lose their CDBG pork barrel in 1981. But it was not to be. Stockman recommended drastic cuts for CDBG, but Secretary of Housing and Urban Development Samuel Pierce fought successfully to preserve the spending. In the end, its funding fell sharply compared to the late 1970s.[89] The program was eventually cut from $6.1 billion in 1980 to $2.8 billion in 1990.[90] CDBG has lived on, 30 years after Reagan's election.[91]

Carter also had direct pork-barrel spending through the Urban Development Action Grant program.[92] UDAG was said to be an anti-poverty program: the federal government provided "ailing cities sufficient resources to overcome hardships being experienced by the poor and near-poor within their bounds."[93] This goal later became less important than spending money to enhance the reelection prospects of members of Congress not representing declining cities.[94] Stockman also sought to eliminate UDAG. Its spending was cut by one-third for 1982, and it would later be cut again in the face of administration requests to terminate the program.[95] UDAG also had political problems. Most of its money went to the declining states of the North and the Midwest, thereby weakening support among members of Congress from other states.[96]

Congress also followed Reagan in reducing spending on several other programs. For example, Reagan won a 32 percent reduction in mass transit spending.[97] Reagan briefly struck a few blows against the intellectual defenders of the old regime.[98] The poverty research industry, however, hardly suffered.[99] In the larger picture, these cuts did not greatly reduce the size of government.

The Reagan administration set out to curb federal spending on higher education and initially enjoyed some success. Between 1980 and 1984, the federal education budget, apart from student loans, fell by 17.7 percent (accounting for inflation). Federal spending on postsecondary education declined by 3.2 percent (including growth in outlays on student loans).[100] Federal changes also had little effect on state spending, the major source of subsidies to higher education. Such spending peaked in 1977 and declined thereafter; Reagan's first term saw little change in this declining trend until a sharp drop in 1984.[101] Two analysts concluded that "education under President Reagan . . . changed a little, but not much. . . . the federal role in education looks very similar to what it did under Presidents Johnson, Nixon, Ford, and Carter."[102]

Overall, discretionary domestic spending dropped about 14.2 percent during Reagan's first year.[103] Discretionary spending for nondefense activities has generally ranged between 3 percent and 4 percent of gross domestic product. From 1975 to 1981, such spending rose to about 5 percent of GDP.[104] In that light, the 1981 reductions returned discretionary spending to the upper end of its range, relative to national income. As Reagan and voters wished, defense spending rose about as much as other discretionary spending had fallen, again relative to national income.[105] This restraint in spending hardly constituted a major threat to the old regime.

Reagan and Stockman decided to try to constrain Social Security. Circumstances seemed propitious, even apart from Reagan's victory.

In 1980, Congress had learned that the Old Age and Survivor's Insurance fund would go broke by 1982; they had found money to cover that deficit but feared renewed shortages. At the same time, members understood that budget discipline demanded control over entitlement spending.[106]

Stockman considered restraining cost-of-living adjustments (COLAs) for Social Security in 1981. Time was not on his side. The deadline for determining the next year's payment was late April. Stockman backed off. Instead, the administration later proposed reductions in Social Security, including penalties for early retirement and reductions in disability benefits. Increasing the penalty for early retirement seemed defensible.[107] They also proposed a three-month delay in the 1982 COLA for Social Security recipients as well as a change in indexing that reduced benefits. Other changes included capping benefits for some families, taxing sick pay, and ending dependent children's benefits for retirees under 65. In part, these proposals were designed to reduce spending and improve the deficit picture. The administration also believed the cuts would save money for future retirees.[108]

The proposals went nowhere, to put it mildly. A week after the proposals were introduced, the House Democratic Caucus unanimously adopted a resolution calling Reagan's changes "an unconscionable breach of faith." They promised not to "destroy the program or generation of retirees." Republicans too ran in fear of the public reaction to the plans.[109] On May 20, 1981, a little over a month after Reagan had been shot, the Senate, with a Republican majority, and the Democratic-controlled House approved nonbinding resolutions rebuking Reagan's Social Security proposals. The administration began to back off from the proposals.[110] A little over a week had passed from proposal to retreat.

Why did Reagan and the GOP retreat so quickly? In early May, during his recovery from being shot, Reagan's approval rating was 68 percent favorable and 21 percent unfavorable. In early June, the ratio had moved to 59 percent favorable, 28 percent unfavorable.[111] GOP pollster Robert Teeter found at that time that the Democrats were doing much better on "helping the elderly and retired" than the Republicans (a 63 to 20 percent advantage). Two-thirds of respondents opposed any cut in Social Security benefits. The Republicans in Congress, not surprisingly, wanted to hear no more about Social Security.[112]

The May debacle was not the end of the Social Security story for Reagan.[113] The program itself was too unsteady to simply leave things as they were out of fear of the American Association of Retired Persons. The previous decade had seen an enormous increase in benefits, promises of a sound financial future followed immediately by an impending deficit, an increase in taxes said to solve the impending deficit, followed in turn by a new recognition of emerging deficits. Reagan and Congress would be forced back to the pension problem in the fall of 1981.

The Tax Story

President Reagan had one great advantage in the struggle over-taxes in 1981: federal taxes had risen well above their long-term trend (see Table 3.1).

Carter's last year in office also saw federal taxes reach their highest level since 1944. In 1978, revenues had been 19.1 percent of gross national product but bracket creep, payroll tax increases, and wind-fall profits tax on oil along with a progressive income tax on rising real incomes had produced a record haul for the government. The normal federal tax burden from 1961 to 1980 was about 19 percent of GNP, almost 2 percent under the 1981 number.[114] The future offered more of the same. The last Carter budget foresaw steady increases in revenue, culminating in taxes taking 24 percent of GNP in 1986.[115] A significant tax cut in 1981 would have done no more than return the federal government tax burden to normal. A deeper

Table 3.1
TAX REVENUES BEFORE REAGAN

Fiscal Years	Average Federal Tax Burden, % of GNP
1961–65	19.2
1966–1970	19.2
1971–1975	18.6
1976–1980	19.2
1981	20.8

SOURCES: Joseph White and Aaron Wildavsky, *The Deficit and the Public Interest: The Search for Responsible Budgeting in the 1980s* (Berkeley: University of California Press, 1989), p. 333.

cut would have been needed to actually roll back federal control over income.

Traditional Republicans had always said—and repeated the axiom in 1981—that government should cut spending and then reduce taxes to balance the public budget. Reagan believed causality ran the other way: "Government spends all the taxes it gets. If we reduce taxes, we'll reduce spending."[116] The Democrats in 1981 both disagreed and agreed with Reagan. They disagreed, of course, about his desire to cut spending. They agreed, however, with his theory that cutting taxes would lead to constraints on spending. That fear, along with other motivations, fostered their opposition to Reagan's tax cuts.[117]

If tax rates were cut and indexed to inflation, Congress would have to raise taxes to spend more. Congress would have to choose between higher taxes and more spending. Reagan could easily believe that choice would favor lower taxes and, therefore, less spending. What he did not say, but might have, was that lowered taxes would improve public finance: the spending that continued with the lower revenues would more explicitly reflect the opportunity costs to the society. After all, Congress would have to explicitly confront those costs by raising taxes. For Reagan, tax cuts had other advantages. They would also tend to become permanent. Congress had raised taxes during peacetime only during the 1930s.[118]

Reagan perhaps assumed that if Congress cut taxes, it would also cut spending enough to keep spending and revenues roughly near balance. He assumed, in short, that members of Congress would fear incurring deficits and raising taxes more than they would fear the wrath of those who benefited from government spending.[119] If that assumption were not true, his whole strategy for limiting government would fail. Taxes would rise. If taxes did not rise, deficits would provoke borrowing that in turn implied taking money from future taxpayers. If Reagan were wrong about deficits, he might succeed in shifting taxation but not reducing it.

Yet the risk would have seemed to be worth running. In 1981, many people believed previous public deficits had caused inflation. Given the importance of reducing inflation to voters, it seemed unlikely that Congress would run deficits in response to reduced revenue. Congress would have to take the best of a bad lot and truly cut programs to bring spending into line with reduced revenues.

Reagan's strategy for reducing government was similar to Lyndon Johnson's for expanding the state. LBJ believed that creating programs would also create supporters for spending on those programs. The passing of time would thus bring a growing federal establishment that could not be stopped through political means. To avoid deep deficits, Congress would have to find ways to raise taxes to fund the inexorable rise in spending; collective choice would replace private choices. By cutting taxes, Reagan would apply the same logic to control spending. Both assumed American voters and thus Congress would not tolerate deficit spending for long.

Reagan originally proposed to cut individual tax rates 10 percent a year for three years. Reagan could count on only 192 votes in the House; he needed 26 Democratic votes to pass the bill. As he did in seeking spending restraint, Reagan turned to the 47 conservative Democrats, the Boll Weevils. At first, the administration struck a deal with Kent Hance, a Texas Democrat who led the Boll Weevils. This deal both delayed and cut the first year of the three-year reduction. (Hance received a tax break for oil producers as part of the bargain.) This version of the bill also had lower deficit projections, a concern of the Boll Weevils and Senate Republicans.

Getting those lower numbers, however, had required cutting out other tax reductions for business, particularly involving depreciation schedules. Business groups had sought for some time to speed up depreciation, thereby cutting the prices of their equipment. Such changes were thought to lead, not unreasonably, to more investment and higher productivity. The deal with Hance threatened these faster depreciation schedules and thereby business support for the law. Business groups did not much care about the tax-rate reductions, but they did want the new depreciation rules. In the end, business groups proposed moving the last part of the tax credits and depreciation schedules out beyond the third-year budget window where deficit hawks would not have to worry about the budgetary implications. The coalition behind tax cuts regained its stability, but the cost of the package increased in the out years.[120]

As the struggle over the tax bill neared its end, an all-out bidding war broke out to gain the final few votes needed for victory. House Democratic leaders began by offering commodity traders $400 million in tax preferences that the Senate Republican Finance Committee had removed from the tax code to reduce deficit projections. The real industry with power, however, was oil and its regional base. Oil had prospered in the 1970s because of the Organization of Petroleum Exporting Countries. That success, however, came at a cost to other regions, whose voters greatly outnumbered the oil-producing region. Hence, windfall profits taxes in the late 1970s gave some of the gains to the other regions. In 1981, representatives from the oil states decided the fate of the tax bill. The Democrats offered a tax credit against the windfall profits tax that was expected to cost $7.1 billion by 1986. The Senate Republicans briefly increased their bid before running into a filibuster from northern Democrats. It appeared the Democrats had won. But the Republicans did not give up. Instead they embraced almost all the tax preferences offered by Democrats and added more. The tax credit for the oil region rose to an estimated $13 to $16 billion. There were many smaller deals offered by both sides.

Reagan went on television in late July to defend his economic program. He gave perhaps his best speech up to that time. Reagan said: "If the tax cut goes to you, the American people, in the third year, that money . . . won't be available for Congress to spend, and that, in my view, is what this whole controversy comes down to. Are you entitled to the fruits of your own labor or does government have some presumptive right to spend and spend and spend?" The public thought it was entitled to keep the fruits of its labor. Members received a barrage of phone calls and mail supporting Reagan's proposals, favoring Reagan by six to one. But members had other reasons to support the administration. Many programs of interest to their constituents (in one Georgia case, the peanut subsidy) were protected. The administration won by attracting 48 Democrats to its bill while losing 1 Republican.[121]

None of this dealing was pretty, especially for anyone, like David Stockman, committed in principle to limiting government. The negotiation with the oil interests eventually led to saving the oil depletion allowance, which was scheduled to be phased out. Stockman saw the survival of this tax preference as a straw breaking his back: "The depletion allowance was an unjustified and wasteful tax subsidy, a symbol of the corrupt political system that the Reagan Revolution was challenging. And now the revolution had embraced even that in order to win."[122] Later Stockman would say: "I now understand that you probably can't put together a majority coalition unless you are willing to deal with those marginal interests that will give you the votes needed to win. That's where it is fought—on the margins—and unless you deal with those marginal votes, you can't win."[123]

A government that acted on behalf of a majority of voters might eliminate favors like the oil depletion allowance. Stockman accepted the reality of a fragmented polity in which trading favors for the votes needed to make up a majority preserved policies like the oil depletion allowance. The fragmentation and subsequent negotiating also complicated majority rule and protected minorities. The enduring question for Reagan would be what winning meant. Did it reduce the ambit of government? Or would the interests that supported the programs trimmed in 1981 eventually reassert themselves and return the nation to the path of growing government?

The final tax bill included indexing, the three-year tax cuts, an increase in the corporate depreciation allowance, and a major reduction in the top corporate rate (from 70 to 50 percent). Still, the reliance on Democrats had moderated the final product: half the first-year tax-rate cut had been dropped, and the spending cuts had been reduced by more than 20 percent. The law enacted a $37.7 billion tax cut for the next fiscal year. The Economic Recovery Tax Act of 1981 was also expected to return $749 billion to taxpayers over the next five years. The final votes for the law were not close: two-thirds of both chambers of Congress voted for it.[124] Public opinion agreed. Gallup found that the public approved the tax cut by two to one.[125]

President Reagan signed the Economic Recovery Tax Act of 1981 and the Omnibus Budget Reconciliation Act of 1981 on August 13. It is too much to say that the Reagan Revolution ended on that Thursday. It is accurate to say, looking back, that the Reagan administration had constrained federal spending as much as it would. Reagan would spend much of his remaining eight years in office refusing to acquiesce in raising income tax rates. Tax revenues would drop compared to the previous trend. The Carter budget looked forward to taxes equal to 24 percent of GNP in 1986. In 1981, the Reagan people saw revenue dropping to 19.3 percent by the 1984 fiscal year.[126] The government had been denied as much money as it wanted. Would this reduce the size of government?

After Reform

The political agenda comprises the problems and policy proposals being debated at any time by people attentive to politics and policy-making. It is both what people are talking about and how they are talking about it.[127] Control over both the topics and terms of public debate—agenda control—fosters political power and success. Reagan had won the presidency in part because the economy, especially inflation, had been so bad. Reagan had promised changes in spending and taxing that would revive the nation's prosperity. Until September 1981, President Reagan dominated the political agenda of the United States. Such complete control over the public agenda is rare, even for a president. In the fall of 1981, politics began to return to normal in a painful way.

Reagan lost control of the agenda because he did not have control over all policies affecting the economy. The Federal Reserve Board controlled the money supply. From the Nixon administration onward, the Fed had worried a lot about its political standing with each administration and not about the price level. By the 1980 election, inflation seemed out of control.[128] During the 1970s, expert opinion slowly concluded that inflation was largely a monetary phenomenon. In 1981, the Federal Reserve under Paul Volcker acted on that consensus and sharply restricted growth in the money supply. It persisted in this policy well into 1982, largely because the Fed lacked credibility in fighting inflation; earlier efforts had culminated in a premature loosening of the monetary supply and renewed inflation. In 1981, the Fed persisted in its tight policy until there was "unmistakable evidence of real progress in reducing inflation."[129] The Federal Reserve thereby induced the most severe contraction of the economy since the 1930s.[130] In the final quarter of 1981, GNP fell at an annual rate of 4.7 percent.[131] Things would get worse until November 1982, when the downturn ended.[132] The unemployment rate averaged 9.7 percent in 1982 and peaked at 10.8 percent in November, when congressional elections were held.[133]

Economic decline translated into political weakness for the president. In August, when Reagan signed the tax and spending reforms, 60 percent of the public approved of his job performance. As the economy slowed, public approval declined. By the end of 1981, 49 percent approved of Reagan. Throughout 1982, his approval rating steadily declined, finally reaching bottom in January 1982, at 37 percent.[134] Tax and spending cuts no longer dominated public discussions.

People in Washington—Congress, the media, and inevitably the White House—began talking about federal deficits, a theme that would stay near the top of the public agenda for the next 17 years. In a recession, government receives less tax revenue than forecast and spends more than planned on unemployment insurance and other programs. This recession also changed expectations about budget deficits. The 1983 deficit exceeded the Congressional Budget Office's 1981 estimates by nearly $40 billion.[135] The deficit was expected to be $300 billion by 1988. Just as Congress and other members of the political class had come to believe that something had to be done about spending and taxes, they decided in late 1981 that something had to be done about the deficit. "The answer to deficits," Reagan said in his 1982 budget message, "is economic growth and indefatigable efforts to control spending and borrowing."[136] Yet he could not find a majority for further significant cuts in spending, and economic growth had not revived. He and the Congress were left with tax increases as the only way to "do something" about the deficit.[137]

Democrats did not wish to raise taxes going into the 1982 elections. House leaders, where revenue and appropriation bills should start, waited for the Republican Senate to act (and garner blame from voters). The Senate Finance Committee agreed on a three-year, $98 billion increase. The two parties struggled over raising corporate taxes. In the end, Reagan had to lobby for a bill raising taxes (but not tax rates).[138] He gave cover to Democrats who voted for the increases. Reagan found harder going on the Republican side but eventually found the GOP votes in the House to get the bill through; Senate Republicans stayed together enough to pass the bill with significant Democrat support.[139]

The Tax Equity and Fiscal Responsibility Act of 1982 raised many taxes.[140] The tax increases fell on business groups that had done well in 1981. Defense spending also grew more slowly than Reagan had hoped. Joseph White and Aaron Wildavsky argue that in 1981 and 1982, an idea of fairness informed congressional decisions. Both business and defense had done well in 1981 because they had done poorly in 1970s; both could argue that fairness required some concessions from Congress. Spending on social welfare had risen during the previous decade; in the circumstances of 1981, fairness suggested some constraint in such outlays. In 1982, winners and losers changed seats in part for the same reason: business had done well and should now lose, while the poor were protected from further constraint on redistribution.[141]

This "fair shares" story is not complete. Some tax preferences persist for democratic reasons. Many voters pay no taxes on health care benefits from their employer, pay reduced taxes on the interest on their home mortgage, and pay no taxes up front on their retirement savings. All those preferences might have been reduced or eliminated to deal with the impending deficits, but no rational politician running for office would have punished large numbers of their constituents by eliminating such preferences.

Why did the tax-rate reductions of 1981 survive? Increasing rates lacked congressional support.[142] The president cared more about the tax rates than he did about other tax increases; his veto also protected the rates. That leaves the question of why the 1981 rates attracted enough support to sustain a veto, while other tax increases did not. The 1982 tax increases fell on businesses. In general, "big business" is politically unpopular, and many judge its interactions with government, especially on tax policy, as corrupt or nearly so.[143] Americans see individuals differently; in the United States, only rich leftists wish to impose equality of income and wealth. Most voters care little about material inequalities.[144] Business had little chance against individuals, if someone had to pay higher taxes.

The same Congress voted on the 1981 tax cuts and the 1982 tax increases. Twenty-seven percent of its members changed their minds in 1982 and voted for higher taxes. Fifty-three percent maintained their position from 1981 (including 25 percent who opposed the 1981 cuts). Twenty percent were against both bills: the increase and the tax cut.[145] The members who switched from supporting tax cuts to favoring tax increases in 1982 were more moderate ideologically and less likely to believe that Reagan received a mandate in 1980.[146] Over 86 percent of those who switched were Republicans. They gave two major reasons for voting for a tax increase in 1982. Ninety percent said it would stimulate the economy; 82 percent said their vote went along with opinion in the district.[147]

These lost Republican votes were crucial. Republicans cast only *three* votes against the administration during key votes on Reagan's economic program in the spring and summer of 1981. In 1982, Republican cohesion faltered. Northeastern Republicans were likely to oppose the president on votes concerning his economic policies. They returned to their old habit of moderately supporting social welfare programs, votes that seemed prudent in light of economic difficulties and the upcoming 1982 elections. Outside the Northeast, Reagan did better with his 1981 supporters. These members, Barbara Sinclair suggests, saw the 1980 election as a mandate for a policy change rather than as support for President Reagan. Consequently, they continued to support the larger program even when Reagan's own authority and influence were waning.[148]

The Republican Party often professed (and sometimes professes today) to be a party that favors reducing government. In truth, the Republican Party may be less enamored with an expanding welfare state than Democrats are, but in power they generally accept its political reality. Eisenhower had not bothered the New Deal, and Nixon's expansions of government were noted earlier. As David Stockman discovered, many Republicans and some members of Reagan's cabinet swiftly came to the defense of the old regime in its moment of need.[149] The extraordinary unity Reagan achieved early in 1981 changed many Republican votes from their natural tendency to support the status quo. Moreover, the price of GOP unity was bought by "opening up the soup kitchen" at crucial times.[150] Once circumstances turned against Reagan and he lost control of the agenda, these Republicans reverted to form and supported the old regime.

None of this should be surprising. The two major parties reflect ideological as well as regional, class, and religious differences. The task faced by a member of Congress, however, is remaining in office first and then, so far as possible, enacting into law a set of principles or ideals. When ideals conflict with that reelection goal, a member does what he or she must to win office again. The persistent problems of the old regime in the 1970s created an opportunity for Ronald Reagan. Offering an answer to those problems reconciled the Reagan economic proposals to the reelection needs of liberal Republicans and conservative Democrats. Yet that reconciliation depended on the promise of an improving economy, which meant the recession of late 1981 and 1982 strained and then dispersed Reagan's 1981 coalition.[151]

Yet the circumstances of 1982 did force Congress to address spending, even spending on entitlements. Medicare costs had been rising quickly, and Congress agreed they had to be controlled. The costs were rising "largely because under the third-party payment system, neither providers nor consumers had to worry about costs." The Reagan administration wanted to do so by cutting Medicare benefits and raising patient costs. Congress would have none of it. Eventually, Congress decided to regulate prices rather than allow costs to fall more on consumers. Their conference agreement set limits on hospital prices and physician fees.[152]

The changes would cut spending for the programs by an estimated $14.4 billion over the three years, nearly two and a half times the amount pruned from the programs in 1981. Most of the spending reductions made by the bill—$13.3 billion—came in Medicare, the largest part of the restraint coming in the last year. These were hardly drastic cuts. Even with the proposed reductions, federal spending on the two programs was expected to be $72.7 billion in fiscal year 1983 and $79.6 billion in FY84, compared to $68 billion in FY82.[153]

About 47 million people would be covered by one of the two programs in 1983.[154] More importantly, Medicare or Medicaid recipients were about 28 percent of the voting-age population. Medicare recipients alone (29 million voters) constituted about 1 in 5 voters in 1982.[155] Congress wanted the burden of controlling costs in these programs to appear to fall on health care providers rather than on voters. Providers would presumably be forced to give the same health care for less remuneration than in the past. This appearance of savaging providers and saving recipients meant Congress could try to control spending on health care entitlements.[156]

The deficits did improve the prospects for another part of Reagan's economic agenda. In 1982, the Senate passed a constitutional amendment to require a balanced federal budget by a vote of 69 to 31, 2 more than necessary to send an amendment to the states. In the House, the balanced budget amendment had been confined to the House Judiciary Committee, which was dominated by opponents of the reform. Eventually, supporters of the amendment obtained the needed votes to discharge it and bring about a floor vote. In the end, the House voted 236 to 187 for the amendment, or 46 votes short of the needed two-thirds majority.[157]

1982 proved to be the zenith of the amendment's prospects in the Reagan years. The amendment movement lost momentum in 1984 when courts raised questions about ballot initiatives rather than state legislatures petitioning for a convention.[158] Eventually, the amendment would be superseded by congressional attempts to tie itself to the mast of budget constraints. Once the Democrats returned to the majority in the Senate in 1986, the balanced budget amendment had little hope of passing.

The administration also retreated on Social Security in 1982. By late September 1981, Reagan went on television to announce a new deficit reduction plan. He also mentioned Social Security but only to speak of his surrender. He would support restoring the minimum benefit in the program, which Stockman in July had persuaded Congress to eliminate. Reagan also decided to appoint a commission to deal with Social Security's impending financing crisis. Its current financing problems would be dealt with for the time being by borrowing from the Medicare fund, which still had a surplus.[159]

The resolution of the struggle over Social Security's minimum benefit is instructive. The term "minimum benefit" might suggest an impoverished older person barely hanging on. In fact, many recipients of the minimum benefit were government workers who retired and then worked long enough in the private sector to qualify for Social Security benefits. Most recipients were, as Stockman later put it, "double dippers," middle-class people taking advantage of generous government retirement rules. Under Reagan's proposal, people who received the minimum benefit and had no other income qualified for an equal sum from the means-tested Supplemental Security Income program.[160] The minimum benefit had become, in short, largely a middle-class benefit sold politically as help for the needy.

That image would be enough to partially save the benefit in 1981. Political calculation also argued for the benefit. The alternative for the truly needy was a means-tested part of Social Security. Recipients would be as well off as before, but Social Security itself might be politically worse off. Supporters of Social Security from the start believed that a program for the poor would be a poor (i.e., not especially generous) program. If any part of Social Security, even the relatively obscure minimum benefit, were replaced by a means-tested alternative, the program itself might eventually come into question. The public outcry about the needy and the private concern about a political foundation of the Democratic Party led the House of Representatives to quickly restore the minimum benefit for everyone. The Senate took longer and ultimately restored the benefit for current recipients while denying it to those who started in 1982.[161]

The pressures created by impending deficits brought the Congress back to Social Security in 1982. Reagan and his budget team went along when Domenici proposed and passed a plan that included about $40 billion in Social Security savings over the next three years.[162] Both parties were reluctant to take on the Social Security issue. Both waited for the other to make the first move. When the GOP did so, the Democrats pounced. Democratic Sen. Donald Riegle said, "This is a time bomb designed to raid and loot the Social Security system." Sen. Robert Byrd added, "The President proposes to mortgage the future of the elderly to keep alive the folly of his Kemp-Roth tax cut." Sen. Moynihan went deeper to the same end: "There is a social contract in this nation, and Social Security is one of the most important elements in it." Sen. John Chafee, a Republican from Rhode Island, remarked that Social Security was "essential" to the well-being of many elderly citizens.[163] An anonymous White House aide correctly noted that the Republicans had just given the Democrats an issue "that they're going to beat our brains out with."

Chafee was hardly a typical Republican senator, but he was not alone. A Cleveland Republican said, "I think any substantial cuts in Social Security would be devastating at the local political level." Republican senators from contested states (Chafee, John Heinz of Pennsylvania, David Durenberger of Minnesota) all opposed the bill. The coming election and the presumed difficulties facing the GOP were on many minds. Clarke Reed of Mississippi, who served on the Republican National Committee, stated the day after the Senate Budget Committee plan was announced, "GOP members of the SBC better think about losing four or five senators and being back in the minority."[164] Lowell Weicker of Connecticut was emphatic: "I am totally unwilling to in any way even imply cuts in Social Security benefits."[165] The plan emerged on May 5 from the SBC. House GOP leaders rejected it on May 11. The Senate Budget Committee took out the Social Security provisions on May 18.[166]

What to do? Reagan had created a national commission in December 1981. Alan Greenspan was appointed chair.[167] His charge was to find a politically plausible way to stabilize the financing of the program. The membership itself assured the president that its recommendations would be politically plausible. The program itself did not come into question.

Why did the Democrats agree to do anything about the program? During the 1970s, inflation outran wages by some distance, creating continual shortfalls in Social Security financing. Confidence in the system was falling: the number of people who had "only a little" or "no" confidence in the ability of the system to pay benefits when they retired had risen by 50 percent from 1979 to 1983. This lack of confidence combined with a concern about the long-term solvency of the system convinced even proponents that something should be done. In other words, they wished to shore up the credibility of the system in public opinion by doing something that could be presented as saving Social Security.[168]

The National Commission on Social Security began work early in 1982. It came up with a package that included tax increases, delays (really cuts) in cost-of-living adjustments, and taxation of benefits.[169] As in the past, new taxpayers were brought into the system; they paid taxes now and received benefits later, thereby making the system seem stable for the time being. For the first time, benefits were taxed with the money going back into the "trust fund." The taxes constituted a net loss of benefits for more affluent recipients.[170] The report appeared, as planned, more than two months after the congressional elections of 1982.

For those interested in reducing the size of government, the package was largely a defeat. The cost-of-living adjustment did reduce spending over time, but taxation of benefits and a payroll tax increase augmented the growth of government. The package was a victory for those who sought to maintain benefits. However, if the taxing of benefits counted as a benefit cut, then the real decrease in benefits ($70 billion) was greater than the increase in taxes ($58 billion).[171]

The "reforms" of 1983 may have fostered larger government. The increase in taxes went into the "trust fund," or reserves for the program. Social Security revenues, however, are part of a unified budget for the federal government. Increases in the payroll tax for Social Security thus increase the revenues available for federal spending. Over the history of the program, Congress has tended to spend these reserves.[172] The buildup of reserves foreseen by the 1983 commission thus gave Congress the means to spend more generally now rather than to meet specific obligations to recipients later.[173] If payroll taxes had not created a Social Security surplus, Congress would have had to raise taxes to pay for the spending that was in fact covered by the surpluses. Matching the costs (economic and political) of taxes to the marginal spending might well have led to less spending in the years after 1983.

The commission offered both sides cover from attack, a kind of bipartisanship. Unlike in 1981, Republicans in Congress were not exposed to political recriminations. Democrats could not attack them for raising the retirement age because Speaker O'Neill had signed on. Republicans could not complain about higher taxes because Democrats had supported Ronald Reagan's plan.[174] Responses to the deal are revealing. A Reaganite said, "Once we stopped being revolutionaries and started being system conservers, it was a tremendous accomplishment." A Democrat remarked: "We even cut social security. We just didn't say we were doing it. Everyone agreed to say we weren't doing what we were doing."[175]

The political logic of Social Security governed this deal. The commission's recommendations applied to the very long run; by 2030, most Social Security benefits would be taxed, thereby reducing the net benefits to those *future* recipients.[176] People whose pension benefits are cut in 50 years are barely old enough to vote, too young to vote, or unborn. Imposing costs on them 50 years hence hardly represents political courage. The administration had tried to appeal to the young as a political means to constrain Social Security spending. Health and Human Services Secretary Richard Schweiker argued that Reagan's original proposals would mean a young person entering the work force in 1982 would pay over $33,000 less in Social Security taxes during his or her lifetime, a reduction of 10 percent. Reagan was offering a tax cut for future workers and recipients.[177] The offer did not work. Legislators respond to incentives defined by the next election. American government is biased toward choosing "policies with favorable short-term results and with consequences beyond the term of office of the policymakers."[178] In this case, the president and Congress used a commission to come up with a back-loaded proposal.

It is easy to criticize Stockman for seeing Social Security in narrow budgetary terms and Reagan for not pursuing a fundamental reform of the system like privatization. But public support for fundamental reforms did not exist in 1981. Until 1973, the program had been hailed as a success: the program paid a handsome return on "contributions." Even the emerging deficits and financial problems of the 1970s could not overturn the support for the program. Recognizing that reality, Reagan had promised not to cut, much less end, Social Security.[179] A greater leader might have seen and grasped the opportunity for fundamental reform of the program. But maybe no such opportunity existed in 1981. Reagan had constrained the program in the future. Such constraint itself was unprecedented. That act tended to preserve the system from the consequences of its contradictions. Reagan had become a reformer of the central entitlement of the old regime.

A Radical Gambit

By 1980, the state role in American government had all but ended. It was "taken as axiomatic that the federal government shall initiate policies and programs, shall determine their character, shall delegate their administration to the states and localities according to terms that it alone determines, and shall provide for whatever intervention on the part of its administrative agencies as it deems necessary to secure compliance with those terms."[180] The states were, at best, administrative units subservient to Washington's commands.

Reagan spoke of radical change. "It is my intention . . . to demand recognition of the distinction between the powers granted to the federal government and those reserved to the states or to the people," Reagan said in his inaugural address. "All of us need to be reminded that the federal government did not create the states; the states created the federal government."[181] Reagan believed the Framers "intended for the states to participate in the federal system as full-fledged partners with the national government." In his view, the national government was sovereign within its delegated powers, but the Framers thought the states should be equally powerful and have considerable discretion in exercising their reserved powers. For the Framers, Reagan thought, most of what government should do was local and hence fell within the proper ambit of state and local governments. The states would be the senior partner in the state-local relationship. Reagan thought the Framers believed it would be easier to hold officials accountable if they were closer to the voters. Citizens also want efficient government relatively free of waste, fraud, and abuse; state and local governments were less prone to such pathologies. Reagan also thought decentralization would enable government to respond as well as possible to public problems.[182] Reagan believed his New Federalism might decrease the size and influence of the federal government.[183]

Reagan's first budget proposed consolidation of dozens of federal categorical grant programs into block grants to state and local governments. Block grants serve broad purposes, such as health, education, or law enforcement. The money must be spent on programs for such purposes; state or local officials decide how the money is used. Categorical grants can be used only for specific programs as directed by Congress and the federal agencies that write the regulations to implement the laws passed by Congress. Categorical grants come with national control and money. "Categorical grant programs burden local and state governments with a mass of federal regulations and federal paperwork," Reagan said in his nationally televised economic address February 18, 1981. Converting these programs to block grants, the president said, would "reduce wasteful administrative overhead and . . . give local government entities and states more flexibility and control." [184]

Reagan initially achieved some of his federalism objectives. The 1981 budget act reduced federal grant-in-aid expenditures by $6.6 billion, the first reduction in decades. Reconciliation in 1981 also consolidated 77 categorical grants into 9 block grants and eliminated another 60 categorical grants. By 1983, the number of categorical grant programs administered by the federal government had fallen to 313.[185] Williamson would later report other achievements: "Dozens of relief actions were taken to reduce the regulatory burden on state and local governments, and the administration made it clear through hundreds of different actions that it was committed to reversing the forty-year trend of power centralization in Washington."[186] As with other budget votes, conservative House Democrats were essential to Reagan's success with federalism.[187]

Others doubted that the wins on federalism translated into a more limited federal government. The budget changes had changed responsibilities and spending priorities, but "they had done little to check the trend toward centralization of political authority in the American System." The presidential initiatives barely reduced federal involvement and did not address "the ongoing erosion of state authority in congressional and federal court decisions." Hence, "the events of 1981 have had the net effect of continuing the decline in the growth of government, while also continuing the tendency to perceive and organize intergovernmental powers along centralized lines."[188]

The next year, in the teeth of the economic contraction, Reagan used his State of the Union address to propose a more extensive New Federalism program that would have turned over nearly $50 billion in programs and tax sources to the states and local governments over a period of eight years. The initiative comprised "the swap" and "the turnback." Under the swap, the federal government was to take full responsibility for Medicaid (it was a shared responsibility between the states and the federal government), thereby saving the states their portion of the cost of this program. This change was thought to save the states $19.1 billion in FY84. However, the states would take up full responsibility for Aid to Families with Dependent Children and food stamps (then fully paid for by the federal government). The additional cost to the states for these two programs was projected to be $16.5 billion in the coming fiscal year. The turnback proposed phasing out approximately 40 federal education, transportation, community development, and social service programs. The federal government would provide financing for the states to fund these programs or to use the money in other ways.[189] The swap and the turnback would have profoundly changed fiscal federalism, the financial relationship between the federal government and state and local governments.[190] The states would have been empowered again.

Reagan devoted time and effort to the federalism proposal. He met with the nation's governors, state legislators, mayors, county officials, and township officials. The "New Federalism negotiations" had been promised in the State of the Union message.[191] The administration did not include in the negotiations the national interest groups that had worked to create and sustain the programs in question. They assumed, probably correctly, that these groups would work intensely to continue the status quo. The administration thought state and local officials could be persuaded to support the plan, thereby circumventing interest groups' demands.[192] Yet the state and local officials that Reagan was counting on could not be persuaded to support the innovation.

The president and the states deeply disagreed about what level of government should be responsible for social welfare programs.

Reagan believed income maintenance programs (Aid to Families with Dependent Children, food stamps, and Medicaid) should be the responsibility of state and local governments. Most state and local officials thought that demand for such programs came from national factors, which implied the programs should be a national responsibility. Reagan agreed to take on Medicaid in return for the states taking food stamps and AFDC. Later, Reagan also agreed to take food stamps out of the swap. That did not produce a deal. The failure was not surprising. Governor Scott Matheson, the head of the National Governors Association, told the president, "The Governors are unanimously on record as opposing the transfer of income maintenance to the states."[193]

In the end, despite all the negotiations and compromises, the New Federalism initiative did not come close to passing. The swap aspect of change attracted opposition from the National Governors Association, the National Conference of State Legislatures, the National League of Cities, the National Association of Counties, and a number of key members of Congress.[194] State officials had been open to changing the federal system in 1981.[195] Why did they reject the swap?

The states did not want more responsibilities in tough times.[196] Nor did they wish to raise the taxes needed to finance their end of the swap. By one estimate, Reagan's initial and second proposals required substantial tax increases in the states.[197] Richard Williamson, Reagan's adviser on the project, also thought the chances of passing the changes suffered along with the economy. The administration was also pursuing budget cuts, and Congress had passed cuts in spending for state and local governments that were larger than the administration requested. The struggle also became more partisan, and many of the governors faced election in 1982, a difficult year for incumbents, and wished not to make things worse through budget cuts caused by changes in federalism.[198] In Congress, votes on the New Federalism were similar to the 1982 votes favoring tax increases. Eastern Republicans, representing free-spending states dependent on federal subsidies, abandoned Reagan. Congress also voted on particular programs and grants rather than for or against an omnibus reconciliation.[199]

In 1983, Reagan proposed more limited reforms in federalism. He called for consolidating 34 programs into 4 block grants. Congress ignored the proposal. The window of opportunity for radical change in the relationship between the states and national government had closed.[200]

Informed observers concluded that despite the changes enacted at Reagan's behest, "the basic contours of the federal system were not markedly different. No real devolution of power had been accomplished."[201] The Reagan administration claimed to have provided regulatory relief for state and local governments in 24 cases; however, only four of those involved reducing regulations on the states.[202]

Yet Reagan could count some successes along with these disappointments. The Reagan program limited federal subsidies for state spending.[203] Reagan's efforts also reduced federal control over grants to the states. Reconciliation in 1981 also consolidated 77 categorical grants into 9 block grants and eliminated another 60 categorical grants. By 1983, the number of categorical grant programs administered by the federal government had fallen to 313.[204]

How did the states respond? Liberal states in good fiscal condition replaced the federal cutbacks. The programs that did the best "were those in areas of traditional or longstanding state and local government activity that had a politically strong constituency and/or provider group." Health care and capital spending did better than other programs. Scholars studying the Reagan initiatives concluded that federalism had changed: state governments were more likely "to play a larger role as the federal government pulled back. Decisions about strategies to 'cope' with federal aid cuts were often made at the state level, and local governments often turned to their state government to deal with problems and needs in the areas in which the federal government was pulling back."[205] Power and responsibility did return in some measure to the states, and that revival did not necessarily lead to policies that Reagan would have supported. Many states and localities raised taxes as well as cut spending.[206]

The failure of his New Federalism proposal deprived Reagan of the chance to fundamentally change the foundations of the old regime. The New Federalism initiative would not only have devolved power from Washington but also set up competition among the states, thereby holding down redistribution of income and wealth. This dynamic might have reversed the nationalizing trend that began with FDR. Congress was unlikely to surrender its own power, at least to the states. For their part, the states had no interest in a swap that did not help their budgets. Reagan might have mollified the concerns of state and local officials by making the swap more attractive financially in the short term, but such compensation would have required more federal spending, not less. Reagan's moderation in taxation had deprived his administration of the money to spend on such compensation.[207]

Such compensation might have eased the way to a New Federalism. But it would have also undermined the reforms. The New Federalism proposal offered two ways to reduce the ambit of the federal government. It would renew and empower the states, enabling them to reclaim their traditional role in a federal system, a role that would limit the federal government. That shift of responsibilities—the swap—would also reduce the spending (and taxing) of the federal government; both would be carried out outside Washington. State officials wanted both control and "free" money. Had they been compensated to take back the programs, would the states actually have become independent of the federal government? Of course, the federal largesse might be transitional, but temporary spending from Congress tends to become permanent. The cuts in spending and empowerment of the states in the New Federalism had to be accomplished together to achieve Reagan's goal of limiting the national government. It would have been difficult in normal times to accomplish both, given history and the power of inertia. In a bad economy, Reagan had little chance to bring about radical change.

The Politics of Trade

Reagan's commitment to individual liberty implied free movement of goods, services, and people across international borders. Ideas notwithstanding, the early Reagan record on trade and immigration focused on restricting liberty in trade and employment. The libertarian writer Sheldon Richman complained in 1982 that Reagan had pursued neomercantilism in trade policy marked by a "churlish jingoism" along with broad restrictions on immigration.[208] Reagan's early record supports Richman's complaint.

Reagan first provided protection to the U.S. auto industry in May 1981. Rising gasoline prices had spurred demand for smaller, more fuel-efficient cars, which in turn rewarded Japanese importers while harming domestic auto companies. During the 1980 campaign, 30 percent of American autoworkers were redundant. Reagan said in Detroit in September 1981, "I think the Government has a role to convince the Japanese that the deluge of their cars into the U.S. must

111

be slowed while our industry gets on its feet."[209] As with cutting spending, several members of Reagan's cabinet supported larger government. Congress took up an auto import quota bill that would have cut Japanese imports by 15 percent through 1983. The Japanese understood the risk and "voluntarily" restricted imports by 12 percent through 1985, when they expanded to 2.3 million units. Import prices went up, consumer welfare declined, and U.S. auto companies enjoyed regained profitability. The Japanese responded by exporting more expensive cars and maintaining their import share in the long run.[210]

David Stockman later remarked of the auto import restrictions, "The President was a strong free trader, but he was also a politician, and his political antennae could be tuned to the desired frequency."[211] Good politics did not support good policy. Voters enjoy the wealth produced by market competition free of state controls. But such competition also brings changes: industries fall as well as rise, and individuals lose as well as gain from the "creative destruction" implicit in capitalism. The losers then seek protection from change, in part because they have been told they are entitled to a certain standard of living. Having created a demand for protection, politicians then campaign on promises to implement "industrial policy" or import restrictions.[212]

Reagan's actions may be defended with an eye toward consequences rather than principles. Reagan faced an economic contraction in 1982 that harmed many voters, who in turn might have elected members of Congress who would have expanded state power enormously over economic life to satisfy their constituents' desire for economic security. Reagan could have vetoed the bills offering protection to the steel and auto industries. If his veto had been upheld, international trade would have been freer than under the "voluntary" protectionism he negotiated. But Democrats might have used his veto to win a larger victory in the 1982 congressional elections and thereafter enacted laws that expanded the intervention of government well beyond Reagan's voluntary agreements. Reagan certainly violated free-trade principles in 1982 and thereafter. He may also have maximized liberty, given the circumstances of the time.

The 1982 Election

The 1982 election should have been an unmitigated disaster for the GOP. It was held during a severe recession. Unemployment was over 10 percent of the work force. The campaign of 1982 focused on the economic policies of the president. The Democrats made the case for their unfairness; the administration urged voters to stay the course. Commentators in the media viewed the election as a referendum on Reagan and his economic policies. Reagan still commanded a majority approval rating (52 percent) but it had fallen, and the gap between approval and disapproval was the lowest in history one year into a presidency. By election day, Reagan's job approval rating was the lowest for a president going into an election since Truman in 1946.

Economic models of election outcomes indicated that the GOP should have received 41 percent of the overall vote, leading to a loss of 50 seats. Other experts estimated that the dire economic conditions should have led to a loss of 58 Republican seats in the House. House Republicans in fact received 44 percent of the vote in 1982 and lost 26 seats. The Senate was a different story. The partisan breakdown in that body remained the same; the GOP enjoyed a seven-seat majority.[213] In these circumstances, the 1982 electoral results should count as a success for the Republicans, House losses notwithstanding. Why did the GOP do as well as it did?

Reagan was lucky in his opponents. The public trusted the Democrats even less than they trusted the Republicans. One-quarter had "a lot of confidence" in Reagan's ability to solve the nation's economic problems. That was bad enough. But only 1 in 10 had the same confidence in the Democrats. One poll showed that 46 percent blamed the recession on "the situation Reagan inherited," while only 33 percent blamed "Reagan and his policies." Another poll showed that 50 percent believed Reagan's policies "needed more time," while only 6 percent thought they were a success. Polls also showed that people opposed higher income and gas taxes, while in the abstract supporting cuts in government spending. There was also little support for cutting specific programs.[214] Many voters, in short, were inclined to give the president's policies more time to work. This division in the electorate held Democratic gains below expectations.[215]

Republicans struggled hard against their circumstances and were helped by Democratic miscalculation. The GOP recruited a group of challengers in 1981, when Reagan was going from legislative victory to political victory, and held most of them the next year, when conditions were less sanguine. The GOP could offer adequate funding for a candidate. The party ran its most experienced group of challengers since 1972. The Democrats also recruited a strong class of candidates. But they faced a funding problem. Democratic incumbents began the cycle in fear of a repeat of 1980, a concern that successful Republican efforts to recruit strong challengers did nothing to soothe. Incumbent congressional Democrats went on "a fundraising binge" and soaked up much of the funding that might have been available for other Democratic challengers once the economy changed and 1982 started looking like a Democratic year. They also had no way to transfer the money already raised from safe incumbents to needy and potentially successful challengers. The Republicans used their fundraising edge well in the final days of the campaign. Experts concluded that the national Republican Party's efforts in the last three weeks kept 10 to 20 House seats in the GOP column.[216] Nearly one-third of Democratic campaign money went to incumbents who won more than 70 percent of the vote, money that was almost completely wasted.[217]

The Republicans did not do as well as they might have, however. Many experts expected demographic change to favor the GOP in 1982. Southern and western states had obtained 17 new districts, and the Republicans hoped to win a majority of them. In the end, the Democrats won 10 of the 17. The recession played a part in this result, but redistricting to favor Democrats also mattered, especially in California. Redistricting, as well as the recession, accounted for this result.[218] The problems with redistricting reflected Republican weakness in state legislatures. Democrats controlled both chambers in 28 states during the redistricting following the 1980 census; Republicans controlled 15 and would lose 4 of them in 1982.[219]

The 1982 results did not favor limiting the federal government. The House itself moved left in 1983. All 26 Republicans defeated in the election had supported the 1981 budget along with its cuts in spending. Moderates who had voted against Reagan in 1982 by and large survived. These changes emboldened the House leadership, who loaded the Budget Committee with liberal Democrats over the next three Congresses.[220] Even though Republicans had avoided a catastrophe, the new Congress would hardly be open to more spending cuts. More taxes had also not attracted much support from voters, and since the Senate had remained as it was, the president could sustain a veto of tax increases in any case. The nation moved away from the Reagan Revolution without endorsing the old regime. Stalemate began.

Conclusion

The years 1981 and 1982 are the most important in the history of the struggle to limit government in the United States. Reagan won a substantial victory by promising to cut spending and taxes. He then carried through on those promises by persuading Congress to lower marginal tax rates and to constrain the growth in federal spending. From 1981 to 1982, federal budget resources dropped by 14.2 percent. He successfully defended the lower tax rates in the face of deficits even as he bowed to political reality and supported other tax increases in 1982.[221] Reagan also contributed to preventing electoral catastrophe for Republicans in 1982.

The record of Reagan's first two years should not be overestimated. During his most successful period legislatively, Reagan was more a reformer of the old regime than a radical undermining it. His most radical proposals—for a balanced budget or a decentralized federalism—came to nothing. His attempts to introduce mild changes in entitlement programs lasted for days, not weeks, on Capitol Hill. His most unexpected achievements restrained spending to comport with historical norms. His tax-rate cuts were followed by tax increases. Even the rate cuts reformed rather than undermined the old regime. They improved incentives for working, saving, and investment, thereby shoring up the old regime.

As an orator, he brilliantly invoked a residual distrust of the government among Americans. Perhaps he realized "in only seven months, a major redirection of the priorities of the American government." But his victories were not truly revolutionary for "he did not change the minds of the American people."[222] Reagan had assumed most Americans did not need to change their minds. They needed only to be freed of the corruptions brought to the few who presided over big government.

His first seven months in office raised questions about his optimism about Americans. They would support limiting government to a point. They would not support even mild reform to programs to which they thought themselves entitled. Innovations that might actually undermine the old regime—balanced budgets and a renewed federalism—did better with the public but not well enough to pass into law. The old regime had fostered support for itself among American voters. FDR had remade Americans in some measure. They both wanted liberty and demanded their due as promised for decades by the leaders of the old regime. Reforms notwithstanding, Reagan still faced the job of not only saving the American people from their government but of also saving them from themselves.

4. Reagan and After

The final six years of the Reagan presidency were marked by economic recovery and political stalemate. The recovery rewarded Reagan with a resounding victory in 1984, a victory that had little meaning apart from a general endorsement of a status quo marked by rapid economic growth. Reagan devoted himself to protecting the decrease in tax rates achieved in 1981. Meanwhile, the spending restraint achieved in that year slowly came undone even as the Democrats remained firmly in charge of the House and, after 1986, also the Senate. Reagan would prove resourceful, however, in finding a way to get liberals to agree to limit government by eliminating tax preferences. The tax reform of 1986 would stand as the major, and perhaps only, achievement in limiting government in Reagan's second term.

By 1988, the United States had neither returned to the 1970s nor entered a new age of limited and popular government. Reagan had changed the trend in spending and taxing. He had solidified skepticism about the beneficence of expanding government. He had done little to end the old regime founded by FDR and continued by LBJ. The Reagan presidency would come to an end in 1990 when his successor agreed to higher tax rates in exchange for the illusion of budgetary restraint. This chapter examines Reagan's continuing struggle to limit government and offers some explanations for his difficulties.

Stalemate

Reagan tried to lead, circumstances notwithstanding. His first budget plan after the 1982 election called for reducing expected spending by $558 billion over the next five fiscal years. Government outlays would increase at the rate of inflation. Defense spending would continue to rise while nondefense discretionary spending, health care spending, and farm price supports would continue to decline. Over the long term, Reagan also proposed savings in Social Security, Medicare, and Medicaid, as well as civil service reforms.[1]

Reagan still had a toehold in public opinion. A small majority in 1983 agreed that the nation should reduce its budget deficit "mostly by cuts in spending." Few people wished for higher taxes even if the revenues were devoted to reducing the deficit. One-third of respondents did support reducing the deficit by both cutting spending and raising taxes "about equally."[2] Yet the public desire for spending cuts did not comport wholly with Reagan's preferences. Fifty-three percent thought cutting defense spending was the best way to reduce the deficit. Twenty-nine percent preferred cutting "all federal programs other than defense and social security and Medicare." The poll helpfully identified the targets for such cuts as farm supports, veterans' benefits, welfare, education, and transportation.[3]

Public opinion notwithstanding, Reagan's cuts had little support in Congress even from Republicans. Republicans controlled the Senate Budget Committee, which offered a plan to raise taxes by $30 billion while cutting Reagan's defense spending increase in half. By 1988, the Senate plan foresaw $80 billion in new taxes, a proposal not far from the one passed by the Democratic majority in the House.[4] Congress did agree on $12 billion in new taxes apart from another $5.2 billion in new Social Security levies.[5] Tax rates did not rise. Spending was not deeply cut. Washington had reached an equilibrium that excluded both deeply cutting or greatly expanding government spending and taxes. Deficits became a lasting part of fiscal life.

The deficits did create some pressure for controlling spending by the most spendthrift programs. Beginning in 1983, the administration and Congress made progress in constraining Medicare costs.[6] In the early 1980s, spending on health care, public and private, was accelerating at record rates. Medicare's hospitalization insurance trust fund neared bankruptcy at a time when government deficits rose near the top of the national agenda. Something had to be done. The Reagan administration had come into office proposing to introduce market reforms into Medicare. Such reforms, however, would not lead to budgetary savings for some time, and the fiscal crisis of Medicare was at Washington's doorstep. The administration shelved vouchers in favor of price controls.

In 1983, Congress enacted the prospective payment system (PPS) for Medicare hospital costs. The PPS set predetermined rates for hospital reimbursements. In 1983, the new system paid hospitals prospectively per case according to a rate applicable to its diagnosis. The PPS was, in other words, a system of prices administered by the government, the dominant buyer in the market for Medicare services. Government regulation, not choices mediated by markets, constrained Medicare costs after 1983 primarily by reducing operating margins for hospitals treating such patients. Congress transferred authority over Medicare from the Social Security Administration to the Health Care Financing Administration, a new agency focused on cost control. The annual rate of growth of Medicare payments to physicians thereafter dropped by almost half. The administration had become responsible overseers of the welfare state. A similar system of physician payment regulations would later be formulated by Congress and signed by President Bush in 1989. The temporary success with Medicare was budgetary, not philosophical.

Election of 1984

Record aside, Reagan's prospects for reelection improved along with the economy in 1983. Civilian unemployment fell by 2.5 percent. The prime interest rate fell to about half of what it had been in November 1980. The economy began expanding rapidly, growing by 9.7 percent and 7.6 percent in the second and third quarters, respectively, before dropping back to 4.9 percent in the final quarter of 1983. As 1984 arrived, Reagan stood an excellent change of being reelected. The question remained what, if anything, a victory might mean. As it turned out, not much.

Unlike 1980, Reagan did not campaign in 1984 on a specific platform. Instead, his reelection effort emphasized the strong economy and a general appeal to "morning in America." The president made no commitments much beyond "stay the course." He did commit to not raising taxes and to "eliminating wasteful and unnecessary government spending." He opposed cuts in military spending or Social Security.[7] The Reagan of 1980 seemed committed to change. The Reagan of 1984 wanted things to stay the same, not least the occupant of the White House. The Democrats wanted change, of course, but wished to do so by staying the same themselves. They chose Walter Mondale, a traditional New Deal liberal who had served as Jimmy Carter's vice president.

Much of the domestic debate concerned the deficits and how they might be reduced. During a presidential debate, Mondale asserted that "perhaps the dominant issue of our times is: What do we do about these enormous deficits?" Later he was more emphatic: deficits were "the most important single issue of our time." [8] Reagan had changed the agenda of the Democratic Party: the party's presidential candidate said the leading issue of the age was the government's budget deficit and not equality, civil rights, or wealth redistribution.

Mondale promised to cut the deficit by two-thirds in his first term. On the spending side, he promised cuts and pay-as-you-go budgeting. Mondale proposed $100 billion in spending cuts to reduce the deficit. He quickly added, "But I am not going to cut it out of Social Security and Medicare and student assistance and things that people need." The sentence evoked applause. Instead, he would cut the rate of growth of defense.[9] Mondale continually came back to the cuts proposed earlier for Social Security and Medicare, putting Reagan on the defensive about those proposals. Reagan said little about cutting the size of government. Indeed, both candidates favored cutting spending on programs few cared about. But someone, often many people, cared about most programs. We might infer that promising to cut those programs did not seem to be a way to win the election.

Mondale also promised to raise taxes, a move later considered courageous if politically foolish. Mondale could point out that Reagan too had agreed to tax increases in his first term and thus might well do so over the next four years. Of course, Mondale would add that Reagan would tax the average American while leaving "his rich friends alone." Mondale then promised he would not leave Reagan's rich friends alone when it came time to tax; the same would be true for the "corporations and freeloaders who play the loopholes or pay no taxes."[10] Mondale seemed to be saying two things. I will raise your taxes but not really; the rich will pay the most. No one seemed willing to pay for the spending that neither candidate was willing to cut.

Unfortunately for Mondale, deficits did not matter much in the 1984 election.[11] The public when polled said deficits were very bad. They also overwhelmingly supported a balanced budget amendment. However, deficits were not really salient. When asked what the nation's most important problem was, deficits received about 5 percent of responses until early 1984 when they jumped to 12 percent. Reagan also received strong support for his handling of the presidency even though the public thought he had done poorly on the deficit. The latter did not matter that much in the larger picture, especially when the economy was doing better.

What might people be willing to do to reduce the deficit? They were willing to postpone the third year of Reagan's tax cut, at least until they received it. A Roper poll showed that for every three respondents who were willing to pay to reduce the deficit, another five would rather live with the red ink than pay more taxes.[12] On election day, 59 percent of the people who cared most about the deficit voted for Reagan.[13]

Reagan won every state except Minnesota and the District of Columbia (which is not a state but has three electoral votes). He received 59 percent of the vote, which ran just below Lyndon Johnson's 61 percent in 1964. Rep. Geraldine A. Ferraro was the Democratic vice presidential candidate. Female voters, however, preferred Reagan to the Mondale-Ferraro ticket by 57 to 42 percent. One of every four Democrats voted for the Republican ticket. Reagan received at least 60 percent of the vote in two-thirds of the states he won, including later Democratic strongholds like New Jersey.[14]

Taxes did matter. An ABC/*Washington Post* survey asked voters to identify the issue where they most disliked the stand of the candidate they did not vote for. The most frequent response was "tax increases." Of those who gave that response, 92 percent voted for Reagan. The third most frequent response was "government spending." Eighty-four percent of those who selected that issue voted for Reagan. The traditional Democratic issues did not work well against Reagan. Only 6 percent of the survey cited Social Security as the issue they disliked about the candidate they voted against; Mondale received two out of three votes among that 6 percent. Reagan ended up increasing his share of the 60 years old and over vote by 9 percent; Mondale ran five points worse than Carter in that age group. Overall, the senior set swung to the GOP candidate by seven points compared to 1980.[15] At the same time, "The president's reelection campaign had done nothing to convince politicians that voters who chose Reagan were voting to cut domestic programs." Most politicians saw the election as a mandate *against* tax increases but not a mandate *for* anything.[16]

1984 was worse than 1980 in some ways for the GOP. Despite Reagan's large victory, the GOP suffered a net loss of 2 Senate seats; it had netted 12 in 1980. The party picked up 14 House seats in 1984; it had won 34 in 1980. Reagan's first victory had yielded four statehouses, but his reelection saw only one governorship switch to the GOP. In 1980, the Republicans won control of both houses of state legislatures in 15 states; 11 followed in 1984.[17]

Why didn't Reagan's victory translate into Republican gains generally? William Schneider thought incumbency advantage accounted for the relative success of embattled Democrats. The economic good times meant voters favored the political status quo, and, in any case, redistricting meant that few seats were open and contestable.[18]

Perhaps what happened to the Democrats was more important than what happened to the Republicans. At no time during the 20th century had a major party experienced such losses as the Democratic presidential candidates experienced from 1972 to 1984. In two of those contests, the Democratic candidate carried only one state. In three of the four, they carried no more than six states, and then they were running as an incumbent. Even their victory bespoke their weakness: Carter won in the wake of Watergate by just 2 percent.[19] To be sure, the Democrats did offer "a liberal vision that was appealing to certain elite groups and minorities." That appeal was not enough to remain the majority party or to win elections.[20]

In contrast, the Republican future looked bright. Fifty-eight percent of 18- to 29-year-olds supported Reagan. The younger voters were also less tied to party in general and were more likely to identify with the Republican Party (by 39 to 34 percent) and to vote for the Republicans in House races (50 to 41 percent). This support among young people suggested that a realignment might be in the works. Reagan also closed the gap between the Democrats and the GOP in party identification. The differences between the parties after 1984 were roughly half what they had been before that date.[21]

Public opinion offered a mixed picture for advocates of limited government at the end of Reagan's first term. Confidence in the federal government had rebounded smartly.[22] The number of people who thought the federal government had become too powerful had dropped by one-third compared to 1980.[23] In some cases, public opinion evinced more support for government regulation in 1984 than when Reagan began his term. The same could be said of government spending. In 1980, the National Opinion Research Center found on average that 42 percent of the public thought the government was spending too little on the environment, health, education, welfare, and urban aid. This number steadily rose during Reagan's first term, reaching 50 percent by 1984. More general measures of the public mood also indicated support for more spending and rose steadily during Reagan's first term.[24]

This shift in public opinion's favoring more spending may seem incongruous. Reagan was popular. He had always stood against government spending, and his administration had even cut the growth of spending sharply in 1981. Perhaps Reagan's other achievement suggests why public opinion changed. By cutting taxes and decoupling taxation from inflation, the president and Congress told taxpayers that the direct costs of government were capped. As long as the United States could borrow to cover deficits, any additional spending would impose no costs on current taxpayers. Having discovered that the price of additional spending was zero, the public favored more of it. Reagan's hope in 1980 was that restraining taxation combined with a fear of deficits would control government outlays.

Voters no longer saw the GOP as a party of businesspeople and the Democrats as the party of prosperity. The traditional Democratic advantage in party identification among voters also dropped by half during Reagan's first term, a 10 percentage point reduction.[25] The Democrats were no longer the nation's normal majority party: "The electorate is now about one-third Democratic, one-third Republican, and one-third independent."[26] The shift was pragmatic: "More Americans express confidence that the conservative approach—less government—may be the best way to solve the nation's problems. . . . conservatism has been tried and has been found to work."[27]

It is difficult not to rue the path not taken. Reagan may have known from polling that he "no longer enjoyed popular support for a further extension of conservative policies."[28] Reagan might have seized the opportunity presented by a strong economy and his own popularity to try to change the public mood toward a taste for less government. But he did not take that chance. Consequently, he could not claim a mandate for limiting government in his second term.

123

Budget Reform in Congress

In 1985, Reagan again proposed cuts in the growth of federal spending. Congress considered his proposals dead on arrival. Meanwhile, as a percentage of national income, the deficit in 1985 reached its highest level since World War II.[29] In late 1985, Congress voted to raise the debt limit to $2 trillion, double the sum when Reagan entered office. Congress also amended the increase in the debt ceiling with the Balanced Budget and Emergency Deficit Control Act, better known as Gramm-Rudman-Hollings. At the time, many members, not all of them Democrats, thought GRH was less than perfect as legislation. But given the continuing deficits and congressional failure to balance the budget, GRH was, as one of its sponsors said, "a bad idea whose time has come."[30]

GRH was a remarkable law. It was "premised on the notion that if left to its own will, a congressional majority would not be able to control the deficit" and that "Congress could not be trusted to deliver deficit reduction under normal legislative procedures."[31] This notion had ample empirical support. Proponents argued that the delegation of power in GRH to other actors would reduce spending and deficits "because spending powers were taken away from the main source of the problem."[32] The law also had a broader appeal. Public opinion primarily blamed Congress for the deficit problem.[33] In passing a law that limited the power of Congress, members of that institution were only following the judgments of the voters who had elected them.

GRH also reflected the hopes and fears of major players in the budget game. The White House saw GRH as a risk to defense spending, but even if defense were cut, the money would go to reduce the deficit, where in the recent past defense had been cut with no effect on the deficit. Democrats thought that GRH would be the end of the Reagan Revolution since it would lead to defense cuts and tax increases. The Senate's budget leaders also believed GRH would force Reagan to give in on taxes to save defense and compel House Democrats eventually to give in on Social Security to save other domestic spending.[34]

GRH established a ceiling on maximum allowable federal deficits, which were expected to decline to zero by 1991. This requirement ostensibly bound Congress to the mast of deficit reduction: this schedule could not be altered except by supermajorities. GRH also required automatic cuts—a sequestration in federal spending when Congress and the president failed to hit the deficit goals. This procedure was controlled by officials outside of Congress, first by the comptroller general of the General Accounting Office and later by the Office of Management and Budget.[35]

Some members thought GRH would never actually bring about sequestration. It was a doomsday machine: the political consequences of sequestration were so bad that members would be forced to meet the deficit reduction targets through negotiation. It was an attempt to impose budgetary discipline on Congress by making deficit reduction look better to members than the alternative of general reductions in spending.[36]

Yet the automatic cuts would not be "across the board." In the final version of the law, 40 percent of total federal spending would be threatened by sequestration. To get the law passed, spending supported by a majority would have to be exempt from the doomsday device. GRH stipulated that sequestration would split the cuts equally between defense and social spending. The included social programs would thus face a larger relative cut under sequestration since most of the domestic budget had already been excluded from the law.[37]

GRH failed to meet its targets for reducing the federal deficit. The deficit as a percentage of national income did fall after GRH became law. However, it is far from clear that GRH reduced the deficit. It may have been a symbolic gesture that encouraged Congress to reduce deficits more than it would have otherwise (though not enough to the meet the law's targets). The law may have also increased deficits. Members might have concluded that by increasing spending on unprotected programs, they would both decrease the likelihood of sequestration and fund favored programs.[38] Why did GRH fail?

The doomsday machine was not credible. Sequestration required deep cuts in a small number of programs, including defense. At one point, the law would have required a 30 percent reduction in defense and other unprotected spending. Such spending had enough champions in Congress to make such reductions unlikely. Once members knew that sequestration would not work, the process did not deter members from deficit spending.

Sequestration might have worked if it demanded much smaller cuts in a larger number of programs. However, members of Congress wished to protect most programs from even small cuts. GRH thus reflected rather than contested the mentality that led to deficits: members wished to protect programs they favored. Budget rules did not affect the budget choices of Congress; rather, those preferences caused the budget rules (like GRH), and when the two conflicted, the underlying preference for spending on favored programs triumphed.[39]

GRH in various forms would persist for several years. It remained largely an ineffectual congressional gambit. Reagan would look elsewhere for reforms to limit government.

The Tax Reform Act of 1986

For years, congress has offered tax preferences that are said to "allocate benefits among people and groups for social purposes." Such preferences reduce a person's tax liability to the government so long as that person performs some act the government wishes to encourage.[40] The government reduces its cost to individuals or groups in exchange for their doing something the government wants done. Tax preferences represent a kind of social control through offers rather than threats. Is it coercive? Perhaps not. It makes people better off since they have more money than they would have otherwise, and presumably they are willing to do what the government wants in exchange for the "tax payment." The taxpayers are better off and consent to the obligation, which might be nothing more onerous than owning a house.

But tax preferences do not reduce the scope of government in general. Others must pay higher taxes unless spending elsewhere is cut just as much as the tax preference, and tax preferences have no relation to spending cuts. Hence, the coercion implicit in taxation merely shifts from the previously taxed citizen to others, who must pay his or her (former) share. There is no net reduction in coercion by the state.

The ambit of government actually grows through tax preferences. A tax preference, afterall, is not a tax cut. If a tax is reduced, the government loses control over how that money will be spent. With a tax preference, the government expands by hiring new (part-time?) employees in the private sector who are charged with attaining some government-given goal. For example, in 1981, the moderate

126

Democratic alternative tax bill offered small and medium-size businesses "liberalized depreciation and specific incentives for research and technological innovation . . . to rejuvenate America's industrial base."[41]

Tax preferences also obscure the intervention of the government in the private economy. Robert Packwood, a longtime member of Congress and supporter of tax preferences, once said:

> If for some reason we think something needs to be encouraged beyond the marketplace, whether it is for national security, or other legitimate reasons, it seems to me we have two ways to do it. One way is to use the tax code, and the other is a straight out government subsidy or government program. And for years at least, many of us have thought that the tax code was a more effective and efficient way to do it than a government managed, government run, government loaned and on occasion government owned program.[42]

Put this way, tax preferences seem market friendly, a better alternative than state coercion. But control remains with the government, which gets people to do as it wishes. Individuals essentially trade higher after-tax income for less liberty.

Tax preferences also work against limiting government in two other ways. First, they encourage elected officials to extract more taxes than they would otherwise; more tax revenue translates into more offers of tax preferences and thereby a larger ambit of control for elected officials. Second, tax preferences may also lead to higher tax rates than otherwise could be sustained by elected officials. Tax preferences lower the cost of taxes to the recipient, who then has less reason to complain about the taxation. Elected officials might be expected to offer tax preferences to the point that enough opposition to the rate of taxation is bought off to stabilize the system.[43] If tax preferences did not exist (that is, if everyone paid the same rate), existing tax rates might generate enough opposition to induce a lower rate.

It may also be argued that eliminating tax preferences may shore up or even expand activist government. The public did not like the tax code in 1985. Surveys indicated that most saw income taxes as the least fair of all taxes, and only a minority of the public saw cheating on taxes as wrong.[44] Another survey taken the same year found that 81 percent of respondents agreed that "many rich people pay hardly any taxes at all."[45] Tax preferences, therefore, might undermine the legitimacy of taxes, a necessary condition for growth of government.

This concern for restoring public confidence had some appeal to elected officials, who depended on a measure of cooperation from the public to finance their ambitions. Packwood took up tax reform as a way to get lower marginal rates, which in turn would foster a greater public willingness to pay taxes.[46] More generally, those who wished to expand the ambit of government also believed tax reform would help their cause by restoring public faith in government.[47]

This argument runs up against one large empirical problem: the rapid growth of government and an increase in tax preferences went hand in hand during the 1960s and 1970s. Tax preferences do not appear to have stopped the growth of government spending and certainly increased the ambit of public officials.

Eliminating tax preferences—known as tax reform—faced serious opposition. That prospect of losses provided ample reason for the affected groups to organize and defend their preferences. The end of the preferences could reduce taxes on a much larger number of people and firms, but their gains would be relatively small and hardly enough to support lobbying efforts to counter the activity of those who held the preferences. The politics of tax reform are thus the politics of overcoming the "special interests" and the iron logic of political organization and influence.[48] It seemed unlikely that tax reform would ever pass.

Tax reform was not merely the work of devils claiming privileges denied "the people." Many tax preferences assisted large groups of voters. Surveys in the 1980s showed that a majority would do away with the deduction for oil and drilling costs; at the same time, more than 80 percent of respondents wanted to keep the preferences for Social Security benefits, veterans' benefits, and high medical expenses.[49] Two-thirds of itemizing taxpayers took the deduction for state and local taxes, which might be eliminated under a comprehensive reform. Millions of others received untaxed fringe benefits nominally paid for by their employer. Few people thought of these tax breaks as a free ride for a special interest. *Their* tax preferences, of course, were fully deserved.[50]

What would become the Tax Reform Act of 1986 had a bipartisan political pedigree going back at least to the 1970s. Rep. Jack Kemp and Sen. William V. Roth Jr. had proposed a low-rate tax code in 1977 that included existing preferences. In 1982, Sen. Bill Bradley and Rep. Richard A. Gephardt also took up the idea of low rates, not to reduce revenue but rather to remove the incentives for tax preferences.[51] The Reagan reelection team feared that Bradley would convince the Democratic candidate for president to adopt tax reform as a campaign theme. Reagan would need a response, and hence the reform plan rose on the administration's agenda.[52] In January 1984, Reagan called for a broad simplification of the tax code, and Jack Kemp, along with Sen. Robert Kasten (R-WI), followed up in April by introducing a tax bill built around a single, flat rate.[53] As we saw earlier, taxes did matter in the 1984 election, but tax reform largely did not. The issue nonetheless persisted.

Reagan asked his treasury secretary, Donald T. Regan, to come up with a concrete proposal for reforming taxes. Their initial effort reduced corporate and personal tax rates, accelerated depreciation for business equipment (an important part of the 1981 reform), and eliminated the investment tax credit and deductions for state and local income and sales taxes. Personal taxes were expected to be cut by $148 billion, while business taxes would increase by $165 billion.[54] Secretary Regan asked for a simpler and lower personal rate structure than the one initially proposed by his staff. The revised, lower rates came with an increase in the corporate tax from 28 to 33 percent.[55] Business groups opposed the initial proposal; it reduced their existing preferences. In May 1985, Treasury offered a bill that preserved some business preferences and eliminated taxes for the poor while retaining the reduced tax brackets of Treasury I.[56]

Tax reform began in the House. It also almost ended there. Dan Rostenkowski, chair of the House Ways and Means Committee, favored reform but wished to formulate his own bill. He found out what his fellow Democrats on the Ways and Means Committee wanted and then through negotiation and vote trading produced a bill that was strongly partisan. The bill seemed little more than a reshuffling of deductions to favor Democratic client groups. The whole House at first rejected the Ways and Means bill on a procedural vote; the bill lost one-quarter of House Democrats and over 90 percent of GOP members. Reagan then intervened to save the effort. He promised the Senate would forge a better bill more favorable to Republican concerns. Two days after the initial failure, the House voted to send the bill to the Senate.[57]

The Senate Finance Committee started fresh, but once again reform all but died. The committee began writing the bill by *adding* tax preferences valued at $30 billion. The chair of the Finance Committee, Robert Packwood (R-OR), was an unlikely foe of tax preferences. He had championed preferences for sending children to private schools, conserving energy, and encouraging businesses to offer employee health coverage.[58] He and his committee, like Rostenkowski and his, began by assuming the future would be like the past on tax reform, a lot of talk followed by contravening actions. But in the spring of 1986, the future would differ from the past, at least for a while.

Like Rostenkowski in the House, Packwood at first tried to do tax policy the old way. He produced a bill that contained at best marginal reforms formulated through horse-trading with Finance Committee members. The deal turned out to be bad public relations. The politics of taxes had changed for the time being, while Packwood and his committee had stayed the same. The initial Senate bill distributed benefits to various favored causes in the traditional manner.

What was different this time was public attention. Reagan, the media, and some interest groups favoring reform made the Finance Committee actions into a public matter framed as a populist drama: the virtuous and long-suffering little guy was once again done in by the rich insiders claiming special privileges. Yet it is easy to exaggerate the appeal of that populism. Inside Washington, many people, especially in the media, cared about the tax legislation, and their attention tended at first to reduce Packwood's moral and political reputation. The public at large, as almost always is the case, generally knew little about the ongoing struggle.[59] The story that moved Packwood was a populist story for elites.

The Packwood turn toward reform meant in practice that the Joint Tax Committee staff would be writing a bill. Packwood and five members of the Finance Committee met to design a bill that would lower rates and remove preferences. They tried within limits to craft a system in which reductions favored the lowest-income taxpayers and where income from all sources was treated uniformly. The Finance bill established two individual tax rates—15 percent and 25 percent—and a top corporate rate of 33 percent. Economic efficiency would flow from a level playing field. In committee, Packwood required that any amendments be revenue neutral. The reform bill passed the committee largely intact.[60] Packwood transformed his rhetoric in seeking to lead: "By the end of the legislative debate, in fact, Packwood was pushing his bill precisely because he said it offended many economic interests, and thereby represented the triumph of general over special interests."[61]

After two years of work, Congress passed the first complete revision of the Internal Revenue Code since 1954. The new law reduced the top individual tax rate from 50 percent to 28 percent and taxed 85 percent of all individuals at the bottom rate of 15 percent. It reduced the number of brackets to two in 1988, compared to 15 in 1985. The law cut individual tax rates more than either the Reagan plan or the Bradley-Gephardt bill had envisioned.[62] When Reagan took office, the marginal rate was 70 percent for individuals. After tax reform, the top rate was 28 percent. Experts expected that the 1986 law would lead to slightly lower personal tax bills for about two-thirds of all individual taxpayers.[63]

The law was expected to move $120 billion of the total income tax burden from individuals to corporations over the next five years. On the other hand, the new law reduced the top corporate rate from 46 percent to 34 percent.[64] The increases were not the same for all businesses. Agriculture, manufacturing, and trade, which labored under the highest effective rates up to 1986, were expected to see similar or smaller tax liabilities. Among the losers on the business side were oil and mining, utilities, construction, communication, transportation and service industries, real estate, heavy industry, large banks, casualty insurance, defense contractors, and multinational corporations.[65]

The economic interests that normally dominated tax policymaking lost money from tax reform. Thomas Downey, a Democrat on Ways and Means, said: "This tax bill is really a testament to the limitations of special interest groups. They were annihilated. They took a beating the likes of which I could not imagine before it occurred."[66] For a moment, at least, the Stockman critique of American corruption was proved wrong.

Reagan praised the law precisely because it reduced (or seemed to reduce) the progressivity of the tax code. Reagan said on signing the bill, that the "steeply progressive nature of the income tax" had "struck at the heart of the economic life of the individual, punishing his special effort and extra hard work that had always been the driving force of our economy."[67] But many on the left were also satisfied. Henry J. Aaron of the Brookings Institution called the legislation "the most important improvement in the broad-based taxes on individual and corporate income in at least two decades."[68]

Why did tax reform happen? Reagan's leadership was vital. He made tax reform a priority of his second term and stayed behind it despite the doubts of his own party. The Democrats also believed that given Reagan's support, they would be outflanked if they blocked the bill, and tax reform would become a weapon for the popular GOP incumbent to use against the congressional Democrats.[69] Reagan was also willing and able to impose costs on his supporters in pursuit of a larger goal. In tax reform, Reagan sought to transfer taxes from individuals to businesses. That transfer served the larger goal of "a limited domestic government supported by a larger economy that operated under market incentives."

Reagan believed preferences were bad for business, while low taxes were good. He also believed, not without reason, that once tax rates had been reduced, it would be difficult to raise them again. Inflation would not raise them since the rates had been indexed to the price level. To raise revenue, the Democrats had to explicitly raise rates; they could no longer count on simply doing away with tax preferences to find more revenue. That might not matter much if the Democrats could simply raise taxes on the affluent. But significant increases in taxes may require more than attacking the top decile of the income distribution; it may require taxing the middle class.[70] In short, Reagan "traded short-term dissatisfaction among his constituents for a long-term policy structure that fit and favored his ideals."[71]

It would be nice to think that the public rallied to a cause that was popular across the political spectrum, but they did not. When the bill was signed, a poll showed that 19 percent of respondents supported the program, 16 percent opposed it, and 65 percent had no opinion.[72] Most of the public saw the deficit as a much more important issue than tax reform. Fewer than 2 percent of the public named tax reform as the most important national problem in 1985 polling.[73] The law also did little to assuage the public resentment about taxes. In April 1987, surveys found that 74 percent of respondents agreed that "many rich people pay hardly any taxes at all." That was lower than two years previously, when 81 percent agreed to the claim. Congress had moved heaven and earth on taxes to change public attitudes by less than 10 percent.[74]

The Election of 1986

The 1986 elections in the House were uneventful. From 1946 to 1986, the president's party lost an average of 30 House seats at midterm; during a president's second term, the midterm average loss had been 43 seats. Before 1986, the best performance in the House by the president's party had been to lose 29 seats. In 1986, the GOP lost a net of five seats; in general, only six incumbents were defeated.

Why did the House move so little? The economy was in its fourth year of steady growth, per capita incomes rose 3.1 percent during 1986, and Reagan had a 63 percent approval rating on election day. Republicans had also made few gains in the 1984 House elections, so few seats were at risk in 1986. Both parties also mounted few serious challengers, a likely condition for beating an incumbent. Only 19 percent of Republican incumbents faced challengers who had previously held elective office; in 1982, 40 percent had faced experienced challengers, and in 1974, 42 percent had done so. Few challengers were adequately funded, which is not surprising since things were going well in the nation. Moreover, Republicans might well have been discouraged about the chances of beating Democrats who had survived Reagan's 1984 landslide. Democrats were discouraged by the national conditions and the lack of targets.[75]

The story in the U.S Senate was different: Democrats defeated seven Republican incumbents, gained eight seats, and took majority control. The Senate outcome depended on close races going to the Democrats. In 1980 and 1982, most close Senate elections had fallen to the GOP. But in 1986, 9 of the 11 races won by 52 percent or less went to Democrats.[76] American government would be fully divided for first time under Reagan.

Moreover, the large Democratic majorities seemed invulnerable. In 1986, House races evinced the highest rate of reelection in more than three decades: 98 percent. Only eight of the 393 representatives who sought reelection lost: two in the primaries and six in the general election.[77] Sixty percent of the House of Representatives in the 100th Congress would identify with the Democratic Party. In the Senate, the Democrats would have a 10-seat majority. Having recovered from their 1980 debacle, the congressional Democrats seemed ready and capable of protecting most of the old regime.

The Stock Market Crash

During much of 1986, congressional leaders tried to induce President Reagan to join budget negotiations that would lead to a compromise budget deal. They believed a "budget summit" would force Reagan to choose between his desire for higher defense spending and his opposition to the higher tax increase. The congressional leaders believed at the same time that domestic spending had been reduced as much as it could be, given the electoral risks associated with reducing spending. Reagan rejected the summit idea. The Democratic leadership still had another card to play. In October, the automatic cuts mandated by Gramm-Rudman would take effect. Half those cuts would come from the defense budget, which would be reduced by 10.5 percent. To avoid that, congressional Democrats hoped Reagan would come to the table to work out a bipartisan deal on the budget.[78]

Then Black Monday came. The Dow Jones Industrial Average dropped by 22 percent on October 19, 1987. In retrospect, the reasons for the decline remain obscure. Black Monday did not lead to a recession.[79] At the time, however, virtually everyone involved in politics thought the markets were sending the politicians a message to deal with what had come to be known as the "twin deficits," the budgetary and trade deficits.[80] For six years, political leaders had told one another and the public that their fiscal irresponsibility would surely lead to economic disaster. In the nervous days after Black Monday, members of Congress began to believe that disasters, economic and political, so long portended might be arriving. The public was less concerned. On Thursday and Friday of the week that began with Black Monday, the Gallup organization found that 60 percent of Americans thought the stock market crash "does not necessarily indicate a serious downward trend in the economy." Just over 50 percent also believed they would be better off financially in the fall of 1988.[81]

Three days after Black Monday, Reagan agreed to participate in a "budget summit" in response to the market problems. To that moment, Reagan had defended his 1981 achievement of lower tax rates. Now he seemed ready to surrender: "I'm putting everything on the table with the exception of Social Security, with no other preconditions." An increase in taxes seemed inevitable. The negotiators had fashioned a two-year plan to reduce the budget deficit; almost one-third of the reduction came from new taxes. The rate reduction from 1981, however, survived.[82] The administration relented also on defense spending, and the growth in entitlement programs was cut by $4 billion and $6 billion over the next two fiscal years. Social Security and other cost-of-living adjustments in the budget were left alone."[83]

The 1987 budget summit served as an apt bookend for 1981. In 1981, Congress had limited spending and taxation following an electoral mandate. The man who fostered that mandate, Ronald Reagan, believed that lower tax rates would ultimately force lower spending through Congress's fear of deficits. The events of the next six years belied that hope. Congress feared voters would react worse to higher taxes or lower spending than to the future effects of the ensuing deficits. It was only when deficits seemed to be leading, in fact as well as in theory, to economic disaster that Congress and the president acted. Even then, taxes as well as spending would be the way to avert the looming disaster. Congress apparently will lower spending only in the face of a clear electoral mandate or looming economic disaster.

After Reagan

Reagan's vice president, George H. W. Bush, won the presidency in 1988, largely as the candidate of continuity. Reagan had also chosen Bush with the presumed knowledge that vice presidents often succeed presidents. Reagan may have thought Bush was an acceptable leader to continue his work. His endorsement mattered. Reagan enjoyed majority approval of his presidency for almost all of 1988.[84] Of those who approved of Reagan, 83 percent voted for Bush. Political scientist Paul Quirk concludes, "To a great extent, the election outcome was an endorsement of Reagan."[85] Bush won election with 54 percent of the vote.[86]

George H. W. Bush had earned his place as Reagan's heir, and yet reasonable questions remained whether or not he was a Reaganite. He had attacked Reagan's economic proposals as "voodoo economics," a charge recalled thereafter by Democratic campaigns and mistrustful conservatives. His address accepting the Republican nomination both affirmed and denied the limited government part of Reagan's legacy. He invoked the Pledge of Allegiance, the death penalty, voluntary school prayer, gun ownership, opposition to abortion, and prison furloughs. He famously promised to never accept a rise in taxes. Two-thirds of the voters agreed with that position.[87]

But Bush's speech also proposed mainstreaming the disabled, ending ocean garbage-dumping, reducing acid rain, extending racial harmony, and restoring pride and ethics to government service. Bush called for a "kinder, gentler nation," thereby rhetorically backing away from opposition to the welfare state. Bush called for higher ethical standards in government service, thereby indirectly affirming the value of the bureaucracy.[88] Bush may have wished to give the public what it wanted, which led to his incoherent jumble of proposals. Writing in 1989, Jean Bethke Elshtain noted that surveys had shown for a number of years that solid majorities favored national health insurance, job guarantees, and more environmental regulations. At the same time, solid majorities also believe the federal government was too large, spent too much, and interfered too much in people's lives.[89]

The GOP base was changing and with it, the program of its presidential candidate. Pat Robertson, a television personality favored by Protestant evangelicals, ran in the Republican primaries and unexpectedly finished ahead of the vice president in Iowa. This surprise slowed but did not endanger Bush's nomination by the GOP. It did force Bush to spend more resources on that struggle and to give rhetorical support to cultural conservatism, as he did when he accepted the nomination.[90]

The political point had been made: conservative Christians counted in Republican presidential politics. In retrospect, the 1988 general election represented a turning point for the Republican Party. It was the first general election in which Republicans attracted more voters who regularly attended Protestant evangelical churches than the Democrats did. This trend toward the GOP would accelerate over the next decade.[91]

By 1980, Protestant denominations—long a solid source of GOP voters—were rapidly losing their shares of the market for religion.

Evangelical denominations were gaining adherents and would continue to do so for the next two decades.[92] If these rising denominations could be tied politically to the GOP, the party would have demographics on its side in future elections.

Bush's 1988 campaign suggested the search for votes would change the party. Party leaders might consider both evangelicals and limited government advocates as conservatives, but the former hoped to use government to redeem the world by enforcing God's will, while the latter sought to free the individual from government guidance, including on the fundamental issues that defined the Christian right. The big Republican tent had always threatened to become a big fight over fundamentals. In 1988, the third straight GOP victory obscured potential problems for the coalition. In any case, the advocates of both liberty and virtue were more concerned that their new leader had little commitment to either ideal.

Surrender

Congress continued to struggle with the deficit. Outside mechanisms were again created. A commission to study the deficit came to no consensus and was ignored.[93] Summit meetings between Congress and the White House took place as they had in late 1987; on two occasions, such groups came up with proposals that led to bills that reduced the budget deficit. The deficit continued to grow larger. For three years under Gramm-Rudman (fiscal years 1987–89), the deficit came in around $150 billion; this sum was lower than the two previous years. But the deficit blossomed anew during the Bush administration, twice threatening to breach the $300 billion mark.[94]

Bush started his administration by proposing a budget and a series of summits with congressional leaders to agree on the details. The deals that followed did not convince anyone. They were filled with one-time fiscal windfalls and accounting tricks that would get Congress through the Gramm-Rudman process but would have little effect on long-term deficits.[95] In a word, the budget remained a mess.

In May 1990, President Bush called for the third budget summit with Congress in as many years. Democrats feared that tax increases were inevitable and that they would be blamed for them. They joined the summit only on the condition that higher taxes were a subject of negotiation. Conservatives fretted and for good reason. In June, the president endorsed tax increases. He argued that "getting this

137

deficit down, continuing economic expansion and employment in this country" trumped his earlier campaign pledges not to raise taxes. "I knew I'd catch some flak on this decision," Bush said, "but I've got to do what I think is right."

House Republicans immediately sent their president a sharp letter saying they were "stunned" by the statement. Three weeks later, the House Republican Conference passed by a 2-to-1 margin a resolution opposing new taxes to cut the deficit.[96] Eighteen Senate Republicans wrote to Bush stating that they "unequivocally oppose new taxes." A group of House Republicans running for the Senate sent a similar letter.[97] The counterattack against taxes continued in August when House Republican Newt Gingrich called for tax cuts to stimulate growth.

On September 11, Bush told a joint session of Congress that the summit's agreement should include "growth-oriented" tax cuts, including capital gains.[98] The 1990 budget struggle reopened older divisions in the GOP between those who favored tax cuts and those who focused on balancing budgets. It also pitted those who sought aggressive partisan confrontation against those who were ready to compromise with the Democrats. The leader of the partisans, Newt Gingrich, said: "There is a clear difference between those of us who believe passionately in growth incentives and those with the traditional view that reducing the deficit is more important. It's a debate that has been going on for 15 years."[99]

It was a long budget summit. The first part lasted from May until the August recess of Congress. A recession began in July 1990. Congress and the president faced much larger deficit forecasts. Gramm-Rudman would require automatic spending cuts in October to bring the deficit down to the year's target. Gramm-Rudman also had to be modified because its targets had become politically impossible since the required cuts had grown to the $160 billion range for a single year.[100]

The summit considered making recipients pay more for Medicare benefits. That might be done either by raising the monthly premium for Part B, which pays doctors and other providers for outpatient services, or by extending the payroll tax for hospitalization coverage. This restraint on spending made majoritarian sense. Removing the ceiling would affect perhaps one-fifth of the population. But Congress had learned that harming even relatively small minorities could be tricky. In 1989, Congress had taxed wealthier beneficiaries and fostered an angry response that led Congress to repeal the Medicare Catastrophic Coverage Act.[101] Nonetheless, Medicare in part was on the table in 1990. Despite being an entitlement, it was much more vulnerable than Social Security.[102]

Both the opponents of tax increases and of spending cuts found their political voice after returning from summer recess in 1990. But Democrats controlled the House, and the opponents of spending reductions had the upper hand and the loudest voices. Henry Waxman (D-CA) and Sen. Bob Graham (D-FL) heard that the summit might recommend deep cuts in Medicare. A bipartisan group of House members from states with high taxes announced they were ready to vote against the budget agreement if the summit's work restricted federal income tax deductions for state and local taxes. Committee turf also came into play. Members of the House Public Works and Transportation Committee resisted efforts to put new gas-tax revenues toward reduction of the deficit rather than applying them as always toward repairing and building highways.[103]

From the start, the budget deal had little appeal for members of Congress. Members like to do things for their constituents, who in turn vote for them. They do not like to violate the expectations of their constituents, especially when those expectations involve cash or services provided by the government. As the budget summit continued, it was apparent to all that the deal would bring higher taxes and some reductions in spending, including cuts in programs like Medicare or defense. Members would stand for reelection saying, "Here's what I am taking from you, against your expectations," instead of "Look what I've done for you."[104]

October 1 was the deadline for complying with Gramm-Rudman targets, the moment when Congress and the president could reach agreement or drive off the political cliff to finish their long-standing game of chicken. As the deadline approached, the Office of Management and Budget reported that sequestration under Gramm-Rudman would mean slashing in excess of 40 percent from discretionary spending on both defense and domestic programs. Few members of Congress found such cuts tolerable.[105]

Negotiators produced a budget on September 30 that was accepted by the president. The budget deal included a 10 percent surcharge on incomes over $1 million, an increase in the top marginal rate from 28 to 33 percent, an increase in the alternative minimum tax from 21 to 25 percent, an almost 100 percent increase in the Medicare tax base, and a one-year suspension of the indexing of tax rates, which had been enacted in 1981. Reagan's supporters had reason to feel betrayed.

Bush got something for all the tax increases: pay-as-you-go budget procedures (called PAYGO) and spending caps on some spending. PAYGO meant that new spending or programs had to be offset by equal cuts elsewhere in the budget and that tax cuts had to be matched by spending cuts. In other words, tax cuts or spending increases had to have no effect on the budget deficit. The new law also set out spending caps to meet deficit targets that were more flexible than the Gramm-Rudman goals. The bill set a series of caps on spending. However, the president had considerable authority to adjust the caps, which made the threat of a sequester less likely. The president could adjust the caps for many reasons: changes in economic indicators, changes in categorization of programs, changes in credit reforms. He could also exempt "emergency" spending from the overall ceilings; Persian Gulf War funding was an example of such spending.[106]

Of course, there were exceptions to the new rules. The caps did not touch Social Security, Medicare, or other mandatory direct spending, a category that accounted for 60 percent of the federal budget in 1990. The spending limits that did exist, however, were observed largely because they made modest demands on members of Congress; the caps did not require cuts in spending but rather that spending increase at a lower rate than in the past.[107]

Over five years, the 1990 deal was expected to cut defense and discretionary spending by $182 billion and entitlements and farm subsidies by $186 billion. It also reduced interest payments on the national debt by $165 billion.[108] Congress reduced expected government spending by $500 billion over five years.[109] President Bush could thus claim he had reduced spending in exchange for increasing revenues through tax increases.

One problem remained: the deal would have to be approved by both chambers of Congress.[110] Few liked the late September agreement. Both conservatives and liberals rejected the taxes and the spending compromises. Ed Rollins, the cochair of the National Republican Congressional Campaign Committee, advised Republican congressional candidates to oppose the president's budget plan in late September.[111] That was not bad advice for outsiders. Challengers to sitting members from the right would cite the taxes, while challengers from the left would complain of program cuts. A survey revealed that over 400 challengers in the upcoming election opposed the deal.[112]

The budget resolution enacting the deal met bipartisan defeat in the House. Bush then vetoed a continuing resolution. Pressured by public and elite opinion, Congress then put together a new deal that dropped the surtax but put limits on personal deductions, increased the top rate to 31 percent (not 33), limited itemized deductions, and set the capital gains tax rate at 28 percent. The new package relied more on tax increases than cuts in entitlements, which attracted a majority of liberal Democrats and moderate Republicans. The changes in budget procedures survived into what became the Budget Enforcement Act of 1990.[113]

Congress went almost immediately from the budget struggle to an electoral verdict with the midterm election of 1990. After the hoopla, betrayals, and recriminations of the previous two years, the election surprisingly suggested stability in American politics. Of the 407 representatives seeking reelection, 307 had no primary opposition, and overall 67 received more than 75 percent of the primary vote. No senator and only one representative—Donald E. Lukens of Ohio, who had been found guilty of having sex with a minor—lost in a primary. In the general election, few incumbents were defeated.[114]

The GOP lost six House seats and one in the Senate. The Republicans might have expected better results. After all, the Democratic Speaker of the House, Jim Wright, and his closest ally, Tony Coelho, had resigned the previous year as a result of ethics problems.[115] Bush suffered, however, from the denouement of the budget struggle, along with a growing belief that war and recession were coming. The decision to break his promise to oppose new taxes damaged Bush's standing with the public. In the two months from August to October, the CBS News/*New York Times* poll showed that his approval level dropped 24 points to 52 percent (with 37 percent of the people polled disapproving). His level of support then stabilized a week or two before the election—and remained above 50 percent—thereby limiting GOP losses.[116]

The 1990 budget agreement marked the end of the Reagan presidency. Where Reagan had cut taxes and constrained spending in

1981, the first Bush agreed to raise rates (and other taxes) and seemed complacent, at best, about government spending and regulation. Bush's political promise of "a kinder, gentler America" not only criticized Reagan but uncritically equated expanding government regulation with national progress.[117] In part, Bush's path away from Reagan was purely political: he might have believed that the voters wanted more government spending and regulation.[118]

But Bush himself was also different from Reagan. He was at heart a liberal Republican, content to manage the welfare state.[119] He had differences with liberal Democrats, of course, but his most important difference concerned who would hold office, not which ideas would inform policy and politics. Reagan's successor was not a Reaganite, and Reagan himself bore responsibility for the end of his presidency. He had chosen Bush as his running mate, and Reagan should have known that his successor did not share his vision of limited government and individual liberty.

Assessing Reagan

Some have seen Ronald Reagan as "the most ideological President, and the leader of the most ideological administration, in modern American history" who sought to "carry out a mandate for very large-scale change in American politics" by realizing Ayn Rand's "capitalist utopian program."[120] Reagan's admirers agree that his presidency was a turning point in history, a renewal of the American ideal of limited government. While Reagan's rhetoric might have supported such expectations, the concrete details of his proposals suggested a more modest agenda. Keeping this modesty in mind, we might still ask, did Reagan limit government?

Spending

Reagan sought to control spending later by cutting taxes first. The prospect of substantial deficits would force Congress to choose cutting programs, a choice members did not like but would have seen as better than deficit spending.[121] This strategy did and did not work initially. Many programs were sharply restrained in the first two years of the Reagan presidency. Nonetheless, the 1981 tax cuts were three or four times larger than the spending cuts achieved that same year.[122] After the 1982 recession, Reagan had less sway over Congress and thus less power to cut spending. John Cogan and Timothy Muris discovered that overall domestic discretionary spending (including defense spending but not entitlements) grew only slightly less than the inflation rate for the whole economy during Reagan's two terms. By 1989, such spending was almost equal to its 1981 level, adjusted for inflation.[123]

Overall, the Reagan years saw neither growth nor reduction of domestic discretionary spending. However, such conventional budgetary concepts obscure some spending. Cogan and Muris used a more accurate measure of spending and concluded that the "real budgetary resources" available for domestic spending grew in real terms by 14 percent after Reagan's first two years.[124] The programs that made up the other 70 percent of domestic spending grew in real terms by 19 percent over those eight years.[125] For example, spending by the Department of Education rose by 14 percent during the Reagan years, despite Reagan's campaign promise to abolish the department.[126] Hence, "The period 1981–89 is more appropriately characterized as one year of deep budget cuts, 1982, followed by rapid budget growth."[127]

About 15 programs or agencies received hefty real increases of more than 20 percent in budgetary resources during the Reagan era (see Table 4.1).

Of these 15, 12 grew faster than the defense budget during this period.[128]

Other spending also grew. Federal spending on highways increased in real terms by 3 percent, financed by a 5-cent-per-gallon increase in the federal gas tax passed in 1982. Education programs for the handicapped grew by 50 percent in real terms. Biomedical research sponsored by the National Institutes of Health grew by 47 percent. Basic science supported by the National Science Foundation rose by 38 percent. The safety programs and general operations of the Federal Aviation Administration increased by 36 percent. Funds for the federal prison system rose by 206 percent. The Women, Infants, and Children's program that provides nutritional assistance to pregnant women and newborns increased by 54 percent after inflation. The budget of each of these programs grew faster than defense during the Reagan years.[129] Spending on agricultural subsidies also rose more than any of these discretionary items. Over the eight years, Martin Anderson notes, spending on farm subsidies went up 252 percent. Spending on welfare increased 44 percent during those same eight years.[130] Some spending was cut. The large

Table 4.1

MAJOR BUREAU INCREASES IN BUDGETS (billions of 1989 dollars)

Bureau	1981	1989	% Change
Federal Prison System	0.5	1.6	206
Immigration and Naturalization Service	0.5	1.1	120
Court of Appeals	0.6	1.1	83
Internal Revenue Service	3.3	5.2	58
Handicapped Education	1.4	2.1	50
National Institutes of Health	4.9	7.2	47
House and Senate accounts	0.7	1.0	43
National Aeronautics and Space Administration	7.8	10.9	40
Alcohol, Drug Abuse, and Mental Health Administration	1.3	1.8	39
National Park Service	0.8	1.1	38
National Science Foundation	1.4	1.9	36
Federal Aviation Administration	4.8	6.5	35
Federal Medicare/Health Care Financing Administration	1.3	1.7	31
Veterans' medical care	9.3	11.6	25
Environmental Protection Agency	4.6	5.6	22

SOURCE: John F. Cogan and Timothy J. Muris, "Changes in Domestic Discretionary Spending during the Reagan Years," in John F. Cogan, Timothy J. Muris, and Allen Schick, *The Budget Puzzle: Understanding Federal Spending* (Stanford, CA: Stanford University Press, 1994), p. 98.

decreases in community and planning development, the Urban Mass Transit Authority, and the Army Corps of Engineers mostly affected spending on localities. As noted earlier, the Urban Development Action Grant program (in community planning) was terminated; it had spent $1 billion annually in 1981. Community development block grants were sharply cut. The Corps of Engineers was cut in real terms by $1 billion, thereby cutting back on harbor dredging, flood control, and dam construction and renovation. The federal government also cut back sharply mass transit operating subsidies for city and regional governments and delayed approval for matching money for building more mass transit. In total, the Corps of Engineers and mass transit programs were cut by $7 billion during the Reagan years.[131]

The concern over energy that gripped the 1970s ended, so Congress cut $6 billion in real terms from the Department of Energy's energy supply and research and development programs along with the Strategic Petroleum Reserve. The low-income home energy program also lost 1 billion in constant dollars during the Reagan era. This is not surprising. During the same period, energy prices had fallen by 50 percent compared to prices in the rest of the economy.[132] The real cut of $6.5 billion for the Labor Department came from terminating the Comprehensive Employment and Training Act. Another $800 million came out of refugee assistance, but this too is misleading: the 1981 baseline reflected a large one-time funding increase to deal with the refugees from the Mariel Boatlift.[133]

Eight budget bureaus received major real cuts in spending during the Reagan era; they account for 76 percent of all cuts in the domestic discretionary budget for the period. These eight areas lost 26 billion in constant dollars from 1981 to 1989, which accounts for roughly three-quarters of the cuts to domestic discretionary spending during that period. If you exclude these programs, the rest of the domestic discretionary budget increased in real terms by 19 percent. The Reagan administration cut about 50 percent in real terms from programs that made up about 30 percent of all domestic discretionary spending.[134]

Earlier pages recounted the difficulties Reagan faced in cutting back entitlement spending. The budgetary outcomes for these programs should not be surprising. Between 1980 and 1987, the three largest social welfare programs (Social Security, Medicare, and other health care spending) increased their spending by 84 percent, a total of $145 billion. In 1980, the nation spent $40 billion more annually on these social welfare programs than on defense; by 1987, after a steep increase in defense spending, the nation still spent $37 billion more each year on these entitlements.[135] Social Security, in particular, appeared invulnerable to spending restraint in the 1980s. Medicare and Medicaid present a more mixed picture. Surprisingly, in the Reagan period, Medicaid often appeared more resistant to spending restraint than Medicare.[136]

Even in the discretionary domestic budget, a relatively small part of overall spending, the Reagan administration produced only minor absolute cuts in spending. Budget authority did fall during that period by over 5 percent, but Congress found other means of financing the programs, a form of funding that rose by 27.3 percent during the Reagan era (though just by 2 billion real dollars).[137] The $26 billion reduction in eight of these discretionary programs constitutes 18 percent of the $145 billion increase in entitlement spending during the Reagan years. In any case, the cuts in some discretionary spending merely shifted spending to other discretionary programs so that this part of the federal budget essentially remained the same in absolute terms.

Yet judging the Reagan administration by the standard of absolute government spending may be unfair in several respects. Candidate Reagan also did not promise to cut absolute levels of spending. Instead, he hoped to constrain the rate of growth of federal expenditures while enacting policies to revive economic growth; the result would be a relatively larger private sector and a relatively smaller government.[138] An increase in federal spending thus need not count as a Reagan failure unless it led to a larger government relative to the private economy. Judged this way, the Reagan presidency looks better. Figure 4.1 shows the trend in government spending from 1948 to 1980 extrapolated through the Reagan years (marked by a broken line). All things being equal, in 1980 an observer would have expected total government spending to increase to 34.5 percent of gross domestic product by 1989, if the Reagan era had continued the trend of the previous 30 years. Yet we can see that government spending from 1980 to 1988 (marked by a solid line) departed from the earlier trend.

Interpreting these data requires some care. Government spending actually ran even with or exceeded the longer trend in 1982 and 1983. Those years involved a steep recession, while 1984 and after were marked by strong growth. Since the relative size of government is a ratio of spending relative to GNP, the relative reduction in the size of government may owe more to higher economic growth than to spending constraint. Even so, Reagan still made good on his promise; his program as a candidate promised to reduce the size of government through spending restraint and economic growth.

But even if we imagine that the expansion after 1983 was a normal revival following a steep recession, the question remains of why renewed growth did not return government spending to its earlier trend. In 1989, the answer to this question might have been that spending would eventually return to its earlier trend. The Reagan era would have been simply a somewhat stronger relative decline in the size of government, a decline that was, however, similar to

Figure 4.1
SPENDING AS A PERCENTAGE OF GROSS DOMESTIC PRODUCT, 1980–2005

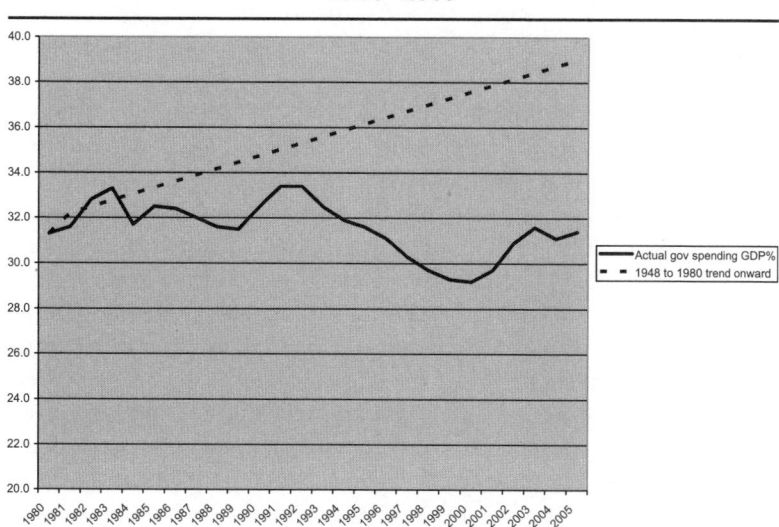

SOURCE: Budget of the United States Government: Historical Tables Fiscal Year 2006, Table 1.3 — Summary of Receipts, Outlays, and Surpluses or Deficits (-) in Current Dollars, Constant (FY2000) Dollars, and as Percentages of GDP: 1940–2010.

earlier relative reductions. Looking at the last two decades of the 20th century does suggest that the Reagan years marked a move off the earlier trend, a noticeable change in course that began around 1980 and continued in the 1990s (see Figure 4.1 from 1989 to 2005).

The Reagan administration did attain its rather limited goal of reducing the relative size of government, in part through what turned out to be modest restraint on the growth of spending along with revived economic growth. The Reagan years did not see what the candidate Reagan did not promise: a significant reduction in the size of government as measured by public spending. The ship of state under Reagan changed course. It did not change direction.

Taxes

In the first instance, cutting taxes reduces government control over the private. By this standard, Reagan brought changes to the nation. Reagan and Congress cut taxes by 23 percent. The federal burden had fallen to 18 percent of GDP by 1986, down from 19 percent when Reagan took office. More or less automatic increases in Social Security and indexation kept the total take near its starting point. However, absent the tax cuts, the total tax would have been 23 percent of GDP.[139] The 4 percent difference covered most of the deficit by 1986.

This suggests two points. First, Reagan did not so much reduce federal tax revenue as keep it steady during a period when it was supposed to expand. Reagan was conservative in tax policy outcomes; he more or less continued the past at a time when the future seemed likely to bring a much higher federal tax burden. Second, the deficits that appeared early in the Reagan years came largely from expansions in federal spending rather than reductions in tax revenue.[140] Forced to choose between spending cuts and borrowing, the federal government picked the latter to an unprecedented degree. Denying revenue to the federal government did not appear to constrain spending.

This outcome contravened Reagan's larger political program in an important but largely unnoticed way. Public deficits have to be financed by issuing government debt. Later in time, taxpayers—though not the current cohort of taxpayers—have to pay back both the borrowed sums and the related interest. Taxes are reduced but only for the current cohort. The costs of current spending are thus shifted to future taxpayers, which is to say there was no tax cut across time or, ultimately, across generations.

Shifting the tax burden across generations may seem objectionable at first glance: like Social Security, it imposes costs on future generations who have no voice in the matter. But a case could be made for such taxes. If tax cuts hold down government spending to a lower path across time than it would be otherwise and such constraint (compared with an alternative higher path of spending) offers benefits to both current and future generations, imposing some of the cost for those benefits on future generations seems reasonable since they could be said to be paying for benefits received. Unfortunately for this thesis, later studies indicate that cutting taxes does not reduce spending in general.[141] Future taxpayers thus probably do not receive the benefits of lower spending for the taxes imposed prior to their lives.

Of course, the loss imposed on future taxpayers could have arisen from a mistaken policy of cutting taxes with the welfare of current and future generations in mind. If so, the attempt to starve the beast would be an honest mistake but not an especially morally objectionable one. If the beast were starved to shift the costs of current consumption (government spending) to future generations, the policy would seem more like a predatory act undertaken by powerful people (the current generation elects officials who make policy) against powerless people (future taxpayers cannot vote).

By the end of the Reagan administration, current taxpayers were paying for about 80 percent of the total government budget.[142] Most voters, it would seem, wanted more government than they were willing to pay for and were also willing, if not eager, to overcome that mismatch by shifting its costs into the future. Ethics aside, this poses an important question about government. If voters are not willing in some measure to pay for what government provides, should we believe voters actually want such services or goods. After all, this history suggests that voters are not willing to pay the total costs of providing what government provides. Government thus appears to be either a fiscal illusion or a free ride, or both. Neither premise speaks well of representative government and the voters and politicians who determine its course.

Reagan did change public perceptions of taxes and government. Before Reagan, the expansion of the federal government through increased spending seemed natural and benevolent. By 1990, even Reagan's critics would note "a general feeling that more is not necessarily better when it comes to government."[143] The older view that more government was always better flourished because its costs were hidden: taxes rose through inflation and concomitant bracket creep. Reagan's first tax reform dispelled this illusion and forced taxes to the center of the political stage. After the 1986 reform, the top tax rate was less than half that in 1980, and most of the resources wasted on seeking tax preferences had been freed for more productive uses. Reagan's aide and sometime critic William Niskanen concluded in 1988, "For the most part, the structure of the federal tax code is now simpler, fairer, and of lower cost to the economy than in 1981."[144] Reagan also disrupted the prior consensus favoring a sharply progressive tax code, a consensus rooted ultimately in the politics of envy.[145]

Institutions and Culture

Candidate Reagan also promised to change the "rules of the game" in politics. These changes sought to modify and constrain the old regime of expanding spending and regulation. Reagan proposed several reforms designed to constrain the federal government: supermajorities in Congress to approve appropriations bills and a renewed federalism fostered by devolution of federal programs. He also put forth an "Economic Bill of Rights" to be added to the Constitution to provide economic liberty with the same standing that civil liberties received in the courts of the old regime.[146]

Some parts of his reform package did not attain serious consideration: the supermajority for appropriations, constitutional limits on the income tax, and the legal proscription of wage and price controls. Reagan pushed the line-item veto in several State of the Union addresses. At the height of his popularity, even Reagan could not persuade Congress to report a line-item veto amendment out of committee.[147] Following the 1984 election, the Senate narrowly sustained a filibuster of a line-item veto.[148] The administration made serious efforts to enact a balanced budget amendment and to revive federalism. Both efforts failed.

Did Reagan change the political culture of the United States? The evidence suggests diverse answers. Polling responses indicate that the number of people who wanted more government spending grew with each passing year in the Reagan presidency.[149] A similar result marked ideological self-identification among Americans. During most of the Reagan years, the number of people claiming to be liberals rose and the number identifying as conservatives fell.

Yet after Reagan, conservative self-identification resumed its long-term rise among Americans, and liberalism renewed what would become a 50-year-long decline in adherents.[150] The conservative trend in the 1990s might be seen as a legacy of Reagan and his policies; certainly conservatives in that era did all they could to identify their politics with the former president. We will return to the question of liberalism in the 1990s in the next chapter. It is worth noting, however, that Reagan did not actuate the rise of conservatism or the decline of liberalism among Americans. The great divergence between the two happened in the 1960s; after that, the trends toward more conservatives and fewer liberals continued.

Reagan did do much to redefine the federal government. FDR and LBJ told Americans the state could provide them with security and opportunity. Reagan asked whether the government might also threaten liberty, opportunity, and wealth. By 1990 or so, the older programs that spread the wealth around remained, but Americans had a more balanced and complex view of Washington than they had embraced in 1975, not to speak of 1965. Many Americans had concluded that the state could be both their friend and a threat to their hopes and their well-being. Reagan had articulated that danger, but it may be that the national experience from 1965 to 1980 gave credence to his arguments. Reagan was both an effect as well as a cause of a longer conservative trend in American politics.

What explains Reagan's limited success at limiting government? The first answer may be found in Reagan's 1980 election campaign. Candidate Reagan promised to restrain the growth of government, not roll back the state. But candidate Reagan also promised to enact reforms that would constrain government spending and taxing. These changes did not happen. Year after year, the Reagan administration proposed cutting or eliminating spending on everything from small programs like the Legal Services Corporation or vocational education to large programs like Medicaid, student aid, or the Economic Development Administration.[151] In other words, the Reagan administration seemed willing to bring about significant cuts in federal spending.[152]

Yet after 1981, these budgets and their cuts were considered "dead on arrival" on Capitol Hill. In part, the opposition in Congress to spending restraint came from partisan and ideological considerations. The Democratic Party from FDR to LBJ had built and defended the regime that Reagan's budgets, if enacted, would vitiate. After 1981, however, partisanship offers a less convincing explanation. William Niskanen noted:

> There turn out to be relatively few consistent fiscal conservatives in the administration or in either party in Congress. Many of the smaller programs that constitute the American welfare state were created under Republican presidents and continued to be defended by Republicans in Congress. All too often, the conservatives in both parties were more protective of programs that served their own states and favored constituencies than of their commitment to a responsible fiscal policy.[153]

151

Niskanen's explanation was more than a conjecture. In 1986, Sen. Pete V. Domenici (R-NM), then chair of the Senate Budget Committee, bundled together 43 administration proposals to terminate federal programs and offered them as an amendment to the budget resolution to show how little support they had. The amendment was rejected by the Senate by a vote of 14 in favor and 83 against.[154]

Why would representatives nominally committed to limiting government support such programs? Government policies can offer concentrated benefits to smaller groups at a higher total cost to a larger group; for example, trade protectionism rewards managers and workers at firms exposed to international competition at a large cost to consumers. The benefits provide an incentive for the groups to organize and take on the costs of political action. The costs of awarding such benefits to interest groups are spread out over the general population, thereby providing little incentive for the average citizen to actively oppose the special interest benefits. In other words, politics may have perverse logic, whereby the costs and benefits of political activity favor the triumph of relatively small groups. This logic suggests why cutting programs was and remains so difficult. People who benefit from the programs have strong incentives to organize and lobby for their continuation. The much larger number of voters who would benefit on the whole from cutting or ending such spending has relatively small incentives as individuals to become organized and press for cutbacks.[155]

David Stockman provides a slightly different interpretation of interest groups based on his experience in the Reagan years:

> Economic governance must consist of a fundamental trade-off between capitalist prosperity and social security. As a nation we have chosen to have less of the former in order to have more of the latter. Social Security, trade protectionism, safety net programs, UDAG urban Development Action Grants and farm price supports all have one thing in common. They seek to bolster the lot of less productive industries, regions, and citizens by taxing the wealth and income of everyone else.[156]

For Stockman, interest groups reduced the overall wealth of the nation in order to reward less productive people, industries, and regions. Government was not corruption or "organized thievery." It was a kind of compensation for those who lose out from economic changes.

This view of government implied a change of mind also about the American people. They were no longer the decent bourgeoisie of Michigan who, given a chance by a strong leader, would vote to cut back on government. The people were, as the 1980 version of David Stockman might have said, part of the problem. They would not save the nation from a corrupt capital.

This argument goes too far. Farm subsidies have persisted long after the transition from an agricultural to an industrial society; indeed, the subsidies live on in the post–industrial age. Trade protection often persists well beyond any reasonable adjustment period for firms facing competition. Social Security may have cushioned the blow of lost savings during the Great Depression, but it grew popular by paying recipients far more than they had contributed and then persisted because each generation had to pay pensions to current retirees, thereby creating an expectation of later support. Programs may well begin by compensating voters for losses from valuable changes in the economy and then persist well beyond this period, all the while taxing those who create or adapt well to such changes.

The old regime was built politically on entitlement expectations and concomitant spending. Reagan did not eliminate or significantly restrain major entitlement programs. Reagan did attempt, more than once, to constrain Social Security spending, and each time was met by an overwhelming political reaction that cowed most congressional Republicans almost immediately. His failures led to a commission that both raised taxes immediately and limited pension spending a generation hence. A decade earlier, Congress and the president had agreed to increase Social Security by 20 percent in a single year. In that light, Reagan's mild reforms might count as a major success, but they can hardly be called radical. Spending on Medicare and Medicaid grew at a slower rate than in earlier years. The programs themselves persisted.

Were these entitlements an expression of the will of the people? Certainly Reagan could not find a majority for even minor reforms to Social Security, though Congress did support minor constraints on Medicare and Medicaid spending. Over time, Social Security had created its own support by changing the expectations of the American people. Americans no longer expected to provide wholly for their own retirement. In theory, many expected to provide for retirement through government, not on their own. In fact, for much of the time before and after Reagan, Americans received Social Security benefits that reflected large, politically imposed returns. The old regime had done its work in corrupting the American people.

Conclusion

Ronald Reagan was considered both dull and evil by many in Washington. Yet Reagan had a better sense of his own achievement than most people. In his 1986 annual budget message, Reagan said:

> The past 4 years have also seen the beginning of a quiet but profound revolution in the conduct of our Federal Government. We have halted what seemed at the time an inexorable set of trends toward greater and greater Government intrusiveness, more and more regulation, higher and higher taxes, more and more spending, higher and higher inflation, and weaker and weaker defense. We have halted these trends in our first 4 years.[157]

Later he might have added that his administration had also rid the nation of a welter of tax preferences that extended state control over much of the economy.

Reagan did not come close to overturning the old regime. Its main policies and institutions resisted his efforts. Given that, Reagan's successes at cutting taxes or constraining spending tended to stabilize the old regime by making the economy more productive and the state less wasteful. In that light, Reagan turned out to be a reformer of the old regime. He was a reformer despite himself, since Reagan did wish to fundamentally change the nation and even tried to do so at some political cost. Reagan did show that liberty and limited government still had some appeal to Americans, if not so much to George H. W. Bush. Who might take up that challenge?

5. Revolution?

The struggle to limit government did not end with the retirement of Ronald Reagan and the election of George H. W. Bush. What had been primarily an economic crisis for the old regime in the 1970s became a political crisis in the late 1980s. The renewal of the struggle began as a crisis of legitimacy for national institutions, not least of which was Congress. This crisis would be resolved for a time by electing a Republican House of Representatives. The end of decades-long domination of the legislature by the party of the old regime held out the possibility of deep changes in politics and policy. The American people had grown increasingly discontented with politics in the early 1990s. They seemed ready to limit a corrupt and incompetent federal government. They elected a House of Representatives apparently ready to act on their desire. Did anything change?

Signs of Instability

At the start of 1992, the future held promise of being like the past. The long budget struggle appeared to have ended with higher taxes and spending caps in October 1990. Nonetheless, the Republican incumbent seemed likely to win reelection. The Gulf War early in 1991 had routed Iraqi troops from Kuwait, and the president could plausibly claim credit for adroitly managing the unwinding of the Soviet empire after 1989. Bush's approval rating hit 89 percent in early March 1991 and remained around 70 percent in the early fall.

Congressional incumbents rarely lost. From the mid-1960s through the late 1980s, the margins by which incumbents were reelected increased, though less clearly in the Senate than in the House.[1] Voters seemed to favor incumbency more than party affiliation.[2] The Democrats enjoyed significant majorities in the House (and often also in the Senate) during this period. Incumbent success suggested continued domination of Congress by Democrats.

But the future turned out to be unlike the past. Bush's successes hurt him politically. Republicans promised to provide national security. If threats to the nation no longer existed (the Soviet Union) or were defeated (Saddam Hussein), what could the president offer the voters in 1992? Not prosperity. The U.S. economy contracted slightly in the first half of 1991 and grew weakly thereafter. Unemployment remained stuck at an uncomfortable 6.8 percent. Bush had also lost core Republican support by agreeing to tax increases in 1990.

The public was losing faith in Congress and the federal government more generally. In 1990, the average share of the vote for incumbents declined by nearly 5 percentage points. This outcome reflected larger trends in public opinion. Earlier in the year, polls had found a rising distaste for incumbents and for Congress.[3] In March 1992, public approval of the performance of Congress reached its lowest point ever. Normally, such disapproval did not matter to individual members; the public disliked Congress the institution while approving of their own representative. Yet the same poll found for the first time that fewer than half the public approved of the performance of their individual representatives.[4] Almost all measures of distrust of Washington were rising throughout the late 1980s and early 1990s.[5] The government appeared to be suffering a serious crisis of legitimacy.[6]

The skepticism about Congress was well founded. In April 1989, the House Committee on Standards of Official Conduct reported that House Speaker Jim Wright (D-TX) had violated congressional ethics rules 116 times during the 1980s.[7] Wright soon became the first Speaker of the House to resign.[8] About the same time, Tony Coelho (D-CA), the third-ranking House Democrat, also resigned from Congress following ethical questions about his financial dealings.[9]

The ethical problems of Wright and Coelho arose in part from Congress's effort to deal with the savings and loan catastrophe. The savings and loan industry had been troubled since the inflation of the 1970s.[10] During the 1980s, Congress passed two major laws covering losses in the industry. Congress was then drawn into oversight and regulation of the industry. As night follows day, scandals appeared, the most important of which involved the Keating Five. The "Keating" in question was Charles H. Keating Jr., who managed the Lincoln Savings and Loan, an S&L that proved to be the greatest strain on the federal budget. Five U.S. senators had met with banking regulators in 1987 on Lincoln's behalf; the five had received $1.3 million in campaign contributions from Keating. Congress investigated the five senators for two years. In the end, the Senate Ethics Committee reprimanded Alan Cranston (D-CA), and it criticized in writing the four other senators—Democrats Dennis DeConcini of Arizona, John Glenn of Ohio, and Donald W. Riegle Jr. of Michigan, and Republican John McCain of Arizona—for acting on Keating's behalf.[11]

The Keating Five, Wright, and Coelho were not the only congressional misbehavior cases in the news. During the late 1980s and the early 1990s, as the *Congressional Quarterly* noted, "two senators were indicted on criminal charges; a House member was acquitted after a volatile trial; two of the House's former officers pleaded guilty to crimes stemming from their service; and three former House members were convicted and sentenced to prison."[12] A scandal involving no criminal acts, however, did the most political damage to the largest number of members of Congress.

In September 1991, the General Accounting Office revealed that members of Congress had written 8,331 bad checks in 1990 against their accounts in the House bank and that the bank had covered these overdrafts without penalty or interest. The Speaker and the minority leader at first tried to keep secret the names of the malefactors; a group of younger Republicans demanded disclosure, and the leaders eventually complied. In April 1992, the House Ethics Committee disclosed 325 current or former members who had caused one or more overdrafts. Forty-six sitting representatives had written 100 or more overdrafts. Public outrage spread at what many Americans saw as another abuse of power.[13]

Congressional wrongdoing combined with invulnerable incumbents actuated the term limits movement in the early 1990s.[14] Proponents of term limits argued that mandatory retirement from Congress would bring new people and viewpoints into Congress, reduce the drive for reelection, and control federal spending. They noted that federal spending and the average length of a congressional career had grown in tandem, perhaps because the longer members served, the less likely they were to question the spending demands of interest groups and government agencies.[15]

Beyond the spending question, the term limits movement posed a radical challenge to a government founded on administrative

157

expertise and legislative professionalism.[16] Term limits proponents lauded instead the political amateur, the "citizen legislator." Faced with evidence of public corruption, Americans should turn to untainted and capable outsiders. Could they do worse than Jim Wright and his wife's alleged no-show job or the Keating Five's waste of $2 billion in taxpayers' money?

Would this lead to constraints on government spending and taxing? Many proponents thought so. Voters were thought to want limited government. The term limits advocates shared David Stockman's earlier faith that the people remained uncorrupted by the old regime. The people certainly appeared to be disgusted by the government they had.

If the people did not want more government, why did they reelect incumbents who voted for more spending? Term limits proponents argued that the power of incumbency enabled members to follow their desire for unlimited government rather than the voters' desire for constraint. Big government came from the ambition of career politicians, not the true desires of Americans. The problem lay with institutions, not the people.

Term limits would reform institutions by preventing incumbents from amassing the powers of office. Term limits would also foster more competition for office since more seats would fall open, and open seats were generally more competitive. Freed of incumbent power, the people empowered by term limits would bypass corrupt pols and reclaim their birthright of liberty. Term limits were almost always enacted by direct democratic means, like the ballot initiative. The term limits movement was at once populist, thoroughly democratic, and hostile to the old regime.

Term limits appealed to voters. Colorado limited the terms of its congressional delegation in 1990. Two years later, 14 states, including larger states like Ohio, Michigan, and California, passed ballot initiatives to limit the number of years that House and Senate members could serve. Almost all were supported by more than 60 percent of the voters. These new laws meant that 181 members of Congress would eventually serve under some limit on their terms.[17] Moreover, the term limits movement seemed to be just starting. People who hoped to limit the federal government seemed to have found an institutional reform equal to their ends.

Agents of Change

In 1980, dissatisfaction with the status quo led to the election of Ronald Reagan, an outsider in origins and ideas. In 1992, a similar dissatisfaction could not turn to a Republican presidential candidate offering the prospect of cutting back on government. George H. W. Bush was unavoidably the candidate of the status quo, and that in more ways than one. Political struggle threw up four alternatives to Bush, only one of whom would seek to sustain the struggle for limited government.

Gingrich

From 1960 to 1994, Republicans never held more than 44 percent of House seats.[18] The average Republican representation was much worse during this era: 39 percent of the whole. This weakness fed on itself. Candidates run to hold office and enact policies. Most Republican candidates had little chance of beating an incumbent, and those that did had little hope of enacting policies. Many potentially strong Republican candidates had better things to do with their careers.

The region that might be open to a message of skepticism about the federal government—the South—had long been a Democratic bulwark grounded in local party and government officials. Democratic control in the region continued despite Reagan's electoral successes. The House GOP was strong in the Northeast and parts of the Midwest, both largely filled with voters who had supported the New Deal. In this context, the House GOP leadership cooperated with their Democratic counterparts to attain a small measure of influence. Weak and conformist, the GOP in Congress seemed likely to remain permanently in the minority.

In March 1989, House Republicans narrowly elected Newt Gingrich their new whip. He defeated Ed Madigan of Illinois, an exemplar of conciliation toward the Democratic majority. Gingrich was no conciliator. He asked: "If all we have to offer as Republicans is simply half of the corrupt liberal welfare state, that's crazy. There has to be fundamental reform."[19] Gingrich had been building the party outside of Congress. From 1986 until 1995, he led GOPAC, a political action committee funding and advising state and local GOP candidates, a major effort to improve the quality of GOP challengers in House elections. Gingrich and his cohorts in the Conservative

Opportunity Society had also come up with policy alternatives, most outside the mainstream. Gingrich had learned from Reagan's problems that Republican majorities in both houses of Congress were necessary to limit the federal government.[20]

Gingrich's victory in the whip election suggested that a slim majority of House Republicans would stand behind a domestic agenda that directly challenged the old ways of the Democrats, not least their traditional faith that higher federal spending led to higher reelection rates for incumbents (and the common good). The GOP would offer itself less as a collection of individuals skilled at constituent service and more as a party with an agenda for action that would be accountable to its majority.[21] This concept of majority rule, somewhat at odds with American government, explains some of Gingrich's successes and failures.

Gingrich was thus the true heir to Reagan's legacy. With him and his efforts to build a congressional majority, the struggle for limited government would find its new general.

Clinton

In 1991, after victory in the Gulf War, challenging George H. W. Bush seemed futile to most leading Democrats. They stayed out of the race, opening the way for the governor of Arkansas. Bill Clinton called himself a "new Democrat," thereby rejecting the old Democrats who had lost three straight presidential elections. Clinton promised to set aside liberal orthodoxy and "reinvent government." He sought votes of groups who had abandoned Democratic presidential candidates since the late 1960s.[22] Clinton also needed to win the nomination, which meant appealing to primary voters, who were primarily on the political left. A measure of ambivalence would mark Clinton's candidacy and presidency from the start, an ambivalence that owed as much to his circumstances as to his character.

Clinton's ambivalence toward the old regime—his rejection and affirmation of the traditional doctrines of his party—informed his acceptance speech to the Democratic convention during the summer of 1992. Clinton described himself as "a product of the American middle class" who would accept the nomination "in the name of all the people who do the work, pay the taxes, raise the kids and play by the rules—the hard-working Americans who make up our forgotten middle class." In doing so, Clinton said goodbye to his youth and to the left wing of the party shaped by the 1960s. The radicalism of that era had preached contempt for the bourgeoisie and bourgeois values. This contempt never completely defined the party, in part because the children of the 1960s grew up to be middle-class, save for believing they were not. The party's leaders did not exactly portray the middle class as selfish and heartless—the rich would play that role in their drama—but clearly few Democrats thought the well-being of the bourgeoisie should be the primary concern of the left in power. By saying he sided with the middle class, Clinton signaled his willingness to take risks with his own party.

Clinton directly attacked the old regime and its ideals: "There is not a program in government for every problem." Clinton called his proposal a "New Covenant, a solemn agreement between the people and their government, based not simply on what each of us can take, but on what all of us must give to our nation." Clinton said he and Gore offered "a new choice based on old values. We offer opportunity. We demand responsibility. . . . The choice we offer is not conservative or liberal; in many ways it's not even Republican or Democratic."[23]

On the other hand, Clinton offered a list of traditional liberal angels: "every child in America tonight who's out there trying to grow up without a father or a mother," "our best people who are falling into poverty," and "family farms," "the minorities . . . the liberals . . . the poor . . . the homeless . . . the people with disabilities . . . the gays." These groups were also presented as usual as victims of the Republicans.

Clinton also conjured up familiar demons of the left: "the forces of greed and the defenders of the status quo," "politicians in Washington," "big insurance companies and the bureaucracies," "special interests . . . and lobbyists," "health care profiteers," and "the wealthiest few." To this list Clinton would add several demons absent from the standard Democratic catalog: fathers who abandon their children, the federal government, big bureaucracies, both public and private, and famously, "welfare as we know it." Both liberals and conservatives could be pleased as long as they ignored what the other side wanted to hear.

Clinton, the new Democrat, had not redefined the political world. He had embraced it and all its contradictions: freedom, democracy, individual rights, free enterprise, economic opportunity, and social justice. If he won, Democratic activists might expect Clinton would not be constrained by his gestures of accommodation to the realities of attracting independent and middle-class voters. There was a risk. Everyone heard those words of accommodation and moderation; those who doubted "social justice" mattered above all else—a considerable majority of the American electorate—might take offense if Clinton forgot his promises once in power.

Buchanan

Patrick Buchanan had been a political insider from early in his life. Having been educated at Georgetown and Columbia, Buchanan first worked as an editorial writer before becoming in his late 20s an assistant to Richard Nixon and then serving as speechwriter and adviser in Nixon's administration. Buchanan then wrote a nationally distributed newspaper column before joining the Reagan administration at the start of its second term as presidential adviser and director of communications.[24]

In 1992, Buchanan ran for the Republican presidential nomination. He lost in New Hampshire, but in receiving 37 percent of the vote, Buchanan did "better than expected" and thereby gained the attention of the media and the president. By late April, however, he acknowledged that the GOP would again nominate Bush.[25]

Buchanan had made much of Bush's betrayal on taxes in 1990. Apart from taxes, Buchanan had never been much of a limited government man. In the Nixon administration, Buchanan had argued that the television networks held an "an ideological monopoly" over political information and that the views of "middle America" were not aptly represented. The government, he suggested, should act to break this monopoly.[26] Bullying the media on behalf of a sitting president does not bespeak a mind devoted to liberty or limited power for the state.

Buchanan's speech at the 1992 GOP convention bespoke a conservatism that was at best indifferent to liberty.[27] The words "free" and "freedom" appear in two sentences in the speech, which comprise 26 words out of the 2,600 in the speech. Buchanan stated that he and his followers stand "against the amoral idea that gay and lesbian couples should have the same standing in law as married men and women." His entire speech affords pride of place to traditional morality and religion.[28] The most famous words in the speech deftly summarize Buchanan's point of view:

> My friends, this election is about more than who gets what. It is about who we are. It is about what we believe and what we stand for as Americans. There is a religious war going on in this country for the soul of America. It is a cultural war as critical to the kind of nation we shall be as the Cold War itself, for this war is for the soul of America.

Buchanan's candidacy reflected the rise of Christian conservatives in the Republican Party. They did not have the power to nominate the party's candidate. They did have the power to make trouble and thus to be heard and to be influential.

But Buchanan's speech raised questions about the GOP and the ongoing hope for limited government. How could a nation organized around individual liberty be involved in a cultural civil war? In a nation based on liberty, individuals would attend to their own souls as they saw fit. The government itself would be a soulless instrument to their ends. Buchanan's alternative reflected a different outlook, a political theology of social conservatism informed by Christianity.

Perot

Ross Perot was an unlikely politician. He had never tried to win election to office. His policy views were somewhat unclear apart from a deep concern with the budget deficit. He had no social or geographic constituency. Perot was hardly mediagenic. Yet he had advantages. The public did not like the status quo; Perot appeared different from the typical candidate. He offered plain talk and straightforward prescriptions for government failure. Not least of his advantages: he was extremely wealthy and could fund his own campaign for the presidency or any other office.[29]

He focused on limiting the deficit. He called for a steep increase in the gas tax to raise $150 billion in revenues to that end.[30] Perot also opposed the North American Free Trade Agreement with Mexico and Canada, thereby siding with trade protectionism. In 1993, he undertook a crusade to defeat NAFTA in Congress.[31] Perot was a populist, who argued that government failed because officials ignored common sense. Like many populists, he was not much of a limited government man.

Perot showed surprising strength early in 1992. In April, 12 percent of the public said that they knew "quite a bit" about Perot, while

25–30 percent of the public in most polls supported the Texan. By June, he was all but tied with Bush thanks to his appearances on talk shows and news programs. An early June poll showed him leading the presidential race, with 39 percent supporting Perot, 31 percent Bush, and 25 percent Clinton.[32] More than one-fourth of the Democratic primary voters in New Jersey, nearly one-third in California, and nearly one-half in Ohio told exit polls on June 2 that they preferred Perot to Clinton. And one-third of the Republican primary voters in New Jersey and Ohio and close to one-half in California indicated a preference for Perot over Bush.[33]

Summary

The incumbent president's leading competitor for the Republican nomination saw the presidency as a combination of politician and pastor, tending to the nation's soul. Another candidate, Ross Perot, combined a concern for unchecked spending and deficits with an economic nationalism and populist demeanor. Among the presidential candidates, Clinton ironically showed how much Reagan had changed the nation: the Democratic candidate for president paid an ambivalent homage to limited government and other conservative themes. Reagan's true successor was not running for president. Newt Gingrich had led the revolt against Reagan's tax increase in 1982. He was more Reagan than Reagan. Now he led the minority party in the House. The Reagan legacy needed a president; it would receive a Speaker of the House.

Change Did Come in the 1992 Elections

Clinton's victory in 1992 ended the Democrats' 16-year exile from the White House. In some ways, his victory was remarkable. He won a plurality among independents, a feat not accomplished by a Democrat since 1964. Clinton ran almost even with Bush among white voters, again the best performance by a Democrat since 1964. The economic situation, as always, mattered a lot: those who said their family's financial situation was getting worse—one-third of all voters—voted overwhelmingly for Clinton. Fears about the economy fostered Clinton victories in nine states that voted Democratic for president for the first time since 1964.[34]

The Republican Party and its presidential vote changed significantly from 1988 to 1992. The proportion of Republicans identified as Protestant evangelicals doubled in those four years; about one in five Republicans was an evangelical by 1992.[35] The number of actual Republican voters in the presidential contest showed the same doubling from a higher base line: in 1992, one in four Bush voters was an evangelical who regularly attended church. For Reagan in 1980 (as for Nixon in 1972), the comparable number had been around 12 percent.[36] Not surprisingly, the incumbent president in 1992 did well in the South, where he won more than two-thirds of his electoral votes. Where Reagan had been western and relentlessly economic, the post-Reagan GOP candidate seemed likely to be southern and religious. The results of 1992, however, raised questions whether a post-Reagan candidate could win the votes of independents and the suburbs, key voters in the long trend of Republican presidential electoral successes.

For all the talk, however, the political order seemed remarkably stable. The incumbents' share of the total vote dropped, and the power of incumbency became less overwhelming. In 1988, 13 percent of House incumbents won with less than 60 percent of the major party vote; in 1990, that same number had increased to 19 percent. In 1992, it went up again: 28 percent won with less than 60 percent of the vote. These signs of greater competition in congressional elections did not translate into a large loss of seats for House incumbents; 93 percent who stood for reelection succeeded. Incumbent senators also did relatively poorly compared to earlier years.[37]

Not much changed from a partisan perspective in the 1992 Senate elections. The Democrats went in and came out with 57 seats. In policy matters, the Senate on the whole had shifted to the right a bit. The House results were similar for the Democrats. The Democrats lost on net 10 House seats. Sixteen of their incumbents lost, and on average the losers were more liberal than the Democrats who won. The Republicans who won were much more conservative than the Democrats they beat.[39]

Clinton hardly had a mandate. He garnered 43 percent of the total vote, a small plurality even by the standards of American presidential elections. Clinton's share was smaller than Dukakis's by 3 percentage points. Yet 43 percent was good enough against an incumbent who received only 38 percent of the vote, 16 percent lower than in 1988. The 19 percentage points lost by both parties compared to 1988 had gone to Perot. Overall, 57 percent of the electorate had voted for a serious presidential candidate other than

Bill Clinton. Looked at this way and taking into account the weak economy, the electorate had given an ambivalent candidate an ambivalent endorsement.

Clinton in Power

Having run as a "new Democrat," Clinton governed from the left and set about reviving and expanding the old regime. He issued executive orders regarding abortions performed in military hospitals, federal funding of fetal tissue transplant research, and the importation of RU-486, the abortion-inducing drug. He then signed into law the Family and Medical Leave Act, a policy long sought by the left wing of his party. He promised to sign an executive order ending the ban on gays in the military. He sent Congress proposals on education and an economic stimulus package. In his first State of the Union address, Clinton proposed tax increases of $236 billion over the next five years. The higher taxes hit the top 1 percent of the income distribution, corporations, and users of energy through a Btu tax. The stimulus fell victim to a Senate filibuster but further defined the new president as a big spender. The president also assigned priority to health care legislation over welfare changes. A significant part of his proposed spending cuts came from the Pentagon.[40] As it worked its way through Congress, the Clinton proposals took on a partisan as well as an ideological bent. The budget package passed without a single Republican vote.[41]

Clinton believed his election marked a renewed call for expansive government, especially in health care. Polling seemed to support him. A few weeks after his initial speech on the subject, a significant plurality of the public supported his health care proposal. That made sense. Polls had found for some time that in the United States and elsewhere, the public supports a universal right to medical care. Yet Clinton was misled on two points. First, public support for a universal right to health care exists in abstraction from its costs. When costs are added—in other words, "in reality"—perceptions changed.[42]

Beyond that, Clinton also misread the public's attitude toward the federal government. The public might wish for universal coverage, but once it became clear that Clinton was proposing a large increase in the power of the federal government, support for his plan declined. As Karlyn Bowman remarked, the public in 1994 continued to see the federal government as a source of problems rather than a problem solver. Once the Clinton plan became a big government plan, public support eroded.[43] Nine months after Clinton introduced the plan, its public support had flipped: a significant plurality opposed the effort in July 1994. The Clinton administration abandoned the effort a few months later.[44]

This unhappiness with the federal government went beyond health care. The Democratic pollster Stanley Greenberg found after the election that an "extraordinary" 56 percent of voters said they were self-consciously "casting a vote of dissatisfaction . . . about the mess in Washington."[45] Reviewing the evidence, three political scientists concluded that the public was dissatisfied with the federal government and virtually everyone connected with it.[46] This unhappiness suggested a desire for limits. The *New York Times* found a week before the election that "by a 2-to-1 margin, people believe that Government should be less involved in solving national problems."[47]

Moderate voters could be excused for assuming that Clinton had misrepresented his intentions in 1992. Indeed, as early as the summer of 1993, voters were rapidly concluding Clinton was an old-fashioned "tax and spend" Democrat. [48] Public approval of Clinton's performance would fall to 50 percent by September 1993, and remain there for most of the next year. Thereafter, as the midterm elections approached, Clinton's approval ratings would begin to fall again into the mid-40s.[49] On election day, 50 percent of the voters said they "disapproved" of Bill Clinton. Of that number, 82 percent voted for Republican candidates.[50] Congress shared the public's ire with Clinton. If anything, the public liked Congress less than their new president.[51] The public had rapidly lost faith in the return to unified government under the Democrats.

The Contract

The most honored of political aphorisms may be "all politics is local." House members believe their electoral fate depends on constituent service and benefits rather than fealty to a partisan or philosophical program.[52] "All politics is local" did not hold out much hope for a Republican takeover of the House in 1994. The Democratic majority was, and had been for generations, in control of the funding and institutions of constituent service.

Newt Gingrich and the Republican House leadership rejected much about American politics, not least that "all politics is local." They tried to nationalize the 1994 election from the start, in part through the Contract with America.[53] The contract comprised 11 bills that Republican congressional candidates vowed to bring to a vote on the House floor within the first 100 days of the next Congress if the Republicans took over.[54] The contract provides a sense of why the GOP appealed to the electorate in 1994.

The Contract with America sought a Republican majority. It avoided issues and policies that might preclude a Republican victory. What had been and would be major issues for social conservatives— abortion and homosexuality—did not appear in the contract. The planks that involved culture had wide support. Few people were happy with the increase in crime, and welfare reform had long enjoyed majority support. "Family values" appeared in the contract as the Family Reinforcement Act, which offered assistance for adoption, better enforcement of child support, and protection for children from the pornography trade.[55]

The contract included planks designed to limit the federal government in economic life. For example, the Job Creation and Wage Enhancement Act plank of the contract contained "a variety of tax-law changes and federal bureaucratic reforms designed to enhance private property rights and economic liberty and make government more accountable." The contract remained silent, however, about constraining entitlement programs and spending, the most important factors increasing federal spending and regulation.[56]

The public had little faith in Congress as an institution, so it was not surprising that the contract focused on procedural reform.[57] Republicans promised on their first day in power to pass eight reforms that would change congressional procedures.[58] They also promised a renewed vote on a balanced budget and line-item veto amendments to the Constitution, both of which were seen as ways to control spending.[59] The contract also promised a vote on two joint resolutions to pass constitutional amendments to impose term limits on House and Senate members.[60]

Beyond its contents, the Contract with America itself implied a profound institutional change in U.S. politics. It set forth a program to be enacted by a unified party who obtained a majority of seats in an election. The contract was a tactic for fighting an election in a parliamentary system. The limits of that change were evident from the start. The signers of the contract could promise to enact changes in congressional procedures that lay within the power of the House. The United States remained a system of divided powers, including legislative powers. Yet the contract suggested, and GOP leaders may have come to believe, that a victory in 1994 would allow Republicans to push limited government reforms from the House of Representatives.

The Republican campaign assumed that popular rule and limited government had been reconciled. The contents of the contract were popular, and its authors might well have believed that its institutional changes, rooted as they were in greater accountability to the voter, would be both popular and reinforce the policy initiatives designed to cut back on federal power. Like Reagan, the 1994 Republicans sought to cut government in response to popular concern. Could Gingrich succeed where Reagan had failed?[61]

Election Results

The results of the 1994 election are well known. Fifty-four seats switched parties in the House of Representatives, returning control to the GOP for the first time since 1955. It was the greatest party shift in a House election since the election of 1948, when the Democrats won 75 seats. In the Senate, 9 seats changed from Democratic control to Republican.

Nationally, support for Clinton's agenda in marginally Democratic House districts correlated well with a Democratic defeat. Controlling for other factors in 1994, a Democratic incumbent who supported Clinton's policies had a 47.7 percent chance of being reelected. Incumbents are almost always reelected, but a 10 percent increase in support for Clinton increased the likelihood of a Republican victory in a district by 11.6 percent.[62] Clinton had cost his party vulnerable seats in the House and thereby control over Congress.

The results had a partisan and philosophical bent. Thirty-four incumbent Democrats had lost their seats while no Republican in power had met defeat.[63] As the *Washington Post* noted:

This was not just an "anti-incumbent" vote. The incumbents who were defeated this year were Democrats—and in particular Democrats in Congress. . . . The change called for went

169

almost uniformly in one direction, and that was against liberalism and toward the right.[64]

Republican congressional candidates received 52 percent of the total vote while the Democrats got 45 percent; the Republican share increased by 6 percent over 1992.[65]

More than party and philosophy separated the new majority from the old. Some Republicans had been concerned that the GOP had too many inexperienced challengers for House seats in 1994. In the preceding 50 years, inexperienced challengers had been only one-fourth as likely to beat incumbents as experienced challengers. But it did not matter in the end. Of the Republicans who won their races, fewer than half had any electoral experience, fewer than one-fourth had experience in state legislatures, and fewer than 10 percent had experience in the majority party of a state legislature.[66]

Many of the new members saw themselves as outsiders; their lack of experience counted as a virtue. The 1994 class "were drawn together by a widely shared conviction that the nation needed to be rescued from impeding doom." The capital, filled with professional politicians and their abettors, represented for them a major reason for the nation's plight. Skeptical of government, they nonetheless believed that dedicated individuals could win office, overhaul the government, and change the political system: the 1994 group "saw themselves refusing to play the game of bargaining favors with interests groups contrary to the general best interests of society. They would not go politically native in Washington and become part of the problem like the Democrats who preceded them." The older virtues of the insiders—negotiation and skill at compromise— were not sought or encouraged.[67]

The 1994 class also believed, not without reason, that they had been given a mandate by the voters.[68] But what sort of mandate? Should they renew the Reaganesque effort to cut back on the federal government?

The Revolution

On November 9, 1994, the day after the election, Bill Clinton remained a skillful politician. He responded to a question by saying the American people "want a smaller government that gives them better value for their dollar, that reflects both their interests and their values, that is not a burden to them, but empowers them."

Clinton summarized the lesson he took from the electoral debacle: "the third thing the voters were saying . . . is there are things we expect government to do, but we don't think government can solve all the problems. And we don't want the Democrats telling us from Washington that they know what is right about everything. We want the government to be smaller. We want it to be more efficient. We want it to create opportunity, to empower us. And we want it to demand responsibility of people who aren't behaving responsibly."[69] Clinton mixed efficiency and smaller government while gesturing toward a more active government that "empowers" people. For the moment, his emphasis would be on smaller government, but he made sure that the old regime remained alive at the moment of its most severe illness.

Like a newly elected president, Newt Gingrich claimed a mandate. His commission was to save America:

I think it's important to recognize that what is ultimately at stake in our current environment is literally the future of American civilization as it has existed for the last several hundred years. . . . we have to simply, calmly, methodically reassert American civilization and reestablish the conditions, which I believe starts with the work ethic. . . . we have to think through what are the deeper underlying cultural meanings of being American and how do we reassert them.[70]

Gingrich's call for renewal was also a call to reject "those who argued for counter-culture values, bigger government, redistributionist economics and bureaucracies deciding how you should spend your money." Gingrich's analysis of their errors is instructive:

It is impossible to take the Great Society structure of bureaucracy, the redistributionist model of how wealth is acquired, and the counter-culture value system that now permeates the way we deal with the poor, and have any hope of fixing them. They are a disaster. They ruin the poor, they create a culture of poverty and a culture of violence which is destructive of this civilization, and they have to be replaced thoroughly from the ground up.[71]

"From the ground up"? In the headiness of the moment, Gingrich gestured toward a conservative transformation of society. If bureaucracy, redistribution, and countercultural values went away, would the older virtues return? Were the American people still healthy in their mores after three generations under the old regime? If not, how might a Republican Congress (or the federal government) foster their renewal? And would fostering of that renewal comport with a constrained vision of government?

Gingrich's cultural conservatism differed significantly from Patrick Buchanan's of two years earlier. In 1992, Buchanan appealed to a Christian vision of America enforced by political power. Just as the Contract with America had avoided core concerns of the Moral Majority, Gingrich overlooked Christian virtues and appealed to the work ethic, a cultural norm shared by people of many faiths or no faith at all. Where Buchanan spoke of "our people," Gingrich appealed to cultural meanings that belonged to all Americans. Both were fighting a cultural war against the 1960s, but Gingrich's secular traditionalism transcended Buchanan's sectarian bellicosity.

Even at that heady moment, the new Speaker of the House was honest. He spoke of the costs of limited government:

> Jefferson understood that you had to have limited but effective government precisely in order to liberate people to engage in civic responsibility, and that the larger government grew, the more you would crowd out civic responsibility, and that in the end, you could never replace civic responsibility with professional government. . . . this means that my challenge to the American people is real simple. You really want to dramatically reduce power in Washington? You have to be willing to take more responsibility back home. You really want to reduce the bureaucracy of the welfare state? You have to accept greater responsibility back home.

Gingrich was taking risks here. If "back home" meant a shift of power to the states, the Reagan experience suggested that governors and their votes wanted power over programs funded by someone else. If "back home" meant the individual household, voters were being called on to take responsibility for their own lives, for the risks as well as the rewards. It cannot be said that Gingrich told Americans freedom would be a free lunch. He offered his revolution as a challenge to them. That challenge would not necessarily foster political popularity.

172

The Revolution in Power   The Contract with America made the Republicans seem more unified than they were. Gingrich and much of the leadership embraced limited government and private enterprise. A large number of House Republicans were social conservatives focused on threats to traditional morality.[72] Moderates were the other GOP faction that mattered. Gingrich's effort to become GOP whip had attracted significant support from GOP moderates, who constituted 11 percent of the House caucus by 1994. Moderates were tired of being excluded from all influence and saw Gingrich as a leader who might create a majority for the GOP. They liked the procedural reforms in the contract.[73] Republican unity in 1994 and 1995 thus owed a great deal to the history of abuse by the Democratic majority. Absent that majority, would the new GOP majority hold together enough to limit the power of the federal government?

The Contract with America had promised several changes to the tax code: a $500-per-child tax credit, an end to the marriage tax penalty, new savings vehicles for the middle class, the repeal of the 1993 tax increases on Social Security benefits, and tax incentives for private long-term care insurance.[74] In 1992, Clinton had proposed a middle-class tax cut and then abandoned it once in office in pursuit of deficit reduction. In 1995, he was again ready for some easing of the tax burden for most voters.[75] A tax cut seemed likely, but the details remained in question.

On the spending side, Gingrich promised that there would be a "pretty big" package of spending cuts early in 1995. He remarked: "This is a genuine revolution. We're going to rethink every element of the federal government. We're going to close down several federal departments."[76] The GOP leadership was discussing proposals to abolish the Departments of Energy and Housing and Urban Development.[77] What Reagan had promised, Gingrich seemed intent on delivering.

He was confident that most voters wanted a revolution, and his faith fostered a strategy. Gingrich said on election night: "If you are going to operate with his veto being the ultimate weapon . . . you have to find a trump to match his trump. And the right not to pass money bills is the only trump that is equally strong."[78] Would Congress withhold money to the point of shutting down government? Gingrich said it would. He remarked, "I'm not sure the President will want to be in the position of shutting down the government in order to block something that most of the people in the country want."[79] Gingrich intended to call "the people" on their professed desire for a more limited federal government.

The budget numbers in 1995 set the stage for the government shutdown drama.[80] The tax cuts proposed by the GOP meant that entitlement spending would have to be cut. The GOP leadership had taken Social Security off the table so that Medicare and Medicaid spending would have to be reduced. But Clinton sought to increase such spending.

The Republican leadership thus had to choose from three ways forward. They could bargain with Clinton to get a deal he could sign. That tactic would probably mean compromising on spending cuts. They could attempt to put together a budget bill that would attract enough support to override his veto. Finally, they could let him veto a budget and then take credit for doing what they said they would do even though they could not override the veto. Having taken credit, however, they would then have to compromise or the government would shut down, absent a continuing resolution to provide enough money for brief periods.

In early May 1995, the House and Senate Budget Committees reported their budget resolutions for the next fiscal year. The House budget would have abolished the Departments of Commerce, Education, and Energy. The House would also have eliminated 14 agencies and 284 federal programs. As in 1982, Gingrich aspired to be more Reagan than Reagan. The Senate would have terminated more than 150 federal programs.[81]

The Republicans eventually passed a reconciliation budget that foresaw $894 billion in cuts to projected federal spending by 2002, leading to a $4 billion surplus. The bill proposed reducing projected welfare spending by $82 billion, Medicare by $270 billion, and Medicaid by $163 billion, and reducing agricultural subsidies with an eye toward eliminating them. Where Reagan had proposed minor constraints on Social Security, Gingrich was ready to take on Medicare.

By 1996, Medicare was expected to cover 36 million people at a cost of $178 billion, or 11 percent of total federal spending. It was the fourth-largest federal outlay. The other three—Social Security, defense, and interest on the debt—had been exempted from budget discipline by the 1994 Republicans. After moderating in the second half of the 1980s, Medicare spending on hospitalization insurance had returned to near double-digit annual increases or above from 1992 to 1994.[82] The GOP had to deal with Medicare or give up all hope for fiscal discipline. They eventually decided to restructure the program to reduce spending over seven years. To say the GOP was taking a risk was an understatement. The largest previous reduction in Medicare had been $56 billion in five years enacted in 1993.

Gingrich and his allies had learned from Clinton's health care debacle that the relevant interest groups should be part of the political solution so that they would not later become part of the problem. How could health care providers be persuaded to accept the largest reduction ever in Medicare spending, cuts that included lower payment rates to doctors and hospitals? The Republican leadership decided to work closely with the interest groups to ascertain their desires and to give enough compensation to make the larger cuts tolerable. The strategy worked.[83] The president also wanted to constrain Medicare spending. He offered to cut $124 billion over seven years, largely by reducing payments to providers. The two sides did differ on more than the total sum of cuts. The Republicans wanted medical savings account and more contributions from more affluent elderly voters. Clinton rejected both.[84]

Clinton promised to veto the bill. If Clinton vetoed the budget, the government would shut down, more or less. On November 14, 1995, over 14 million nonessential government employees were sent home. The struggle then began in earnest. The two sides began to blame each other for the shutdown in the media. The Republicans were at a disadvantage since the budget bill cut taxes by $245 billion over seven years. It was easy to demagogue. Rep. Pete Stark (D-CA) said Republicans "have decided to reward their rich friends and stick it to the women and sick people."

Another continuing resolution kept the government open. Clinton rallied public opinion, and his approval ratings climbed above 50 percent for the first time in more than a year. Worse, surveys showed that Clinton and the Democrats had a 23 percent margin among the public on who could best handle the deficit. The continuing resolution expired, leading to parts of the government again closing down. Early in 1996, more continuing resolutions followed to keep the government open, and Clinton offered a balanced budget proposal that included cuts in Medicare, Medicaid, and welfare that were half as large as those proposed by the GOP. In the end, the Republicans proposed more cuts in spending than Clinton: $99 billion more in Medicare over the period, $65 billion more in Medicaid, $88 billion more in discretionary spending, and $37 billion more in welfare. The Republicans also sought $154 billion more than Clinton in tax cuts.

The battle over interpreting the gridlock continued. Clinton won over public opinion. The president's approval ratings improved through much of the battle. In the spring and fall of 1995, Clinton's approval rating was on average 4 percent greater than his disapproval. Shortly after the shutdown, the gap grew to more than 7 percent. By early December, he was 11 percent ahead. Gingrich went the other way. His disapproval rating was 11 points greater than his approval number by early 1995. In mid-November at the time of the first government shutdown, 60 percent of respondents disapproved of the Speaker, 33 percent more than approved. His ratings did not rebound.

Losing the battle for public opinion, the Republicans relented and sent Clinton appropriations bills. He vetoed what he did not like, thereby protecting federal spending on education, job training, and the environment. The original Republican proposals for cuts in entitlements could not pass. The budget did contain a reduction in domestic spending from earlier baselines. But the programs Clinton had sought to protect survived intact, and the new majority had suffered terrible political damage. A 1994 freshman House member concluded that the budget confrontation "was a disaster . . the momentum of 1994 came to an end."[85]

Some argue that the outcome of the shutdown struggle shows Americans truly want big government. When the GOP freshmen actually offered the public smaller government, voters rebelled and took Clinton's side in defense of their entitlements.[86] This story does not account for two facts. Before 1994, Clinton had offered the public more government paid for by debt and taxes on the rich. He became unpopular and fomented an electoral debacle for his party. Second, Clinton himself was offering constraint on Medicare spending in 1996, though not nearly as much as the Republicans. His victory in the public relations battle over the shutdown may indicate the public wanted less constraint in Medicare than the Republicans offered. It does not show that the public at that time hoped to maintain or expand the welfare state.

Richard Fenno, a political scientist who has studied Congress for decades, argued that the budget confrontation disaster arose from the new majority's ignorance of the legislative process. "Budget politics is always incremental politics. You can't possibly run a revolution through the budget process." From the beginning, the House Republicans wanted to bring about quick changes. They were not inclined, therefore, to accept or take credit for incremental steps toward their goals, steps that would keep them in control of the public debate and moving toward a unified Republican government. The Republicans could have declared victory at various points. The president did submit a balanced budget, accepted reductions in Medicare, and set a seven-year timetable for a balanced budget. The Republicans could have gotten a lot more than anyone would have thought they might at the start. But they refused to recognize a compromised but real victory.[87]

The experience of the Contract with America also misled the freshmen who had no other experience of governing. Fenno noted that the new majority "came to the budget conflict with an exaggerated idea of their capacity to shape outcomes, an unrealistic idea of how much they could win through a refusal to compromise, and an underdeveloped idea of what the business of governing looked like in the world beyond the House." They refused to compromise and thus forced the shutdown.[88] For Fenno, the Republicans failed because they did not know how to govern and refused to learn.

The class of 1994, in other words, lacked enough cynicism to succeed politically. The new members feared the United States was losing its way, corrupted by insiders in the capital. They resolved to run as outsiders free from the taint of Washington, to ask for a mandate from the nation, and to enact that commission without delay or compromise. The 1994 Republicans were radical and populist: they believed the people wanted to be free of their government and that the House GOP had a mandate to attain that end.

In retrospect, Gingrich may be accused of letting ardency for his cause overcome prudence in pursuit of change. Indeed, Gingrich was an idealist. He saw the struggle with Clinton in terms of keeping promises: the people "are counting on us keeping our word because they actually believe we are different."[89] He was both similar to and different from the president. Clinton had promised to change both national politics and his party. He was cynical enough to succeed but not competent to govern, at least at first. The Republicans had run against Clinton. Their refusal to compromise contravened his incompetent cynicism. Moreover, doing the right thing did not yet seem to contradict political prudence. Polls had shown for some months that the public had tired of big government. Clinton himself would famously declare as late as his 1996 State of the Union address that "the era of big government is over."[90] What people might tell a stranger over the telephone and what they might believe when faced with a concrete possibility of program cuts need not be the same. Gingrich believed what many, perhaps most, Americans professed from 1993 onward: the era of big government was over. That faith, in retrospect, was his major failing.

The budget confrontation marked the first step toward President Clinton's reelection in 1996.[91] Clinton adopted a strategy of "triangulation," which involved opposing the extremes of American politics. Newt Gingrich was one of those extremes; the other was, as in 1992, the left wing of the Democratic Party. He repudiated the left by getting behind several conservative and popular policy initiatives: welfare reform, V-chips in televisions to allow parent to screen program content, curfews for teenagers and school uniforms, mandatory drug tests for 16-year-olds applying for driver's licenses, and a balanced budget proposal.

His differences with Gingrich were more concrete and significant. The president carefully avoided supporting actual constraints on environmental regulation. He proposed more subsidies for college students.[92] Clinton gave in to conservatives, in other words, on the style but not on the substance of policy. Moreover, even his concessions tended to expand government in one way or another though the motives behind the expansion seemed "conservative."

Clinton's rebound owed as much to a revived economy as to his political skills. By the fall of 1996, the economy was growing at nearly a 5 percent annual rate. The voters noticed. One poll found that the 60 percent of the respondents who said that the economy was doing well heavily favored Clinton. The president was twice lucky with the economy. In 1992, the exit polls found that fewer than 20 percent said the economy was doing well, and the dissatisfaction of so many helped the challenger to the White House.[93]

Clinton easily won reelection.[94] His victory was large but incomplete. He did not win a majority of the popular vote, and his party did not win control of Congress.[95] Seventy Republican freshmen ran for reelection. Fifty-nine of the freshmen won reelection, an 84 percent reelection rate. These freshman incumbents, on average, received about the same proportion of the vote in their districts as they had in 1994. The freshmen thus did 5 percent better than their fellow Republicans.[96] Republican voting records were quite conservative; over 90 percent of the GOP House voted conservatively more than 80 percent of the time.[97] Looking at the election results, analysts found no evidence that these voting records hurt Republican incumbents in moderate to liberal districts.[98] The 49 percent vote share captured by the Republican congressional candidates exceeded candidate Robert Dole's vote by 8 percent.[99] In many ways, the GOP freshmen were similar to what other freshman members at other times had experienced.

What can be said about the Republican Party and religious voters in 1996, especially evangelical Protestants? The data support three propositions. First, the proportion of evangelical Protestants who regularly attend church and identify with the GOP continued to rise in 1994 and 1996. Where just over one in three such voters identified with the GOP in 1988, fully half did so in 1996 (and slightly less than half in 1994).[100]

Second, the proportion of Republican identifiers who were Protestant evangelicals who regularly attend church rose rapidly from 1988 to 1992, leveled off in 1994, and rose sharply again in the 1996 election. Between 1988 and 1996, the proportion of Republican identifiers composed of evangelical Protestants who regularly attend church doubled, from just over 12 percent to 25 percent. In the previous two decades (1968 to 1988), such evangelicals had formed only a marginally larger part of the group of all voters who identified with the GOP.[101]

Third, the evangelical contribution to the Republican presidential vote had also roughly doubled between 1988 and 1996; the increase in such voters within the coalition, however, had leveled off between 1992 and 1996. Once again, this rapid rise in evangelical commitment to the GOP followed 16 years of little or no increases in this measure.[102] This rapid change in the composition of the Republican coalition coincided with GOP candidates' losing two consecutive presidential elections for the first time in 30 years.

The 1996 results offered little evidence that the voting records or government shutdown of the 1994 class prevented more than a handful of Republicans from being reelected to Congress. The electorate said no to Clinton in 1994, no to the House GOP in 1995, and yes to both in 1996. The voters seemed to like the new status quo of divided government, particularly when it came with economic growth well above the historical average. No one had won completely and no one had lost. The growth of the federal government had been constrained, especially compared to Clinton's expansive hopes in 1992, but the limited government promised in 1994—agencies ended and all that—had also not happened.

In 1994, Republicans had both run and largely tried to govern as the party of Reagan, not as the party of Pat Robertson. They had promised limits on government and institutional reforms associated with reductions in spending and taxing. Reagan had praised traditional morality, condemned contemporary decadence, and rarely acted on his praise or condemnation. That mixture of promises and performance reflected the relative power of traditional morality in the GOP.

By 1996, the party of Reagan was much less Reaganite: it had become more the party of the two Pats, Robertson and Buchanan. Evangelicals had become much more important generally and at the margin to Republican candidates. Like Reagan, however, Newt Gingrich and the GOP leadership had talked more about traditional morality than acted to enforce it. How long could Republican leaders continue to give religious voters little in return for their votes?

Beginning of the End   The 1996 election broke the deadlock over the budget. In May 1997, the president and congressional Republicans announced that a deal was at hand to balance the budget by 2002 while cutting taxes. The performance of the economy had brightened expectations; in 1996, gross domestic product had grown by 4.5 percent after adjusting for inflation.[103] The future also looked better to the forecasters. As budget negotiations neared their end, the Congressional Budget Office had increased its five-year revenue estimates by $225 billion.[104]

Clinton and the Democrats got more money for some programs for the poor. The Republicans made some progress on the spending. The budget included the most extensive changes in Medicare since 1965. As with Reagan, these "cuts" involved limits on increases in spending rather than actual reductions from prior levels of outlays. Medicare was changed to include more managed care options and a small initiative creating tax-exempt medical savings accounts. The bill also cut projected spending on Medicaid by about $10.4 billion by 2002. Most of these savings depended on reducing payments to states for hospitals that had more poor patients than average.[105]

Republicans made good on their 1994 promises to cut taxes. Overall, the final budget bill included $95 billion in net tax cuts over five years, growing to $275 billion over 10 years. Republicans attained the largest reduction in capital gains tax rates since 1981. Gross tax cuts in the final package were about $152 billion over five years, with an offset of $56 billion in tax increases, according to estimates by the Joint Committee on Taxation. Over 10 years, the gross tax cut was projected to be $401 billion, with $126 billion in offsetting tax increases.[106]

But the tax story is not that simple. Much of the law rolled back the reduction in tax preferences gained in 1986. The GOP backed a capital gains tax exemption for profits from the sale of a primary residence, a $500-per-child tax credit, a significant increase in the tax exemption for estates, and an expansion of tax-preferred individual retirement account savings plans. Clinton obtained new tax incentives for education.[107]

In late July, GOP leaders brought the spending side of the budget to the House floor. Members gave themselves a standing ovation. John Kasich, the chair of the Budget Committee, proclaimed "the dawning of a new era, an era where we recognize the limits of government." The Senate passed the spending bill the next day with both liberals and conservatives on board. The same mix of left and right passed the conference report on the tax bill the same day by an overwhelming margin.[108] The long struggle over the deficit appeared to have ended with the projected end of the deficit itself.

Gingrich had reason to be satisfied. The legislation was a part of the policy agenda that House Republicans promised to voters if they took control of Congress. The agreement would have been a career achievement for any Speaker, and especially for one who had emphasized the issue in the first place.[109] Yet Gingrich had also become one of the nation's most detested politicians. Polls showed fewer than 35 percent of the public approved of his performance. He also largely did not win back the affections of disgruntled House Republicans, many of whom had gradually lost faith in his leadership in struggles with the president.[110] Gingrich was the face of 1994, but the ideals of that time and that new majority involved more than one man. Apart from the lost battle over the government shutdown, how far did the 1994 group cut government, if at all?

The Revolution's Record   The politics for the Republican 1994 revolution are not especially pleasing to the devotee of limited government. The revolutionaries seem to have lost most of the major battles. Did they lose the war? I examine first the institutional changes they sought followed by the much longer list of policy reforms.

The Balanced Budget Amendment required support from two-thirds of the House and the Senate to send it to the states for their approval or rejection. Moderate and conservative Democratic votes were necessary, but the conservative Democratic Caucus did not support the original GOP amendment because it included, as the Contract with America had promised, a supermajority (three-fifths of those voting) requirement for raising taxes. (The same proposal Reagan had made in 1978!) After some bargaining, the GOP settled for the Democratic version instead of the status quo; the amendment went to the Senate with 300 House votes in its favor.[111] The limit on taxation had been jettisoned.

In the Senate, the needed votes for the amendment belonged to moderate and conservative Democrats who knew the proposal had majority support in the Senate and in the nation as a whole. Democratic leaders argued that the amendment would threaten Social Security if it were treated as part of the budget. Crucial votes would appear if Social Security were exempted. Since the surplus from the payroll taxes assigned to Social Security covered spending in other areas, taking Social Security out of the unified budget would require large tax increases or program cuts, the prospect of which would reduce support for the amendment. The amendment picked up 14 Democrats while losing the vote of Republican Mark Hatfield, thereby ending up one vote short of success. Half the Democrats who voted for it were up for reelection in 1996. Six other Democrats who had voted for the amendment in 1994 voted against it in 1995; none of the six was facing election in 1996.[112] Other reforms were enacted and thereafter failed.

As far back as 1978, Reagan had proposed giving the president the power to veto specific spending in an appropriations bill—the line-item veto—to cut spending. The 104th Congress did not propose a line-item veto amendment to the Constitution. Instead, it would allow the president to offer rescissions that would take effect unless Congress blocked them by a supermajority vote. This change attracted a majority in the House but did not emerge from conference until a year later. In the end, the line-item veto passed with strong Republican and modest Democratic support.[113] President Clinton used the veto rarely to little effect on spending. The Supreme Court eventually declared the line-item veto unconstitutional.[114]

Of all the reforms in the Contract with America, the vote on limiting congressional terms seemed least likely to attain a majority. Most of the new House majority had made politics their livelihood and hoped to do so into the future. The older members were unlikely to accept constraints on their tenure or to admit, as term limits advocates argued, that long stays in office corrupted incumbents and fostered the growth of big government. With the 1994 election over, even GOP leaders like Richard Armey seemed to be having second thoughts on term limits: "Now, with Republicans in Congress, I don't feel as much a need for it, but I'll vote for it."[115]

The outlook for limiting congressional terms worsened early in 1995 when a bare majority of the Supreme Court held that the states could not change the qualifications (including limiting terms) for serving in Congress. Supporters could only limit terms by amending the Constitution. Two months before the Court's decision, a proposed constitutional amendment had failed in the House for lack of the necessary two-thirds majority.[116] In the end, a constitutional amendment to permit term limits fell 63 votes short of the needed votes in the House. The outcome reflected both Democratic unity in opposition and divisions within the GOP majority, primarily between older and more junior members.[117] Later efforts to enact an amendment did worse.[118]

The new majority held to its pledge to hold votes on all parts of the Contract with America. They also quickly enacted institutional changes that lay within their power. These included eliminating standing committees, cutting congressional staff, disclosing committee votes by members, rotation of committee chairs, limiting the term of the Speaker, and other reforms.[119] These changes in the rules governing Congress made the legislature more transparent and more centralized. They also made it easier for the leadership to control the House, which might make reductions in government more likely if the leadership sought them.

Why did the GOP effort at institutional change fail so badly? The faith in the line-item veto was misplaced. The difficulties with the other two constitutional amendments were not surprising. The 1994 election results suggested the possibility of radical changes in American institutions and policies. Those institutions, however, were designed to stop radical changes of any sort, in part by requiring a broader consensus than a simple majority. The new majority was hardly united on all matters. The newly elected members sought power in part to save the nation by enacting significant changes. Older and more moderate House Republicans wanted power for the same reasons most Democrats did: they wished to rule. They did not necessarily want to change the world they had adapted to and mastered. 1994 did empower a majority in the House on some issues. It did not produce enough votes, however, in favor of significant institutional changes that might have had the most radical and lasting changes. Did the 1994 group change policy, if not institutions?

Gingrich's desire for change faced another obstacle created by the Constitution: the president and his veto. At first, Bill Clinton did not seem to matter much. Gingrich, along with many other people, assumed Clinton would not block the GOP agenda for fear of crossing the new majority and thereby ensuring the defeat of his bid for reelection in 1996.[120] Had Clinton persisted in his hubris of 1993, these expectations about his irrelevance would have proved correct. Clinton would prove, however, he could adapt to the new majority in ways that would frustrate their desire to limit the federal government.

From the start, Gingrich decided that the Contract with America would stay clear of Social Security. He opened the 104th Congress by saying, "I think Social Security ought to be off limits, at least for the first four to six years of this process, because I think it will just destroy us if we try to bring it into the game."[121] When the new Congress met early in 1995, more than half the budget (Social Security, defense, and interest on the national debt) could not be constrained.[122] Not surprisingly, the GOP platform in 1996 pledged allegiance to Social Security.[123]

As ever, the political logic of Social Security worked against fundamental reforms. As noted earlier, the program had experienced both short- and long-term problems in the 1980s. Its reserves had shrunk to just six months in 1986. By the 1990s, however, its reserves had rebounded smartly. No immediate crisis existed, although the program's long-term prospects remained problematic. Yet in 1995, as in 1935, the future had little leverage on the present. More Social Security revenue meant more money to spend on constituents; both Democrats and Republicans responded to the short-term incentive, and new spending on disabilities and pensions rose in 1994 and 1996. By 1998, one-tenth of the reserves had been diverted to other related spending.[124]

Social Security also affected other efforts to constrain spending. Democrats, as mentioned, argued that the balanced budget constitutional amendment would require cuts in Social Security; they hoped to use popular support for the latter to contravene popular support for the former. The tactic worked, as the amendment came up one vote short in the Senate, in part because no way could be found to remove Social Security from deficit calculations.[125]

It is true that members of Congress lacked courage on this issue, but they had reason to fear the electorate. In late 1994, at the high point of public skepticism about big government, a CBS News/*New York Times* poll found that while 81 percent of Americans supported the balanced budget amendment, 30 percent or fewer remained in favor when told the amendment might require cuts in Social Security, Medicare, and education.[126]

The politics of Social Security appeared on a predictable path in 1997. In the short term, members would obey powerful political incentives and do nothing, save claim someone else was threatening Social Security. Meanwhile, the system's funding problems would slowly come forward in time until some Congress at some point would have no choice but to deal with Social Security. But a future crisis had little to do with current politics and elections.

Then in 1998, the politics seemed to change at the behest of Bill Clinton. The president held a series of town meetings to build public awareness of the funding problem and support for policy changes. He also proposed "saving Social Security first," a skillful political gambit. His 1999 State of the Union address proposed that the government invest part of the Social Security surplus in the private capital markets.[127]

Clinton had another surplus in mind, the newly appearing surplus in the federal budget. He was concerned that the surplus might lead to tax cuts. After all, if the government had more than enough money to cover its expenses, voters might wonder why the surplus was not returned to taxpayers. Clinton preferred that the government spend this money rather than give it back to voters.

He had learned an important lesson from the balanced budget amendment debate: you need a popular program to beat a popular idea. Hence, Clinton proposed "saving Social Security first." Sixty percent of anticipated federal budget surpluses over the next 15 years would be set aside to "save Social Security."[128] Money set aside in this way, of course, could not fund tax reductions. (It did not matter, of course, that taxes collected for Social Security had never been set aside but rather used for new spending.)[129] Clinton was betting that forced to a choice, taxpayers would favor Social Security over tax cuts.

On the other hand, Clinton had given legitimacy to a somewhat private solution to the long-term funding of Social Security. To be sure, private markets would remain under government control, but public pensions in the United States would no longer be solely a preserve of the federal government.[130] Clinton had given only a little ground, and his plan was essentially a bait and switch that appeared to be a significant reform while continuing on the path to fiscal crisis. For all that, Clinton had signaled a willingness to admit the legitimacy of private saving and private pensions.

House Ways and Means Committee Chair Bill Archer (R-TX) and Social Security Subcommittee Chair E. Clay Shaw (R-FL) responded to Clinton's overture by proposing that individuals be allowed to invest, through a refundable tax credit, a part of their payroll taxes in private capital markets. The plan was not as radical as it might appear; it remained a public-private scheme since individuals would only be allowed to choose from a government-approved list of investment possibilities, and individuals would not actually own the earnings from the accounts. Moreover, the Archer-Shaw plan stipulated that no one would receive a lower pension benefit under the proposed system than they would have gotten under current law, thereby creating a moral hazard problem of the first order.[131] Shortcomings notwithstanding, Archer and Shaw, like Clinton, seemed to be feeling their way toward a significant departure from the old politics of Social Security.

In 1999, the new House Republican leadership was wary of reform through private accounts. As early as April 1999, the leadership warned Archer and Shaw against moving forward with their private accounts proposal. The leaders were looking at polls that showed that recipients were skeptical of private accounts. The GOP itself was divided over the proposal. On the Senate side, leaders like Trent Lott (R-MS) recalled the difficulties of trying to deal with Social Security early in the Reagan administration and worried about a political calamity. GOP leaders in both the House and the Senate wanted at least some Democratic support for the plans, support that was not forthcoming.

Instead of a broad rewrite of the program, Republican leaders concentrated on ensuring that Congress did not use the Social Security surplus to pay for upcoming spending bills through a so-called lockbox. The lockbox was more public relations than anything else. It put Republicans on the side of "saving" Social Security while putting pressure on the rest of domestic spending. But the lockbox would require deep cuts in domestic spending that members, Republicans included, would only enact if they had no choice. But they had a choice: they did not have to do anything about Social Security because the fiscal train had not yet wrecked. Clinton eventually abandoned his direct investment proposal. By that time, however, the window of opportunity had closed for the time being for changes in Social Security.[132]

Could the GOP have done better in 1999? The Clinton proposal sounded better than it was. While Clinton mentioned private markets, the proposal itself sought to preclude tax cuts and to increase Social Security benefits. The investment of Social Security taxes would also be politically driven, thereby enhancing rather than reducing the ambit of government, politicians, and majorities. Had the Republican leadership been bolder, they might have risked all on the private accounts. But they feared that private accounts might become a rhetorical killing zone for Republicans during the upcoming presidential election. History supported their fears. On the whole, Archer and Shaw, with Clinton's help, did accomplish something: the idea of a private solution of some sort became more acceptable than it had been before 1998.

The struggle over Medicare continued after the government shutdown saga. The Republicans proposed smaller cuts, while Clinton held fast to less constraint on the program. The trustees of Medicare reported that the program would go broke in five years. Everyone blamed everyone else as the presidential election wore on.[133]

The budget agreement of 1997 did better on costs, at least for a while. Congress and the administration believed they had reduced Medicare spending by $112 billion over five years. About one-fifth of the savings was expected from expanding managed care in Medicare and introducing medical savings accounts. Another one-third would come from reducing hospital costs by reducing various payments to these institutions. A final large portion of the restraint would come from "reducing payments for doctors, durable medical equipment, laboratory services, and ambulatory surgical services; and by changing reimbursement methods for outpatient services and therapists."[134]

Congress had not addressed the program's funding problems. It did appoint a commission to study the problem, a common way of kicking various cans down the road.[135] Solving the next crisis of Medicare funding would be someone else's electoral headache. The 105th Congress could claim credit for staving off the immediate collapse of the system. By historical standards, that was indeed an achievement, but that judgment reflects more than anything else the low expectation of congressional performance fostered by the electoral logic of entitlement programs.

The spending restraint lasted two years. In 1999, Congress gave back $16 billion of the earlier reductions over five years. In 2000, both parties in Congress became even more forthcoming. The federal budget had gone into surplus. Meanwhile, the managed care plans set up in the 1997 law had started dropping out of Medicare because the payments were said to be too low and the administrative burdens too costly. Government experts predicted that in early in 2001 an additional 115 plans would drop Medicare, thereby forcing 934,000 recipients to find other plans. 2000 was, of course, an election year, and members of Congress did not wish to irritate anyone, least of all the elderly. The Republicans and Clinton squabbled over how much of the added spending would go to managed care organizations. In the end, more than $35 billion was added to Medicare.[136]

The GOP story about Medicare from 1995 to 2000 can be summarized briefly. Republicans demanded spending restraint in the range of $270 billion over seven years. After being outmaneuvered by Clinton, they eventually settled for $112 billion in reductions over five years in 1997. By the end of 2000, 46 percent of the 1997 reductions had been given back through increased spending on Medicare.

Why did this happen? Budgetary pressures had abated by 2000. Members felt they had money to spend without causing larger deficits. Medicare beneficiaries, as well as providers, wanted public money for medical care. Republicans could refuse to support this desire for new spending, but Democratic challengers for Congress would be more than happy to promise new money for a program their party had created. Absent a sense of budget constraint, the GOP sought to control the budgetary and electoral damage that might be done by Medicare. This part of the revolution had been, in sum, betrayed by the people. What of government medical care for the poor? Surely it faced severe costs.

Medicaid is a federal-state program to pay for health care for the poor; it also pays for half the nursing home costs of the elderly and the disabled. The program had grown from less than $1 billion in 1966 to over $144 billion by 1995. By 2000, such spending would top $200 billion. From 1966 to 2000, spending on each recipient had risen from less than $200 to more than $6,000. Medicaid spent about $4 per U.S. resident in 1966 and would spend nearly $750 per resident in 2000.[137] During the 1990s, Medicaid spending grew at an average annual rate of just under 11 percent.[138] The history of Medicaid confirmed Lyndon Johnson's faith that programs would grow over time, even if elected officials wished to limit them.

The 1994 class waded into the Medicaid morass. In 1995, the new Congress proposed a "Medigrant" program that would have ended the Medicaid entitlement and put a ceiling on the federal share of such spending. The plan was expected to reduce Medicaid spending by $163 billion over seven years. Clinton vetoed Medigrant. It also had perverse effects on spending. The states knew that if Medigrant became law, 1995 would be the baseline for calculating caps on future spending; hence, the states increased Medicaid spending in 1995 to increase future aid.

The 1997 budget agreement gave the states the option of establishing managed care programs for Medicaid recipients without seeking waivers from the federal government. The move was expected to cut costs. Congress also reduced payments to states with hospitals that provided health care to the poor or uninsured. By 2000, half of all Medicaid recipients were in such programs.

The agreement also created a new entitlement, the State Children's Health Insurance Program, which allocated nearly $40 billion in new spending over the next decade to fund health care for approximately 3.4 million children who did not qualify for Medicaid.[139] The agreement was expected to constrain Medicaid spending by $7 billion, in part because SCHIP spending was funded by an increase in the federal cigarette tax, which would reduce smoking and thereby health care costs for the program.[140]

Why did SCHIP pass the Congress? The struggle over SCHIP became defined as a fight for children and against tobacco. The program began life in the Senate with bipartisan sponsors, Ted Kennedy (D-MA) and Orrin Hatch (R-UT). Hatch said that "he was offering the legislation to prove that the Republican Party 'does not hate children,' and he added that 'as a nation, as a society, we have a moral responsibility' to provide coverage for the most vulnerable children."[141] Here, the Republican wound was self-inflicted. According to Hatch, if Republican members refused to enact SCHIP, they hated children. Hatch was hardly to blame for this childish account of the issue. Democrats had worked hard for some time to redefine redistribution as a benefit to children who, after all, bore no responsibility for their conduct or for the conduct of their parents. The Democrats' wish to redistribute wealth or fund services for the poor could thus avoid the opprobrium usually associated with welfare spending.

Tobacco provided a convenient villain. Ted Kennedy and his fellow Massachusetts senator, John Kerry, had introduced a bill in late 1996 that proposed paying for health insurance for children through a tobacco tax, a levy already in place in their state. Kennedy then sought out Republican senators who in the past had voted against tobacco interests and were open to supporting children's insurance. Hatch's Mormonism led him to favor both restrictions on tobacco and insurance for children. His conservative reputation also helped the cause.[142] The sponsors eventually found seven other Republican senators to support their proposals. With all 43 Democrats voting yes, the new GOP votes would seal a majority for the bill, at least in theory.[143]

With the tax in place, opponents arguing against raising taxes could be portrayed as favoring big tobacco over little children. Moreover, advocates of the new spending argued that the tax would prevent some teens from starting to smoke. Kennedy and Hatch then put together a coalition of 150 interest groups to push the legislation. They immediately sponsored a newspaper advertisement that posed the rhetorical question: "Senators, who do you stand with: Joe Camel or Joey?" The ad included pictures of the Camel cigarette character and of an innocent child in a cowboy hat.[144] As Kennedy said during the struggle: "Remember Harry and Louise, the ad characters that had helped defeat Clinton's health care proposal in 1993? Well, now it's Joe Camel and Joey."[145] Hatch also tried to redefine cigarette taxes as a "user fee," paid only by smokers, who made up one-fourth of the population.[146]

The opponents of the bill did not recover from this initial definition of the issue. In the Senate, some argued that raising the tobacco tax would reduce smoking and thus reduce state revenues. So what? Hatch retorted. Do we really want to kill people to keep money flowing to the states? House Republicans were in a much more difficult spot: by the time the Senate tax bill had arrived in the House, polls showed that 60 to 70 percent of Americans supported higher tobacco taxes, a burden that would fall on 25 percent of the population.[147] Republicans were reduced to agreeing to the tax while arguing that it should not go to spending on children. The program was signed into law with $24 billion in new spending and a 15-cent tobacco tax increase.[148]

Several factors contributed to the political success of SCHIP. As with increased Medicare spending, the emerging federal surplus opened up the Treasury. The Republicans were divided, particularly between the House and the Senate; senators were more favorable to new spending on this issue. Ted Kennedy was much more skillful than any of his Republican opponents. He created in part the division in the Republican ranks by recruiting Hatch and other GOP senators. Together with Hatch, he defined the issue so senators (and to some extent, all members) were forced to choose between sick children and companies selling a product that caused cancer. Kennedy also moved public opinion toward tobacco taxes, widely considered a just punishment to purveyors of tobacco. That move was crucial. American taxpayers could afford to be sentimental about sick children if they believe someone else would be required to pay for their health care. Kennedy was offering much of the nation a free lunch. Republicans could not outbid him.

Welfare was one policy area where there was significant reform. From the New Deal onward, the federal government redistributed wealth to the poor through Social Security, food stamps, Medicaid, housing programs, and job training. One program—Aid to Families with Dependent Children—was commonly called "welfare." As its name suggests, AFDC sought to redistribute wealth to assist dependent children, understood as children "deprived of parental support or care because their father or mother was absent from the home, incapacitated, deceased, or unemployed."[149] Grants were given to the states to support the program.

Congress created AFDC as part of the Social Security Act of 1935, but welfare did not enjoy the long-term political success of its siblings. AFDC posed a moral problem for Progressives. Where Social Security might be thought of as just compensation for a lifetime of work, welfare was an alternative to work, a way to avoid personal responsibility for obligations voluntarily undertaken. AFDC deeply contravened American norms. It was, however, an entitlement and thus available to all who met specific criteria set by law. The program continued to impose burdens on taxpayers while gradually losing legitimacy with voters.

Democrats tried to connect AFDC to work. Jimmy Carter tried to distinguish those who deserved taxpayer support from those who did not. When running for president, Carter promised "a complete overhaul of our welfare system" and proposed a system that would separate the employable from the unemployable poor.[150] Carter's comprehensive effort failed, and a more incremental proposal failed in the Senate late in his administration.[151]

Reagan's 1982 budget cut benefits for welfare and emphasized work in exchange for benefits, along with allowing the states to experiment with training and other programs designed to promote self-sufficiency. Reagan followed Carter in exempting caregivers for small children from the work requirements; as a result, only about 800,000 of the 10 million people on AFDC rolls would have to work or face a cutoff in aid.[152] Like some parts of federal spending, AFDC had been constrained, but it remained in place. Here again, Reagan's radicalism was more in the eyes of his enemies than in reality.

Reagan returned to welfare reform in his 1986 State of the Union address. The renewed struggle began on the same (and only) common ground that had existed since 1967: parental support orders should be enforced. Beyond that, liberals wanted more and more uniform benefits while conservatives wanted working recipients, lower costs, and more experimentation from the states. In the end, conservatives won on work (one parent in two-parent welfare families had to work at least 16 hours per week) and lost on the overall cost of the bill. Liberals did not like the work requirement but gave in since the law gave recipients more money, medical benefits, and job training.[153] The 1988 law was praised as an example of governance and bipartisan compromise.

It did not take welfare off the public agenda. In the 1992 campaign, Bill Clinton signaled his moderation by promising to "end welfare as we know it." Reforming welfare, however, was not a priority for the new administration. His first proposal harkened back to Carter. Recipients would be required to find work within two years of accepting welfare. Those who could not find work would receive a job subsidized by the federal government. The federal government would also subsidize job training and childcare for welfare recipients.

Clinton served up the proposals with new rhetoric. Only a few years earlier, Democrats had called work requirements "slavefare"; many still did in 1994. Clinton said in contrast: "We propose to offer people on welfare a simple contract. We will help you get the skills you need, but after two years, anyone who can go to work must go to work—in the private sector if possible, in a subsidized job if necessary. But work is preferable to welfare. And it must be enforced."[154] The language of work might enable Clinton to get new education and welfare spending by the public.

The competing Republican proposal departed from past initiatives, even in the Reagan era, by focusing on illegitimacy and on limiting welfare spending. The Personal Responsibility Act sought to overhaul "the American welfare system to reduce government dependency, attack illegitimacy, require welfare recipients to enter work programs and cap total welfare spending." It also gave states much more control over benefits and work programs, especially with regard to AFDC.[155] The Contract with America also identified AFDC as a failed program that had exacerbated social pathologies. It advocated denying welfare to noncitizens as a way to save $22 billion over five years. Most taxpayers in 1995, it might be said, would be surprised to learn that noncitizens received billions of dollars in welfare from the federal government.

Clinton vetoed the first welfare reform to pass Congress.[156] He had stopped reform temporarily, in part because the struggle over the government shutdown obscured the welfare issue. But he was playing a dangerous game in a year he would face the electorate. Taking the side of welfare recipients could cost any president votes if not reelection. Clinton was more vulnerable. He had promised to end welfare and then blocked all attempts to end it.

As the election drew near, both Clinton and many Democrats abandoned opposition to welfare reform. Clinton's decision to sign the bill brought grief from some Democrats. Some Senate Democrats, led by Daniel Patrick Moynihan of New York, opposed any end to a federal entitlement to welfare. Other Democrats in both chambers of Congress resisted restraint on spending on food stamps and on welfare for noncitizens. The prominent leftist Marian Wright Edelman said the president's decision to sign the reform "makes a mockery of his pledge not to hurt children. It will leave a moral blot on his presidency and on our nation." The Urban Institute, the research organization created by the Johnson administration, came to the defense of this New Deal entitlement by estimating that the reform would throw nearly 2.6 million people, including 1.1 million children, into poverty.

Democrats in Congress had given up on the entitlement to welfare. Other Democratic senators were willing to take a chance on reform, not least because the current program had turned into a perennial electoral liability for the party. Newt Gingrich provided an accurate assessment of the outcome. Clinton had decided to affirm welfare reform "because he can't avoid it and get re-elected."[157] No politician could be elected by promising to cut the pension payments provided by the Social Security Act of 1935; 60 years later, few politicians could be reelected by promising to defend payments to AFDC clients. The result of the welfare reform vote and its emphasis on work suggested that American political culture was healthier than one might think.[158]

Can we determine the effects of welfare reform? The number of families receiving welfare declined by more than 50 percent from 1994 to 2004; enrollment comprised 2.2 million families in 2004 compared to a zenith of 5.08 million in March 1994. In 2002, the Council of Economic Advisers concluded that time limits alone brought about more than 10 percent of this decline from 1993 to 1999. Other economic research suggested that roughly half the decline in the caseload during the 1990s came from fewer new recipients entering the programs.[159]

This decline in the number of recipients did not mean the federal government (or governments more generally) no longer redistributed money to the poor. In the 2002 fiscal year, experts estimated that federal funding for the poor amounted to over $44 billion; total spending on services and case benefits for the poor reached almost $170 billion. Of this, just over $13 billion in state and federal money was spent through the Temporary Assistance for Needy Families program, which replaced AFDC.[160] The largest redistribution comes from the Earned Income Tax Credit, which is offered to those who earn relatively low wages. In 2004, 22.3 million tax filers received $40.6 billion through this mechanism. Poor families with one child garnered on average a credit of $1,728, and families with two or more children received $2,669.[161] In some cases, benefits rose sharply from 1994 to 2000: the maximum Earned Income Tax Credit for families with two or more children, for example, rose by more than 50 percent during that period.[162]

As the number of AFDC/Temporary Assistance for Needy Families recipients fell, work increased. The participation rate of single mothers grew from 44 to 66 percent between 1994 and 2001, a greater increase than any other group of women experienced over this period. By 2004, their labor force participation had fallen to 61 percent, which was still well above where it had been in the early 1990s. Their incomes grew also, and increases in their earnings were larger than the decline in welfare benefits. Poverty rates among single-mother households dropped to record low levels by the end of the 1990s and remained well below earlier levels in 2004. Poverty among households headed by single mothers fell to historically low levels by the late 1990s. Some experts continued to be concerned about poverty among working mothers, while others argued that the effects of welfare reform on their children were largely unknown.[163] The experts who had predicted a catastrophe after the 1996 reform turned out to be wrong.

Welfare reform did not get government out of the business of controlling the conduct of the poor or of spending money on their welfare. The reforms built on a conservative cultural foundation were accepted by everyone, including Bill Clinton.[164] As Clinton put it, the poor had a legitimate expectation of public support, and taxpayers could legitimately expect the poor would improve their lives through work.[165] Instead, the states would require the poor to work and would give them benefits to make them productive enough to support themselves and their children.

Did welfare reform cut back the powers of the federal government? Recipients left (or did not enter) the welfare rolls rapidly after 1996. The welfare rolls were smaller; fewer people became dependent on AFDC. The federal government, as we have seen, continued to spend a great deal of money (including direct redistribution) on the poor. The reform also assumed that the federal government should reinforce widely held norms through policy choices. Welfare reform was not a policy of ending welfare and letting people live with the consequences of their choices. Instead, it ended welfare to affirm the superiority of a way of life defined by work and personal responsibility. Welfare reform worked against corruption and for the virtues that undergirded limited government, not to mention prosperity. Welfare for the relatively well-off, however, remained.

In April 2008, Congress passed a new farm subsidy law providing over $5 billion in direct payments annually, mostly to a small number of wealthy farmers. Tom Harkin, a Democratic senator from the largely rural state of Iowa, said of the bill: "It doesn't make sense, but farmers continue to get it. . . . People love free money."[166] Farm subsidies are common internationally, although they complicate liberalizing international trade and thereby reduce human welfare. Domestically, such programs "typically transfer income from consumers and taxpayers to farm operators, especially to owners of farmland and other resources used in farm production." Those who pay this welfare—consumers and taxpayers—are a large group and thus incur small per capita costs. Recipients of farm subsidies are politically mobilized and active, while those who pay for this redistribution remain inattentive of their losses and thus politically inert.[167] In light of this iron law of misrule, it is amazing that the 1994 Republicans not only attempted to eliminate but also succeeded in eliminating farm subsidies—for a time.

An earlier chapter discussed the origins of farm subsidies and regulation in the New Deal. Since 1973, the federal government offered "deficiency payments" to farmers that equaled the difference between a "target price" and the national average market price for a commodity. Congress set target prices well above market prices. This subsidy led to higher production of food, which in turn depressed prices. The secretary of agriculture was required in some situations to limit the acreage farmed. Some of the costs of the intervention thus fell on consumers. The government also offered marketing loans tied to a target price in local areas. The deficiency payments alone cost $30 billion from 1991 to 1995.[168]

In 1996, Congress tried to liberalize agriculture by enacting the Federal Agriculture Improvement and Reform Act. It replaced deficiency payments with "market transition payments," which were phased in over six years. These latter subsidies were neutral toward production and thus reduced the incentive to keep land idle. The Agriculture Department also lost the power to limit the acreage farmed.

Why did the new majority undertake such a difficult task as reducing farm subsidies? The budget was tight, and deficits seemed to matter to the public. The majority had committed to markets replacing government. Recipients of farm subsidies had a weak case, their persistence notwithstanding. The reformers also had some luck. Farmers were doing well in 1996. The payments planned by the act were larger than the deficiency payments they would have received under the old policies. In exchange for this windfall, farm interests would accept the longer-term savings and efficiencies of liberalizing agriculture.[169]

Richard Lugar (R-IN), the chair of the Senate Agriculture Committee, concluded: "From now on, the federal government will stop trying to control how much food, feed and fiber our nation produces. Farmers will be producing for the market, rather than being restricted by federal government supply controls, for the first time since the Great Depression."[170] The ambit of the federal government appeared to have been restricted, the "free money" notwithstanding. It was an astonishing moment in American political history, but a wholly misleading one. The law overlooked what economists call the "time consistency" problem.[171]

The new law was costly. It authorized about $56 billion over seven years for farm and forestry programs, with additional money for nutrition programs. The Congressional Budget Office reported that the law would save $2.1 billion compared with previous farm programs. Farmers were supposed to receive an estimated $5 billion in *additional* payments in 1996 and 1997, when market prices were expected to be high, and lower payments later in the decade, even if market prices dropped. Some Democrats promised to revisit the issue and repeal the bill if they controlled Congress: "The minute that those of us who think this is a bad farm bill have enough strength in Congress, we will move quickly. We will have another day."[172] The law ended, or seemed to end, six decades of government intervention in the production and pricing of wheat, soybeans, rice, and corn. Dairy, sugar, and peanuts escaped radical reforms. Most Republicans supported the changes; some Democrats, though not most, voted for the law.[173]

It was remarkable enough that Congress had taken farmers off the federal dole. Could government resist the demand for new subsidies if the agricultural economy went bad? In 1998, foreign demand for American food fell, and prices followed. Farmers still had their loan program, which the Agriculture Improvement and Reform Act had not touched. Lobbyists for farmers demanded direct assistance to meet the "crisis" of falling prices. President Clinton and Congress complied, offering $25 billion in "emergency" payments along with enhanced (and ironically named) "market transition payments." "Emergency" was more than an adjective; it exempted the payoffs from budget rules. Between the new subsidies and the windfall from transition payments, farm aid actually increased after 1996.[174]

The Agriculture Improvement and Reform Act was the greatest threat to farm subsidies since the New Deal. In 1996, farm prices were high, public budgets were tight, and politics tended toward free markets. The recipients of farm subsidies overcame these circumstances by promising to "stop drinking" at a future date if Congress would keep the bar open with more booze for the time being. In 1998, when the time came to stop drinking, the world had changed, and Congress could not make good on its 1996 intentions. Farm prices were low, and farmers were struggling. The federal budget had turned toward surplus, which allowed Congress to avoid tough choices. The highly mobilized farmers beat the uninformed consumer.[175] Worse was still to come.

The 1994 majority promised to impose cost-benefit analysis on federal regulations and, more generally, to reign in regulation "to create additional jobs, enhance wages and recognize private property rights."[176] It tried to force federal agencies to assess the risks that new regulations ought to address and laid out a specific process for analyzing the costs and benefits of such rules. The House Republicans also proposed protecting private property rights by enforcing the Fifth Amendment, which required "just compensation" to land-owners when government regulations reduced the value of their property. The House quickly passed a bill to make good on these promises.[177]

The reform effort, however, faced opposition in the Senate from Rhode Island's John H. Chafee, who chaired the Environment and Public Works Committee, and at the White House.[178] Ultimately, the Senate passed a regulatory bill with numerous amendments limiting the reforms of environmental regulations.[179]

Other unpleasant surprises awaited reformers. In July, the House removed parts of an appropriations bill that would have prohibited the Environmental Protection Agency from implementing some aspects of existing laws.

By the end of 1995, a *Congressional Quarterly* reporter would write, "After a year in office, the GOP has virtually nothing to show for its ambitious environmental agenda, which was to have included rewrites of water, hazardous waste and endangered species laws." House Speaker Newt Gingrich (R-GA) conceded that "we mishandled the environment all spring and summer." The problem, however, ran deeper than mistakes by the leadership. The Republican caucus was not unified in opposition to environmental regulations. Forty moderates from the Midwest and Northeast wished to move carefully and slowly in reforming the environmental laws; another 70 Republicans from the West or rural districts wanted more reforms, more quickly. The leaders could not get this fractured group behind reform bills that would also pass the Senate.[180] Hence, the Environmental Protection Agency's budget avoided significant cuts, the Endangered Species Act remained largely unchanged, and oil did not flow from the Alaskan wilderness.[181]

Republicans, among others, had complained about the slowness of new drug approvals at the Food and Drug Administration, but Congress did not eliminate or even reform the FDA. However, the pressure it put on the agency did lead to improvements in speeding up approval of some new drugs to head off legislative changes[182] Such changes notwithstanding, the FDA of this period will be remembered most for declaring tobacco an addictive drug and approving sweeping new tobacco regulations.[183]

Republicans might also claim to have fostered some constraint on workplace regulations. The top two proposals on the agenda of the

Occupational Safety and Health Administration were for increasing penalties by 5 percent and bolstering enforcement. The new majority proposed cutting back on OHSA's regulatory ambit, and 1995 brought more talk from the agency of consultation and training. OSHA officials argued the changes came before the 1994 elections.[184]

The 1994 Republicans did restrain the administrative state. A scholar of the federal bureaucracy remarked in the fall of 1996: "Congress can take a lot of credit for creating a climate that has changed the agencies' most substantive processes. The regulatory agencies have become much more cautious. Fewer rules have been generated. There are fewer new regulations. It's just self-preservation. Any reasonable bureaucrat now knows there's trouble down that road."[185] Yet the change was by its nature temporary. If a Republican majority was not tightly overseeing federal officials, they might well return to their old ways of attacking business and expanding the scope of their authority.

The Great Society had created or expanded many government agencies. Almost all the Great Society agencies survived the Reagan presidency, although, as noted earlier, some received less support. Did the class of 1994 do any better?

Consider housing policy and the Department of Housing and Urban Development, a Great Society anachronism. The class of 1994 wanted to but did not eliminate HUD. It did stop Clinton's plans for more HUD spending, and the new majority's influence forced the Clintonites to move right even without a legislative mandate. Henry Cisneros, the secretary of HUD, started talking about demolition of public housing, law enforcement, and budget restraint instead of building more units and preservation.[186]

The first HUD budget after the 1994 election reduced the agency's funding by 25 percent.[187] With HUD, as with much else, the Senate proved more moderate than the House in seeking reform. It took three years for both chambers to agree to a housing bill. The bill that did pass devolved some power over public housing away from the federal government. It also sought to diversify public housing by allowing more near-poor in while increasing vouchers. The law amended but did not repeal the Housing Act of 1937.[188] The House Republicans changed federal housing policy. They even reduced spending and control by Washington over housing. But the programs once in question survived.

Federal intervention is energy markets had grown quickly in the 1970s. Clinton promised in his 1992 campaign to increase the budget for civilian research at the Department of Energy and direct it away from nuclear weapons research toward "industrial competitiveness," the Internet, clean-running automobiles, and alternative energy sources.

The Republicans fought back. They demanded the elimination of the department. This wish met two obstacles. First, the Department of Energy enjoyed significant support in the Senate. Second, the freshmen had not worked out the details of abolishing the agency; they had not refined the proposal to the point of identifying where surviving DOE programs would be moved.[189]

Instead of abolishing the agency, the House committee reduced its spending by 7 percent from the previous year. The Senate balked at the cut and restored funding. Eventually, a conference between the two chambers added over half a billion dollars to the House number. The final number reduced DOE spending by 3.5 percent compared to the previous year.[190] Reducing spending by an agency must count as a success, given the history of increases in most programs at most times, but cutting just over 3 percent of a budget is a long way from abolishing an agency.

Having failed to eliminate the agency, they turned to oversight, holding hearings on DOE's waste of taxpayer money. House Republicans repeatedly called for the head of DOE, Hazel O'Leary, to resign. They also used the spending power. A DOE official compared 1993 to 1995: "There was real momentum growing toward new and different goals. That momentum has completely disappeared for the sake of the institutional survival of the agency." In May 1995, O'Leary announced that she would close over 20 agency offices, reduce employment by 3,788, or 27 percent, and save $1.7 billion over five years. Thereafter the savings pledged by the department grew to $10.5 billion.[191]

The DOE story, however, did not end well. DOE began to spend more on research on nuclear weapons. This story of a Clinton defeat becoming a victory for big government was written primarily by Pete V. Domenici, the chair of the Senate Budget Committee and a veteran of the Reagan era budget battles. His state, New Mexico, had two of DOE's three major nuclear weapons labs. Domenici wished to increase DOE's spending for 1997 by a quarter of a billion dollars more than Clinton's request.[192] The struggle over DOE eventually reflected a Republican priority. That priority, however, was not spending less. The voters of New Mexico and their relative prosperity mattered more than ideals like liberty and limited government.

Lyndon Johnson proved to be prescient regarding public television. The Corporation for Public Broadcasting, the government institution responsible for public television, had begun with little funding. By 1995, public television had become a $2 billion undertaking.[193] The 1994 class had hoped to eliminate public broadcasting. It survived, but not without difficulties.

In the final budget battle, 133 House Republicans voted on the floor to completely cut off funding for CPB.[194] The House ultimately passed an appropriations bill that cut CPB funding by 24 percent, a large cut by Washington standards but far from 100 percent, the promise made at the start of 1995 by the GOP leadership.[195] The Senate ended up passing an appropriations bill that included $20 million more for CPB, a 17 percent cut over current spending. The final budget rescinded $55 billion in planned spending by CPB over several years.[196] The struggle had achieved something, but it had also taken its toll.

Why did public television survive? Its supporters used a version of the Washington Monument strategy. If someone proposes cutting government spending, federal officials respond by proposing to close the Washington Monument to tourists to save money. When threatened with cutbacks, government employees and their supporters offer to eliminate their most popular programs, not their least defensible. The public (or some of the public) then rally to the cause of the popular program, and both the popular program and the wasteful effort survive the budget knife.

The supporters of public television raised the possibility of eliminating *Sesame Street*, a popular program for children.[197] The Republicans were thus cast as villains who wished to harm children and not accidentally deny their parents some free time. Just as the later SCHIP struggle had pitted tobacco companies against children, the Republicans found themselves squaring off against Big Bird.

By March 1996, the House GOP had decided to reform rather than eliminate public broadcasting. But again, the Senate precluded even this modest reform of CPB, largely because Sen. Larry Pressler, a Republican from South Dakota, faced a tough reelection battle. The previous year, Pressler had been attacked for supporting reforms of public television. His vote was crucial to the reform effort in committee. The effort to eventually remove public funding from CPB came up short in committee.[198]

Congress settled on an annual appropriation of $250 million for CPB. It had been cut for two straight years compared to its budget baseline and its starting point of $315 million in 1995.[199] But CPB had not been eliminated or even cut severely. Like Amtrak, the public train service that Reagan promised to end, CPB had built up enough support among officials and some of the public to survive in 1995.

To be sure, if CPB had been eliminated, some taxpayer at some future point would have had slightly lower taxes to pay (or perhaps we could say a current taxpayer would have less debt to be concerned about and less motivation to save to meet future public obligations). But that small sum now or in the future mattered little compared to the intense losses imposed on a few people by eliminating CPB. Those who loved Big Bird were a special interest, though not a particularly effective one, relatively speaking, but one that had more clout than the generals.

Defense spending dropped during the 1990s. The defense budget declined by just under 17 percent from the last Reagan budget in 1989 to the last Bush budget for 1993. From 1993 to 1998, spending on defense again declined by about 13 percent. The administrations of both George H. W. Bush and Bill Clinton proposed declining budgets for the 1990s; indeed, the Clinton administration proposals differed little from the long-term expectations of the Bush presidency. The Republican Congress after 1994 did add some funding to Clinton requests from 1996 to 2001, but the increases amounted to perhaps 3 percent of the overall outlays.[200] The budget year that would eventually include September 11, 2001, saw Congress add 1.5 percent to Clinton's final defense budget request.[201]

The restraint on defense spending thus cannot be credited to one party or the other; if anything, the Democrats deserved marginally more praise for reducing spending. But a larger factor mattered more than the hopes and machinations of either party: the threat posed by the Soviet Union had ended, along with the nation itself, in 1991. Absent that threat, the United States had reason to spend less on defense. In that light, the $300 billion defense budget of 2001 might seem an apt exemplar of bureaucratic success in sustaining spending whatever might happen. Nonetheless, the decline in defense spending, supported by both parties, remains the most remarkable sustained reduction in the federal government in the years after Ronald Reagan became president.

Conclusion

The party that controlled the House of Representatives from 1995 to 1997 tried to continue to fulfill Reagan's legacy. It truly sought to turn back the growth of government in many ways. We have seen that these efforts often fell short. That is not surprising. Many elected that year had radical hopes for reducing government to the boundaries set out in the U.S. Constitution. The failure in radical hopes is an old story, one that Newt Gingrich himself foresaw in November 1994 when he said of Washington: "This is a city which is like a sponge. It absorbs waves of change, and it slows them down, and it softens them, and then one morning they cease to exist."[202] The institutions of the federal government—a moderate Senate, a skilled president, and established organized groups— absorbed and slowed the hope to limit government in the 1990s. After the budget agreement of 1997, this hope to limit political power would be replaced by new aspirations that seemed to offer better prospects of winning elections.

6. The Politics of Moral Renewal

Republicans faced a political crisis that began after the 1996 elections and extended throughout 1998 and the elections of that year. In response to that crisis, the Republican leadership began to look for other foundations for their coalition and eventually new leadership. In 1998, these leaders sought to strengthen their hold on power by responding at last to the desires of social conservatives. In 1998, the Republican majority moved to impeach a president for sins that led to crimes. The gambit did not work. In that same year, the next Republican presidential candidate would seek a new foundation for what he hoped would be an emerging GOP majority. In 1997, a post-Reagan Republican Party came into view, a party that would rule until 2006.

The Turn

Republicans' problems began with their leader, Newt Gingrich, who admitted ethics violations. The sudden admissions of guilt surprised many House Republicans, who had defended Gingrich for two years. They had believed, not without reason, that his ethics investigation was highly partisan and nothing more. But in part, the probe had also turned out to be correct. The 1994 majority had promised a cleaner and more responsive House. Many were themselves idealistic about the prospects for changing, indeed for saving, the United States. Gingrich had not turned out to be corrupt; he had proved to be less than observant of the rules of the House. The Gingrich result, for all the partisanship, must have dejected more than a few of the class of 1994.

Gingrich soon developed other problems with his troops, problems created in part by his pursuit of a budget deal. House Republicans who still believed in the ideals of 1994 became increasingly frustrated. Gingrich and the other leaders, in this view, were becoming corrupted by their desire for power and by the ways of Washington. About a dozen sophomores in the 105th (supported by 20 other members originally elected in 1994) met regularly to come up with ways to refuse and resist the new corruption. Most of these rebels had been among the Speaker's most stalwart admirers during the early days of the 104th Congress.[1] The Republican coalition that favored limiting government began to fracture.

There were early signs of trouble. In March 1997, 11 House Republicans voted against a rule for consideration of House funding of committees to protest their moderating leadership. Gingrich then seemed to be backing off on tax cuts.[2] Subsequent debates within the GOP caucus evinced broader support for the 11. The turning point for the rebellion came later in the spring. A spring flood in the upper Midwest goaded the House to send money to midwestern farmers and flood victims. Instead of allowing a quick passage, the GOP leadership added provisions to the flood relief bill, one of which would have set up an "automatic CR" as a budget management tool for the House. This CR (or continuing resolution) reflected lessons learned in the earlier struggle with Clinton. It provided for automatic funding for government agencies at existing levels if budget negotiations hit an impasse and a regular appropriations bill was not enacted by the start of the next fiscal year. Republican leadership decided that if government shutdowns were bad for their image, then the public would like the idea of a guarantee against shutdowns, but one that might persuade the president to support budgets favorable to the GOP. The automatic CR tried to weaken the president's hand in budget negotiations. It gave House Republicans a worst-case scenario—continuation of current spending—that held the line on spending increases for parts of the federal bureaucracy. The president, in contrast, probably favored such increases. In any case, he would have reason to agree to any budget slightly better than the automatic CR. The House Republican leadership also knew that they would be happier with either an automatic CR or a budget negotiated under the gun of an automatic CR than they were under the current system in which the failure of negotiations led to a government shutdown and an outcome favoring the president.

Bill Clinton also understood the implications of an automatic CR: it would limit his leverage over budget outcomes compared to the status quo of a government shutdown as the last resort. Hence, Clinton would normally veto any bill with an automatic CR. The Republican leadership thus decided to attach the automatic CR as a provision to the flood relief bill. They were hopeful that the president would not risk public disapproval by vetoing a bill to help disaster victims. The proposed automatic CR was smart legislative politics. The 1994 leaders were improving their political skills.

Smart maneuvers required party unity, and the House GOP was not unified more generally. Members objecting to the moderating trend of the leaders chose to make a stand. Forty-three Republican members voted against the procedural rule to guide debate on the flood relief bill. Several GOP sophomores led this insurrection, and they were joined by Tom DeLay, the majority whip. Some of the rebels recalled the Speaker's recent unwillingness to back their opposition to a dam project in California. Others complained that the leadership did not explain their tactics.

With the flood relief bill tied up by internal GOP struggles, the public relations disaster that Republicans had planned for Clinton fell on the House majority. The media message was not good: the House Republicans were willing "to let thousands of people in North Dakota live in temporary shelters if need be" to attain their political objectives. One poll found that 55 percent of respondents blamed Republicans for delaying the disaster aid, compared with only 25 percent who blamed Clinton. In the end, Gingrich once again had to back down and send the president a flood relief bill without riders.[3] More and more, Speaker Gingrich appeared incompetent as well as too moderate to many GOP members.

Voters had also become a problem. Certainly, many Americans still doubted the morality or competence of the federal government. Many voters might say they would like a smaller government; indeed, many had told survey researchers something like that in the months before the 1994 election. In 1997, an ambitious Republican politician could recall, however, that the people had not supported limiting government in the government shutdown struggle or in the many minor fights over programs. In 1997, the public mood had begun to change. The public no longer wanted less government. One measure of the public mood shows no consistent trend in the second half of the 1990s. Yet, looked at in two-year averages, we can now see that 1997 marked the beginning of a shift toward more public support for spending.[4] Politicians specialize in detecting changes in the public mood. In 1997, the public had begun to move away from limited government. With their House leadership in shambles, Republicans were not in a good position to lead and sustain support for limiting the federal government. The only relevant question might have been: should they resist or follow the incipient changes in the public mood? Politicians do not sustain a career by opposing what voters want. The Republican majority began to follow the public.:

Following the budget agreement, the GOP majority lacked interest in continuing to pursue limiting government. Its members could go to the electorate in 1998 and say they had balanced the budget, one major concern of voters in 1994. The budget situation seemed much less critical. For the first time in more than a generation, the appropriate federal agencies began projecting budget surpluses. Members of both parties were freed from deficits and their progeny, spending caps. By 1998, the surplus had reached $70 billion, and everyone, the GOP included, had ideas about how to spend the money. Taxes might have been cut, but congressional Republicans had been outmaneuvered by Clinton and his demand to "save Social Security first."[5] Congress passed a $217.9 billion transportation bill that increased spending on highways and mass transit by 40 percent. Actual outlays violated the spending caps enacted a year earlier in the budget agreement.[6] No one cared.

Budget discipline disappeared in other ways. The next year's budget included a $21 billion supplemental funded by the emerging surpluses. Congress defined most of this spending as "emergency" spending to avoid the budget caps.[7]

Both parties got a piece of the growing federal pie. No one seemed interested in reducing the size of the pie. Consider the political logic of this outcome. Republican members—or indeed, a member of either party—might have refused to vote for programs that would benefit his or her constituents directly. Two conclusions then follow. The members of Congress who were willing to vote for more spending would have more money to spend on their constituents. Second, challengers might emerge contending that the members who stuck to the principle of limited government had failed to procure benefits for their constituents. If elected, the challenger would not fail to bring home the bacon. In this context, new taxes need not be mentioned: there was a surplus to be spent. A member inclined to vote against more spending would thus decide after due consideration to vote for more spending to avoid these two unpleasant outcomes. This grim political logic underlay the outburst of spending in 1998.

This logic also raised a question. The Republican brand had stood for constraining spending and cutting taxes. Now spending seemed the road to a permanent majority for the GOP (or at least, the path toward maintaining its control of Congress). The Republican brand needed to change; Republicans needed to become a different party, more friendly to government and thereby more electorally successful than they would be if they remained committed to constraining spending. Ironically enough, it was President Clinton who set the GOP on the road to its new identity in early 1998.

Impeachment

1998 began with revelations about the president's sexual affair with a White House intern. It ended with the House of Representatives voting to impeach the president on two counts, one for perjury and the other for obstruction of justice.[8] In between, the GOP did poorly in the midterm congressional elections and replaced its leader from the 1994 takeover of Congress. Punishing sin, not containing power, seemed to have become the primary concern of the GOP. As we have seen, this turn toward faith had been coming since 1990, when Christian conservatives began flocking to the GOP. This first essay at a post-Reagan identity for the GOP did not end well.

The details of President Clinton's conduct in 1996 need not be recalled.[9] He faced allegations that he had perjured himself while testifying before a grand jury investigating sexual harassment charges against Clinton. An independent counsel, Kenneth Starr, was investigating the perjury question and whether Clinton had also obstructed justice.[10] Almost a month after Clinton admitted lying to the public, Starr reported 11 specific charges that the president had lied under oath, obstructed justice, and suborned perjury from his personal secretary. Clinton argued that his conduct was bad but a private matter. Starr had made the case for lawbreaking and, hence, a public interest in the case. Congress was faced with the question of impeachment.

The U.S. Constitution states that the president "shall be removed from office on impeachment for, and conviction of, treason, bribery, and other high crimes and misdemeanors."[11] Were Clinton's actions "high crimes and misdemeanors"? But that was not the question. Politics, informed by public opinion, would decide whether Clinton should be removed from office.

Polls showed that most of the public held Clinton in low regard and did not trust him. Other polls showed that his approval ratings had steadily risen throughout the year.[12] Two-thirds of the public were also against impeachment.[13] Clinton had one great advantage: for three out of the four quarters of 1998, the economy grew by more than 5 percent on an annual basis.[14] Strong economic growth prompts public content with the status quo, including the president. Clinton's foibles on the morality front had not precluded prosperity. In any case, while concern about moral and cultural decline grew during this period, it never came close to being as important to the public as the economy or entitlement issues.[15]

The House GOP, polls notwithstanding, moved ahead with impeachment. Perhaps the public mood was changing, leading to a large Republican majority.[16] Perhaps voters would punish the president's party for his conduct.[17] The impeachment effort, however, appealed to an intense minority. Committed evangelical Christians had become an ever-larger part of the Republican base. These voters needed a reason to vote. Most religious people in 1998 approved of Clinton's job performance in 1998, thought the Lewinsky matter was private, judged the president to be immoral, and opposed impeachment. The one exception was "committed evangelical Protestants," a majority of whom favored impeachment and linked the Lewinsky matter to presidential job performance.[18] For evangelicals, impeachment rewarded their loyalty after years of being ignored by the GOP.[19]

The significance of the impeachment effort should not be discounted. FDR built the old regime on promises of government provision of prosperity and security. Ronald Reagan argued that liberty would be more likely to bring sustained prosperity. Newt Gingrich had agreed with Reagan in 1994. In 1998, however, he saw government as a means to private virtue through public shaming and punishing a cad. The Republicans were offering a different kind of politics, one more concerned with morality than with prosperity. They were groping toward a new regime founded in traditional virtues, a politics that could not be called libertarian. The moral drama of impeachment, however, failed utterly as political gambit.

A president's party usually performs poorly in elections held in the middle of his second term.[20] A result even half as good as the historical average would have created a Republican House majority that might persist for a generation or more. History did not repeat itself.[21] Turnout had shifted away from the GOP, and the impeachment gambit had not mobilized even the evangelicals. In a historical year, the election outcomes suggested continuity. The Democrats picked up five House seats, and the partisan division of the Senate remained unchanged. Over 98 percent of congressional incumbents who ran won reelection.[22] The president's party had *won* House seats in his second midterm election.

Gingrich resigned as Speaker of the House and leader of the Republican Party. For all his shortcomings, Newt Gingrich had been a man of ideas who pursued a politics of ideas, not least of which was the idea of limiting government. Dennis Hastert (R-IL) became Speaker with the support of Tom Delay, the man who more than any other had brought about the impeachment vote in the House.[23] Hastert sought to "get things done" by calling on a large network of personal relations built up in over a decade in Congress. His first mentor had been Robert Michel, the Republican minority leader who had been willing to go along with the Democratic majority. Hastert was a dealmaker; he was unlikely to go to the ramparts to repel the invasions of Big Government.

DeLay was a partisan whose major concern was finding the votes to get the GOP agenda through the House. He was tough, effective, and unsentimental in making the deals that made the majorities that advanced the Republican agenda. He did not lack a political vision. He was a conservative who respected markets and wished to limit government in some ways.[24] But Delay was also the exemplar of the new Republican politics of moral renewal. After the 1998 election, House Republicans might have abandoned the impeachment inquiry for lack of votes. *Congressional Quarterly* explained why impeachment went forward:

> Activists on the right, the conservative-dominated Judiciary Committee and DeLay quietly brought the party together. They painted Clinton's alleged perjury as not just a political or legal issue, but part of a pattern of lies and a sign of a moral decline in society that had to be checked.[25]

The events of 1998 had handed the Republican revolution over to a skillful leader—Tom DeLay—dedicated to social conservatism and limited government, in that order. The impeachment project now seems foolish, at least to the politically astute, but those who pursued Clinton thought morality and society itself depended on their efforts, political consequences notwithstanding. They saw themselves practicing a politics of moral renewal. Republicans under Reagan had sought to overturn the old regime in favor of prosperity and liberty. The post-Reagan party had taken its first steps toward a very different political vision.

Compassionate Conservatives

The founder of the post-Reagan Republican Party and the most radical American leader since Lyndon Johnson began his national political career by being elected governor of Texas in 1994. As governor, George W. Bush pursued tax cuts, education reform, and bipartisanship while seeking votes from Hispanics. In 1998, Bush won reelection with almost 70 percent of the vote. His total included almost half the Hispanic vote and over one-quarter of the African-American vote.[26] Bush won big even as the House GOP floundered. His main adviser, Karl Rove, thought Republican successes on welfare, taxes, and crime had taken the party's issues off the table.[27] Instead, the public was now concerned about education, Social Security, and health care, all issues largely associated with the Democrats. Rove concluded that the GOP had to change, but "we don't have to deny our roots. What we've got to do is find a way to make them relevant to a changing demography, to a changing economy, to a changing set of political circumstances and break out of a routine of talking about things that the American people no longer find relevant."[28] The shift in public mood first sensed by the congressional Republicans in 1997 now informed presidential politics.

Bush had a new philosophy and a new agenda for the new circumstances: "compassionate conservatism."[29] Conservatism now needed qualification. The Democrats had long styled themselves as the party of compassion.[30] Perhaps Bush was both liberal and conservative. In fact, compassionate conservatism was more than a slogan.[31] It grew out of Marvin Olasky's books, *The Tragedy of American Compassion* and *Compassionate Conservatism*. Candidate Bush provided a foreword to the latter repudiating both big government and those who "are content to let markets be our only guide." The needy in American deserve "our care" and "compassionate conservatism is a conservatism that cares about them." To be sure, Bush favors a government that knows its limits; government cannot "put hope in our hearts or a sense of purpose in our lives." Those tasks belong to religious institutions and charities. Government is charged with helping the American people show their natural compassion for the needy.[32] Bush offered a third way between big government and the market, an alternative that seemed conservative and yet differed from the limited government conservatism of Reagan. Bush's philosophy made room for the state as funder and monitor of civil institutions.[33] From the moment he appeared on the national stage, Bush repudiated the older conservatism of individual liberty and limited government."[34] He "wanted to use the resources of government to build a moral society, encourage government to use the resources of faith-based groups, and use the bully pulpit of the presidency to expound God's teaching on the sanctity of life."[35]

Bush's religious conservatism would seem to stand in complete opposition to the ideas and intimations of the old regime. Contemporary liberals are resolutely secular. When Lyndon Johnson declared war on poverty, he hoped the poor would become materially better off and vaguely more spiritual, perhaps by communing with the beauty of nature. He did not worry at all about their souls or their character. Yet the crusading zeal of the contemporary liberal often differs little in fervor from that of those eager to spread the message of religious salvation. This perception should not be surprising. Historians recall that progressivism included the Social Gospel movement, which urged Christians "to focus on salvation in this life, in the form of social goods achieved through the state."[36] In this regard, Bush might be called a progressive conservative. He wished to restore the lost politics of the Social Gospel, the hope to realize Christian ends through government action. Bush's progressivism necessarily rejected individualism and limited government.[37] He looked instead to ideas that fostered the old regime as a foundation to transcend both it and the hope for limited government.

Karl Rove saw the political potential of compassionate conservatism.[38] The House impeachment inquiry had mixed religion and politics to the political detriment of the GOP. Compassionate conservatism hoped to show a different side of religion: the Good Samaritan coming to the aid of the vulnerable and transforming their lives through love.[39] Compassionate conservatism also appealed to Roman Catholics, voters who compose one-quarter of the population.[40] Catholic doctrine endorsed left-leaning economic policies with socially conservative ethical precepts. Democrats claimed Catholic votes with compassionate economic policies. Bush offered both compassion and moral traditionalism. Compassionate conservatism also appealed to the material interests of Christian conservatives, especially those who were in the business of helping the poor. In 1990, the Department of Health and Human Services would spend just over $400 billion.[41] A small portion of that sum would greatly increase funding for religious charities. Finally, compassionate conservatism tried to cut into an emerging gender gap among voters. From 1976 to 1988, Republican presidential candidates had received around half the female vote. In 1992 and 1996, Bush and Dole garnered far less than 50 percent of that vote.[42] The Bush campaign of 2000 hoped that a softer conservatism that came "from the heart" would attract women back to the GOP.[43]

Bush's speech accepting the nomination reflected this turn away from the older outlook.[44] To be sure, the speech included several traditional conservative positions.[45] In general, however, the tone and substance of the speech greatly differed from Reagan's call for a return to limits on government. Bush associates laissez faire with indifference and counsels subsidized charities as the solution to poverty. Education also figured prominently in the speech; the candidate saw federal efforts in education as a response to poverty.[46] Apart from the tax cuts and glancing reference to entitlement reform, Bush sounded like a moderate churchgoing liberal with doubts about Big Government: government should not so much protect rights to life, liberty, and property as oversee social work with a spiritual bent funded by taxpayers.

Candidate Bush only mentioned Reagan twice in his acceptance speech: once in regard to the end of the cold war and once in praise of his optimism.[47] Both mentions are significant for understanding the Bush presidency. George W. Bush could not win the presidency by promising to defend voters from the Soviet Union; that battle had been won, and the electorate's gratitude toward the GOP, assuming it ever existed, hardly mattered by 2000. Reagan's optimism was a personal virtue with putative political appeal. How the man stood—upbeat and optimistic—mattered a great deal more to Bush than what he stood for. In Bush's truth, Bush repudiated sotto voce the Reagan aspiration to limited government and individual liberty.

The struggle for power that followed the 2000 election is well known. Commentators have paid less attention to the less spectacular aspects of the voting. The Republicans did poorly in Congress, losing four seats (and their clear majority) in the Senate and two seats in the House. The House majority first gained in 1994 had steadily declined.[48] The number of voters identifying themselves as Republicans had also declined.[49] Bush did well among independents. Such voters rated Bush higher than any GOP presidential nominee since 1988, and he garnered the highest proportion of the independent vote of any Republican candidate since that era.[50] The proportion of women voting for the Republican presidential candidate also edged up compared to 1996 but only attained the level of 1992, itself far below the female GOP vote in the 1980s.[51] Without compassionate conservatism, Bush might argue, he would not have done so well among independents, and without their votes, he surely would not have won at all. Yet he had still not won a plurality of the vote, and the GOP itself had not arrested its decline with a gentle (or earlier, a harsh) mixing of religion and politics. Something more was needed to bolster the prospects of the post-Reagan party.[52]

Bush in Power

Bush was true to his campaign promises in the early months of 2001. Bush moved quickly to support education reform. Schools that came up short would face an exit of students through public school choices or private school vouchers.[53] The president was more interested in national testing: he would not, as Undersecretary of Education Eugene Hickok later put it, "sacrifice accountability on the altar of school choice."[54] While the House was at work, the Senate had come under Democratic control when James Jeffords of Vermont shifted parties. The Senate version of the education bill included higher spending and no vouchers.[55] Some more conservative House Republicans resisted the new centralization over education. The Bush team sought Democratic votes to replace them and ended up with a bill mandating testing without vouchers.[56] The two versions of the bill went to a conference committee. President Bush fashioned the bipartisan coalition that ultimately saw the bill through Congress. He created that coalition by obtaining the votes of Republican members while abandoning traditional Republican concerns regarding accountability and federalism in education.[57] For Bush, compassion meant more education spending and more centralization of

215

power over education in Washington. He cared about vouchers and private choice, but he cared more about accountability and political success. His fealty to his priorities meant his administration abandoned the cause of limited government.

Bush also remained true to his promise to support religion in a new war on poverty. On January 29, 2001, he signed two executive orders, one creating a White House Office of Faith-Based and Community Initiatives and the other establishing centers in five cabinet departments to cut back on regulations that prevented religious groups from offering drug treatment and prisoner rehabilitation programs. The next day, he proposed that Congress enact tax incentives to encourage charitable giving and expand "charitable choice," a part of the 1996 welfare reform that allowed religious groups to apply directly for federal funds for welfare-to-work and drug treatment programs. Charitable choice permitted religious groups to receive federal money to deliver social services without altering the religious content from their programs.[58]

Many people opposed tax funding of programs with religious content. Some senators also conjectured that the bill would exempt religious groups from the anti-discrimination laws. But some religious groups worried that the proposals would make churches and charities dependent on the government and politics; others, including Marvin Olasky, argued that the proposal would lead to discrimination among religions. Bush's proposals barely passed in the House and became stalled in the Senate during the summer of 2001.[59] The religious aspect of compassionate conservatism failed quickly.

The "compassionate" part did well, if we equate compassion with increased federal spending. The 2001 budget resolution called for increasing Medicare spending by $313.7 billion over 10 years, including a $300 billion reserve fund for a Medicare prescription drug benefit. Congress also spent more to restore payments to Medicare home health care providers. These commitments reflected a Bush promise during his campaign.[60] The post-Reagan Republican Party had moved from symbolism and rhetoric into concrete action. Big Government conservatism was born.

Not all Bush's proposals departed from traditional Republican ideas, at least on the surface. He proposed tax cuts and higher defense spending as promised. But Bush's tax cuts were different from Reagan's in two ways. Reagan and members of his administration argued that reducing tax rates would reward work and innovation, thereby contributing to national welfare from the supply side. George W. Bush supported his tax reductions with Keynesian arguments: they would increase consumer spending and disposable income while countering an economic slowdown.[61] The Reagan administration had thought tax cuts would both reduce the burden of government directly and ultimately constrain spending. Keynesian justifications aside, Bush's tax cuts were more like fulfilling a promise to a valued member of the coalition. They had no connection to constraining government because George W. Bush had not promised to constrain government. His other promise to propose private accounts for Social Security received no attention from the president.

Perhaps this shift toward government activism reflected electoral and political realities. We noted earlier that the public mood became more favorable toward government spending in 1997. Bush's message on the campaign trail reflected that shift. His actions in 2001 and 2002 adapted to the public mood as a means to political success. Unfortunately for Bush, the data do not support this defense of his first two years in office. The public was actually less favorable toward government activism in 2001 and 2002 than it had been at any time since the budget deal of 1997.[62] In other words, from the perspective of 2001 and 2002, the trend in public opinion was away from more government. That downward trend would be short-lived, but no one knew that in 2001 and 2002. From the standpoint of limited government conservatism, Bush may be criticized for missing an opportunity in 2001 and 2002. He acted on the public mood of 1998 and 1999. In doing so, he failed to detect the possibilities of 2001 and 2002. Bush the politician undertook an expansion of government that was not necessary to placate the public.

How did George W. Bush relate to the old regime before September 11, 2001? He would seem to be more a friend than an enemy of the old regime. Unlike Reagan, who spoke of restoring liberty, Bush spoke of compassion delivered by government or by public subsidies. But his support for an active federal establishment concealed his radicalism. Bush could not be a reformer like Reagan. He sought a government that pursued neither liberty nor prosperity. In the end, Bush saw public policy as a means to religious virtue. In his presidency, both in word and deed, Christian evangelicals found a new Republican seeking to realize their political aspirations. Of course, the first ninth months of Bush's presidency revealed the difficulties of founding a new regime, given the secular character of the old regime and an underwhelming mandate from the electorate. But Bush had the aspirations of a founder of new regime, and the events of September 11th would offer an opportunity to act on that ambition.

After September 11th

Many Americans now look back on September 11th as a day that changed everything. Much did change, of course. The nation gained for a while a novel sense of vulnerability and concomitant desires for justice and security. For that reason, September 11th was both a tragedy and an opportunity. Pearl Harbor marked the beginning of a war that consolidated and perhaps extended the life of the old regime. September 11th might also have consolidated great changes in American politics. George W. Bush saw in the aftermath of that day the possibility of a new regime founded on compassionate conservatism writ large.

Attacks on the homeland of any nation sometimes end a government, but they rarely limit its ambit. In a democracy, the government responds by striving anew to offer security to voters, and that quest generally requires more power for public officials, putatively to protect against future attacks. Just over a week after the attacks, Attorney General John Ashcroft asked for new law enforcement powers, many of which had been proposed by the department for years. The attorney general asked for broader powers to search, to wiretap, and to surveil the Internet, to hold noncitizens indefinitely, and to use information gained by foreign intelligence. Ashcroft also sought tougher penalties for terrorism and procedural changes like consolidated judicial appeals. Congress held few hearings and worked in secret; the Patriot Act passed in late October about seven weeks after the attacks. The Senate resisted Ashcroft's proposals more than the House, but neither resisted all that much; Sen. Orrin Hatch (R-UT) would say the bill contains "virtually everything that Attorney General Ashcroft and the Bush administration have asked for."[63] The final bill changed the administration's proposals slightly and then passed both houses by large margins.[64] The federal government had new powers to prevent terrorism.[65]

The tasks and ambit of government grew even more in foreign policy. In the 2000 presidential debates, candidate Bush could adumbrate what had become a typical Republican outlook on foreign affairs: realistic in ends, limited in scope, and concerned about the military. Bush promised to use force "if it's in our vital national interest, and that means whether our territory is threatened or people could be harmed." He added that the mission should be clear and an exit strategy in place. Bush remarked, "I would be guarded in my approach." He was also guarded about using force to build nations: "I would be very careful about using our troops as nation builders. I believe the role of the military is to fight and win war and therefore prevent war from happening in the first place."[66]

Bush's views then fit well with the doctrine of realism, which supports foreign policies, including the use of force, that relate to a nation's vital interests.[67] Realism had become associated with conservatism by 2000, especially after the Clinton administration intervened in the Balkans' struggle in the absence of a vital American interest. Bush's outlook on foreign policy was hard: it was rooted in power, national interests, and prudence.[68]

This outlook also implied that those who made foreign policy would recognize the limits of government. Humanitarian interventions would have no place in a restrained foreign policy agenda founded on realism. The nation would not use force to realize democracy and human rights or to save foreigners from their despots. In a major foreign policy speech during the 2000 campaign, Bush mentioned democracy only once and then merely as a means to defend the core American ideals of individual freedom and dignity.[69] The realism of the early Bush months did not see the use of force as a way of remaking the world toward democracy.[70]

Foreign policy did not matter much then; the cold war had ended a decade earlier, and the United States had enjoyed declining defense budgets and no real challenges to its preeminence. Foreign policy offered few electoral opportunities. No foreign power threatened (or could be imagined to threaten) the security of American voters. Politicians could not win election or reelection promising to protect such voters from foreign threats. Prudence was required to avoid messes like Somalia, but prudence produced few votes. The Bush administration said little about extending compassionate conservatism to foreign policy. Voters simply did not care, and no one believed that softness and compassion for foreigners would sell on election day.

Bush's realism in foreign policy had shallow roots in his politics and his optimistic personality.[71] Bush the candidate had endorsed a crusade funded by taxpayers to save the poor, a soft crusade informed by compassion and a novel mixture of the state and religion. Bush himself did not have strong views about international affairs.[72] This indifference should not surprise anyone. He had been a governor and had risen to prominence through domestic innovations in domestic policies and in image. Three months after endorsing realism, in his first statement as president-elect, Bush suggested "the essence of compassionate conservatism" comprised among other things "a bipartisan foreign policy true to our values and true to our friends, and . . . a military equal to every challenge and superior to every adversary."[73] Values, not interests, had begun to define American foreign policy. What might the values of compassionate conservatism imply for American foreign policy?

The first response to the attacks comported well with foreign policy realism and domestic popularity. He ordered a war against the perpetrators of September 11th and invaded Afghanistan, the country that had given al-Qaeda support and sanctuary. The American military did what it does better than anyone ever: killing people and destroying property. Both were done to exact retribution and to properly price future threats. By the end of 2001, the United States had conquered Afghanistan and routed for the time being both al-Qaeda and its former sponsors, the Taliban. The politicians remained aloof and did not worry whether the carnage improved anyone's spiritual life. By December, all national surveys reported that the president's approval ratings were above 80 percent.[74] For the moment, the war in Afghanistan was a political success, and the 2002 midterms suggested a rising GOP.

The realism of the war in Afghanistan set limits on its utility as a political and electoral gambit. Having conquered the country, President Bush faced unpalatable choices. The U.S. military could stay in Afghanistan to keep a peace and to transform a failed state into an American ally; the former task would have continual costs in lives, while the latter should have seemed unlikely, given the history of the country. On the other hand, the military could leave Afghanistan under the control of American allies in the war, the various warlords and faction leaders that might exercise authority in the postwar era. Neither option bode well for the upcoming American elections. Bush's father had conquered Kuwait in 1991. That remarkable victory had not mattered at all to the outcome of the 1992 presidential election. Bush's father had also seen off the Soviet threat without fostering lasting public support for his party or his presidency. George W. Bush had temporarily reversed Republican political decline. But the fix might have seemed likely to be only temporary.

American leaders were worried about Saddam Hussein's Iraq before September 11th. American policymakers had long sought a peaceful and stable Middle East with open access to Persian Gulf oil at relatively stable prices. The first Bush administration had fought a war to expel Iraq from Kuwait to preclude a presumed threat to that national interest. The Clinton administration also valued regional stability. Like their predecessors, the Clintonites saw Iraq as a profound threat to regional stability.[75] The Clinton administration continued the Bush administration strategy of containing Iraq until an opportunity arose for Saddam's overthrow or in the parlance, regime change.[76] The Clinton policymakers hoped regime change would come from indigenous forces.[77] The administration did not seriously consider an attack to change the Iraqi regime followed by an occupation and transition to a government more suited to American interests.[78] Some conservatives complained that Clinton's efforts at containment relied too much on international institutions and diplomacy. The Clinton administration's putative commitment to regime change, these critics argued, should be taken more seriously, perhaps by actively supporting an Iraqi opposition.[79]

Another group of critics— the neoconservatives—saw American foreign policy and Iraq differently. They agreed that Iraq threatened American interests. They denied, however, that American foreign policy should be guided by interests alone. Instead, they spoke of a foreign policy infused with moral clarity and moral purpose. By that, neoconservatives meant the United States should actively promote "American principles of governance—democracy, free markets, respect for liberty" through its foreign policy.[80] This sense of moral clarity, however, did not require immediate regime change among America's enemies; the nation should pursue policies "*ultimately* intended . . . to bring about a change of regime."[81] Two leading neoconservatives, Robert Kagan and William Kristol, saw an idealistic foreign policy as a way to improve the nation and the individual:

> A true "conservatism of the heart" ought to emphasize both personal and national responsibility, relish the opportunity for national engagement, embrace the possibility of national greatness, and restore a sense of the heroic, which has been sorely lacking in American foreign policy—and American conservatism—in recent years.[82]

Kagan and Kristol had titled their 1996 *Foreign Affairs* article "Toward a Neo-Reaganite Foreign Policy," implying that their call for a moralistic, crusading foreign policy represented the true legacy of the former president. Reagan had come to power with a promise to renew the struggle against Soviet power by increasing defense spending. He had called the Soviet Union an "evil empire" and acted forcefully in Central America and Libya.[83] Yet Reagan soon attracted criticism from the neoconservatives. He invaded Grenada but carefully avoided direct military confrontation with the Soviet Union. The invasion itself was more like an application of the Monroe Doctrine than an attempt to build democracy.[84] His second secretary of state, George Schultz, was a moderate conservative who believed that the evolution toward democracy should come from within nations and not be imposed from the outside by force.[85] Reagan's secretary of defense, Caspar Weinberger, set out six tests for the use of armed force by the United States, rules that contained phrases like "vital interest" and "last resort."[86] Realism rather than a crusade marked Reagan's foreign policy.

The differences between Reagan and neoconservatives went beyond realism and idealism in foreign policy. Neoconservatives believed that the United States and its people were in decline; the optimistic Reagan believed the growth of government had not corrupted the virtues of the people.[87] Reagan was an exemplary American conservative who celebrated individualism and the concomitant ideal of limited government. Left to their own devices, individuals will rise to greatness or, at the very least, to the pursuit of happiness. In the larger history of ideas, American conservatism had much in common with classical liberalism. In Europe and elsewhere, conservatism had cast a cold eye on individualism; the individual freed from tradition and social structure lacked direction and became miserable and anomic.

The older generation of neoconservatives—led by Irving Kristol—was more conservative in this European sense than liberal in the American way. For the senior Kristol, individuals who live their lives in pursuit of self-interest achieve only an ephemeral self-gratification and end up living empty and meaningless lives. This degradation of the individual brings with it a decline of society as the moral and social bonds necessary to a healthy public order are destroyed by the pursuit of individual concerns.[88]

Arresting this decadence poses a great challenge to modern liberal societies. For neoconservatives, part of the answer to moral decay is recovering the founding ideals of the American republic, not least a republican virtue that links individuals to a larger social and yet liberal whole. But a look backward to 1789 is not enough; that is the failed hope of the older limited government ideal. Modern politics demands a pursuit of progress in the future. In foreign policy, the nation acted as an agent of progress. Neoconservatives endorse a nationalism informed by ideals that motivate commitment and action from individuals. Americans might thus overcome their excessive individualism through a commitment to the larger nation and its ideals.[89]

The neoconservative policy prescriptions of 1996 reflected the philosophical wariness of the 1970s: American greatness in foreign policy might be the antidote to American decay fostered by a pervasive individualism. Americans would find their redemption, as the president would say in his 2002 State of the Union address, by becoming a nation that serves goals larger than the self.[90] In this light, we can see why a neoconservative foreign policy appealed to George W. Bush. Both neoconservatives and Christian conservatives saw a nation in decline. Both believed that decay could be arrested and reversed by government action. Both rejected the individualism and restrained government that had guided the conservatism of Reagan and earlier Republicans. Neoconservatism offered in foreign policy, as compassionate conservatism had in domestic matters, a fundamental break with Reaganite orthodoxy.[91]

The 15 months between the initial victory in Afghanistan and the invasion of Iraq saw the president and his foreign policy cadre appeal to both interests and ideals. The appeals to interest are hardly surprising: national leaders are supposed to protect voters from being killed by foreigners, whatever other tasks the government might undertake. The invasion of Afghanistan related to al-Queda and hence to protecting the nation against terrorism. The Bush administration set about showing that Iraq as well threatened vital American interests.[92]

Yet as neoconservatives had hoped, the confrontation with Iraq transcended mere interests. President Bush's State of the Union address in 2002, delivered one year before the Iraq invasion, recalls Kristol and Kagan's admonition for moral clarity in foreign affairs:

> America will lead by defending liberty and justice because they are right and true and unchanging for all people everywhere. No nation owns these aspirations and no nation is exempt from them. . . . America will always stand firm for the non-negotiable demands of human dignity, the rule of law, limits on the power of the state, respect for women, private property, free speech, equal justice and religious tolerance. America will take the side of brave men and women who advocate these values around the world, including the Islamic world, because we have a greater objective than eliminating threats and containing resentment. We seek a just and peaceful world beyond the war on terror.[93]

Threats and containment, key concepts in the realist lexicon, no longer guided American foreign policy. Eight months after Bush's 2002 State of the Union speech, his preface to the nation's official National Security Strategy restated his idealism now conceived as America's mission to do good in an evil world:

> Freedom is the non-negotiable demand of human dignity; the birthright of every person—in every civilization. Throughout history, freedom has been threatened by war and terror; it has been challenged by the clashing wills of powerful states and the evil designs of tyrants; and it has been tested by widespread poverty and disease. Today, humanity holds in its hands the opportunity to further freedom's triumph over all these foes. The United States welcomes our responsibility to lead in this great mission.[94]

The document itself took up Bush's themes:

The U.S. national security strategy will be based on a distinctly American internationalism that reflects the union of our values and our national interests. The aim of this strategy is to help make the world not just safer but better.[95]

In pursuit of those nonnegotiable ends, the United States would take up the task of remaking the Middle East. The consequences of the coming crusade, it was promised, would be worthy of a great nation. As the United States went to war in Iraq, neoconservatism had become the vision and strategy behind the invasion and what was taken to be the subsequent effort at nation-building.

Domestic affairs garnered few headlines as the nation went to war. Yet in line with Bush's commitments, the government continued to expand in defense and elsewhere. Nondefense discretionary spending began to rise relative to the post-1980 years.[96] In early 2002, No Child Left Behind passed, increasing both spending and national oversight in education. Business failures and scandals at Enron and WorldCom brought new regulations on corporate governance and accounting firms. The Enron affair then contributed to Congress's passing the McCain-Feingold campaign finance law, which enacted new restrictions on political speech. [97] In domestic as in foreign affairs, Congress and the Bush administration had taken up a crusading, Progressive mien, determined to set the particulars of the world right at home and abroad. Bush also refused to constrain Congress's worst inclinations. He signed a 10-year farm bill expected to cost $190 billion.[98] Perhaps the Bush administration could boast of enacting new policies. The innovations, however, were not in pursuit of limited government.

President Bush and the Republicans in Congress entered the 2002 election offering voters security from terrorism. The president had tried to expand that hope for protection into something more. The Bush Doctrine proposed to remake the Middle East, the world, and American foreign policy. But the Bush vision for foreign engagement was also a gambit for domestic politics, an effort to attract a lasting majority dedicated to compassion at home and abroad. Bush offered Americans the chance to participate in a heroic adventure to make the world better. On the home front, government had begun to expand, ostensibly in pursuit of virtue.

The 2002 election outcomes were widely considered a success for the president and his party. Republicans picked up six House and two Senate seats. The former strengthened their hold on the House after three declining elections, while the latter returned control of the Senate to the GOP. It was the first time since 1934 that a president's party had picked up seats in both houses of Congress in a midterm election. In the previous three elections, the overall GOP advantage in votes for House candidates had been less than 1 million. In 2002, their total vote count was 3.6 million more than the Democrats. [99]

These results were normal in one sense.[100] Most congressional elections from the 1970s onward ended with small changes in the partisan divide. Knowing that, one might predict some gains or losses for the Republicans in the House and a close battle for control of the Senate, which is what happened. The Republicans were also less likely to lose a large number of seats since Bush's victory in 2000 had not brought about many Republican congressional victories in districts or states that normally voted Democratic or were competitive. His lack of coattails in 2000 implied fewer targets for the Democrats in 2002.[101]

Redistricting may have mattered. Normally, the first congressional election after a redistricting sees a larger than usual number of incumbents lose their reelection bids. Incumbents are often not totally familiar with their new districts, which in any case may have fewer voters from the member's party. Demographic change also deprives some states of representation, thereby forcing incumbents to run against one another. When districts were redrawn after 1990, 111 House seats were won in 1992 with less than 55 percent of the vote, and 43 incumbents were defeated, 19 in the primaries and 24 in the general election. Some thought the 2000 redistricting focused more on protecting incumbents and less on gaining partisan advantage. In 2002, 50 House members won with less than 55 percent of the vote, and just 16 incumbents were defeated, 8 in both the primaries and the general election.[102] It may be that a pro-Republican bias in redistricting helped preserve their House majority in 2002.[103]

The economy, in contrast, worsened Republican prospects. The economy grew 1.6 percent in 2002 after expanding only 0.8 percent in 2001.[104] Normally, a weak economy translates into a poor public assessment of the performance of the dominant party. In 2002, the economy and presidential approval went separate ways. His approval ratings were good, especially in light of the economy. But a 60 percent approval rating had not led to gains for the president's party in congressional midterms except in 1998.[105] Clinton's party had done well in 1998 with a strong economy and an unskillful opposition; Bush's party won about as many seats in Congress in 2002 with a bad economy. Year 2002 makes a stronger case for presidential approval making a difference in the election. In September and October 2002, just over 60 percent of the nation approved of Bush's performance as president. His approval rating had declined since the spring by about 10 points, but Bush's support was strikingly strong given the weak economy and considerably higher than in the late summer of 2001.[106]

Bush's popularity, however, did have an effect on the 2002 outcomes. Consider two worlds, one imagined and one real. In the imagined world, September 11th does not happen and the Bush administration continues along its earlier path. The president's approval ratings stay in the low 50s and then decline with the economy in 2002. Statistical models of midterm elections indicate that in the likely event that Bush's approval ratings were below 50 percent, the Republicans would have lost control of the House in 2002.[107] Now consider the real world and the effects of terrorism:

> The shock of September 11 and the president's forceful response to the crisis rallied the entire nation to his side. The terrorist attacks radically altered the context in which people responded to the approval question; the president was now to be evaluated as the defender of American democracy against shadowy foreign enemies rather than as a partisan figure of questionable competence and legitimacy.[108]

The economy mattered less to Americans after September 11th. Before the attacks, Bush's overall rating was on average 8 percentage points higher than the public rating of his performance on the economy; afterward, it became on average 21 points higher.[109] The attacks also put terrorism at the top of the public agenda, and majorities thought the GOP would do a better job of dealing with terrorism and related issues (including Iraq and foreign affairs generally) than the Democrats.[110] Bush's popularity among Republicans also helped give the GOP a significant edge in turnout.[111]

Why did the public approve of the president? His response to September 11th had been pleasing. That response may be divided into concrete actions to secure America against terrorism and a larger, prospective agenda that promised war, progress, and democracy. It seems likely that the approval rating reflected Bush's actions in foreign affairs (notably the war in Afghanistan) and internal security.

What about the prospect of war in Iraq? Polling from just before the 2002 election indicates that about 50 percent of the public thought there was enough of a link between Iraq and terrorism to justify a military attack on that nation.[112] About half the respondents to a CBS/*New York Times* poll thought Saddam Hussein was personally involved in the September 11th attacks.[113] Just after the election, two-thirds of respondents believed Iraq currently had weapons of mass destruction.[114] In October, the nation was evenly divided on the question of whether the United States had "done all it can do to solve the crisis with Iraq diplomatically."[115] In the weeks before the election, support for military action against Iraq rose to around 60 percent.[116] This support declined, however, if the question of war included a reference to troops or, especially, to "thousands of American casualties."[117] As late as February 2003, respondents remained divided about whether Iraq's development of weapons required immediate military action.[118] For all that, large majorities of Americans were convinced before and shortly after the 2002 election that war between Iraq and the United States was inevitable.[119]

Did the Bush political strategy after September 11th succeed? The public approved of Bush's performance as president but remained ambivalent about war with Iraq. President Bush had called for a crusade to liberate and democratize the Middle East, if not the world. I have found no evidence of public support or resistance to this larger vision in the fall of 2002.[120] Bush had succeeded politically not because he was a compassionate conservative or a warrior for democracy but rather because he offered protection from foreign and domestic threats. His hope to found a new Republican majority and, indeed, a new political regime was floundering even at the moment of his greatest political success, the 2002 elections.

The war with Iraq remained the Bush administration's major priority after the 2002 election. Its efforts at persuading the public to go to war had some success from November 2002 to March 2003. More Americans believed Iraq had weapons of mass destruction.[121] The view that the United States had done all it could diplomatically to avert war also found more adherents during this period.[122] The belief that the Iraqi threat required "military action right now" had attained a bare majority by March.[123] Respondents who believed the nation should try to achieve its goals without force dropped rapidly but remained a majority of the respondents in March.[124] More people also came to think that Bush had made an adequate case for war during these months.[125] It is also true that large majorities—in the 60 and 70 percent range—came to support using military force against Iraq in the first quarter of 2003.[126] Yet responses changed considerably when survey firms asked whether respondents would support or oppose the war if there were thousands of American casualties. Given that condition, support for the war barely rose in early 2003, and a bare majority remained opposed.[127]

As war approached, Bush also moved on the domestic political front. When running for president, Bush had supported new federal spending to subsidize purchasing prescription drug coverage by private insurers for the poor.[128] The president and his Republican allies could expect a favorable response by voters, especially older ones, to his overture: per capita spending on prescription drugs had increased annually by 13 percent or more each year from 1998 to 2002.[129] Majorities supported adding this benefit to Medicare, especially when costs were not mentioned.[130] Bush and the Republican Congress "committed $400 billion to a prescription drug benefit, established a new entitlement in Medicare, and provided federally subsidized drug coverage for all enrollees and supplemental coverage for low-income beneficiaries."[131] These benefits were expected to increase Medicare spending by 30 percent over the next decade.[132]

Bush's willingness to proposal and to support an expansion of the welfare state surprised many people. It should not have. Bush had worked hard since 1998 to avoid being seen as traditionally conservative in the sense of trying to limit government. Bush had run against such conservatism to gain the Republican nomination. He had turned his back on a prudent realism in foreign policy in search of a permanent majority and a new regime. In that context, offering a large new entitlement to buy votes normally purchased by Democrats fit well with Bush's larger agenda and political style.[133] None of this had much to do with limiting government: securing voters against terrorism and medical expenses required more spending and thus more government.

The Bush administration did have difficulty passing the new entitlement. Liberals in Congress found its provisions too spare, while more than a few House Republicans recalled older ideals and doubted the wisdom of expanding Medicare coverage. The administration sought support from powerful groups engaged in struggles over health care policy. The American Association of Retired People endorsed the plan with the expectation that it would do nothing to change the existing Medicare program and that its benefits would expand over time; AARP had read its LBJ and learned the lessons of past policy battles. It also got an enhanced subsidy for the poor in the new benefit package. The pharmaceutical industry sought to preclude two outcomes: government control over drug prices and federal permission to purchase medication from firms in other nations. The 2003 bill included neither. Managed care firms and private insurance companies won a larger portion of the Medicare pie and more subsidies to participate in the growing Medicare market. Employers received more than $70 billion in subsidies to maintain retiree insurance for prescription drugs. Physicians had been set for a 4.5 percent reduction in payment rates; instead, they obtained a 1.5 percent increase. Small business owners and advocates of consumer-driven health care obtained expanded health savings accounts. Hospitals won higher reimbursements for care and a halt to constructing specialized hospitals that might effectively compete for the same patients. Health care providers in rural areas received hefty subsidies.[134]

The bill passed after Herculean efforts by the administration, not least in the House, where the final roll call of votes remained open longer than any other in history. The final votes were roughly along party lines.[135] The administration argued that enacting the law would ensure Bush's reelection and that the GOP had gone too far politically to turn back: if they failed to pass the bill, voters might turn on their president and his party in 2004.[136] The bill had another advantage for all members: the "pay-as-you-go" budgetary rules enacted in 1990 had expired a year earlier. Congress could vote for the new prescription drug entitlement without imposing new taxes on seniors or taxpayers generally or cutting other parts of Medicare or other domestic programs.[137] This desire for benefits without costs reflects American public opinion on the Medicare issue.[138] Finally, the bill might co-opt a normally Democratic issue. If the GOP were trusted as much as the Democrats on health care and more on national security, might not the party of Roosevelt and Johnson become a permanent minority? Republicans might have asked in response: how would the party of Reagan then differ from the party of Roosevelt and Johnson?

Some on the left were unhappy with the law. They believed the benefits were too spare and the concessions to the hated pharmaceutical industry too large. They also believed the law transformed medical care into a private good when it should be publicly funded and publicly provided. Jonathan Oberlander lamented: "The medicare Modernization Act takes market-based reform in Medicare to a new level. . . . There is no Medicare drug plan directly offered by the federal government; drug coverage in Medicare has effectively been privatized."[139]

For the left, symbolism mattered more than reality in this regard. The federal government established the plan and collected the premiums that paid for part of the benefits; the taxes that would pay the rest would also be taken by the federal government and not voluntarily; the benefit was publicly funded in large measure. The left also tended to equate private firms and their interests with free markets and limited government. The efforts of the pharmaceutical firms did constrain the federal government. Price controls on prescription drugs would have been an expansion of the ambit of government; avoiding such oversight thus limited the state. Its other efforts increased the scope of government. The 2003 law prohibited competition with existing pharmaceutical firms by prohibiting voluntary exchanges of money for medicine across borders. This limit on competition would create above-average returns for the pharmaceutical firms. Those returns should be protected, it was argued, to provide capital for the expensive research needed to produce new generations of medicines. The constraints on markets were an attempt by the government to ensure that an industry had the "correct" amount of capital for investment, an effort to manage the industry for the longer term. Such efforts may be confused with free markets if one forgets the large ambit of government power. Congress also did little to enhance the overall role of private health insurance in Medicare.[140]

The new entitlement appeared to be politically perfect. It provided benefits to virtually every organized interest, including the most powerful, elderly voters, without immediately imposing costs on anyone. Some conservatives resisted the expansion of the welfare state, but many relented to the political logic of Bush's reelection strategy. Some even hoped to control Medicare costs through privatization. The iron logic of electoral success prevailed.

What of Christian conservatives? Karl Rove, the president's political adviser, stated several times that 4 million evangelicals had stayed home on election day in 2000. Bush's reelection depended on getting those voters to the polls.[141] The campaign faced two questions. How could the president motivate evangelical voters? How could evangelicals be prompted to the polls while alienating as few other voters as possible?

Opposition to gay marriage answered the motivation question. Polls indicated that 65 percent of Protestant evangelicals opposed any legal recognition of gay relationships, including civil unions. Eight percent of this group favored gay marriage. Being against gay marriage had its risks. Thirty-eight percent of Americans opposed gay marriage, 31 percent favored it, and another 31 percent supported civil unions for homosexual couples. Other parts of the electorate are secular or liberal on this issue. Secular voters respond badly to religious appeals in elections. Liberal voters may profess a faith but deny that government should enforce religious doctrines.[142] A direct and candid opposition to gay marriage would both attract and repel voters.

The Bush campaign talked about the president's opposition to gay marriage to evangelicals but not to the rest of the nation. The president himself rarely mentioned this position. Little was heard on television about the issue: only nine ads from the presidential campaigns, parties, and interests groups touched on gay marriage in the 2004 struggle.[143] Instead of broadcasting, the campaign targeted telephone calls and direct mail to membership lists of churches and other relevant organizations. Christian conservatives and evangelicals received direct and customized appeals to vote, arguments rooted in religious faith.[144] Several states at issue in 2004, including Ohio, had initiatives before the voters proposing to prohibit gay marriage. The Bush effort would supplement the interest created by the initiative campaigns. The Republicans veered away from compassionate conservatism toward the tactics of 1998. For some voters, they offered to defend the tenets of traditional Christian morality against forces tending toward cultural decay.[145] Unlike 1998, however, the appeal went to some and not all voters. The political lesson of the 1998 election had been learned.

We should wonder whether terrorism, prescription drugs, and foreign crusades had much to do with the 2004 election. George W. Bush ran for reelection at a propitious time. Overall, the nation's wealth grew much faster than at any time since the late 1990s. The economy expanded by more than 3 percent over the year; growth was especially strong in the second and third quarters.[146] Economic models of presidential elections predicted a substantial victory for the president; based on economic conditions, Ray Fair, an economist at Yale University, estimated that Bush would receive 57.7 percent of the two-party vote for the presidency.[147] In fact, Bush received 51.3 percent of the two-party vote in 2004.[148] This 6.4 percent difference of the two-party vote means Bush received almost 8 million fewer votes than he should have garnered given the favorable economic conditions. The surprise in 2004 was not that Bush won. The surprise was how close the election was. The question remains, what could have accounted for the loss of 8 million votes? Looking away from the general conditions of the election, what policy or combination of policies might have cost Bush votes?

Apart from economic problems, and later prosperity, George W. Bush's first term was marked by September 11th and the wars in Afghanistan and Iraq. Public approval of Bush's performance as president rose sharply twice: after September 11th and at the beginning of the Iraq War. In both cases, Bush's approval ratings were well above the averages for popular presidents in recent memory. However, his ratings began to fall at almost the moment he declared victory in Iraq. This decline in public approval continued unabated until the end of 2003. Thereafter, about half or slightly less than half of Americans approved of Bush's performance. Disapproval had also risen sharply during this period. His loss of approval did not preclude reelection; his approval rating remained higher than incumbent presidents who had lost their bids for reelection. But his popularity was clearly below that of most presidents who had won reelection.[149]

Public opinion about Bush's handling of the Iraq War explains much of this decline in his popularity. The proportion of the public that approved of Bush's handling of Iraq declined by 30 percentage points from the beginning of the war until the late summer of 2004. The decline was steady save for a brief upturn when Saddam Hussein was captured. His general approval rating followed a similar path, although the decline reached only a little more than 20 percentage points.[150] Taking into account other factors, every 100 deaths of American soldiers in Iraq cost Bush 3 percentage points in his public approval of his handling of the war.[151] In late October 2004, Bush's overall approval rating would have been "on the order of 58 percent were it not for the casualties suffered in Iraq."[152] Fifty-eight percent approval fits well within the range of previous presidents who handily won reelection. A later study would find that a one-point drop in public approval of Bush's handling of Iraq translated into a one-third of a point drop in his overall approval rating; the effects of the former on the latter are cumulative, however, which suggests that a one-point drop in approval on Iraq led to a one-point fall in Bush's overall approval.[153]

Some argue that the war in Iraq and Bush's case for war ultimately helped his reelection campaign. They note that President Bush did win reelection despite the rise in American casualties. They argue that voters who believed the war was "the right thing to do" supported Bush even when the casualties mounted and that such support persisted even when controlling for party identification.[154] It is also far from clear that the war mattered as much as the economy in 2004.[155] Unfortunately, the authors do not offer evidence that this view of the war predicts voting for Bush if we control for short-term economic conditions.[156]

The marginal effects of beliefs about the rightness of the war matter little in the larger picture of the 2004 election. It is true that about half of Americans on election day in 2004 still believed the war in Iraq was the "right thing to do," but that proportion had dropped precipitously since March 2003. The number of Americans who thought the war was a mistake had risen by a similar number. By election day, the nation was evenly divided about the rightness of the Iraq War.[157] A 50 percentage point gap in public opinion favoring the rightness of the war had turned into essentially no gap at all. Surely more than a few of those who changed their view of the war might have voted for Bush, absent that change. The Iraq War was anything but a political success for Bush in 2004, in large part because ever-fewer people believed the war had been the right thing to do.

The prescription drug benefit did not help Bush's cause. The public did not like the new benefit. In a survey conducted at the time President Bush signed the law, 47 percent of senior citizens opposed the changes, and only 26 percent approved. Among people of all ages who reported closely following the Medicare struggle, 56 percent said they disapproved of the legislation, and 39 percent supported it.[158] When asked whether the new law would benefit Medicare participants or prescription drug companies, half the respondents said drug companies. The proportion who thought it would help people on Medicare dropped by almost a third (from 36 percent to 25 percent) from 2003 to 2004.[159]

One poll indicated that the drug benefit had done little to redefine the two parties. The prescription drug benefit was signed into law in December 2003. For example, in January 2003, Democrats held a 15-point advantage on the health care question.[160] In February 2004, respondents accorded Democrats a 21-point lead over Republicans (52 percent to 31 percent) on which party would do a better job on health care issues.[161] As we shall see, this situation did not change later.

Bush had not co-opted a signature Democratic issue. He *had* shifted the Republican Party to the left, in fact if not in the minds of liberal commentators. What he *had not* done was convince many Americans that the program would work. Yet the prescription drug law probably accounts for no more than a few of Bush's missing votes in 2004. Apart from a benefit for the poor, the law had not yet gone into effect. Absent actual results, the bill is unlikely to have cost the president a significant number of votes.

The moral conservatism of the Bush administration, exemplified above all in the support for bans on gay marriage, might have convinced secular voters to support Kerry or to stay at home. It appears that Bush both gained and lost voters in states having an initiative vote on banning gay marriage. His opponent, John Kerry, did not benefit from the voters repelled by Bush's moral conservatism. Bush's position did keep some more secular Republicans at home, but it attracted more evangelicals and thus, on net, appeared to add to Bush's votes.[162]

This examination of the 2004 election began by asking why Bush won reelection narrowly rather than widely as predicted by economic conditions. Factors like the prescription drug benefit and opposition to gay marriage had minor effects on the outcome. The war in Iraq drove down the president's approval ratings and ultimately reduced his vote share compared with what a strong economy and no war would have predicted. It is possible, though unproved, that the president avoided defeat by retaining enough votes of people who believed Iraq had been the right thing to do. It is more likely that the strength of the economy arrested the president's slide near the edge of the electoral cliff. In either case, the president was sliding downhill when he should have been enjoying an untroubled walk toward victory.

The 2004 election offers little support for President Bush's effort to refashion the Republican Party. He did win reelection, but he won *despite* rather than because of the issues he hoped would define the post-Reagan GOP. Compassionate conservatism rapidly fell apart when translated into policies, and religious issues had to be handled carefully to avoid costing the GOP votes. The prescription drug benefit had largely not gone into effect in 2004, and public opinion seemed doubtful if not hostile to the policy. In any case, the public still trusted the Democrats much more than the GOP to deal with health care. Bush's largest gambit—the Iraq War and the larger crusade for democracy throughout the world—had cost his campaign millions of votes. Economic growth had saved Bush from his own follies, domestic and international. But those follies hardly laid a sound foundation for a permanent Republican majority, much less for a new regime that combined crusades at home and abroad.

President Bush had won reelection. His victory, however, had little meaning. Americans voters were deeply divided in 2004, not least over the war in Iraq. Bush sought to claim some meaning for his victory in his second inaugural address. He began by signaling that what had been important in his first term would remain essential during his second term: national security and foreign affairs. His rhetoric remained the same as it had been since early 2002: "The survival of liberty in our land increasingly depends on the success of liberty in other lands." Foreign policy was a "mission" dedicated to advancing ideals, a mission that happily had become "the urgent requirement of our nation's security." Foreign policy was no longer a limited matter, a management of intractable problems and conflicts, seeking to vindicate national interests. Instead, foreign policy sought "to seek and support the growth of democratic movements and institutions in every nation and culture, with the ultimate goal of ending tyranny in our world." That task, not surprisingly, would be "the concentrated work of generations." Just as the president in 2002 had demanded service to goals higher than the self, he now challenged young people to "make the choice to serve in a cause larger than your wants." Sixty-four percent of Bush's address was given over to such exhortations toward an international crusade for freedom. The crusade was the first thing he mentioned, and clearly, judging by the valued time given to the topic, the most dear to the president's heart. This mission also occupied the last 19 percent of Bush's speech.

Apart from the crusade for liberty, Bush devotes 17 percent of his speech to domestic matters, and here his post-Reagan preoccupations dominated. The president notes that politics depends on character, which in turn is "built in families, supported by communities with standards, and sustained in our national life by the truths of Sinai, the Sermon on the Mount, the words of the Koran, and the varied faiths of our people." Compassionate conservatism appears in explicit opposition to the older individualism: "In America's ideal of freedom, the exercise of rights is ennobled by service, and mercy, and a heart for the weak. Liberty for all does not mean independence from one another." One paragraph obliquely mentions the ownership society and the reform of entitlement programs along with the putatively higher standards for education. His recognition of Christian conservatism would take up almost 40 percent more space in his second inaugural than his restrained endorsement of the ownership society.[163]

Bush's call for a renewed crusade for freedom continued to fail politically. Ever-fewer Americans believed the war in Iraq had been "the right thing to do," although the rate of decline in support slowed. By the middle of 2007, 40 percent of Americans thought the war in Iraq had been the right thing to do; 55 percent found the war a mistake.[164] About the same proportion of the nation believed then that "it was worth going to war in Iraq." Public approval of Bush's handling of the war in Iraq fell even more: by the start of 2007, 25 percent of the public approved of the president's work. This measure would recover a bit but remain well below his support on election day in 2004.[165] Not surprisingly, his general approval rating also sank during this period; by the middle of 2007, a little more than one-third of the nation approved of the president's performance in office.[166] Having barely won reelection, he would begin his second term with relatively little political capital to spend on new initiatives.[167] His Iraq adventure had also alienated independents and Democrats, the two groups whose support he would need to reform entitlements.[168] Most of his capital had already been spent in Iraq; the rest would slowly be frittered away in that dark land and dubious enterprise.

Bush had spoken for several years about building an "ownership society" that encompassed several policies to encourage personal savings for health care expenses and retirement. Bush proposed allowing people to create and fund private accounts from taxes that would otherwise go to Social Security. Before the 2004 election, he supported new savings vehicles that might eventually begin privatizing Social Security.[169] In his 2005 State of the Union address, Bush set out his Social Security proposal. He proposed no changes in the program for current recipients and others nearing retirement. His plan would allow younger Americans to invest part of their payroll taxes into personal retirement accounts. The proposal was hardly a full privatization. Individuals could only invest part of their payroll deduction and then only in a restricted set of options decided on by the government. The earnings from the private accounts would then replace benefits owed to the individual by Social Security.[170] To his credit, Bush sought to reform an essential part of the old regime.

Politically, Bush faced a difficult task reforming Social Security. The program had existed for 70 years. Those who contribute to it early in life assume they have a right to whatever benefits Congress enacts later in life. Changing the program may thus be perceived as introducing an overt measure of risk to "benefits earned."[171] FDR had designed the program to persist long beyond his presidency. Creating a sense of desert protected the program from future reformers. Voters might accept that risk to "benefits earned" if the program were likely to fail otherwise. Social Security's future financing difficulties were well known, but the future is not now, and the history of policymaking about Social Security (and much else) indicates that Congress only acts when no other choice exists. Absent changes, the program would become insolvent eventually, but eventually would not arrive before the first Tuesday after the first Monday in November 2006. The elderly were unlikely, to put it mildly, to accept the risk of changes in the program in order to achieve benefits for future generations.[172] Younger voters might support reforms, but they voted far less often than the elderly and the near-elderly.

Public opinion offered mixed signals. Some were optimistic. In September 2004, 58 percent of respondents to a Pew poll expressed supported for personal retirement accounts.[173] Much of the public also had little confidence in the future of Social Security. Most Americans believed Social Security was in crisis or in serious trouble. Earlier polling had shown deep disagreement among the public about solutions to the program's problems. It had shown majority support for the public's panacea for all problems in public finance: raise taxes on the wealthy.[174]

From the start, the Bush proposal also lacked support from within the GOP. Social Security reform recalled an older Republican Party relatively united around a concern for limited government and individual liberty. Bush's new GOP was built on a concern for moral decay and moral renewal under the guidance of Christian conservatives and neoconservatives. Not surprisingly, leaders of these factions objected to Bush's Social Security plan. Gary Bauer, a former presidential candidate and leader of social conservatives, objected that his constituents feared introducing stock market investments to the pensions system. Bauer demanded that Bush put more effort into supporting a constitutional ban on gay marriage.[175] William Kristol, an architect of Bush's democracy crusade, also opposed reforming Social Security.[176] Republican members of Congress feared that Bush's effort at reform would hurt their chances at reelection. Consequently, they were far from unified in favoring privatization in early 2005.[177]

Congressional Democrats, in contrast, were united in opposition to the proposal. Such moderate Democrats as existed in Congress had little reason to help Bush: he had campaigned overtly and effectively against moderate Democrats in 2004.[178] Bush's proposal attracted the expected interest-group opposition, not least from AARP, which had supported his proposal for a new entitlement to prescription drugs. The powerful lobby for the elderly was joined by labor unions and organizations representing minorities.[179] Bush might have had better prospects with some Democrats: "economic growth and declining unemployment from mid-2003 through early 2007 would almost certainly have provided a good boost to Bush's public approval had it not been overshadowed by the Iraq War, and it is hard to conceive that, without the war, Bush's job approval ratings among ordinary Democrats and independents could have become so abysmal."[180]

The power of the presidency was Bush's major hope for overcoming the odds against Social Security reform. But whatever influence the president might have had was wasted in the Iraq adventure. Bush, Vice President Richard Cheney, and Treasury Secretary John Snow campaigned from February to April in 2009 on behalf of the reform proposal. Their effort received largely positive or neutral coverage in local newspapers and other local media.[181] At the height of their efforts, public support for personal accounts had *fallen* to 44 percent of the public. Some polls suggested that proposals for reforming Social Security lost 10 percentage points of support when respondents were told Bush favored them. In July, Congress moved on. Social Security reform had ended for the time being.[182]

Why did Bush's effort fail? His opponents will say their argument prompted latent public support for Social Security to become manifest and, thereby, fatal to Bush's effort. We have seen that the design of Social Security created support for the program by fostering expectations. For the average voter, his or her expectations about Social Security can change for the better or for the worse. A voter might expect that changes for the better (i.e., benefit increases) will be clearly indicated by politicians. If the nature of the changes is unclear, a voter might assume that a benefit cut is coming since otherwise a benefit increase would have been clearly indicated by politicians. Of course, a reformer might argue that changes in Social Security would improve the prospects of future generations, but voters had learned from the managers of the old regime to believe that their contributions meant they, not future generations, deserved existing (or increasing) pension benefits.

Paradoxically, to reform Social Security, a significant part of the public needed to trust the president and the federal government. They had trusted both for some time after September 11th. By the end of 2004, trust in both was in decline. Distrust of the federal government, a healthy civic virtue, had in some measure impeded the liberalization of Social Security.[183]

The responsibility for the failure lies with Bush himself. He decided to undertake the effort and must have known of its difficulty. Perhaps no president could have overcome those difficulties in 2005, but it is certain that only a president who enjoyed the trust and support of more than a bare majority of Americans could have transformed public opinion in 2005. Bush was not that man. To transform the nation, he would have had to appeal to its finest traditions, not least the expectation of personal responsibility. But Bush had embraced compassionate conservatism and heavy government spending, both of which contravened personal responsibility.

Far more important in explaining Bush's failure was the ongoing disaster in Iraq. From September 2004 until July 2005, public approval of Bush's handling of the Iraq War dropped by 10 percent and for the first time dipped under 40 percent of the nation. During his three-month effort to create support for reform, his Iraq approval numbers matched the downward trend for the September to July period as a whole.[184] The struggle over Social Security reform was not lost in Iraq alone. But the president was proposing that voters accept a significant domestic innovation when his other great initiative was undermining his credibility by the day. The public had largely believed Bush in early 2003 about Iraq and terrorism. Why should they again trust him about a major policy change?

Compared to the Iraq War, the other failures of Bush's second term were minor. The administration's response to Hurricane Katrina in New Orleans appears to have done little, if any, damage to Bush.[185] The Republican Congress intervened in the case of Terri Schiavo, a woman from Florida in a persistent vegetative state since 1990.[186] Polls from early April 2005 showed that a bare majority disapproved of Bush's involvement in the Schiavo case and a large majority (75 percent) disapproved of Congress's intervention. Like the Clinton impeachment, the Schiavo case showed Republicans to be responsive to their Christian conservative base. As in 1998, that responsiveness did not yield political benefits. Ironies also abounded. Bush had offered the electorate a chance to crusade for moral renewal at home and abroad. Several congressional Republicans declined to join the effort. By late 2006, the GOP congressional brand stood for minor scandals and major corruption.[187]

The prescription drug entitlement did little to mitigate the losses caused by these errors. In 2006, only 28 percent of registered voters approved of Bush's handling of the health care issue. At that time, 47 percent of elderly voters trusted the Democratic Party to handle the prescription drug issue; 30 percent trusted the GOP.[188] The Democratic edge with prescription drugs reflected a traditional advantage for the party, an edge that existed before the enactment of Medicare Part D.[189] In any case, Gallup found that almost a majority of respondents thought the program was not working.[190] On the whole, Republican support for the drug benefit did little if anything to change public views about the GOP and health care.

The politics of the drug benefit are not complex. Eighty percent of the public favored adding this entitlement to Medicare.[191] Yet much dissatisfaction greeted the new benefit. Why was it unpopular? About two-thirds of all voters, not just the elderly, took an unfavorable view of the prescription drug benefit because "it did not provide people on Medicare enough help with their drug costs."[192] Bush had initially proposed a $400 billion benefit; in the end, the law was expected to cost more than $500 billion. His opposition, however, had proposed a benefit that would cost $800 billion.[193] Compassionate Bush Republicans would find it difficult to outbid compassionate Democrats for the votes of the elderly. Providing something, but not enough, need not garner a vote if the other party is offering something more.

Exit polls in 2006 showed that majorities of the electorate disapproved of how Congress was handling its job, of the U.S. war in Iraq, and of the direction of the nation. A significant majority (59 percent) thought the war in Iraq had not improved national security. Meanwhile, public approval of President Bush's general performance and his handling of Iraq declined steadily throughout 2006, reaching new lows on both measures around election day.[194] The exit polls also revealed that almost 40 percent of the electorate strongly disapproved of the Iraq War , almost all of them Democrats. (Asked their opinion of the president, 29 percent of the electorate replied "angry.") The Republicans did not completely lose their advantage over the Democrats on the terrorism issue. More people said the Republicans would keep the nation safe than said the same of the Democrats; a majority, however, did believe the Democrats would keep America safe.[195]

The GOP faced an electorate where its previous strengths had dissipated, and its opponents were angry and mobilized. The results were predictable. The GOP lost 6 seats on net in the U.S. Senate and with them, control of the body.[196] The Democrats gained 28 seats in the House, along the way defeating 21 Republican incumbents; most elections in recent years had resulted in overall incumbent losses in the single digits. The Democrats had effectively nationalized the contest by making local races into referendums on President Bush and his party in Congress.[197] Given the unpopularity of the incumbent, the results were perhaps better than might have been expected.[198] George W. Bush's effort to fashion a post-Reagan GOP had come to an end. It had lasted eight years.

Conclusion

George W. Bush both accepted and rejected the old regime. He largely accepted its emphasis on active government as a way to promote the welfare of individuals. He also accepted the implication of his views: government should not be limited to protecting life, liberty, and property. Bush rejected the old regime's justification for its programs and policies. His most important innovations did not seek to augment prosperity. They sought instead to save all God's children from moral decay at home and political tyranny abroad. Bush also tried to mildly reform Social Security, a core part of the old regime. His effort came relatively late in his presidency, which indicated both the difficulty of the task and his attachment to other, more important priorities. The Bush administration, like others, was often overtly political. His tax cuts and prescription drug benefit belong in this category. Taken as a whole, Bush adumbrated a new regime that rejected both FDR and Reagan. In that regime, had it come to pass, individuals would live for a larger whole. Crusades for virtue at home and democracy abroad would raise Americans up from moral decline and realize the promise of the older progressivism.

Bush's aspiration to found a new regime failed. The crusade for democracy in Iraq enervated the Bush administration and ended Republican control of Congress. The war did enormous damage to the Republican Party's standing with the public; support for the GOP fell along with Bush's approval ratings.[199] In Bush's second term, the Democrats enjoyed a steadily rising advantage in the number of people identifying with their party compared to the GOP; by election day 2008, the gap was 12 percent.[200] The Bush years wiped out the relative gains in party identification made by the GOP beginning with Reagan.[201]

The Iraq War was initially presented as a defensive war against an emerging threat that would culminate, if not checked, in more

September 11ths. This justification for war offered voters security at a price. The war was also presented as a vindication of democracy and an unchanging moral code. This justification for war offered voters a chance to improve the lives of foreigners along with the satisfaction of having done the right thing.

The security rationale for the Iraq War turned out to be wrong. The democracy promotion justification proved to be difficult and costly. One could argue that the Iraqi people were better off without the Saddam Hussein regime. But that improvement in their welfare came at a steep and rising price to American voters. Politicians have to at least promise voters that in exchange for their vote, they will receive something they want, at a low price. Many voters clearly did not care all that much about the welfare of Iraqis or a feeling of having crusaded on behalf of righteousness.

Christian conservatism turned out to be more of a political problem than a foundation for an enduring majority. Christians lost a fair fight in trying to impeach Clinton for sinning. The Shiavo case indicated the political consequences of mixing religion in politics. Both impeachment and the Shiavo case suggest that many Americans see a zone of privacy that should exclude politics infused with religious conviction. Compassionate conservatism fostered political opposition and quickly came to nothing largely because many Americans wish to maintain Jefferson's wall of separation between church and state. The years after 1997 offer little hope that Christian conservatism will lead to political success.

Other Bush policies failed in different ways. The efforts to assimilate the old regime to conservative ends—education reform and the prescription drug benefit—came to nothing politically. Bush's effort to reform Social Security indicated how deeply entrenched the old regime had become.

7. Conclusion

Over 40 years, beginning in the 1930s, American politicians created a regime of institutions and politics rooted in progressive ideology and ideals. The old regime opposed the American constitutional order that limited government in pursuit of individual liberty. It promised prosperity through government management of the economy as well as security through the appearance of self-help and through government health care programs. In the 1970s, the economy rapidly declined, and the old regime fell into crisis, thereby fostering the rise of Ronald Reagan. This book has recounted the struggle Reagan and some of his successors mounted against the old regime. It is now time to draw some conclusions and perhaps some lessons for those who still hope to live in a society of free and responsible individuals.

What Next?

I begin by considering the two major political parties in the United States. The two parties primarily seek to win elections and hold power. To accomplish that, they adopt ideas and agendas they believe will attract majority support. The major parties are thus the most likely means to actual changes in institutions and policies, especially in a polarized polity like the United States. By looking at what the parties have done since 1980, we might gain some insight about their futures as a means to limiting government.

As a candidate and as president, Ronald Reagan embodied a central tension of the struggle to limit government. His rhetoric and proposals looked toward a revival of limited government and thereby to an end of the old regime. At the same time, Reagan the candidate embraced the goal of prosperity rather than liberty. He meant to make people wealthier through less government while protecting Social Security. In that way, Reagan proposed both to undermine and to reform the old regime.

Reagan the reformer made a difference. The share of national wealth taken by government changed around 1980.[1] Had the earlier trends in spending and taxing simply continued, the federal government would have been perhaps 25 percent larger than it was at the end of the second Bush's term. On its terms—as set out in Memorandum No. 1 by Martin Anderson—the Reagan administration succeeded: it reduced the government share of national wealth. That success might appear to be a limited achievement. But it might not have happened at all: the trend before Reagan suggested government would grow ever larger. One could argue that Reagan saved the old regime by introducing mild fiscal reforms. It is possible that if spending and taxation had continued to grow along the lines of the decades before 1980, the old regime would have experienced another, more serious crisis. Since his policies precluded such a crisis, we can see Reagan in another light as a reformer (and upholder) of the old regime.

The Reagan years and the first Congress after the 1994 elections were also more politically successful than many critics now recall. Reagan sustained more than enough popularity in 1981 to cut government spending and tax rates. He and the GOP did better than they should have in the 1982 elections, given the depth and length of the recession at that time. The 1994 Republicans did lose a high-wire struggle with Bill Clinton over Medicare and cuts to spending, but that struggle did lead to some constraint on spending. The GOP did well in the ensuing congressional elections of 1996.

From the summer of 1997, Republican leaders began to repudiate the older concern for limited government and individual liberty. The public mood seemed to favor more spending. Republicans sought a new agenda based on the concerns of a different group of voters than those who had supported Reagan and Gingrich. They sought to punish the sins and abuses of Bill Clinton through impeachment, a move that reflected the concerns of the GOP's new evangelical voters. George W. Bush ran against the older Reaganite themes, not least of which was limited government and free markets. Bush enjoyed success for a time in transforming the GOP into a party of compassionate conservatives at home and crusading progressives abroad. Bush adumbrated a new regime and might have become the FDR of evangelical and neoconservative aspirations.

Some Republicans argue that the Republican Party should persist in the pursuit of virtue at home and democracy abroad. The purest statement of "staying the course" can be found in *Grand New Party* by Ross Douthat and Reihan Salam.[2] The authors argue that Republicans need to win back the votes of the working class, which today "is defined less by income or wealth than by education—by the lack of a college degree and the cultural capital associated with it."[3] The working class is—or should be—Sam's Club Republicans. This group is experiencing a "crisis of insecurity and immobility."[4] Douthat and Salam mention markets favorably from time to time, but by far most of their efforts go toward outlining how an activist (and expanding) government can win over its working class. Every other page of the last three chapters outlines a new initiative, sometimes of great complexity, to help the target group. The authors have in fact created an agenda for a Republican Party that has largely abandoned all commitment to limiting government. What they offer instead is the promise of cultural stability and economic security through state action.

David Frum also advises staying the Bushian course. He notes that Bush recognized the exhaustion of Reaganism and tried to escape the dead end of conservatism.[5] According to Frum, Bush was right to reject Reagan. The limited government ideas Reagan stood for addressed the problems of two generations past, not the problems of the coming century.[6] A more principled, more Reaganesque agenda, Frum argues, would have led to a political defeat greater than any suffered by George W. Bush.[7] For Frum, the times now call conservatives to change and adapt or watch their ideas and party become irrelevant.[8] Liberty is not threatened today in the United States: "the ideal under threat today is not the nation's liberty, but the nation's security, its unity, its effectiveness and . . . its beauty." To meet these new problems (and win elections), the GOP should jettison individualism and become what it has always been, "the party of American democratic nationhood." Being the party of the nation means valuing "public service as much as private wealth creation" and appreciating "the duties of government" as much as "the rights of the marketplace."[9] Frum then endorses "reforms": universal health insurance, rising living standards, a renewed war on terror,[10] and a conservative environmentalism.

Those who advocate staying the Bushian course might consider its political consequences. Bush's revisions came close to destroying the party politically. The Republicans followed the loss of control of Congress in 2006 by losing the presidency (and more congressional seats) in 2008. These losses do not convey the depth of Republican troubles. By 2009, the GOP held 178 seats in the House, the lowest number since the late 1980s and early 1990s. From Reagan onward, Republicans had narrowed the gap in partisan identification. After 2004, "Democrats have reclaimed most of the ground they lost during the Reagan era" by opening up a 5- to 10-point lead in partisan identification in the population.[11] The GOP had not been in such bad shape since the 1970s.

The Bush innovations accomplished little for his party. Religious voters received neither lasting programs nor authority to remake the culture. Congress removed the conservative aspects of education reform, and the Medicare drug benefit convinced few voters that Republicans were better than Democrats on health care. This willingness to expand government for political reasons led to a loss of all discipline. In his last year in office, George W. Bush expanded the ambit of the federal government in unprecedented ways. By the middle of 2009, the government ended up "owning controlling interest in an insurer (American International Group) and a car company (Chrysler), and big chunks of another car company (General Motors) and a big investment house (Citigroup)."[12] It is said the ends can justify the means in politics, but Big Government conservatives gave up on the goal of limited government in pursuit of majorities. They ended up with neither limited government nor enduring majorities.

Putting aside matters of principle, we might wonder if staying the Bushian course can consistently win elections. Republicans ran on a Big Government conservatism agenda for almost 10 years before the electoral debacle of 2006. In those years, only the midterm elections of 2002 were an unqualified success, and those races were run in the shadow of September 11th, a time when national security and terrorism were the most important issues for voters. The gains in that election should be balanced against the huge electoral losses that grew out of the Iraq adventure.

Judging times and circumstances can be a perplexing business. Consider the case of Richard Nixon. He adapted his administration to the times as he saw them and offered voters an expanding government, a realist foreign policy, and recognition of socially conservative values. In retrospect, Nixon's approach failed and not just because of Watergate. The old regime was entering a crisis, difficulties that would bring Ronald Reagan to the presidency and not Gerald Ford, John Anderson, or Charles Percy. Those who urge staying the course with Bush now tell the GOP to follow Nixon, not Reagan.

Like Nixon from 1968 to 1971, Douthat, Salam, and Frum fashioned their proposals during bad times for limited government, 2005 to 2008. Their proposals are rooted in pessimism about the electoral possibilities of the older agenda: voters want more government, not less, and the GOP must adapt to those desires. In the run-up to the 2008 election, the public mood did favor more spending. That preference, however, was far less intense before Obama's election than it had been before the victories of Clinton and LBJ. Moreover, such trends in the public mood are generally followed by a shift toward a preference for less spending.[13] Those loyal to Bush's legacy may be simply repeating the best thinking of GOP consultants in 1999.

Might the Republicans become Reaganite again? These pages suggest how darkly the shadow of the past falls on the present. So it is with the Republican Party. Wars to save American culture and foreign nations have proved to be an electoral disaster for the GOP. That failure does not necessarily mean the party will change course. Over the last two decades, conservative Christians have become a much more important part of the Republican Party and its organization. They will demand that party candidates and leaders continue to fight the culture wars. The GOP also remains wedded to an interventionist foreign policy. Here, the outlook is more hopeful. Surely it will be some time before "being strong on national security" translates into humanitarian interventions to save backward regions from their history. Moreover, the Reagan and Gingrich eras show that the GOP can be "strong on national security" while lowering defense outlays.[14] If social immoderation and failed wars have led to electoral disaster, perhaps the GOP might try Reagan's agenda of liberalizing markets, social moderation, and prudence in foreign affairs.

Given the record of the George W. Bush administration, we might ask whether the Democrats are the true party of limited government. The history recounted here provides a quick answer. The Democrats are the party that built and sustained the old regime. Apart from supporting some deregulation in the late 1970s, the Democratic Party has supported more, not less, government. When Republicans held Congress, a large majority of Democrats in Congress opposed most efforts to cut programs or spending. Democrats showed less resistance to tax reductions, at least in the early 1980s. When Democrats held the presidency and the Republicans controlled Congress, President Clinton largely offered promises of limited government combined with astute resistance to any real cutting of programs or taxes. He won the struggle over the government shutdown by defending higher levels of Medicare spending, and he precluded tax cuts by calling for Congress to "save Social Security first." Earlier, when Clinton was unencumbered by a Republican Congress, he proposed a sharp and fast expansion of spending and government power. More recently, many Americans initially saw Barack Obama as "a new-style Democrat who will be careful with the public's money."[15] Like Clinton, Obama proposed expanding government subsidies and management for health care along with a cap-and-trade program that asserted collective control over the energy sector.

Even when a majority of Democrats vote to limit government— as they did with the Tax Reform of Act 1986—they sought thereby to curb the power of business or special interests. They did not support such reforms to cut back on government control of the economy. On budgetary matters, what seems to be the case actually is: the Democratic Party is a party pursuing progressivism, a vision that has come to mean helping the oppressed and harming the oppressor. More specifically, the Democrats remain the party of the old regime that promises to help those who do not do well under laissez faire.[16] They are not inclined to "allow to do" and, indeed, tend instead to "not allow to do." More generally, Democrats presume that individuals and property should be under government control absent strong arguments to the contrary. That presumption might be overridden, for example, if private control over resources contributed more to economic growth than other alternatives, including government control of those resources. On economic issues, the Democratic Party represents old ideals with proven electoral appeal. Liberty from coercion by government is not among them.

The Democrats have a reputation for reticence in the use of force in international matters. The Clinton administration used force in Kosovo but avoided a sustained intervention. Yet Democrats are first and last progressive, and while Vietnam may still cast a shadow on their leaders, progressivism as a governing ideal was from the start imperialistic in foreign affairs.[17]

Iraq was a progressive war, as George W. Bush made clear: the nation should conquer another country in self-defense *and* to improve the world (or at least, the region). The war would be a humanitarian effort against an undoubted tyrant. Perhaps its Progressive roots (along with electoral concerns) prompted the Clinton administration to support regime change in Iraq as a matter of policy if not practice. The Democrats largely supported the actual decision to authorize war with Iraq in 2002.[18] As noted in Chapter 6, they also supported regime change in Iraq during the Clinton administration.

Does Democratic secularism serve the cause of liberty better than Republican culture wars? It might seem so. But progressivism often seems to be a religion for secular people, and many seem ready to use government to enforce its doctrines. For example, Democrats are given to paternalism in most matters not involving sex. They desire to manage people's eating and exercise, thereby improving their health. Democrats are also likely to use government to change people's ideas about the good life, especially when such ideas contradict ideas about the good life held by key Democratic constituencies.[19]

These considerations do not lead to absolute conclusions. Democrats may sometimes support libertarian proposals for egalitarian reasons. When they do so, as with tax reform in 1986, both parties might vote for restricting government management of the economy for different reasons. Republicans may persist in cultural reform rather than market liberalization. If so, they are likely to become a permanent minority party. The Republicans were the *only* party that proposed, pursued, and passed actual constraints on government spending and taxing after 1980.

Beyond the parties, there is the question of the voters. If a majority of voters truly want to cut back the federal government and persist in that desire, both parties will respond. Based on the period covered in this book, we might surmise that the Republicans would propose cutting spending and regulations while the Democrats would temper their plans for increasing spending, taxes, and the role of government. Such majority support existed at times in the era covered by this book, but it proved fleeting at crucial moments. We will never know what might have happened absent the steep recession of 1982, but we do know that Clinton won the battle over Medicare in 1995. Have Americans lost a desire for limited government?

The People

Ronald Reagan and David Stockman thought government had grown too large. They believed also that Americans had not been corrupted by life in the old regime. Cutting back the federal establishment would follow the will of the people. That faith in Americans was perhaps not wholly wrong, but it was too optimistic. The institutions and policies of the old regime created both a politics of entitlement and a people who favor the persistence of such benefits. In that way, the old regime partially changed the American character; it fostered dependence on government among a people culturally disposed toward liberty. Nonetheless, about 14 percent of Americans can be called libertarian in that they support both free markets and social tolerance.[20] Can anything be done to temper and change the desire of Americans for public largesse?

The government offers benefits to Americans along with costs. If those costs and benefits were internalized—that is, if each taxpayer or household pays the costs of the services and benefit government provides—there could be little reason to object to government spending. But government does not internalize its costs and benefits. Instead, it offers benefits to the many at a cost to the few (majoritarian abuse of power) or benefits to the few at a cost to many (special-interest politics). The former would seem to be the normal outcome in a democracy. In fact, we have seen that many of the policies of the old regime offer concentrated benefits to highly organized groups and then pass the costs of those benefits to most of society. Reform is difficult: the highly organized are heard from because they may lose significant benefits while the large majority has little to gain and remains silent.

Reagan tried to cut spending with a novel strategy: if taxes were cut, Congress would not have money to spend and would have to choose between current spending and deficits. He assumed Congress would choose the former given the electoral risks associated with the latter. This strategy had an additional advantage: as we saw, voters wanted taxes cut in 1978. They also wanted more spending on specific programs. The Reagan strategy, had it worked, would have cut this Gordian knot in a politically successful way. Taxes would have been reduced, thus pleasing the public, while Congress would have had little choice but to cut programs, and public displeasure would have then fallen (mostly) on Democrat members of Congress.

Congress had two options to escape this trap. It could have raised taxes on affluent taxpayers to pay for spending and thereby avoided deficits. President Clinton and a Democratic Congress pursued this strategy in 1993; President Obama mooted the idea in 2009. Taking from the rich, however, did not cover the spending, imposed economic costs (and perhaps political costs). The alternative was to continue spending, hold taxes steady, and borrow the difference. Government can borrow, of course, and the development of global credit markets has permitted revenues to run below public spending most of the time since 1980.

Reagan's gambit failed: spending was not brought into line with the taxes people were willing to pay. Borrowed sums must also be repaid with interest.[21] All things being equal, earlier cohorts pay lower taxes than they would have if they had paid for all government spending, and later taxpayers make up the difference with interest. Over a longer period, if spending remains the same, a tax reduction shifts rather than reduces the taxes owed by voters. If cutting taxes had forced Congress to spend less, taxes would have been lower than they otherwise would have been, and tax cuts now would have been compatible with lower taxes later, even given minor deficits.

Perhaps the Reagan strategy had a fatal flaw. If a business cuts prices, it will induce more demand for a product or service, all things being equal. If it raises prices, demand will fall. Cutting taxes reduces the price for government; citizens will want more of government at the lower price. Lower prices and more government might seem to be what voters want, leading politicians of both parties to offer more programs for a lower price in taxes.[22] In fact, empirical studies indicate that reducing taxes has not led to lower spending.[23]

This theory would suggest the opposite: if taxes (prices) are raised, demand for government will fall. If spending falls, the total cost of government, now and later, will also fall compared with a world with lower taxes (now), stable (or rising) spending, and borrowing. As noted earlier, the 1970s saw rising taxes across the board for Americans, a development that appeared to foster Ronald Reagan's election victory and early political success.

Perhaps higher taxes are the way to lower spending and lower taxes overall and thus the way to a more limited government or, at least, to a government that would be smaller than it would have been otherwise over the long run. Increased taxes would accomplish this by fomenting resistance to current spending. This argument assumes reasonably that voters really do not want the current level of spending since they are evidently not willing to pay for it.[24] Forced to pay for current levels of spending, they will rebel and tell their representatives to spend less to a point that they are willing to fund. Both taxes and spending would then fall to this lower point. The new government budget would be both smaller and more efficient in that voters would be willing to pay for what government provided and not shift the costs to future taxpayers.

This argument for lowering spending makes sense assuming that all voters are equally taxed to pay for increments of government spending. In that world, more spending leads to more taxes, and thereafter to voters' giving voice if they are paying for more government than they want. But we do not live in that world. In reality, some voters pay more taxes than others. In general, a majority of voters paid a little less than 3 percent of all income taxes in 2007. The top 10 percent of earning households accounted for just over 70 percent of all income taxes that year. The average tax rate on the bottom 50 percent was 3 percent, on the top 10 percent, just under 19 percent.[25] More specifically, perhaps one-third of households pay no federal income taxes at all.[26] In sum, the suppliers of tax revenue will be a different group of people than the consumers of public spending. The costs of government will therefore not be fully internalized, and spending would not be constrained.

These considerations suggest that the costs of government should be spread widely. A flat tax on consumption—a tax on what people spend rather than on what they earn—would seem to affect everyone.[27] After all, everyone spends money. It need not, however, spread the costs of government to all voters. Such a tax would include an exemption for some spending and could impose different levels of taxation on increased consumption.

Nonetheless, a genuine flat tax—a constant tax rate—would spread the costs of government to all its citizens.[28] The flat tax would also be a reform that removed tax preferences from the code. If all this could be accomplished, the spending induced by organized groups would lead to increases in taxes for everyone, including the groups seeking the increased spending. If a reasonably flat tax could be achieved, we would know whether people actually want as much government as we have.[29] The logic of concentrated benefits and shifted costs indicates that Americans will not want as much government as they have.

The Next Crisis?

We might wonder if more dramatic changes were possible. Reagan the revivalist and enemy of the old regime failed. The federal government still spends trillions of dollars, much of it borrowed. Few programs or program areas were eliminated or even cut significantly. The major entitlement programs—Social Security, Medicare, and Medicaid—remain in existence and largely unreformed. Reagan and Gingrich did not roll back the state to its constitutional limits or to a libertarian ideal. Both politicians talked of radical change and a renewed liberty. Whatever their intentions, they—Reagan especially—ended up as reformers whose innovations shored up rather than ended a regime in crisis.

Yet for all its persistence, the old regime has problems. We begin with its age. The government of the United States changed in important ways in the 1860s and the 1930s. This suggests two thoughts. First, a set of institutions and policies—a regime—does not last for long periods in the United States. Second, the old regime fashioned during the New Deal is over 70 years old and has persisted slightly longer than the Constitution of 1789 and the post–Civil War political order.[30] Yet time itself did not bring change in the 1860s and 1930s: slavery, differences in economic development, progressivism, and policy errors—among other factors—contributed to the political changes noted earlier. Does the history of the progressive regime suggest weaknesses that might foster its end?

The regime promises continual prosperity through government management of the economy. Economic difficulties, if they persist, become more than bad times; they can become a failure of government and raise questions about its validity. As we have seen, the malaise of the 1970s made Reagan's presidency (and subsequent reforms) possible. Other changes happened at that time. The failure of Keynesian economic management shifted authority over the economy to the Federal Reserve Board and monetary policy. Just as fiscal policy seemed to have solved all economic problems in 1965, the monetary authorities appeared to have induced a "great moderation" by 2005. It is possible that the Fed will take the blame for the financial and economic crisis of 2008, especially if subsequent Fed actions lead to renewed inflation or poor economic performance. If both fiscal and monetary policies and the institutions that control them have lost credibility, how can the old regime perform its central task of fostering prosperity?

A second weakness concerns the political legitimacy of the old regime. The last 30 years have seen two low points of public trust in the federal government. The first came about the time Reagan won the presidency. The second fell in 1994.[31] In some measure, this weakness comes from simple partisanship; people do not trust the government when their enemies have power. Beyond that, the government appears unable to persistently convince a majority that federal officials can be trusted to do the right thing. Such persistent doubt about the federal government has not ended the old regime. But it may reflect a larger weakness.

Americans have shown a great deal of trust in the federal government twice in recent history: in the years before 1963 and for a period after September 11th. In both cases, Americans had a sense of common purpose rooted in a sense of external threat (the Soviets in the earlier case, terrorists in the latter). In time, the policies to deal with that threat provoked conflict, as did disagreement over domestic policies. Such unity about national goals is the exception, not the rule, in the United States. As we have seen the federal government usually pursues many purposes through many policies. Absent agreement about ends, the federal government will always be pursuing ends and policies that many people disagree with. Many Americans may much of the time conclude that the federal government is not doing "the right thing." The federal government will normally be active and distrusted, apart from times of national threat and common purpose. Perhaps that distrust will slowly sap the old regime of its legitimacy.

A third weakness is fiscal. For most of the years covered by this study, spending by the federal government has exceeded its revenues. The difference has been covered by borrowing. Clearly, the old regime has both fostered and responded to a sense of entitlement to government benefits. It has not found a way to convince Americans to pay for the spending done by the federal government, perhaps because only a minority trusts the federal government. This failure should raise questions about the old regime. A business that must continually sell its products for less than it costs to produce them would eventually go out of business. Government can continue in business because some of its costs can be shifted to future taxpayers who have no say about current budgets. Deficits raise questions, in other words, about the quality of consent to the old regime.

As a political fact, deficits and borrowing have proved to be remarkably stable since 1980. For voters and candidates, tax increases are bad, and spending cuts would harm specific constituencies. Deficits are said to be bad but, as a matter of fact, remain an unproven harm. Something like this may be what former vice president Cheney had in mind when he said Reagan had shown deficits don't matter. If nobody loses an election because of deficits, perhaps the future will be like the past, and the old regime will remain stable even if the public debt grows.

The fiscal future of the United States, however, may not be like the years covered in this book. Already, obligations incurred during the George W. Bush years are expected to add trillions of dollars to the public debt in the next few years, thereby raising the ratio of public debt to national output by over 50 percent.[32] The Obama administration may add expensive commitments in health care spending.[33] In any case, the new spending may well follow LBJ's expectation: it will gain supporters and continue to expand. Beyond that, the core spending programs of the old regime—Social Security, Medicare, and Medicaid—are expected to grow relative to gross domestic product by 30 percent over the next 10 years and nearly 50 percent over the next 25 years.[34] By that time, federal spending alone would rise to over 27 percent of GDP, perhaps one-third higher than the range experienced during the years covered in this book.[35] State and local spending would be on top of that. Put otherwise, federal spending would rapidly return to the upward trend of 1948 to 1980 and then go well beyond that.

The future will thus present the same choices with rising fiscal pressures. We have little experience of federal taxes taking over 20 percent of GDP, let alone 27 percent. We might recall that Carter foresaw taxes rising to 24 percent of GDP in his last budget. His electoral fate may have been related to his plans. Voters may reject candidates who impose dramatically higher taxes.

As we have seen, Congress has not been able to cut Social Security spending except for outside a 20-year window. It has not been able to consistently restrain Medicare and Medicaid. Indeed, the federal government under both parties has added (or is likely to add) expensive new entitlements in health care. A fear of voters, especially elderly voters, informs the calculations of most candidates for national office. The federal government and the people who elected it clearly prefer deficits to the alternatives.

What might change this trajectory? The first ancient régime may have fallen because it reached an upward bound on its ability to borrow.[36] Almost all of the past 30 years in American politics suggests the federal government will continue to prefer borrowing to tax increases or spending cuts until an upper bound on borrowing is reached.[37]

A public financial crisis of this kind might lead to default or inflation. More likely, it might lead to efforts to constrain borrowing before government reaches the upper bound to borrowing. Those efforts may lead to much higher taxes or much lower spending, or some combination of the two. Much higher taxes would lower economic growth, thereby raising more questions about the competence of the old regime in its central preoccupation. Steep spending cuts will antagonize constituents and disappoint their expectations of entitlement. Perhaps the unhappiness will be great enough to bring about the end of *our* old regime.

Conclusion

The future of limited government depends on the answers to two as yet unanswered questions. Will the failures of the progressive regime bring its end and the start of something new? Its crises and failures have not yet proved deep enough to foster deeper changes. Do the American people still wish to live under a more limited government that offers more liberty if less of other goods? At various times over the past 30 years, American voters have answered both yes and no to this question. The future may require an end to their ambivalence.

Notes

Chapter 1

1. See the list in Eldon J. Eisenach, *The Lost Promise of Progressivism* (Lawrence: University Press of Kansas, 1994), pp. 31–38.

2. Herbert Croly, *The Promise of American Life* (New York: Capricorn Books, 1964). All subsequent parenthetical references in this section are to this edition. For Croly's influence, see Eisenach, *The Lost Promise*.

3. Thurman Arnold, *The Folklore of Capitalism* (New Haven, CT: Yale University Press, 1938), p. 389.

4. For Croly, the only road to "political salvation" was that "the American democracy should become in sentiment and conviction frankly, unscrupulously, and loyally nationalist." Croly, *Promise*, p. 267. See also p. 209: "The proposed conception of democracy is . . . not so much socialistic, as unscrupulously and loyally nationalistic."

5. Eisenach, *The Lost Promise*, p. 102.

6. Alan Brinkley, *Liberalism and Its Discontents* (Cambridge, MA: Harvard University Press, 1998), p. 18. Brinkley notes the common view that the early New Deal did not have a coherent ideology. Ibid., p. 37.

7. Ibid., p. 26. See also William E. Leuchtenburg, "The New Deal and the Analogue of War," in *The FDR Years* (New York: Columbia University Press, 1997), pp. 35–75.

8. Brinkley, *Liberalism*, p. 25.

9. Ibid., p. 28.

10. See *Statistical Abstract of the United States 1940* (Washington: Government Printing Office, 1941), p. 634.

11. Brinkley, *Liberalism*, p. 31.

12. James W. Ely Jr., "Property Rights and Democracy in the American Constitutional Order," in *Institutions of American Democracy: The Judicial Branch*, ed. Kermit L. Hall and Kevin T. McGuire (New York: Oxford University Press, 2005), pp. 493–505.

13. See *A.L.A. Schechter Poultry Corp. v. United States*, 295 U.S. 495 (1935). See also Ely, "Property Rights," pp. 506–7.

14. *United States v. Butler*, 297 U.S. 1 (1936), 67.

15. *United States v. Carolene Products Co.*, 304 U.S. 144, 152 (1938).

16. James W. Ely Jr., "Introduction," in *The Guardian of Every Other Right: A Constitutional History of Property Rights*, 3rd ed. (New York: Oxford University Press, 2007). Following FDR's victory over the Court, the NRA would not be revived. When the AAA proved unconstitutional, farmers were strong enough politically to induce Congress to enact a new law. Brinkley, *Liberalism*, p. 31.

17. Gene Smiley, *Rethinking the Great Depression* (Chicago: Ivan R. Dee, 2002), p. 100 and generally chapter 3.

18. Gene Smiley, "The Great Depression," in *The Concise Encyclopedia of Economics*, ed. David R. Henderson, 2nd ed. (Indianapolis: Liberty Fund, 2008), p. 230; and Brinkley, *Liberalism*, p. 39.

19. Brinkley *Liberalism*, p. 45.

20. Ibid.

21. Ibid., p. 46.

22. Ibid., p. 51.

23. Ibid., p. 52.

24. Ibid., p. 50.

25. Ibid., pp. 58–59.

26. Ibid., pp. 52–55. But see Robert Higgs. Wartime Prosperity? A Reassessment of the U.S. Economy in the 1940s," *Journal of Economic History* 52 (March 1992): 41–60.

27. Douglass North, *Institutions, Institutional Change and Economic Performance* (Cambridge: Cambridge University Press, 1990), p. 3.

28. Brinkley, *Liberalism*, p. 28.

29. Ibid., p. 33 and sources cited.

30. The "Townsend Old Age Revolving Pension Plan" proposed that every citizen over 60 should be entitled to $200 each month; they would be required to spend the sum within 30 days. Senator Huey Long also proposed a "share the wealth" program. H. W. Brands, *Traitor to His Class: The Privileged Life and Radical Presidency of Franklin Delano Roosevelt* (New York: Random House, 2008), p. 403.

31. Arthur J. Altmeyer, *The Formative Years of Social Security: A Chronicle of Social Security Legislation and Administration 1934–1954* (Madison: University of Wisconsin Press, 1966), p. 11.

32. See Julian E. Zelizer, *Taxing America: Wilbur D. Mills, Congress, and the State, 1945–1975* (New York: Cambridge University Press, 2000), p. 59.

33. Brinkley, *Liberalism*, p. 24.

34. Robert M. Ball, longtime SSA head, in 1974, quoted in Martha Derthick, *Policymaking for Social Security* (Washington: Brookings Institution, 1979), p. 416.

35. Derthick, *Policymaking*, pp. 231–32.

36. Altmeyer, *Formative Years*, p. 26.

37. Ibid., p. 29. Altmeyer argues that the secretary of the treasury alerted FDR to the deficit. Merrill Murray suggests Daniel Bell, the director of the Bureau of the Budget, was the likely culprit. Merrill G. Murray, "Social Insurance Perspectives: Background Philosophy and Early Program Developments," *Journal of Insurance* 30 (June 1963): 191.

38. Murray, "Social Insurance Perspectives," p. 192. J. Douglas Brown of Princeton University testified in favor of an eventual deficit. Brown was an outsider to the Social Security program who functioned as an insider promoting its political agenda. See Derthick, *Policymaking*, pp. 100–4.

39. Altmeyer, *Formative Years*, pp. 29–34.

40. Derthick, *Policymaking*, p. 45.

41. As it happened, the initial rise in tax rates was repeatedly postponed and did not start until 1950. Derthick, *Policymaking*, p. 215.

42. Murray, "Social Insurance Perspectives," p. 192.

43. Some in the insurance industry protested that the large reserves would facilitate expansion of benefits. Program advocates responded by spending more of the money sooner. Derthick, *Policymaking*, p. 143.

44. Ibid., p. 197.

45. Paul Peretz, "Social Security and Political Investment," *Polity* 30, no. 1 (Autumn 1997): 95–96.

46. Derthick, *Policymaking*, 21–37; on "religious zeal," see p. 24; on "religion," see p. 31. The first appointees to the agency were drawn from the Committee on Economic Security. Ibid., p. 28.

47. Ibid., p. 66.

48. Ibid., p. 74.

49. Ibid., p. 88.

50. Derthick also establishes that expert critics were either co-opted into support for the program or ignored. Since advocates of the program controlled the flow of information to policymakers, they could choose experts sympathetic to their preferences as participants in policymaking. Ibid., p. 182.

51. Peretz, "Social Security and Political Investment," p. 96.

52. Derthick, *Policymaking*, p. 223.

53. Quoted in ibid., p. 166.

54. Ibid., pp. 199–201.

55. Ibid., p. 204.

56. Ibid., p. 82.

57. Ibid., p. 47.

58. Some two decades after the founding of the program, conservative Republicans held hearings meant to establish the facts about Social Security and thereby discredit it. This was a high moment of political naiveté. The Republicans believed that if the public knew the program was funding benefits much higher than its contributions, the program would lose public support. Derthick, *Policymaking*, p. 154.

59. Ibid., pp. 47–48. In the early years of the program, Congress refused seven out of nine times to let the Social Security tax rise. See ibid., p. 216.

60. Ibid., p. 202.

61. Geoffrey Kollmann and Carmen Solomon-Fears, "Major Decisions in the House and Senate on Social Security: 1935–2000," Congressional Research Service, CRS Legislative Histories RL30920, March 26, 2001, http://www.ssa.gov/history/reports/crsleghist3.html.

62. Derthick, *Policymaking*, p. 267.

63. Ibid., p. 269.

64. Ibid., p. 235.

65. *Congressional Record*, October 5, 1949, p. 13940, quoted in ibid., p. 242. Later during the Great Society period, a White House task force would assert the same point about current young people. See Hugh Graham, *The Uncertain Triumph: Federal Education Policy in the Kennedy and Johnson Years* (Chapel Hill: University of North Carolina Press, 1984), p. 144.

66. Derthick, *Policymaking*, p. 248.

67. Murray, "Social Insurance Perspectives," p. 190.

68. As asserted by Derthick, *Policymaking*, p. 417.

69. Ibid., pp. 5–6.

70. Ibid., p. 8. Lindbeck remarks, "Indeed, most social security systems in the real world seem, when introduced, to have given heavy over-compensation to those who dominated voting when the systems were introduced, which most likely facilitated their introduction in the first place." A. Lindbeck, "Redistribution Policy and Expansion of the Public Sector," *Journal of Public Economics* 28 (December 1985): 325.

71. Derthick, *Policymaking*, p. 270.

72. Ibid., p. 417.

73. Ibid., p. 376.

74. Ibid., p. 412.

75. Ibid., pp. 240–41.

76. Ibid., p. 418.

77. Randall B. Woods, *LBJ: Architect of American Ambition* (Cambridge, MA: Harvard University Press, 2006), p. 433.

78. LBJ quoted in Doris Kearns Goodwin, *Lyndon Johnson and the American Dream* (New York: St. Martin's Press, 1991), pp. 286–87.

79. Graham, *Uncertain Triumph*, p. xxii, referring to an essay by an official in the LBJ administration: Douglas Cater, "The Political Struggle for Equal Educational Opportunity" in *Toward New Human Rights: The Social Policies of the Kennedy and Johnson Administrations* (Austin: Lyndon B. Johnson School of Public Affairs, University of Texas at Austin, 1977).

80. Paul Pierson, "The Rise and Reconfiguration of Activist Government," in *The Transformation of American Politics: Activist Government and the Rise of Conservatism*, ed. Paul Pierson and Theda Skocpol (Princeton, NJ: Princeton University Press, 2007), pp. 19–20.

81. *Public Papers of the Presidents of the United States: Lyndon B. Johnson, 1963–64*, vol. 1, entry 357 (Washington: Government Printing Office, 1965): 704–7, http://www.lbjlib.utexas.edu/johnson/archives.hom/speeches.hom/640522.asp.

82. "Millions of Americans have achieved prosperity, and they have found prosperity alone is just not enough. They need a chance to seek knowledge and to touch beauty, to rejoice in achievement and in the closeness of family and community." LBJ quoted in John A. Andrew III, *Lyndon Johnson and the Great Society* (Chicago: Ivan R. Dee, 1998), p. 20.

83. Ibid., pp. 13–14.

84. Ibid., p. 13. See also Joseph Califano's remark that LBJ had "an insatiable appetite for a program to cure every ill he saw, or to solve a problem that some Oval Office visitor or wire service story had just brought to his attention. . . ." Joseph Califano Jr., "The Ship Sails On," in *Lyndon Johnson Remembered: An Intimate Portrait of a Presidency*, ed. Thomas W. Cowger and Sherwin J. Markman (Lanham, MD: Rowman & Littlefield, 2003), p. 167.

85. Andrew, *Lyndon Johnson*, pp. 183–84.

86. Andrew remarks that the Great Society, in LBJ's mind, was a "spiritual and moral crusade." Andrew, *Lyndon Johnson*, p. 16.

87. A plethora of books take up that task. A good analysis that suggests further reading may be found in Hugh Davis Graham, *The Civil Rights Era: Origins and Development of National Policy, 1960–1972* (New York: Oxford University Press, 1990).

88. *Public Papers of the Presidents: Lyndon B. Johnson*, vol. 1, entry 357, pp. 704–7, http://www.lbjlib.utexas.edu/johnson/archives.hom/speeches.hom/640522.asp.

89. James Heckman and John Donohue, "Continuous versus Episodic Change: The Impact of Civil Rights Policy on the Economic Status of Blacks," *Journal of Economic Literature* 29 (December 1991): 1603–43.

90. Civil Rights Act of 1964, Title II.

91. Civil Rights Act of 1964, Section 703(j). See the explication in Steven F. Hayward, *The Age of Reagan: The Fall of the Old Liberal Order: 1964–1980* (New York: Random House, 2001), pp. 26–27.

92. Lyndon Baines Johnson, "To Fulfill These Rights," commencement address at Howard University, June 4, 1965, in *Public Papers of the Presidents of the United States: Lyndon B. Johnson, 1965*, vol. 2, entry 301 (Washington: Government Printing Office, 1966), pp. 635–40.

93. Andrew, *Lyndon Johnson*, p. 57.

94. See "Message to Congress: Johnson's March 16 Message on Poverty," CQ Electronic Library, *CQ Almanac* online edition, originally published in *CQ Almanac 1964* (Washington: Congressional Quarterly, 1965), http://library.cqpress.com/cqalmanac/cqal64-1302599 (accessed May 12, 2008), for the following references.

95. "The Congress is charged by the Constitution to 'provide . . . for the general welfare of the United States.' Our present abundance is a measure of its success in fulfilling that duty. Now Congress is being asked to extend that welfare to all our people." Johnson, "Message to Congress."

96. For "national headquarters," see Johnson, "Message to Congress"; and Andrew, *Lyndon Johnson*, p. 65.

97. W. B. Dickinson Jr., "Urban Renewal under Fire," in *Editorial Research Reports 1963*, vol. 2 (Washington: CQ Press, 1963), http://library.cqpress.com/cqresearcher/cqresrre1963082100 (accessed May 15, 2008). James Baldwin remarked that "urban renewal means Negro removal." Herbert J. Gans, a sociologist of the left, studied a Boston urban renewal effort and concluded: "By and large, the planners and caretakers were wrong. The West End was not really a slum, and although many of its inhabitants did have problems, these did not stem from the neighborhood." But it was Jane Jacobs who gained lasting fame for opposing clearance of a large tract in the West Village in Manhattan. "There is a quality even meaner than outright ugliness and disorder," Jacobs wrote, "and this meaner quality is the dishonest mask of pretended order, achieved by ignoring or suppressing the real order that is struggling to exist and be served."

98. "Housing, Demonstration Cities Bill Enacted," CQ Electronic Library, *CQ Almanac* online edition, originally published in *CQ Almanac 1966* (Washington: Congressional Quarterly, 1967), http://library.cqpress.com/cqalmanac/cqal66-1301250 (accessed May 15, 2008).

99. Roy Wilkins, the head of the NAACP, agreed: "We must consider the city and its inhabitants in the context of what is going on in the whole nation and treat their problems in a comprehensive manner that has as its objective the solving of the problems of America—poverty, health, education, housing, unemployment, transportation, racial discrimination in all its ramifications and many others." He continued, "Anything less than a national plan . . . will fall short of meeting the needs of our cities." National commitments, national plans; the war metaphor was inescapable. Robert Kennedy spoke of a need for a "master plan" and then invoked what would become a ubiquitous call to action: "We're not using the kind of imagination we used on the Marshall Plan or to win World War II." "Problems of the Cities Highlighted," CQ Electronic Library, *CQ Almanac* online edition, originally published in *CQ Almanac 1966* (Washington: Congressional Quarterly, 1967), http://library.cqpress.com/cqalmanac/cqal66-1301283 (accessed May 15, 2008). LBJ would call for "rational design" of cities in his "Model Cities" speech. See "Message to Congress: Proposes 'Demonstration Cities' Program," CQ Electronic Library, *CQ Almanac* online edition, originally published in *CQ Almanac 1966* (Washington: Congressional Quarterly, 1967), http://library.cqpress.com/cqalmanac/cqal66-1299640 (accessed May 15, 2008).

100. Andrew, *Lyndon Johnson*, pp. 142–43.

101. The legislation emerged from recommendations by a special Task Force on Urban Problems, created by LBJ in 1965. The leader of the task force was Dr. Robert C. Wood, chair of the Political Science Department at the Massachusetts Institute of Technology. The next year, Wood became undersecretary of the Department of Housing and Urban Development. See "Housing, Demonstration Cities Bill Enacted." The administration had also proposed "new towns" legislation, primarily to subsidize private investment in creating new cities that were thought to be necessary to relieve population and other pressure on urban areas. One developer testified before Congress that the sums for the new towns were entirely inadequate. He noted, "What was needed . . . was a multi-billion dollar federal mortgage insurance program to create entire new cities 'in the middle of nowhere.' " The "new towns" bill was passed in 1966 and limited to a six-year duration. It required the approval by local governing bodies of nearby areas and by the state governor. The funding was also inadequate to utopianism; the bill limited to $250 million the maximum amount of all insured loans that could be outstanding at any one time. Ibid.

102. "Problems of the Cities Highlighted," CQ Electronic Library, *CQ Almanac* online edition, originally published in *CQ Almanac 1966* (Washington: Congressional Quarterly, 1967), http://library.cqpress.com/cqalmanac/cqal66-1301283 (accessed May 15, 2008).

103. Andrew, *Lyndon Johnson*, p. 140.

104. "Problems of the Cities Highlighted." See also Andrew, *Lyndon Johnson*, p. 139; by 1966, urban relief appeared "to be another program chiefly for African Americans."

105. See "Problems of the Cities Highlighted." Sen. Abraham A. Ribicoff (D-CT), chair of the Government Operations Subcommittee on Executive Reorganization, held 26 days of hearings between August and December 1966 on the problems of American cities. In announcing the purpose of the hearings, Ribicoff said cities were being neglected "at our national peril," and he would conduct an "in-depth" study of the federal government's role in solving urban problems.

106. See Lyndon Baines Johnson, "Address at Johns Hopkins University: 'Peace without Conquest,' " April 7, 1965, in *Public Papers of the Presidents: Lyndon B. Johnson*, vol. 1, entry 172, pp. 394–99. The analogy to the Great Society may have come from Secretary of State Dean Rusk, who argued for "a program for South Vietnam akin to the War on Poverty to win over the Vietnamese people." Rusk thought the program should include land reform, slum clearance, low-cost housing, improved water supply, rural electrification, and long-term industrial development. See Dror Yuravlivker, " 'Peace without Conquest': Lyndon Johnson's Speech of April 7, 1965," *Presidential Studies Quarterly* 36 (2006): 471. For more on the emphasis on rural electrication, see ibid., pp. 471–72. The speech also reflected the older progressive tradition of Wilsonian internationalism. See Orrin Schwab, *Defending the Free World: Kennedy, Lyndon Johnson and the Vietnam War 1961–1965* (Westport, CT: Praeger, 1998), p. 155.

107. The speech was a great success with the American media and public. In particular, the Eastern Establishment media lauded Johnson's plans. See Yuravlivker, "Peace without Conquest," p. 474. Yuravlivker remarks: "Johnson did not make the speech solely to swing public opinion in his favor. He also endeavored to reassure himself and the country of the positive reasons for America's involvement in Vietnam: not just to protect freedom from aggression, but to build infrastructure and achieve his cherished goal of lifting people from poverty." Ibid., p. 480.

108. Andrew, *Lyndon Johnson*, p. 160.

109. Robert Samuelson, *The Great Inflation and Its Aftermath: The Past and Future of American Affluence* (New York: Random House, 2008), p. 52.

110. Andrew, *Lyndon Johnson*, p. 8.

111. Ibid., pp. 14–15.

112. Derthick, *Policymaking*, pp. 5–6.

113. Ibid., p. 344.

114. President Dwight Eisenhower, July 14, 1954, quoted in James L. Sundquist, *Politics and Policy: The Eisenhower, Kennedy, and Johnson Years* (Washington: Brookings Institution, 1968), p. 292.

115. Jonathan Oberlander, *The Political Life of Medicare* (Chicago: University of Chicago Press, 2003), p. 29; and Derthick, *Policymaking*, p. 327.

116. The National Council of Senior Citizens said at the time that the election gave the bill a net gain of 44 votes in the House. Democrats favoring the bill also gained two seats on the House Ways and Means Committee, which had temporarily delayed matters. See Sundquist, *Politics and Policy*, p. 317.

117. Derthick, *Policymaking*, pp. 328–34.

118. Oberlander, *Political Life of Medicare*, p. 30.

119. James Q. Wilson, *Political Organizations* (Princeton, NJ: Princeton University Press, 1995), p. 332.

120. Derthick, *Policymaking*, p. 332.

121. Graham, *Uncertain Triumph*, p. xvii.

122. Ibid., p. xv. More generally, LBJ pushed through Congress 60 education bills by the time he left office. Andrew, *Lyndon Johnson*, p. 130.

123. Graham, *Uncertain Triumph*, p. xvi.

124. During the 1960s, federal aid to schools and college increased sixfold. As part of that surge, aid to elementary and secondary education rose sevenfold. Federal programs also increased quickly from 20 to 130 and were located in more than a dozen departments. Ibid., p. xix.

125. Andrew, *Lyndon Johnson*, p. 121.

126. Graham, *Uncertain Triumph*, pp. 206–10, 215.

127. Ibid., p. 213.

128. David B. Walker, *The Rebirth of Federalism: Slouching toward Washington* (Chappaqua, NY: Chatham House, 2000), p. 123.

129. Ibid., p. 124.

130. Ibid., pp. 124–25.

131. Much of this coercion targeted racial discrimination in the states. As time passed, however, policymakers increasingly concluded the states were performing poorly even in areas properly within their ambit. See quotation from Alice Rivlin in R. Shep Melnick, "From Tax and Spend to Mandate and Sue: Liberalism after the Great Society," in *The Great Society and the High Tide of Liberalism*, ed. Sidney M. Milkis and Jerome M. Mileur (Amherst: University of Massachusetts Press, 2005), p. 393.

132. Walker, *Rebirth*, p. 124.

133. Melnick, "From Tax and Spend," p. 392.

134. "The most effective way of making everybody serve the single system of ends toward which the social plan is directed is to make everybody believe in those ends.... it is not enough that everybody should be forced to work for the same ends. It is essential that the people should come to regard them as their own ends." Friedrich Hayek, *The Road to Serfdom* (Chicago: University of Chicago Press, 1944), p. 153.

135. In 1960, for every faculty member in U.S. higher education, there were 9.5 students. By 1970, the ratio was 1 to 17.7 students, a ratio that would be roughly sustained during the 1970s. See Table 156, "Historical Summary of Faculty, Students, Degrees and Finances in Institutions of Higher Education: 1869–70 to 1987–88," in National Center for Education Statistics, *Digest of Education Statistics 1990* (Washington: U.S. Department of Education, February 1991), p. 166.

136. By 1970, 2 million federally funded grants, loans, and interest subsidies would be available to one out of every four college students. Federal funding contributed $9 billion in university facilities. Andrew, *Lyndon Johnson*, pp. 126, 130; and Graham, *Uncertain Triumph*, p. xiv.

137. Graham, *Uncertain Triumph*, p. xv.

138. The percentages are 7.7 (1960), 16.2 (1980), and 24.4 (2000). See Table 2, "Percent of the Population 25 Years and Over with a Bachelor's Degree or Higher by Sex and Age, for the United States: 1940 to 2000," Decennial Census of Population, 1940 to 2000, U.S. Census Bureau, Washington.

139. See National Center for Education Statistics, *Digest of Education Statistics 1990*, Table 156, p. 166.

140. Policies are often vetted (and hence potentially vetoed) by policy communities. See John W. Kingdon, *Agendas, Alternatives and Public Policies*, 2nd ed. (New York: Longman, 2002), pp. 117–20.

141. On the number of students, see "Enrollment in Postsecondary Institutions, Fall 2006; Graduation Rates, 2000 and 2003 Cohorts; and Financial Statistics, Fiscal Year 2006," NCES 2008-173, U.S. Department of Education, June 2008, Table 1, p. 4, http://nces.ed.gov/pubs2008/2008173.pdf. For the faculty number, see "Employees in Postsecondary Institutions, Fall 2006, and Salaries of Full-Time Instructional Faculty, 2006–07," NCES 2008-172, U.S. Department of Education, March 2008, Table 2, p. 5, http://nces.ed.gov/pubs2008/2008172.pdf.

142. Thomas J. Kane and Peter R. Orzag, "Higher Education Spending: The Role of Medicaid and the Business Cycle," Brookings Institution Policy Brief no. 124, September 2003, Figure 1, p. 2. Kane and Orzag conclude that Medicaid spending was associated with the relative declines in higher education spending.

143. Two others would be chaired by a staff member of the Brookings Institution and the head of the Carnegie Corporation. Graham, *Uncertain Triumph*, pp. 58–59. Of the 13 original task forces, 46 of the 124 members were professors, half of whom came from Ivy League schools plus Massachusetts Institute of Technology. Federal government employees took up 33 places. Nine individuals on the task forces came from law firms and business corporations. Ibid., p. 62.

144. Richard Goodwin, the White House's liaison to the task forces, thus wrote to LBJ about the education task force: "The work will be helpful in the campaign, and we will make use of the individual task force members." See Graham, *Uncertain Triumph*, p. 69.

145. Ibid., pp. 134–136.

146. Ibid., p. 137. In one case, academics used their access to seek favors for their institutions. A second task force on education in the Johnson administration included several academics from nominally private universities. These members strongly supported general federal aid to private universities and recommended radical increases in such aid amounting to 10 percent of instructional costs plus $100 for each student. The group also recommended establishing a National Social Science Foundation. Ibid., p. 173.

147. Harry McPherson, a leading adviser to LBJ, recalled academic influence on the administration. When meeting with Harvard faculty, "most of the men around the table spent almost as much time in Washington, advising departments and Budget Bureau committees, as they did in Cambridge. Graham, *Uncertain Triumph*, p. 167.

148. A survey from the early 1960s found that Democrats outnumbered Republicans by three to one. See Daniel B. Klein and Charlotta Stern, "Professors and Their Politics: The Policy Views of Social Scientists," *Critical Review* 17, nos. 3–4 (2005): 259. Before the 1960s, the universities also provided a living and a platform for Progressive experts out of power. Wilbur J. Cohen, a member of the Social Security elite, left the Eisenhower administration for a professorship at the University of Michigan. From there, he continued to be involved in the politics and administration of the Social Security agency. He then returned to government in a high post in the Department of Health, Education, and Welfare, ending up as secretary. His work was always intensely political and consisted of expert knowledge of the legislators that oversaw Social Security. See Derthick, *Policymaking*, pp. 52–53.

149. The generational hypothesis may be found in David O. Sears, "The Persistence of Early Political Dispositions: The Roles of Attitude Object and Life Stages," *Review of Personality and Social Psychology*, vol. 4, ed. Ladd Wheeler (Beverly Hills: Sage Publications, 1983), p. 81. See also Klein and Stern, "Professors and Their Politics," p. 287. Klein and Stern do not find a statistically significant difference in the propensity to vote Democratic among academics who received their degree before 1968, from 1968 to 1980, and thereafter. Older academics are less likely than the radical era academics to vote Democratic, whereas the later academics are more likely to vote Democratic. The results, however, are not close to statistical significance as can be seen by the relevant z-values. See Klein and Stern, "Professors and Their Politics," p. 288, Table 14.

150. The number of full-time faculty increased by 71,000 from 1970 to 1975; over the next five years, full-time faculty increased by 10,000. From 1980 to 1986—the last year comparable figures are available—full-time faculty hiring would remain flat. See Table 206, "Full-Time and Part-Time Senior Instructional Faculty in Institutions of Higher Education, by Employment Status and Control and Type of Institution: Fall 1970 to 1987," in National Center for Education Statistics, *Digest of Education Statistics 1990* (Washington: U.S. Department of Education, February 1991), p. 219.

151. Klein and Stern, "Professors and Their Politics," p. 264, Table 3.

152. Ibid., p. 271. Economists tended to support government activism less.

153. J. David Gillespie, *Politics at the Periphery* (Columbia: University of South Carolina Press, 1993), p. 83.

154. David Stoesz, *Quixote's Ghost: The Right, the Liberati, and the Future of Social Policy* (New York: Oxford University Press, 2005), p. 82.

155. Alice O'Connor, *Poverty Knowledge: Social Science, Social Policy, and the Poor in Twentieth-Century U.S. History* (Princeton, NJ: Princeton University Press, 2001), p. 213.

156. See the origin of this theory: M. E. McCombs and D. L. Shaw. "The Agenda-Setting Function of Mass Media," Public Opinion Quarterly 36 (1972): 176–87. For later work on agenda building and the media, see Doris A. Graber, *Mass Media and American Politics*, 6th ed. (Washington: CQ Press, 2002), pp. 175–86.

157. The freedom of the press does not mean its members are neutral in political struggles. Journalists were vital members of the Progressive coalition who "directly and successfully challenged the political parties as the primary engine driving the political agenda and the national mobilization of public opinion." Eldon J. Eisenach,

"Progressive Internationalism," in *Progressivism and the New Democracy: Political Development of the American Nation*, ed. Sidney M. Milkis (Amherst: University of Massachusetts Press, 1999), p. 232. Progressivism "emerged from a new sense of professionalism and professional values in endeavors ranging from the Christian ministry and the academy to journalism and public administration." Alonzo L. Hamby, "Progressivism: A Century of Change and Rebirth," in Milkis, *Progressivism and the New Democracy*, p. 72. Journalists investigated businesses and decried the corruption in government. But when Progressives came to power in the New Deal, the press settled into two generations of complacency toward presidents. In domestic affairs, journalists were valuable allies of the incipient Great Society. Television had covered state violence against civil rights demonstrators in the South, thereby helping to pass the Civil Rights Act and the Voting Rights Act. Leading newspapers endorsed LBJ's education bill. Robert Dallek, *Lyndon B. Johnson: Portrait of a President* (New York: Oxford University Press, 2004), p. 194.

158. By 1966, the nation had 124 public television stations and 350 public radio stations. State and local government provided 60 percent of the public television funding and the federal government another 17 percent. Most of the support for the radio stations came from the universities where they were located. "Congress Creates Public Broadcasting Corporation," CQ Electronic Library, *CQ Almanac* online edition, originally published in *CQ Almanac 1967* (Washington: Congressional Quarterly, 1968), http://library.cqpress.com/cqalmanac/cqal67-1313387 (accessed June 3, 2008).

159. Irwin Unger and Debi Unger, *LBJ: A Life* (New York: John Wiley, 2000), p. 433.

160. This question was raised during the floor debate in the U.S. Senate. John O. Pastore (D-RI), chair of the Commerce Subcommittee on Communications and floor manager of the bill, replied "that this issue was the one that had aroused the most concern and discussion in the hearings and in Committee and that the bill represented what the Committee felt was the best guarantee possible" against such abuses. See "Congress Creates Public Broadcasting Corporation."

161. "Message to Congress: Johnson on Education and Health," CQ Electronic Library, *CQ Almanac* online edition, originally published in *CQ Almanac 1967* (Washington: Congressional Quarterly, 1968), http://library.cqpress.com/cqalmanac/cqal67-1312057 (accessed June 3, 2008).

162. The law also set up a 15-member board of directors for the CPB, which was appointed by the president and confirmed by the Senate. (The Republican members of the first board included the Progressive Oveta Culp Hobby, Eisenhower's secretary of health, education, and welfare.) It stipulated that no more than eight directors could come from the same political party. "Congress Creates Public Broadcasting Corporation."

163. Congress authorized $20 million for the coming fiscal year. The following year Congress raised funding by 50 percent to $30 million annually over the next two years. The next requested authorization grew even faster, $155 million over two years. By 1972, however, public broadcasting had become more controversial. President Nixon ultimately signed a one-year authorization of $45 million, which was again 50 percent higher than the previous two years. Congress then followed up the next year by authorizing $130 million for the following two fiscal years, slightly under a 50 percent annual increase. In the wake of Watergate, CPB finally attained its primary long-term goal of receiving multiyear funding from 1976 to 1980. The funding began around $90 million and rose to $160 million in the final fiscal year. However, the rate of increase in the funding began to slow during this period. The

first two years offered increases of 38 and 25 percent followed by three years in the 15 percent range. See "Public Broadcasting," CQ Electronic Library, *CQ Almanac* online edition, originally published in *CQ Almanac 1969* (Washington: Congressional Quarterly, 1970), http://library.cqpress.com/cqalmanac/cqal69-1248022 (accessed June 3, 2008); "Public Broadcasting Funds," CQ Electronic Library, *CQ Almanac* online edition, originally published in *CQ Almanac 1970* (Washington: Congressional Quarterly, 1971), http://library.cqpress.com/cqalmanac/cqal70-1293317 (accessed June 3, 2008); "Revised Public Broadcast Bill Passed after Veto," CQ Electronic Library, *CQ Almanac* online edition, originally published in *CQ Almanac 1972* (Washington: Congressional Quarterly, 1973), http://library.cqpress.com/cqalmanac/cqal72-1250666 (accessed June 3, 2008); "Public Broadcasting Corporation," CQ Electronic Library, *CQ Almanac* online edition, originally published in *CQ Almanac 1973* (Washington: Congressional Quarterly, 1974), http://library.cqpress.com/cqalmanac/cqal73-1228481 (accessed June 3, 2008); and "Public Broadcasting," CQ Electronic Library, *CQ Almanac* online edition, originally published in *CQ Almanac 1975* (Washington: Congressional Quarterly, 1976), http://library.cqpress.com/cqalmanac/cqal75-1212230 (accessed June 3, 2008).

164. Quoted in Goodwin, *Lyndon Johnson*, p. 159.

165. Allen Matusow, *The Unraveling of America: A History of Liberalism in the 1960s* (New York: Harper Torchbooks, 1986), p. 438.

166. Allen Matusow remarks that Nixon "was a political technician to whom ideologies and beliefs meant little." Allen Matusow, *Nixon's Economy: Booms, Busts, Dollars, and Votes* (Lawrence: University Press of Kansas, 1998), p. 2.

167. Nixon sought "judicious expansion of the welfare state" because he knew "that spending money was more popular than pinching pennies." Ibid., p. 35.

168. As late as 1969, the future of the economy still seemed bright. Some in the Nixon administration argued for raising taxes on business to spend money on the poor. As the left-leaning Herbert Stein explained, "There were more important things at this juncture in history to do with the Federal budget, with the national output, than to make even more rapid a rate of growth that is already very rapid or making larger a gross national product in 1975 or 1980, which already in any case is going to be a staggering size." Ibid., p. 42.

169. Ibid., pp. 40–43.

170. Ibid., p. 52.

171. Ibid., p. 117.

172. Ibid., pp. 120–23.

173. Ibid., pp. 145–47.

174. In August 1971, Congress gave the president the power to impose mandatory controls on wages and prices for six months. Ibid., p. 67. Surveys indicated that 50 percent of Americans favored a wage-price freeze. Ibid., p. 113.

175. Ibid., pp. 157–63.

176. Ibid., p. 193.

177. Theodore J. Lowi, "Two Roads to Serfdom: Liberalism, Conservatism and Administrative Power," *American University Law Review* 36 (1987): 298.

178. Pierson found the same growth by looking at spending on regulation and government employment in regulatory functions. Of these, environmental regulations have been the most expansive: employment in environmental regulation quadrupled in the 1970s and then grew another 50 percent from 1980 to 2004. Pierson, "Activist Government," pp. 24–25.

179. Clifford Winston, "Economic Deregulation: Days of Reckoning for Microeconomists," *Journal of Economic Literature* 31 (1993): 1263.

180. Theodore J. Lowi, *The End of Liberalism: The Second Republic of the United States*, 2nd ed. (New York: W. W. Norton, 1978), pp. xi–xii.

181. Paul J. Quirk and Joseph Hinchliffe, "The Rising Hegemony of Mass Opinion," in *Loss of Confidence: Politics and Policy in the 1970s*, ed. David Brian Robertson (University Park: Pennsylvania State University Press, 1998), pp. 27–28.

182. "Presidential Statement to Congress: Nixon's Environmental Reorganization Plan," CQ Electronic Library, *CQ Almanac* online edition, originally published in *CQ Almanac 1970* (Washington: Congressional Quarterly, 1971), http://library.cqpress.com/cqalmanac/cqal70-1290928 (accessed July 30, 2008). See the analysis in Lowi, *The End of Liberalism*, pp. 119–120.

183. Lowi, *The End of Liberalism*, pp. 114–16.

184. Ibid., pp. 116–18.

185. Ibid., pp. 119–20.

186. "Tax Policy, 1969–1972 Legislative Overview," CQ Press Electronic Library, CQ Congress Collection, originally published in *Congress and the Nation, 1969–1972*, vol. 3 (Washington: CQ Press, 1973), http://library.cqpress.com/congress/catn69-0008168114.

187. "Tax Policy, 1973–1976 Legislative Overview," CQ Press Electronic Library, CQ Congress Collection, originally published in *Congress and the Nation, 1973–1976*, vol. 4 (Washington: CQ Press, 1977), http://library.cqpress.com/congress/catn73-0009170509.

188. See Government Accountability Office, "Tax Expenditures Represent a Substantial Federal Commitment and Need to Be Reexamined: Report to Agency Officials," September 2005, Figure 2, p. 22 and Figure 4, p. 26. The trend reported in this document begins in 1974 because the budget reform of that year required an accounting of the number and cost of tax preferences.

189. In the jargon, the program's funding changed from a "partial reserve basis" to a "pay-as-you-go" system (with reserves, on average, only equal to annual payments) based on "dynamic earnings" assumptions in forecasting future revenues for the program. For a complete account of the 1972 increase, see Derthick, *Policymaking*, pp. 358-62; and Quirk and Hinchliffe, "The Rising Hegemony of Mass Opinion," pp. 33–36.

190. Derthick, *Policymaking*, pp. 352–59.

191. Ibid., p. 374.

192. Ibid., pp. 352–59.

193. Other numbers bespeak the expansion of the program during the second phase of the New Deal. The proportion of covered earnings subject to taxation rose to 86 percent, or about 5 percent higher than before. By 1975, the replacement rate of preretirement income had risen to 67 percent for a married man with average earnings and 92 percent for a married man earning the federal minimum wage; the former had risen 50 percent over a decade; the latter by 67 percent. Ibid., pp. 4, 362–63.

194. Ibid., p. 362.

195. This section relies heavily on Dean J. Kotlowski, "Richard Nixon and the Origins of Affirmative Action," *The Historian* 60 (1998): 523–41.

196. Executive Order 11246, September 24, 1965, Part II, subpart B: "The contractor will take affirmative action to ensure that applicants are employed, and that employees

are treated during employment, without regard to their race, creed, color, or national origin." Available at http://www.eeoc.gov/abouteeoc/35th/thelaw/eo-11246.html.

197. See Kotlowski, "Richard Nixon," p. 527; Joan Hoff, *Nixon Reconsidered* (New York: Basic Books, 1994), p. 91; and Graham, *Civil Rights Era*, pp. 284–97.

198. Kotlowski, "Richard Nixon," p. 530.

199. Quoted in ibid., p. 532.

200. Robert B. Semple Jr., "Nixon Gives Views on Aid to Negroes and the Poor: Upgrading Schools," *New York Times*, December 20, 1967.

201. Kotlowski, "Richard Nixon," p. 534.

202. Graham, *Civil Rights Era*, p. 325.

203. Quoted in Kotlowski, "Richard Nixon," p. 535.

204. Ibid., p. 541.

205. In 1960, the violent crime rate per 100,000 population was 160.9; in 1968, the same number was 298.4, an 85 percent increase. Property crimes also increased by 78 percent during the same period. See Bureau of Justice Statistics, http:// bjsdata.ojp.usdoj.gov/dataonline/Search/Crime/State/statebystaterun.cfm?stateid = 52.

206. See, for example, Patrick Devlin, *The Enforcement of Morals* (New York: Oxford University Press, 1965).

207. Matusow, *Nixon's Economy*, p. 3.

Chapter 2

1. Walter Dean Burnham, "The Reagan Heritage," in *The Election of 1988: Reports and Interpretations* (Chatham, NJ: Chatham House, 1989), pp. 1–3.

2. Sidney Verba and others, "Public Opinion and the War in Vietnam," *American Political Science Review* 61 (June 1967): 332. Of those opposing current policy, about 40 percent (or 20 percent of the overall population) favored withdrawal. Ibid.

3. In 1964, 76 percent of Americans highly trusted the federal government; even in 1966, 65 percent had such confidence in Washington. *Percentage within Study Year Table 5A.1*, The American National Election Studies (http://www.electionstudies.org). *The ANES Guide to Public Opinion and Electoral Behaviors* (Ann Arbor, MI: University of Michigan, Center for Political Studies.)

4. The Office of Legal Services in the Office of Economic Opportunity advised its clients to maximize their claims on the older welfare programs, not least Aid to Families with Dependent Children. Theodore J. Lowi, *The End of Liberalism: The Second Republic of the United States*, 2nd ed. (New York: W. W. Norton, 1978), p. 221.

5. Edward Berkowitz, *America's Welfare State: From Roosevelt to Reagan* (Baltimore: Johns Hopkins University Press, 1991), p. 119 and generally pp. 111–19.

6. John A. Andrew III, *Lyndon Johnson and the Great Society* (Chicago: Ivan R. Dee, 1998), pp.68–69.

7. Ibid., p. 73.

8. Berkowitz, *America's Welfare State*, p. 119.

9. Lowi, *The End of Liberalism*, pp. 219–20.

10. Ibid., p. 221.

11. For a good general discussion of the Phillips curve, see Kevin D. Hoover, "Phillips Curve," in *The Concise Encyclopedia of Economics*, ed. David R. Henderson (Indianapolis: Liberty Fund, 2008), pp. 392–96. De Long argues that policymakers of the period "remembered the Great Depression, and took the reduction of unemployment to its minimum as a major goal of economic policy." J. Bradford De Long,

"America's Only Peacetime Inflation—the 1970s," Historical Paper no. 84, National Bureau of Economic Research, Cambridge, MA, 1996, p. 36.

12. Scott H. Jacobs, *Regulatory Reform in the United States* (Paris: Organization for Economic Cooperation and Development, 1999), p. 18.

13. De Long, "America's Only Peacetime Inflation," pp. 3–10.

14. Federal nondefense spending rose from 5.7 percent in 1955 to 15.7 percent in 1975. During the same period, state and local government expenditures from their own resources increased from 5.7 percent of GDP to 9.8 percent. Federal grants to the states rose from 0.6 percent to 2.6 percent of GDP. See Paul Pierson, "The Rise and Reconfiguration of Activist Government," in *The Transformation of American Politics: Activist Government and the Rise of Conservatism* (Princeton, NJ: Princeton University Press, 2007), pp. 21–23. The composition of federal spending changed rapidly, especially during the Johnson and Nixon eras. Between 1965 and 1975, spending on domestic programs rose from 27 percent of the federal budget to 49 percent and from 3.9 percent of gross national product to 7.6 percent. J. D. Aberbach and Burt Rockman, "Governmental Responses to Budget Scarcity—The United States," *Policy Studies Journal* 13 (March 1985): 496.

15. Entitlements rose from 35.2 percent of federal outlays in fiscal year 1967 to 53.6 in 1974 to 55.7 percent in 1980. It consumed roughly 9 percent of GNP. From 1965 to 1975, national defense fell from 10.2 percent of GDP to 4.7 percent. See Joseph White and Aaron Wildavsky, *The Deficit and the Public Interest: The Search for Responsible Budgeting in the 1980s* (Berkeley: University of California Press, 1989), p. 5. See also John E. Chubb and Paul E. Peterson, "Realignment and Institutionalization," in *The New Direction in American Politics*, ed. John E. Chubb and Paul E. Peterson (Washington: Brookings Institution, 1985), p. 27.

16. David Brady and Craig Volden, *Revolving Gridlock*, 2nd ed. (Boulder, CO: Westview Press, 2006), p. 51.

17. Chubb and Peterson, "Realignment and Institutionalization," p. 27.

18. By 1974, transfer payments, which included entitlements, as a percentage of the federal budget had risen by 60 percent since 1964. Jasmine Farrier, *Passing the Buck: Congress, the Budget, and Deficits* (Lexington: University of Kentucky Press, 2004), p. 55.

19. Quoted in Martha Derthick, *Policymaking for Social Security* (Washington: Brookings Institution, 1979), p. 382.

20. Ibid.

21. "Congress Clears Social Security Tax Increase," CQ Electronic Library, *CQ Almanac* online edition, originally published in *CQ Almanac 1977* (Washington: Congressional Quarterly, 1978), http://library.cqpress.com/cqalmanac/cqal77-1202042 (accessed August 14, 2008). See also Derthick, *Policymaking*, p. 382. The next year, many in Congress sought to roll back the tax increases, but the Democratic leadership and President Carter prevented the change. See "Social Security Tax Rollback," CQ Electronic Library, *CQ Almanac* online edition, originally published in *CQ Almanac 1978* (Washington: Congressional Quarterly, 1979), http://library.cqpress.com/cqalmanac/cqal78-1238354 (accessed August 14, 2008).

22. Derthick, *Policymaking*, p. 12.

23. "Long-Term Growth of Medical Expenditures—Public and Private," issue brief, Office of Assistant Secretary for Planning and Evaluation, U.S. Department of Health and Human Services, May 2005, http://aspe.hhs.gov/health/medicalexpenditures/.

24. Brady and Volden, *Revolving Gridlock*, p. 52.

25. Andrew, *Lyndon Johnson*, p. 103.

26. Ibid., pp. 104–8.

27. John D. Klemm, "Medicaid Spending: A Brief History," *Health Care Financing Review* 22 (Fall 2000): 106–8.

28. Brady and Volden, *Revolving Gridlock*, pp. 53–54.

29. Ibid., p. 56.

30. Joseph Califano, *The Triumph and Tragedy of Lyndon Johnson* (College Station: Texas A&M University Press, 2000), p. 284.

31. Presidents Johnson and Nixon were able to pass a steep surtax on individuals and businesses in 1968 and 1969. LBJ had to agree to controls on planned spending, however, to pass the surtax. Nixon had to struggle to extend the tax increase for another year. See "Congress Votes Surtax with Expenditure Controls," CQ Press Electronic Library, *CQ Almanac* online edition, originally published in *CQ Almanac 1968* (Washington: Congressional Quarterly, 1969), http://library.cqpress.com/cqalmanac/cqal68-1283727 (accessed June 9, 2009); and "Congress Agrees to Compromise on Surtax Extension," CQ Press Electronic Library, *CQ Almanac* online edition, originally published in *CQ Almanac 1969* (Washington: Congressional Quarterly, 1970), http://library.cqpress.com/cqalmanac/cqal69-1247937 (accessed June 9, 2009).

32. Brady and Volden, *Revolving Gridlock*, p. 59.

33. Eugene C. Steuerle, *The Tax Decade* (Washington: Urban Institute Press, 1992), pp. 24–25.

34. Brady and Volden, *Revolving Gridlock*, p. 60; and Steuerle, *The Tax Decade*, p. 15.

35. Some exclusions grew during this period, but the most important trend was the decline in value of the personal exemption. In 1948, in all taxpayer categories, 46.8 percent of all income was exempt from taxation. By 1981, taxpayers with four dependents were able to exclude 13.3 percent of their income from taxes. Brady and Volden, *Revolving Gridlock*, pp. 53–54.

36. During the Carter presidency, from 18.3 percent of GNP to 21.4 percent by 1981 and then hitting a new high of 22.1 percent in 1982. "Reagan's 'New Federalism,' " CQ Electronic Library, CQ Researcher Online, originally published in *Editorial Research Reports 1981*, vol. 1 (Washington: CQ Press, 1981), p. 276, http://library.cqpress.com/cqresearcher/cqresrre1981040300 (accessed December 1, 2006).

37. The initiative limited property taxes to 1 percent of "full cash value" as determined by the 1975–76 assessments. California property taxes had averaged about 3 percent. Proposition 13 permitted reassessments only when property was sold. The law also required a two-thirds vote of both houses of the state legislature to levy new taxes and precluded new property taxes. "California's Proposition 13 as It Appeared on California Ballots; Governor E. G. Brown Jr.'s Address before a Joint Session of the State Legislature," CQ Electronic Library, CQ Public Affairs Collection, originally published in *Historic Documents of 1978* (Washington: CQ Press, 1979), http://library.cqpress.com/cqpac/hsdc78-0000107668 (accessed July 28, 2008).

38. "Tax Cut Bill, 1978 Legislative Chronology," CQ Electronic Library, CQ Public Affairs Collection, originally published in *Congress and the Nation, 1977–1980*, vol. 5 (Washington: CQ Press, 1981), http://library.cqpress.com/cqpac/catn77-0010173914 (accessed July 28, 2008).

39. Advisory Commission on Intergovernmental Relations, *Changing Public Attitudes on Governments and Taxes 1980* (Washington: Advisory Commission on Intergovernmental Relations, 1980), pp. 1–2. Another poll in 1978 found that 55 percent of respondents thought the current income tax was unfair. See Everett Carll Ladd Jr.

and others, "The Polls: Taxing and Spending," *Public Opinion Quarterly* 43, no. 1 (Spring 1979): 127.

40. Quoted in Louis Fisher, *Congressional Abdication on War and Spending* (College Station: Texas A&M University Press, 2000), p. 117.

41. Ibid., pp. 118–19.

42. See, for example, James Macgregor Burns, *The Deadlock of Democracy: Four Party Politics in America* (Englewood Cliffs, NJ: Prentice Hall, 1963).

43. White and Wildavsky, *The Deficit and the Public Interest*, p. 13.

44. Farrier, *Passing the Buck*, p. 71.

45. Quoted in ibid., p. 79.

46. Jacobs, *Regulatory Reform*, pp. 18–20.

47. This awarding of privileges became known as "rent seeking" among economists. Gordon Tullock invented the term and the relevant theory. For a good overview of the concept, see David R. Henderson, "Rent Seeking," in *The Concise Encyclopedia of Economics*, ed. David R. Henderson (Indianapolis: Liberty Fund, 2008), pp. 445–46. Henderson aptly bemoans the obscurity of the term "rent seeking" and indicates the connection to "privilege seeking." Another good overview that distinguishes public-interest regulation and private-interest regulation can be found in Sam Peltzman, "The Economic Theory of Regulation after a Decade of Deregulation," in *Brookings Papers on Economic Activity, Microeconomics 1989*, ed. Clifford Winston and Martin Neil Bailey (Washington: Brookings Institution Press, 1989), pp. 1–59.

48. Francisco R. Parra, *Oil Politics: A Modern History of Petroleum* (New York: I. B. Tauris, 2004), pp. 175–77, 220.

49. See Peter M. VanDoren, *Politics, Markets and Congressional Policy Choices* (Ann Arbor: University of Michigan Press, 1991), pp. 39–44.

50. Lowi, *The End of Liberalism*, p. 92.

51. See ibid., p. xi.

52. Lowi cited the language of the Occupational Safety and Health Act: "To assure so far as possible every working man and woman in the Nation safe and healthful working conditions and to preserve our human resources" as well as Richard Nixon's broad mandate for the Environmental Protection Agency. Ibid., pp. 304–5.

53. See the list in Clifford Winston, " Economic Deregulation: Days of Reckoning for Microeconomists," *Journal of Economic Literature* 31 (September 1993): 1265.

54. The nature of that change can be gleaned from a commission report proposing an agenda for a Democratic administration in the 1980s: "Controls over prices, profits, and entry into numerous utility, transportation, and service industries are traditional forms of economic regulation that have often been shown to have a stifling effect on economic initiative and development. Increasingly, we have come to recognize the benefits of substantially reducing most forms of economic regulation. Not only are such programs difficult to administer fairly, but economic regulation often retards innovation, productivity, and competition that would normally lead to better service at lower prices." See "National Agenda for the 1980s," CQ Electronic Library, CQ Historic Documents Series Online Edition, originally published in *Historic Documents of 1981* (Washington: CQ Press, 1982), p. 47, http://library.cqpress.com/historicdocuments/hsdc81-0000110869 (accessed December 1, 2006).

55. Hugh Graham Davis, *The Civil Rights Era: Origins and Development of National Policy, 1960–1972* (New York: Oxford University Press, 1990), p. 373.

56. The interpretation of the civil rights laws (and a moral defense of it) may be found in Andrew Kopelman, *Antidiscrimination Law and Social Equality* (New Haven, CT: Yale University Press, 1996), pp. 1–9.

57. Pierson, "Activist Government," pp. 27–29.

58. Daniel J. Elazar, "Appendix C: Is the Federal System Still There?" in *The Federal Role in the Federal System: The Dynamics of Growth, Vol. 11: Hearings on the Federal Role*, by Advisory Commission on Intergovernmental Relations (Washington: Government Printing Office, 1980), p. 84.

59. Advisory Commission on Intergovernmental Relations, *The Federal Role in the Federal System: The Dynamics of Growth, a Crisis of Confidence and Competence* (Washington: Government Printing Office, July 1980), pp. 5–25.

60. Ibid., pp. 5–6.

61. Stephen Skowronek, "Presidential Leadership in Political Time," in *The Presidency and the Political System*, ed. Michael Nelson, 5th ed. (Washington: CQ Press, 1998) p. 152.

62. White and Wildavsky, *The Deficit and the Public Interest*, p. xvi.

63. Lowi, *The End of Liberalism*, p. 223. President Carter also saw the Democratic Party as "simply a collection of more or less parochial interest groups, committed to inflationary policies and the expansion of the federal bureaucracy and tied to outdated patronage politics." Wilson Carey McWilliams, "The Meaning of the Election," in *The Election of 1980*, ed. Marlene Michels Pomper (Chatham, NJ: Chatham House, 1981), p. 176.

64. Quoted in J. David Hoeveler, "Populism, Politics, and Public Policy: 1970s Conservatism," in *Loss of Confidence: Politics and Policy in the 1970s*, ed. David Brian Robertson (University Park: Pennsylvania State University Press, 1998), p. 83.

65. See ibid., pp. 85–87, for a summary of Kristol's views and Michael Novak's early writings.

66. American National Election Studies, Table 5A.1, *The ANES Guide to Public Opinion and Electoral Behavior*, http://www.electionstudies.org/nesguide/gd-index.htm.

67. The number of people who thought the government was run for the "benefit of all" dropped by two-thirds from 1964 to 1980. Table 5A.2l, *ANES Guide.* The number of people who thought "that people in the government waste a lot of money we pay in taxes" rose by two-thirds during the same period. Table 5A.3, *ANES Guide.* The public believed that the government wasted 52 cents of every dollar according to the median respondent in a November 1979 Gallup poll. White, *The Deficit and the Public Interest*, p. 21. Researchers found a similar rise in the number of people who thought "quite a few" people running the government were crooked from 1964 to 1980. Table 5A.4, *ANES Guide.*

68. Warren E. Miller and J. Merrill Shanks, *The New American Voter* (Cambridge, MA: Harvard University Press, 2003), p. 23.

69. Robert Y. Shapiro and John T. Young, "Public Opinion and the Welfare State: The United States in Comparative Perspective," *Political Science Quarterly* 104, no. 1 (Spring 1989): 83–84.

70. Advisory Commission on Intergovernmental Relations, *Changing Attitudes toward Government and Taxes* (Washington: Advisory Commission on Intergovernmental Relations, 1988), p. 61.

71. Everett Carll Ladd Jr. and others, "The Polls: Taxing and Spending," p. 132.

72. Ibid., p. 134.

73. Erwin Hargrove and James Young, *Jimmy Carter as President: Leadership and the Politics of the Public Good* (Baton Rouge: Louisiana State University Press, 1988), pp. 33–34. Carter was thought of as a conservative since he talked about balanced budgets

and cutting down on bureaucracy. Ibid. At the same time, Carter presented a far-left image to some Democrats. Patrick Anderson, Carter's speechwriter in 1976, reported the following exchange with candidate Carter: "I gave Carter a new book on labor policy by Mark Raskin of the Institute for Policy Studies. 'Do you know IPS?' I asked. 'It's a left-wing think tank. They're usually ten years ahead of everybody else in Washington.' Carter grinned. 'Maybe we can cut that down to five.' " Patrick Anderson, *Electing Jimmy Carter* (Baton Rouge: Louisiana State University Press, 1994), p. 36.

74. Edward G. Carmines and Harold W. Stanley, "The Transformation of the New Deal Party System: Social Groups, Political Ideology, and Changing Partisanship among Northern Whites, 1972–1988," *Political Behavior* 14 (September 1992): 214–15. See also Harold W. Stanley and Richard G. Niemi, "The Demise of the New Deal Coalition: Partisanship and Group Support, 1952–92," in *Democracy's Feast: Elections in America*, ed. Herbert F. Weisberg (Chatham, NJ: Chatham House, 1995), p. 223. Carmines and Stanley remark: "What has changed is the connection between ideology and partisanship. Once loosely connected, ideology and partisanship are now much more tightly bound together, and the close connection has rebounded to the benefit of Republicans." In other words, ideological transformation among southern and northern whites cut across and overrode the social group commitments that underlay the New Deal coalition. The move toward conservatism translated into a partisan change among whites. Ibid., p. 236.

75. John G. Geer, "New Deal Issues and the American Electorate, 1952–1988," *Political Behavior* 14 (March 1992): 56–58.

76. Geoffrey Layman, *The Great Divide: Religious and Cultural Conflict in American Party Politics* (New York: Columbia University Press, 2001), p. 200.

77. Ibid., pp. 171, 173.

78. Ibid., p. 174.

79. Ibid., p. 170.

80. Ibid., p. 173.

81. "Carter's 'Crisis of Confidence' Speech," CQ Electronic Library, CQ Voting and Elections Collection, originally published in *Guide to the Presidency*, vol. 2 (Washington: CQ Press, 2002), http://library.cqpress.com/elections/g2prz2-136-7413-397478 (accessed August 7, 2008). All subsequent references are to this version of the speech.

82. Skowronek, "Presidential Leadership," p. 163. The crisis of confidence theme emerged on the left well before Carter's speech. Richard Nixon would tell aides as early as 1972 that "the huge colossus of government is a mess. The people running it are incompetent and won't change, and the American people don't want to support it." Matusow, *Nixon's Economy: Booms, Busts, Dollars, and Votes* (Lawrence: University Press of Kansas, 1998), p. 204.

83. Brady and Volden, *Revolving Gridlock*, p. 16.

84. Chubb and Peterson, "Realignment and Institutionalization," p. 17.

85. John Chubb and Paul Peterson noted that the House, interest groups, and state governments tended to conserve the older regime, thereby limiting Reagan's power to change the nation. See ibid., pp. 7–9.

86. Eric Schickler, "Institutional Development of Congress," in *Institutions of American Democracy: The Legislative Branch* (New York: Oxford University Press, 2005). pp. 51–52. See also Gary C. Jacobson, *The Politics of Congressional Elections*, 3rd ed. (New York: Longman, 1992), pp. 208–11.

87. See Lowi, *The End of Liberalism*, pp. 277–78, on the continuity of governance between the two parties.

89. Douglas Koopman, *Hostile Takeover: The House Republican Party, 1980–1995* (Lanham, MD: Rowman & Littlefield, 1996), p. 82.

90. Larry M. Bartels, "Constituency Opinion and Congressional Policy Making: The Reagan Defense Build Up," *American Political Science Review* 85, no. 2 (June 1991): 460, Figure 1.

91. From 1932 to 1979, the GOP won only 4 of 12 presidential elections. It controlled 39 percent on average of the seats in the House and 38 percent of Senate seats. See Mark A. Smith, *The Right Talk: How Conservatives Transformed the Great Society into the Economic Society* (Princeton, NJ: Princeton University Press, 2007), p. 5.

92. Graham, *Civil Rights Era*, p. xxiii; on the political logic of government growth, see also Vito Tanzi and Ludger Schuknecht, *Public Spending in the 20th Century: A Global Perspective* (New York: Cambridge University Press, 2000), pp. 14–15.

93. President Carter believed the budget he proposed in 1978 held real spending growth to less than 2 percent and reduced the relative size of the federal government in the economy. "Carter Asks $500.2 Billion in Spending," CQ Electronic Library, *CQ Almanac* online edition, originally published in *CQ Almanac 1978* (Washington: Congressional Quarterly, 1979), http://library.cqpress.com/cqalmanac/cqal78-1237549 (accessed July 29, 2008). In FY79, federal spending relative to national output did go down by six-tenths of a percent. However, the following year, spending rose again, reaching a full percentage point higher than when Carter announced his goal of reducing relative federal outlays. See Table 2.1, "Summary of Receipts, Outlays, and Surpluses or Deficits (-) as Percentages of GDP: 1930–2009," http://www.gpo access.gov/usbudget/fy05/hist.html.

94. See George J. Stigler, "Director's Law of Public Income Redistribution," *Journal of Law & Economics* 13 (April 1970): 1–10. Aaron Director, a professor at the University of Chicago, had founded the law and economics movement. In fact, changes in transfer and subsidies explain most of the growth in the U.S. public expenditures during the 1960 and 1990 periods, as well as for the other wealthy countries of the Organization for Economic Cooperation and Development. Thomas E. Borcherding and Dong Lee, "The Growth of the Relative Size of Government," in *The Encyclopedia of Public Choice*, ed. Charles Rowley and Friedrich Schneider (Boston: Kluwer Academic Publishers, 2004), p. 275. Other explanations of redistribution also focused on the middle class. Sam Peltzman argued that as incomes are more evenly distributed within potential beneficiary classes, the transaction costs of forming successful coalitions fall, making redistributive efforts more effective. He concluded that the growth of government in the post–World War II period depended on the growth of a more homogeneous middle class, which made the middle class more effective politically than the rich and poor. Sam Peltzman, "The Growth of Government," *Journal of Law and Economics:* 23 (October 1980), 209–87.

Chapter 3

1. Joseph White and Aaron Wildavsky, *The Deficit and the Public Interest: The Search for Responsible Budgeting in the 1980s* (Berkeley: University of California Press, 1989), p. 56.

2. "Analysis of the 1980 Presidential Election," CQ Electronic Library, CQ Voting and Elections Collection, originally published in Paul R. Abramson, John H. Aldrich,

and David W. Rohde, *Change and Continuity in the 1980 Elections* (Washington: CQ Press, 1983), http://library.cqpress.com/elections/cc1980-127-6526-380910 (accessed December 19, 2006).

3. Ibid.

4. "The Political Year, 1980," CQ Electronic Library, CQ Voting and Elections Collection, originally published in *Congress and the Nation, 1977–1980*, vol. 5 (Washington: CQ Press, 1981), http://library.cqpress.com/elections/catn77-0010172893 (accessed December 20, 2006).

5. See Warren E. Miller and J. Merrill Shanks, "Policy Directions and Presidential Leadership: Alternative Interpretations of the 1980 Presidential Election," *British Journal of Political Science* 12 (1982): 351.

6. White and Wildavsky, *The Deficit and the Public Interest*, p. 67.

7. The number wishing for less spending went from 45 percent to 49 percent (a 10 percent increase). The number who thought spending should stay the same increased by 7 points to 33 percent. The big change came in the number who thought spending should increase: it dropped by almost half (from 23 percent to 12 percent). See Kathleen Frankovic, "Public Opinion Trends," in *The Election of 1980*, ed. Marlene Michels Pomper (Chatham, NJ: Chatham House, 1981), p. 114.

8. See Warren E. Miller and J. Merrill Shanks, *The New American Voter* (Cambridge, MA: Harvard University Press, 2003), pp. 325–26. See also Everett Carll Ladd Jr., "The Brittle Mandate: Electoral Dealignment and the 1980 Presidential Election," *Political Science Quarterly* 96 (Spring 1981): 21–22.

9. Miller and Shanks, *The New American Voter*, p. 328.

10. White and Wildavsky, *The Deficit and the Public Interest*, p. 70.

11. For the trend in public opinion on defense spending, see Larry M. Bartels, "Constituency Opinion and Congressional Policy Making: The Reagan Defense Build Up," *American Political Science Review* 85 (June 1991): 461, Figure 2.

12. Miller and Shanks, *The New American Voter*, p. 325.

13. Ibid., p. 349.

14. Stimson's public mood index may be found at http://www.unc.edu/~jstimson/Mood5206.xls. See also his discussion in James A. Stimson, *Tides of Consent* (New York: Cambridge University Press, 2004), pp. 76–84.

15. On conservatives, see Stimson, *Tides*, pp. 87–91.

16. Miller and Shanks, *The New American Voter*, p. 322.

17. *Congressional Quarterly Almanac*, 97th Cong., 1st sess., 1982, vol. 37 (Washington: Congressional Quarterly, 1982), p. 263. When Congress initially set the budget targets for Reagan's first budget, Sen. Pete V. Domenici, the Republican chair of the Budget Committee, spoke of a mandate: "The blueprint contained in this resolution is . . . unequivocal. It responds directly to the mandate of the American people and the requests of our president." Ibid.

18. Paul Pierson, *Dismantling the Welfare State? Reagan, Thatcher, and the Politics of Retrenchment* (New York: Cambridge University Press, 1994), p. 117. Some Democratic leaders did argue that polling showed that Reagan did not have a mandate, as an individual or for the policies he was proposing. White and Wildavsky, *The Deficit and the Public Interest*, p. 116. See also, Darrell West's comment that after the 1980 election, "many representatives temporarily perceived the dawn of a new political era, one that would be as important for Republicans as the New Deal period in the 1930s had been for Democrats." Darrell M. West, *Congress and Economic Policymaking* (Pittsburgh, PA: University of Pittsburgh Press, 1987), p. 60.

19. Gerald M. Pomper, "The Presidential Election," in *The Election of 1980*, ed. Marlene Michels Pomper (Chatham, NJ: Chatham House, 1981), p. 93.

20. Miller and Shanks, *The New American Voter*, p. 355.

21. Gerald Pomper, "The Presidential Election," p. 74.

22. White and Wildavsky, *The Deficit and the Public Interest*, p. 158.

23. Andrew E. Busch, *Ronald Reagan and the Politics of Freedom* (Lanham, MD: Rowman & Littlefield, 2001), p. 6.

24. White and Wildavsky, *The Deficit and the Public Interest*, pp. 272–74.

25. On his radio show in 1978, Reagan said, "I criticize those I believe are turning away from and repudiating the very principles which brought us greatness, eroding individual freedom, robbing us of independence and the right to control our destiny." Kiron Skinner, Anelise Anderson, and Martin Anderson, eds., *Reagan's Path to Victory: The Shaping of Ronald Reagan's Vision: Selected Writings* (New York: Free Press, 2004), p. 253.

26. Irving Kristol, *Two Cheers for Capitalism* (New York: Basic Books, 1978).

27. The text may be found at http://www.reagan.utexas.edu/archives/speeches/1981/12081a.htm.

28. As governor of California, Reagan had combined conservative rhetoric with moderate actions on issues like abortion. See John Micklethwait and Adrian Wooldridge, *The Right Nation: Conservative Power in America* (New York: Penguin Press, 2004), p. 90.

29. David Stockman, *The Triumph of Politics: How the Reagan Revolution Failed* (New York: Harper & Row, 1986), p. 33.

30. Ibid., p. 36.

31. He ran twice more in 1978 and 1980, both times receiving more than 70 percent of the overall vote. See "House General Elections, Michigan, 1972–1980 All Districts," CQ Electronic Library, CQ Voting and Elections Collection, originally published in *CQ Voting and Elections Collection (Web Site)* (Washington: CQ Press, 2003), http://library.cqpress.com/elections/avg1972-3MI3 (accessed August 21, 2008).

32. Stockman, *The Triumph of Politics*, p. 36.

33. Reagan has been called "a sectarian with an ecumenical style." Micklethwait and Wooldridge, *The Right Nation*, p. 90. The relationship between Reagan's liberalism and the Protestant Ethic is suggested in Carl N. Degler, *Out of Our Past: The Forces That Shaped Modern America* (New York: Harper & Row, 1984), p. 6.

34. The memo is reproduced in Martin Anderson, *Revolution: The Reagan Legacy* (Stanford, CA: Hoover Institution Press, 1988), pp. 114–21. This section draws heavily on this document. One scholar has noted that unlike other candidates for the presidency, Ronald Reagan used his campaign to lay the groundwork for his term in office. He developed a policy agenda that was bold, ambitious, and clear. He also tried to develop popular and elite support for his agenda. Later it became clear that many of the proposals that marked the Reagan administration were already present in 1980. West, *Congress and Economic Policymaking*, p. xi.

35. As Reagan put it in his address to the Republican presidential nominating committee: "We will also work to reduce the cost of government as a percentage of our gross national product." Quoted in West, *Congress and Economic Policymaking*, p. 29.

36. Some have incorrectly argued that traditional conservatives would have counseled constraint (more saving, less consumption) to deal with inflation. In this view, Reagan rejected that path in favor of less restraint: "self indulgence takes the place of self denial." See Wilson Carey McWilliams, "The Meaning of the Election," in *The*

Election of 1980, ed. Marlene Michels Pomper (Chatham, NJ: Chatham House, 1981), pp. 183–84. Yet from the start, the Reagan team planned to reduce spending as part of the answer to inflation.

37. Anderson, *Revolution*, pp. 117–19.

38. The Reagan campaign did not create another strategy paper focused on maximizing liberty; it was not among the "three most important" issues facing the campaign in 1980. The other two papers concerned foreign and defense policy and energy policy. See Anderson, *Revolution*, p. 113.

39. See Mark A. Smith, *The Right Talk: How Conservatives Transformed the Great Society into the Economic Society* (Princeton, NJ: Princeton University Press, 2007), pp. 141–42, for a comparison of Reagan and Goldwater.

40. Stockman, *Triumph of Politics*, p. 135.

41. Some analysts would later question the significance of the Senate results. Gary Jacobson noted that GOP Senate candidates did not win a majority of votes nationwide. Their Senate victories were concentrated in small states and were won by narrower margins. They won 11 of the 14 contests in which the victor received 52.1 percent of the vote or less. Properly distributed, 50,000 votes would have given the Democrats a 54–46 majority. Gary C. Jacobson, *The Politics of Congressional Elections*, 3rd ed. (New York: Longman, 1992), p. 196.

42. "Analysis of the 1980 Presidential Election," CQ Electronic Library, CQ Voting and Elections Collection, originally published in Paul R. Abramson, John H. Aldrich, and David W. Rohde, *Change and Continuity in the 1980 Elections* (Washington: CQ Press, 1983), http://library.cqpress.com/elections/cc1980-127-6526-380910 (accessed December 19, 2006). See also Lance T. LeLoup, "After the Blitz: Reagan and the U.S. Congressional Budget Process," *Legislative Studies Quarterly* 7 (August 1982): 330.

43. "Congressional Elections of 1980: Outcomes," CQ Electronic Library, CQ Voting and Elections Collection, originally published in Abramson, Aldrich, and Rohde, *Change and Continuity in the 1980 Elections*, http://library.cqpress.com/elections/cc1980-127-6530-380984 (accessed December 20, 2006).

44. Ibid.

45. White and Wildavsky, *The Deficit and the Public Interest*, p. 73.

46. "Congressional Elections of 1980: Outcomes."

47. *Congressional Quarterly Almanac*, vol. 37, p. 18-E.

48. Ibid. This category included the synthetic fuels program funded by the Department of Energy, loans offered by the Import-Export Bank, and loan subsidies made through the Economic Development Administration.

49. Reagan also proposed to cut federal subsidies to education while returning power over education to state and local governments. He also asked for cuts to subsidies to the arts and humanities. Reagan proposed reducing eligibility in some programs, including food stamps, welfare, and school lunches. Those removed from the programs, he said, were not in real need, were abusing the program, or could afford to pay for the benefit. Reagan also proposed reducing Trade Adjustment Assistance to the level of all other unemployment benefits. *Congressional Quarterly Almanac*, vol. 37, pp. 16-E, 17-E.

50. "It is a soak the poor and give it to the rich proposition" (Steelworkers President Lloyd McBride) and "Robin Hood in reverse" (American Federation of Teachers leader Albert Shanker). White and Wildavsky, *The Deficit and the Public Interest*, p. 113.

51. "Reagan's 'New Federalism,'" CQ Electronic Library, CQ Researcher Online, originally published in *Editorial Research Reports 1981*, vol. 1 (Washington: CQ Press,

1981), pp. 16-E, 17-E, http://library.cqpress.com/cqresearcher/cqresrre1981040300 (accessed December 1, 2006).

52. "Budget, Fiscal Year 1982," CQ Electronic Library, CQ Public Affairs Collection, originally published in *Congress and the Nation, 1981–1984*, vol. 6 (Washington: CQ Press, 1985), http://library.cqpress.com/cqpac/catn81-0011176436 (accessed December 6, 2006).

53. *Congressional Quarterly Almanac*, vol. 37, p. 16-E.

54. Reagan predicted a 20 percent real increase in output, or a $300 billion addition to the national wealth. The average worker's wage would rise by 8 percent in after-tax dollars by 1985. Ibid., p. 17-E.

55. All in all, Reagan proposed that the federal government spend $695.3 billion and tax $650.3 billion in FY82, leaving a deficit of $45 billion. These numbers would lower the growth rate of federal spending to 6.2 percent in FY82 compared to an 11.6 percent growth rate proposed by President Carter in his last budget. Reagan wanted to spend $26 billion more on defense along with increases in the current budget. The expected growth in government revenues would drop from 17.2 percent under Carter to 8.3 percent. "Budget, Fiscal Year 1982."

56. Reagan mentions the political difficulties of cutting spending: some members "have heard from constituents . . . afraid that social security checks . . . were going to be taken away from them." *Congressional Quarterly Almanac*, vol. 37, p. 16-E. Stockman later noted that Reagan proposed to cut government spending back to the level of 1970 while adding additional defense spending. The federal government would then absorb about 18 to 19 percent of GNP. Stockman concluded, "Politically the plan is not that radical." Stockman, *Triumph of Politics*, p. 136.

57. "Congressional Elections of 1980: Outcomes."

58. White and Wildavsky, *The Deficit and the Public Interest*, pp. 155–56.

59. "Congressional Elections of 1980: Outcomes."

60. David Brady and Craig Volden, *Revolving Gridlock*, 2nd ed. (Boulder, CO: Westview Press, 2006), pp. 86–90.

61. Allen Schick, *The Federal Budget* (Washington: Brookings Institution Press, 2000), pp. 105–38. Schick remarks that the reconciliation process may not by law make changes in Social Security, Ibid., p. 127.

62. The political process does not favor program cuts. Generally, they must be fought for one by one, not least because control over the programs (and hence their political support) is divided in the Congress. White and Wildavsky, *The Deficit and the Public Interest*, p. 102.

63. LeLoup, "After the Blitz," pp. 329–30.

64. *Congressional Quarterly Almanac*, vol. 37, p. 245.

65. "The Federal Budget, 1981–1984 Legislative Overview," CQ Electronic Library, CQ Public Affairs Collection, originally published in *Congress and the Nation, 1981–1984*, vol. 6 (Washington: CQ Press, 1985), http://library.cqpress.com/cqpac/catn81-0011176429 (accessed December 7, 2006).

66. See Stockman, *Triumph of Politics*, pp. 159–60; and Eric Patashnik, "Budgets and Fiscal Policy," in *Institutions of American Democracy: The Legislative Branch* (New York: Oxford University Press, 2005), p. 389. Stuart Eizenstat, a domestic policy adviser to President Carter, recognized that the Stockman strategy transformed, however briefly, Congress into a parliamentary system. The strategy gave little time to committee action and put firm constraints on changing the relevant bills. Eizenstat remarked, "Congress would be forced to make the most sweeping changes in a

generation in the substances of federal programs without going through the historic deliberative process to assure sound results or paying heed to the work of its own committees." Quoted in White and Wildavsky, *The Deficit and the Public Interest*, p. 138. Of course, if Reagan and Stockman had followed the "historic deliberative process," the program might never have been enacted.

67. *Congressional Quarterly Almanac*, vol. 37, p. 258. See also LeLoup, "After the Blitz," pp. 328–29; and John E. Chubb and Paul E. Peterson, "Realignment and Institutionalization," in *The New Direction in American Politics*, ed. John E. Chubb and Paul E. Peterson (Washington: Brookings Institution, 1985), p. 22.

68. Brady and Volden, *Revolving Gridlock*, pp. 86–90; and LeLoup, "After the Blitz," p. 326.

69. In 1981, 140 House Democrats were rated as conservative by the American Conservative Union; 80 percent of them supported Reagan's tax bill. Darrell West, "Activists and Economic Policymaking in Congress," *American Journal of Political Science* 32 (August 1988): 668.

70. West, *Congress and Economic Policymaking*, p. 51.

71. Barbara Sinclair, "Agenda Control and Policy Success: Ronald Reagan and the 97th House," *Legislative Studies Quarterly* 10 (August 1985): 305–7.

72. Many opponents of the program believed the bill would hurt the middle class or cast their vote to go along with their party. The opponents rarely said that district opinion influenced their vote (7.3 percent said it did) or that they feared that a vote for the program would lead to electoral retaliation in 1982 (only 1 percent so responded). West, *Congress and Economic Policymaking*, pp. 41–42.

73. Ibid., pp. 43–44.

74. Ibid., p. 54. The importance of grassroots support fit well with the reconciliation strategy of reducing the number of votes on the Reagan economic package. Local activists could rise to the occasion only a limited number of times. See Sinclair, "Agenda Control," p. 294.

75. West, *Congress and Economic Policymaking*, p. 61.

76. See generally, Richard Fenno, *Home Style: House Members in Their Districts* (New York: Longman, 2002).

77. White and Wildavsky, *The Deficit and the Public Interest*, p. 118.

78. Polls in late April showed that pluralities favored both his spending and tax proposals by about three to one. Other findings were amazing. Half of the 38 percent who expected to be personally hurt by the Reagan package approved of his performance as president. By a margin of 54 to 36 percent, respondents disagreed with the proposition that the spending cuts were too drastic. Twenty percent thought they did not go far enough. White and Wildavsky, *The Deficit and the Public Interest*, p. 128.

79. Many policymakers believed that while Reagan had compromised on several minor budget matters, he had achieved "a major change in the direction of government and an abrupt slowdown in the growth of federal spending." *Congressional Quarterly Almanac*, vol. 37, p. 257. Rep. Robert Latta (R-OH) described the final reconciliation package as a bill that would "reverse the 25 year trend toward bigger and bigger government." Ibid., p. 266. The other side of the aisle agreed. Democrat Alice Rivlin, head of the Congressional Budget Office, said Reagan's plan "represented a radical redirection of the federal budget." Ibid., p. 278. Another Democrat, James Jones, chair of the House Budget Committee, called the result "clearly the most monumental and historic turnaround in fiscal policy that has ever occurred." Ibid., p. 278.

80. Stockman, *Triumph of Politics*, p. 223.

81. *Congressional Quarterly Almanac*, vol. 37, p. 255.

82. Ibid., p. 258.

83. White and Wildavsky, *The Deficit and the Public Interest*, pp. 155–56.

84. By 1978, it "provided jobs for more than a million unemployed persons and job training and work experience for thousands more." Paul E. Peterson, *The Price of Federalism* (Washington: Brookings Institution Press, 1995), pp. 61–62.

85. One study of CETA found "that participation in CETA programs was extremely detrimental to the earnings of men, both youth and adults. All the estimated impacts for men were negative, and nearly half were statistically significant." See Katherine P. Dickinson, Terry R. Johnson, and Richard W. West, "An Analysis of the Impact of CETA Programs on Participants Earnings," *Journal of Human Resources* 21 (1986): 64–91. The authors continue, "Although these negative findings may appear unlikely, DJW note that program participation removes the participant from the labor force for an extended period while the nonparticipants are able to gain additional earnings capacity through additional job search and informal on-the-job training." See also Burt S. Barnow, "The Impact of CETA Programs on Earnings: A Review of the Literature," *Journal of Human Resources* 22 (Spring 1987): 158–59.

86. Richard P. Nathan and Fred C. Doolittle, "Federal Grants: Giving and Taking Away," *Political Science Quarterly* 100 (Spring 1985): 53–74.

87. Margaret Weir, "Wages and Jobs: What Is the Public Role?" in *The Social Divide: Political Parties and the Future of Activist Government*, ed. Margaret Weir (Washington: Brookings Institution Press, 1998), pp. 271–72.

88. Raymond A. Rosenfeld and others, "Community Development Block Grant Spending Revisited: Patterns of Benefit and Program Institutionalization," *Publius* 25 (Fall 1995): 56–57.

89. R. Allen Hays, *The Federal Government and Urban Housing: Ideology and Change in Public Policy* (Albany: State University of New York Press, 1995), p. 242.

90. Peterson, *The Price of Federalism*, pp. 62–63.

91. "Community Development Block Grant Program," U.S. Department of Housing and Urban Development, 2009, http://www.hud.gov/offices/cpd/community development/programs/.

92. Alice O'Connor, "Swimming against the Tide: A Brief History of Federal Policy in Poor Communities," in *Urban Problems and Community Development*, ed. Ronald F. Ferguson (Washington: Brookings Institution Press, 1999), p. 112.

93. Max O. Stephenson Jr., "The Policy and Premises of Urban Development Action Grant Program Implementation: A Comparative Analysis of the Carter and Reagan Presidencies," *Journal of Urban Affairs* 9 (1987): 22.

94. Ibid., p. 25.

95. Ibid., pp. 27–28.

96. Ibid., p. 32.

97. "The Federal Budget, 1985–1988 Legislative Overview," CQ Electronic Library, CQ Public Affairs Collection, originally published in *Congress and the Nation, 1985–1988*, vol. 7 (Washington: CQ Press, 1989), http://library.cqpress.com/cqpac/catn85-0012178814 (accessed January 31, 2007).

98. In August 1981, the Reagan administration decided to cut funding to the Urban Institute by eliminating its annual $1.5 million grant. The assistant secretary for planning and evaluation at the Department of Health and Human Services would award funding prospectively by ignoring the intellectual bulwarks of past administrations. Poverty research grants would be smaller, more restricted to specific topics,

and open to bids from institutions unencumbered by "the Great Society view that government alleviates poverty." The Urban Institute lost three-quarters of its federal money—a drop of $8 million—between 1980 and 1982. Alice O'Connor, *Poverty Knowledge: Social Science, Social Policy, and the Poor in Twentieth-Century U.S. History* (Princeton, NJ: Princeton University Press, 2001), p. 244.

99. Sen. William Proxmire (D-WI), successfully persuaded Congress to force the administration to reinstate the $1.5 million contract to the Urban Institute. Progressive foundations immediately offered the Urban Institute nearly $7 million. Other leading research institutions of the old regime (for example, Manpower Development Research Corporation) persuaded state governments to support their work. The Urban Institute also found nongovernment funding for a series of books, *Changing Domestic Priorities*, that "became the closest thing possible to a unified response from the liberal analytic community to the changes Reagan had wrought. . . ." By the mid-1980s, the Urban Institute had recovered much of its support from the federal government. Ibid., pp. 245–46.

100. Denis P. Doyle and Terry W. Hartle, "The 'Safety Net' after Three Years: Income Maintenance and Redistribution Programs in the Reagan Administration: Education," *AEI Public Policy Week*, December 6, 1983, p. 27.

101. The 1984 decline was followed by a sharp increase the next year. See Thomas J. Kane and Peter R. Orszag, "Higher Education Spending: The Role of Medicaid and the Business Cycle," Brookings Institution Policy Brief no. 124, September 2003, Figure 1.

102. Doyle and Hartle, "The 'Safety Net,' " p. 54.

103. John F. Cogan and Timothy J. Muris, "Changes in Domestic Discretionary Spending during the Reagan Years," in *The Budget Puzzle: Understanding Federal Spending*, by John F. Cogan, Timothy J. Muris, and Allen Schick (Stanford, CA: Stanford University Press, 1994), p. 97. The measure here is constant 1989 dollars.

104. Congressional Budget Office, "The Long-Term Outlook for Other Federal Spending," December 2007, Figure 4.1, http://www.cbo.gov/ftpdocs/88xx/doc8877/Chapter4.7.1.shtml.

105. Defense spending rose after 1981 to about 6 percent of GNP following a long-term decline after the Vietnam War. Ibid.

106. Some Republican senators were ready to move on Social Security in 1981. Pete Domenici, the Budget Committee chair, publicly denied that you could balance the budget, cut taxes, and increase defense spending by eliminating "waste, fraud, and abuse." Instead, "you have to restructure the entitlement programs, either by adjusting the inflation indexes or redrawing the eligibility rules." His targets included Aid to Families with Dependent Children, Medicaid, and cost-of-living adjustments for Social Security. White and Wildavsky, *The Deficit and the Public Interest*, pp. 103, 121.

107. Stockman proposed to raise the penalty for early retirement at 62 to the point that there was no actuarial difference between retiring early or at 65. This change would cause "the expected total payout to any recipient to remain virtually unchanged whatever the age of retirement, a sound principle of insurance practice." The change was expected to save between $82 and $110 billion over the next five budget years. White and Wildavsky, *The Deficit and the Public Interest*, pp. 135–36.

108. Health and Human Services Secretary Richard Schweiker argued that the changes would mean a young person entering the workforce in 1982 would pay over $33,000 less in Social Security taxes during his or her lifetime, a reduction of 10

percent. The proposals were a tax cut, at least for future workers and recipients. See *Congressional Quarterly Almanac*, vol. 37, p. 118.

109. Ibid., p. 119.

110. Ibid., p. 284.

111. White and Wildavsky, *The Deficit and the Public Interest*, p. 176.

112. Some state polls showed that "preserving Social Security" ranked second in priority among issues. The Republicans also thought that a near loss in a special election in a normally safe GOP district in Ohio could be attributed to the Social Security problem. The same could be said of a loss in a Mississippi district. David S. Broder, "Reagan Backs Off Televised Speech on Social Security; Reagan TV Speech to Focus on Tax Bills," *Washington Post*, July 26, 1981.

113. The administration began to review the Social Security disability rolls in March 1981. They did so in response to a congressional mandate from the previous year, a mandate that found $2 billion in waste in the program. About 1.2 million recipients were reviewed by the administration; about half were told they no longer qualified for benefits. Of those, 200,000 were reinstated after appealing their cases to administrative law judges. In 1984, Congress made it more difficult for an administration to reduce spending in the disability program. The burden of proof shifted to the government. It had to show that the recipient's condition had improved and that he or she could work before benefits could be cut. In any case, by early 1984, half the states—the states actually carried out the disability reviews—were either refusing to do them or under court order not to do so. This new standard was applied to earlier decisions to cut benefits. *Congressional Quarterly Almanac*, 98th Cong., 2nd sess., 1984, vol. 40 (Washington: Congressional Quarterly, 1985), pp. 160–61. This case shows how difficult cutting Social Security benefits can be, even under a mandate from a Democratic Congress that acknowledges widespread waste in a program.

114. See the five-year averages for that period reported in White and Wildavsky, *The Deficit and the Public Interest*, pp. 332–33.

115. William A. Niskanen, *Reaganomics: An Insider's Account of the Policies and the People* (New York: Oxford University Press, 1988), p. 11. Carter had thus gone from the average tax burden to a significant increase in four years. Because of hikes in Social Security taxes and bracket creep, a family of four with a 1977 income of $10,000 paid 3.6 percent more of its income in taxes over the Carter years (the rise was from 10.2 percent to 13.8 percent). This was an increase of 31 percent. In 1981, the inflation increase (13.3 percent) caused a family of four earning $15,000 to lose $150 in real after-tax income. White and Wildavsky, *The Deficit and the Public Interest*, p. 158.

116. Ibid., p. 170. For Reagan's famous allowance theory of public spending, see ibid., p. 80.

117. Ibid., p. 182.

118. Timothy J. Conlan, Margaret T. Wrightson, and David R. Beam, *Taxing Choices: The Politics of Tax Reform* (Washington: CQ Press, 1990), pp. 19–21.

119. David Stockman also thought substantial tax cuts would require substantial budget cuts because the politicians would have to cut the budgets to avoid national ruin. Stockman, *Triumph of Politics*, p. 68.

120. White and Wildavsky, *The Deficit and the Public Interest*, pp. 159–66.

121. Ibid., pp. 171–80.

122. Stockman, *Triumph of Politics*, p. 262.

123. Quoted in White and Wildavsky, *The Deficit and the Public Interest*, p. 181.

124. Brady and Volden, *Revolving Gridlock*, pp. 86–90. *Congressional Quarterly Almanac*, vol. 37, p. 97.

125. White and Wildavsky, *The Deficit and the Public Interest*, p. 180.

126. Niskanen, *Reaganomics*, p. 11.

127. Sinclair, "Agenda Control," p. 291.

128. Concern about inflation was pervasive. In early 1980, President Carter proposed tightening fiscal policy even though his economic advisers believed a mild recession was in the offing. See Christine D. Romer and David H. Romer, "What Ends Recessions?" NBER Working Paper 4765, National Bureau of Economic Research, Cambridge, MA, June 1994, p. 30.

129. Martin S. Feldstein, *American Economic Policy in the 1980s: A Personal View* (Chicago: University of Chicago Press, 1994), p. 113.

130. Romer and Romer, "What Ends Recessions?" p. 50, indicate that absent this change in monetary policy, the decline in national output would have been half as much as it was in fact. See also Niskanen, *Reaganomics*, p. 228.

131. *Congressional Quarterly Almanac*, vol. 40, p. 89.

132. The recession saw total output go down by 3.5 percent from its prior peak and by 6 percent relative to potential output. See Niskanen, *Reaganomics*, p. 229.

133. See historical table A-3, "Employment Status of the Civilian Noninstitutional Population by Sex and Age, Seasonally Adjusted," Bureau of Labor Statistics, http://www.bls.gov/web/cpseea3.pdf.

134. "Job Performance Ratings for President Reagan," Gallup Poll, Roper Center for Public Opinion Research, http://webapps.ropercenter.uconn.edu/CFIDE/roper/presidential/webroot/presidential_rating_detail.cfm?allRate = True&president Name = Reagan (accessed September 24, 2008).

135. Peterson, *The Price of Federalism*, p. 383.

136. *Congressional Quarterly Almanac*, 97th Cong., 2nd sess., 1982, vol. 38 (Washington: Congressional Quarterly, 1983), p. 9-E.

137. Brady and Volden, *Revolving Gridlock*, pp. 91–93.

138. Reagan faced rebellion in Republican ranks for this. Leading the charge against the bill was Reagan's ally in his 1981 fight for sweeping tax cuts, Rep. Jack F. Kemp (R-NY). On Kemp's side was Gingrich, then only a second-term member. "This is a fight over the heart and soul of the Republican Party," Gingrich said at the time. *Congressional Quarterly Almanac*, vol. 37, p. 29.

139. Brady and Volden, *Revolving Gridlock*, pp. 91–93.

140. Business saw the reductions in the value of depreciation and the investment tax credit. Congress also limited a tax preferences and repealed income shelters for oil and gas companies. Other tax preferences were cut by 15 percent. Congress also eliminated so-called safe-harbor leasing provisions in the 1981 tax bill that allowed firms to sell unused tax breaks. Individuals also paid up. Deductions for health insurance and contributions to corporate pensions were cut. An alternative minimum tax was imposed on some people. Tax collection grew stronger by requiring additional reporting of income, by increasing penalties for noncompliance, and by strengthening Internal Revenue Service enforcement powers. Congress also raised the current 1 percent telephone excise tax to 3 percent and doubled the excise tax on cigarettes from 8 cents to 16 cents a pack. Finally, waiters and waitresses were required to pay their fair share. Restaurants with more than 10 employees were obliged to take 8 percent of their gross income and allocate a share to each employee. The restaurant was required to report that amount under the employee's name to the IRS each year.

The IRS would use the amount reported as a benchmark to measure the accuracy of the amount of tip income reported by the employee. The 1981 tax-rate cuts survived. "Tax Increases Meet Deficit Reduction Target," CQ Electronic Library, *CQ Almanac* online edition, originally published in *CQ Almanac 1982* (Washington: Congressional Quarterly, 1983), http://library.cqpress.com/cqalmanac/cqal82-1163492 (accessed July 3, 2007).

141. White and Wildavsky, *The Deficit and the Public Interest*, pp. 232–33. Donald Regan explained to business groups why the new revenues must come from corporations and the wealthy: "Because of last year's tax and budget cuts, a mistaken impression is abroad that this administration favors only the rich. Business must understand we have to correct this mistaken impression." White and Wildavsky, *The Deficit and the Public Interest*, p. 257.

142. Sen. Ernest Hollings (D-SC) proposed repealing the third year of the 1981 tax cut to increase revenues. The proposal picked up five Republican senators but lost 19 Democrats and failed 32–68. See *Congressional Quarterly Almanac*, vol. 38, pp. 132, 25-S.

143. See Mark A. Smith, *American Business and Political Power: Public Opinion, Elections, and Democracy* (Chicago: University of Chicago Press, 2000), p. 101.

144. Alberto F. Alesina, Rafael Di Tella, and Robert MacCulloch, "Inequality and Happiness: Are Europeans and Americans Different?" Harvard Institute of Economic Research Paper no. 1938, June 2002, http://ssrn.com/abstract=293781.

145. West, *Congress and Economic Policymaking*, p. 91.

146. Ibid., p. 96.

147. Yet actual opinion in their districts about the Reagan cuts was almost exactly the same as opinion in districts whose member voted against the 1982 increases. Grassroots support for the president was slightly less powerful in the districts of those who switched than in the districts whose member continued to support the increases. Ibid., p. 95.

148. Sinclair, "Agenda Control," p. 310.

149. Stockman, *Triumph of Politics*, pp. 401–2.

150. Stockman was called on to "open up the soup kitchen" by California representative Bill Thomas. That meant obtaining the necessary marginal votes to pass a law by giving members on the fence something in exchange for their vote, for example, a $200,000 feasibility study for a water project for their district. See ibid., pp. 221–22.

151. Sinclair, "Agenda Control," pp. 297–98. As political scientist Darrell West remarked, long-term policy revolutions were harder for Reagan than they were for FDR and perhaps, given the short-term factors that inform congressional decisionmaking, no longer possible. West, *Congress and Economic Policymaking*, p. 106.

152. White and Wildavsky, *The Deficit and the Public Interest*, p. 256.

153. Another $1.14 billion was cut from projected spending for Medicaid, the state-federal health care program for the poor. "Congress Votes Cuts in Medicare, Medicaid," CQ Electronic Library, *CQ Almanac* online edition, originally published in *CQ Almanac 1982* (Washington: Congressional Quarterly, 1983), http://library.cqpress.com/cqalmanac/cqal82-1163216 (accessed July 5, 2007).

154. Ibid.

155. U.S. Census Bureau, "Current Population Surveys 1966–2002."

156. The bill's most significant provision, with three-year savings of $4.1 billion, limited inflation adjustments for certain federal retirees. Budget leaders claimed the move was a first step toward controlling automatic increases in federal benefits.

Other major elements of the bill included cuts of $4.2 billion in dairy price supports and $1.9 billion in food stamps during the next three years. "Congress Votes Cuts in Medicare, Medicaid," p. 201.

157. "Balanced Budget Amendment Fails in House," CQ Press Electronic Library, *CQ Almanac* online edition, originally published in *CQ Almanac 1982* (Washington: Congressional Quarterly, 1983), http://library.cqpress.com/cqalmanac/cqal82-1164709 (accessed December 1, 2008).

158. Some thought this failure in Washington would advance the movement to convene a constitutional convention, a legitimate but unused method for amending the Constitution. The movement already had calls for a convention from 32 of the necessary 34 states. "Balanced Budget Amendment," CQ Press Electronic Library, *CQ Almanac* online edition, originally published in *CQ Almanac 1984* (Washington: Congressional Quarterly, 1985), http://library.cqpress.com/cqalmanac/cqal84-1152753 (accessed December 1, 2008).

159. White and Wildavsky, *The Deficit and the Public Interest*, p. 193; and *Congressional Quarterly Almanac*, vol. 37, p. 268.

160. Feldstein, *American Economic Policy*, pp. 40–41; and Stockman, *Triumph of Politics*, p. 216.

161. *Congressional Quarterly Almanac*, vol. 37, p. 117.

162. Reagan supported the Social Security cuts to reduce spending and thereby save the lower tax rates passed in 1981. See "The Federal Budget, 1981–1984 Legislative Overview."

163. Martin Tolchin, "President Pledges to Push Campaign for Budget Plan; Hails an 'Important Step,' " *New York Times*, May 7, 1982.

164. Adam Clymer, "Talk of Social Security Cutbacks Causes Alarm in Ranks of G.O.P.," *New York Times*, May 8, 1982.

165. Martin Tolchin, "Social Security Issue Causing Problems for New Budget," *New York Times*, May 8, 1982.

166. White and Wildavsky, *The Deficit and the Public Interest*, p. 245.

167. See National Commission on Social Security Reform, Executive Order 12335, December 16, 1981, http://www.ssa.gov/history/reports/gspan8.html.

168. White and Wildavsky, *The Deficit and the Public Interest*, p. 315.

169. Chairman Greenspan suggested the commission seek savings in the $150 to $200 billion range, around 14 percent of the projected costs of the programs for 1983 to 1989. The commission also agreed on the size of the long-range problem: 1.8 percent of taxable payroll. Ibid., p. 314.

170. See "Findings and Recommendations," 1983 Greenspan Commission on Social Security Reform, http://www.ssa.gov/history/reports/gspan5.html.

171. White and Wildavsky, *The Deficit and the Public Interest*, p. 323.

172. John F. Cogan, "The Congressional Response to Social Security Surpluses 1935–1994," Essays in Public Policy, Hoover Institution, Stanford, CA, 1998.

173. The revenues from the 1983 tax increase were invested by the Social Security Trust Fund in treasuries and the result was increased consumption rather than investment. See Kent Smetters, "Is the Social Security Trust Fund Worth Anything?" NBER Working Paper 9845, National Bureau of Economic Research, July 2003. Thanks to Peter VanDoren for directing me to this study.

174. Joshua Green, "The Rove Presidency," *Atlantic Monthly*, September 2007.

175. White and Wildavsky, *The Deficit and the Public Interest*, p. 323.

176. Ibid., p. 327.

177. *Congressional Quarterly Almanac*, vol. 37, p. 118.

178. Niskanen, *Reaganomics*, p. 255. Stockman refers to this logic as "backloading." See Stockman, *Triumph of Politics*, pp. 251, 261.

179. White and Wildavsky, *The Deficit and the Public Interest*, p. 121.

180. Daniel J. Elazar, "Appendix C: Is the Federal System Still There?" in Advisory Commission on Intergovernmental Relations, *The Federal Role in the Federal System: The Dynamics of Growth, Vol. 11: Hearings on the Federal Role* (Washington: Government Printing Office, 1980), p. 84.

181. "Reagan's 'New Federalism.' " Daniel Elazar suggests Reagan's view of federalism comported well with the view of James Madison who wrote in Federalist No. 14: "In the first place it is to be remembered that the general government is not to be charged with the whole power of making and administering laws. Its jurisdiction is limited to certain enumerated objects, which concern all the members of the republic, but which are not to be attained by the separate provisions of any. The subordinate governments, which can extend their care to all those other subjects which can be separately provided for, will retain their due authority and activity." Elazar then suggests we might restore a measure of federalism by asking whether a new federal power or national policy actually involves a federal question in Madison's sense. Elazar, "Is the Federal System Still There?" p. 90.

182. J. Edwin Benton, "American Federalism's First Principles and Reagan's New Federalism Policies," *Policy Studies Journal* 13 (March 1985): 569–70. Reagan summarized much of his outlook on federalism in June 1980 in a speech to mayors: "Sometimes I think Congress and Washington regulators lose sight of the fact that Americans live at the local level. This remains true despite four decades of centralization of power and resources at the federal level of government. It is at the local level that their problems occur. And, it is in their individual communities—and not in Washington—that the solutions to these problems will be found. The solutions will be found by mayors like these, and other officials. It is they who best know the unique needs of their separate communities. They are the elected representatives who are most accessible to the people. They are therefore the most knowledgeable and, more important, the most accountable to their constituents. They are in the best position to set and respond to the priorities of their cities—provided they are given the authority and discretion to respond, and greater local access to revenue." Richard S. Williamson, "1980: The Reagan Campaign: Harbinger of a Revitalized Federalism," *Publius* 11 (Summer 1981): 149.

183. Stephen L. Schechter, "The State of American Federalism: 1981," *Publius* 12 (Winter 1983): 1.

184. States would get less money for the programs under the Reagan proposal. For example, the president proposed both giving state and local school districts more control over education and cutting over $106 million in educational aid by consolidating 57 separate school programs into two lump-sum grants. The states also gain more authority over 40 health and social service programs, but they would lose over $2.5 billion in federal aid. In general, funding would be cut by 25 percent, but because of administrative savings by the states, Reagan officials contended that the lower spending "need not result in a reduction of services." Reagan's proposal would reduce federal aid by $2.5 billion in 1982 and by almost $4 billion a year by 1986. The states would have to make up the difference by tightening eligibility requirements, by making their programs more cost efficient, or by reducing payments to recipients. See "Reagan's 'New Federalism.'"

185. Richard L. Cole and Delbert A. Taebel, "The New Federalism: Promises, Programs, and Performance," *Publius* 16 (Winter 1986): 6.

186. Richard S. Williamson, "The 1982 New Federalism Negotiations," *Publius* 13 (Spring 1983): 12.

187. Demetrios Caraley, "Changing Conceptions of Federalism," *Political Science Quarterly* 101 (1986): 60.

188. Schechter, "1981," p. 16.

189. The financing of the turnback was complicated. The turnback would go forward in two stages. Stage one covered FY84 to FY87. During this period, the Treasury Department would administer a trust fund that gave each state an account balance reflecting the federal funds spent on the 40 categorical programs in the state. The states could continue to have the programs administered by the federal government, or they could opt out of one of or all the programs and receive a cash payment to use the funds as they saw fit. The trust fund came from two principal sources: (a) $11 billion out of the $13 billion collected by the federal government in excise taxes on alcohol, telephone, tobacco, and gasoline and (b) approximately $15 billion from the windfall profits tax on oil. Stage two would begin in FY87. The trust fund would have been reduced by 25 percent per year over four years. At the same time, the federal government would have cut excise taxes by 25 percent each year for the states to pick up. For example, the then 8-cent federal tax on a pack of cigarettes would have been reduced by 2 cents in FY87, another 2 cents in FY88, and so on, until the federal government was out of all excise taxes save for 2 cents on a gallon of gasoline (retained as a user fee for the Interstate Highway System). Second, the windfall profits tax would have been phased out by 1991. This was seen as a tax on gasoline, and the states could pick it up easily. Williamson, "The 1982 New Federalism Negotiations," p. 14.

190. Out of approximately $91 billion in grants-in-aid to state and local governments, $19 billion would have become a full federal responsibility (Medicaid), $46.7 billion in programs would have been returned to the states (Aid to Families with Dependent Children, food stamps, and other programs), leaving approximately $25 billion in grants that would have continued as they were under the status quo. Ibid., p. 14.

191. Ibid., p. 11.

192. Stephen B. Farber, "The 1982 New Federalism Negotiations: A View from the States," *Publius* 13 (Spring 1983): 35.

193. Williamson, "The 1982 New Federalism Negotiations," pp. 24–26.

194. J. Edwin Benton, "Economic Considerations and Reagan's New Federalism Swap Proposals," *Publius* 16, no. 2 (Spring 1986): 18.

195. At first Reagan's plan received support from the states. Governor George Busbee of Georgia, chair of the National Governors' Association, said his organization generally supported the president's efforts "to restore balance to the federal-state system" as "a move in the right direction." "Reagan's 'New Federalism,'" http://library.cqpress.com/cqresearcher/cqresrre1981040300 (accessed December 1, 2006).

196. Benton, "Economic Considerations," p. 19.

197. "If state and local governments had assumed fiscal responsibility for the programs destined for transfer to the states under this first turnback proposal and had financed them with tax revenues, it would have necessitated an 18.5 percent increase in state-local taxes in 1982 beyond actual collections." The second turnback proposal "would have necessitated an average state-local per capita tax increase of

$218 (that is, from $1,123 in 1981 to $1,341 in 1982). This would have represented a 19.4 percent increase in state-local tax collections but, more importantly, a considerable increase over 1981 and 1982 levels. . . ." Ibid., pp. 28–31.

198. Williamson, "The 1982 New Federalism Negotiations," pp. 30–31.

199. Caraley, "Changing Conceptions of Federalism," p. 75.

200. Schechter "1981," pp. 3–4.

201. David R.Beam, "After New Federalism, What?" *Policy Studies Journal* 13 (1985), p. 589.

202. Stephen L. Schechter, "The State of American Federalism: 1982," *Publius* 13 (Spring 1983): 8–9.

203. The 1981 budget act reduced federal grant-in-aid expenditures by $6.6 billion, the first in decades. Federal aid as a percentage of total federal spending dropped from its all-time high of 16.8 percent in 1978 to 11.2 percent in 1984. Federal aid as a percentage of state and local receipts fell from 31.7 percent in FY80 to 23.7 percent in FY84. Robert Benenson, "Federalism under Reagan," CQ Electronic Library, CQ Researcher Online, originally published in *Editorial Research Reports 1985*, vol. 1 (Washington: CQ Press, 1985), http://library.cqpress.com/cqresearcher/cqresrre1985052400 (accessed December 1, 2006).

204. Cole and Taebel, "The New Federalism," p. 6.

205. Nathan and Doolittle, "Giving and Taking Away," p. 73.

206. The states responded well and badly to losses in revenue. "In 1983 alone, 38 states raised some form of tax. Even after the economic recovery began, the impact continued. In a study prepared for the U.S. Conference of Mayors, 49 percent of the city officials surveyed said they raised user fees on public services in 1984, 41 percent laid off workers or instituted hiring freezes, 28 percent enacted property tax increases, 40 percent cut services and 11 percent enacted other tax increases." Benenson, "Federalism under Reagan."

207. Pierson, *Dismantling the Welfare State?*, pp. 121–22. Pierson argues also that the New Federalism would have complicated future efforts to intervene in markets and society. It might also have vitiated the political resources of the left, which were concentrated in Washington. It might also have shifted the blame for budget cuts to local administrations. Ibid., p. 156. The Nixon and Ford administrations had coupled spending with block grants to create support for the proposals among state officials. Reagan's proposals changed the focus from federalism to budget issues. Indeed, many thought cutting government spending, not devolution of power, was the point of Reagan's proposals. See Timothy J. Conlon, "Federalism and Competing Values in the Reagan Administration," *Publius* 16 (Winter 1986): 31.

208. Sheldon Richmond, "Examining Reagan's Record on Trade," *Wall Street Journal*, May 10, 1982.

209. John S. DeMott, "In Search of a Trade Policy," *Time*, March 23, 1981.

210. John Sloan, *The Reagan Effect: Economics and Presidential Leadership* (Lawrence: University Press of Kansas, 1999), pp. 197–98. Reagan also used "voluntary" protectionism late in the 1982 midterm campaign. He announced that European steel producers had decided to restrict steel imports to the United States. This agreement precluded a bill in Congress that would have imposed quotas on steel imports. Reagan's sole liberalizing decision in trade policy during his first two years in office involved ending import quotas on shoes from Taiwan and South Korea. Ibid., p. 199.

211. Stockman, *Triumph of Politics*, p. 155.

212. Many Democrats and their labor union allies proposed extensive state control over the economy under the rubric of "industrial policy." Sloan, *The Reagan Effect*, pp. 199–200.

213. Alan I. Abramowitz, "National Issues, Strategic Politicians, and Voting Behavior in the 1980 and 1982 Congressional Elections," *American Journal of Political Science* 28 (November 1984): 711. See also Gary C. Jacobson, *The Politics of Congressional Elections*, 4th ed. (New York: Longman, 1997), p. 142; and "Politics and Issues, 1981–1983," CQ Electronic Library, CQ Voting and Elections Collection, originally published in *Guide to U.S. Elections*, ed. John L. Moore, Jon P. Preimesberger, and David R. Tarr, vol. 1 (Washington: CQ Press, 2001), http://library.cqpress.com/elections/gusel1-152-7223-393089 (accessed December 20, 2006).

214. White and Wildavsky, *The Deficit and the Public Interest*, pp. 204, 299.

215. Abramowitz, "National Issues," p. 717.

216. Jacobson, *The Politics of Congressional Elections*, p. 143.

217. Gary C. Jacobson, "Party Organization and Distribution of Campaign Resources: Republicans and Democrats in 1982," *Political Science Quarterly* 100 (Winter 1985–86): 618.

218. "Budget, Fiscal Year 1982," CQ Electronic Library, CQ Public Affairs Collection, originally published in *Congress and the Nation, 1981–1984*, vol. 6 (Washington: CQ Press, 1985), p. 126. http://library.cqpress.com/cqpac/catn81-0011176436 (accessed December 6, 2006); and "Politics and Issues, 1981–1983."

219. *Congressional Quarterly Almanac*, vol. 38, p. 33b.

220. No member with an ADA score lower than 50 was appointed to the committee. Brady and Volden, *Revolving Gridlock*, pp. 95, 199.

221. Cogan and Muris, "Changes in Domestic Discretionary Spending," p. 97.

222. White and Wildavsky, *The Deficit and the Public Interest*, p. 180.

Chapter 4

1. *Congressional Quarterly Almanac*, 98th Cong., 1st sess., 1983, vol. 39 (Washington: Congressional Quarterly Press, 1984), pp. 425–26. The tax increases were projected to equal $11 and $12 billion in 1984 and 1985 as well as $63 billion in fiscal year 1986. The taxes involved the payroll tax for Social Security, taxes on Social Security benefits, taxes on health insurance premiums, and higher payments for civil service retirement. There were tax breaks too, but they were small compared with the tax increases. Ibid., p. 432.

2. Advisory Commission on Intergovernmental Relations, *Changing Public Attitudes on Governments and Taxes 1988* (Washington: Government Printing Office, 1988), p. 65.

3. Ibid., p. 59.

4. *Congressional Quarterly Almanac*, vol. 39, p. 439.

5. Ibid., p. 444.

6. The following account relies heavily on Jonathan Oberlander, *The Political Life of Medicare* (Chicago: University of Chicago Press, 2003), pp. 120–29. See also Paul Pierson, *Dismantling the Welfare State? Reagan, Thatcher, and the Politics of Retrenchment* (New York: Cambridge University Press, 1994), p. 136.

7. Darrell M. West, *Congress and Economic Policymaking* (Pittsburgh, PA: University of Pittsburgh Press, 1987), p. 31.

8. *Congressional Quarterly Almanac*, 98th Cong., 2nd sess., 1984, vol. 40 (Washington: Congressional Quarterly Press, 1985), pp. 116-B, 109-B, 107-B.

9. Ibid., p. 108-B.

10. Joseph White and Aaron Wildavsky, *The Deficit and the Public Interest: The Search for Responsible Budgeting in the 1980s* (Berkeley: University of California Press, 1989), p. 420.

11. According to Paul O'Neill, treasury secretary in George W. Bush's administration, Richard Cheney once said: "Deficits don't matter. Reagan proved that." Ron Suskind, *The Price of Loyalty: George W. Bush, the White House, and the Education of Paul O'Neill* (New York: Simon & Schuster, 2004), p. 261. That claim might appear to be about their economic effects and hence their political consequences. The 1984 election result supports Cheney's belief.

12. White and Wildavsky, *The Deficit and the Public Interest*, pp. 423–26.

13. Gerald M. Pomper, "The Presidential Election," in *The Election of 1984*, ed. Marlene Michels Pomper (Chatham, NJ: Chatham House, 1985), pp. 60–90, especially 82. See also Scott Keeter, "Public Opinion in 1984," in M. Pomper, *The Election of 1984*, pp. 95–96. Other polls gave Reagan a large lead on the deficit issue throughout 1984. William Schneider, "The November 6 Vote for President: What Did It Mean?" in *The American Elections of 1984*, ed. Austin Ranney (Durham, NC: Duke University Press, 1985), p. 216.

14. *Congressional Quarterly Almanac*, vol. 40, p. 5-B.

15. G. Pomper, "The Presidential Election," p. 67; Keeter, "Public Opinion in 1984," p. 96; and Schneider, "The November 6 Vote for President," p. 231.

16. White and Wildavsky, *The Deficit and the Public Interest*, p. 422.

17. Schneider, "The November 6 Vote for President," p. 205. *Congressional Quarterly Almanac*, vol. 40, pp. 7-B, 13-B, 3-B.

18. Schneider, "The November 6 Vote for President," p. 213.

19. *Congressional Quarterly Almanac*, vol. 40, p. 3-B.

20. Ibid., p. 243.

21. G. Pomper, "The Presidential Election," p. 70.

22. In 1980, surveys found that 78 percent of the public believed the government wasted "a lot of the money we pay in taxes." In 1984, 63 percent held that view. During the same period, the belief that "you can't trust the government in Washington to do right most of the time" dropped from 73 percent to 51 percent. Schneider, "The November 6 Vote for President," p. 228.

23. J. Merrill Shanks and Warren E. Miller, "Policy Direction and Performance Evaluation: Complementary Explanations of the Reagan Elections," *British Journal of Political Science* 20 (April 1990): 161.

24. The proportion who said more government regulation of "the health and safety of working conditions" grew by one-quarter during that period. The number who said that there was too much government regulation of the auto industry dropped by one-third during Reagan's first term. See the measure of the public mood toward spending created by James Stimson of the University of North Carolina, Chapel Hill: http://www.unc.edu/~jstimson/Mood5206.xls. The higher the trend line, the higher is public support for more spending. By 1984, this support for higher domestic spending was greater than at any time since 1973 when the questions first appeared. Support for spending declined for some time before Reagan's election. After 1980, support increased. See Schneider, "The November 6 Vote for President," p. 228.

25. Ibid., p. 160.

26. Ibid., p. 239. See also Shanks and Miller, "Policy Direction," p. 149.

27. Similarly, J. Merrill Shanks and Warren Miller concluded: "Ronald Reagan came into office with a large victory that can be partially attributed to preferences for a more conservative direction in federal policy. He implemented several such changes, to the point where popular preferences about policy change more frequently called for shifts in the liberal (as opposed to conservative) direction, but his 1984 victory was partially due to widespread support for current policies. From this perspective, the Reagan administration seems to have positioned itself fairly close to the political centre of gravity in the autumn of 1984." Schneider, "The November 6 Vote for President," p. 205.

28. "The 1984 election was a vote of approval for the apparent successes of Reagan's policies and administration, but it was not a mandate for further policy changes in a conservative direction." Shanks and Miller, "Policy Direction," pp. 227, 229.

29. David Primo, *Rules and Restraint: Government Spending and the Design of Institutions* (Chicago: University of Chicago Press), p. 112.

30. *Congressional Quarterly Almanac*, 99th Cong., 1st sess., 1985, vol. 41 (Washington: Congressional Quarterly, 1986), p. 459.

31. Jasmine Farrier, *Passing the Buck: Congress, the Budget, and Deficits* (Lexington: University of Kentucky Press, 2004), pp. 83–84.

32. Ibid., p. 125.

33. Ibid., pp. 98–99.

34. White and Wildavsky, *The Deficit and the Public Interest*, pp. 445–46.

35. Farrier, *Passing the Buck*, p. 37; and *Congressional Quarterly Almanac*, vol. 41, p. 425. The new law set maximum allowable federal budget deficits as follows: for FY86, $171.9 billion; FY87, $144 billion; FY88, $108 billion; FY89, $72 billion; FY90, $36 billion; and FY91, zero. Budget resolutions could not exceed these levels and had to contain reconciliation instructions to achieve the targets. *Congressional Quarterly Almanac*, vol. 41, p. 459. The courts quickly invalidated this procedure for automatic cuts. GRH empowered the administration's Office of Management and Budget and the Congressional Budget Office each year to review progress toward meeting the law's deficit target. The sums OMB and CBO believed were necessary would be averaged and then reviewed by the General Accounting Office, which would inform the president whether automatic cuts were necessary. The courts concluded that "GAO was a congressional, not an executive branch, agency that had no right under the doctrine of separation of powers to order the president to do anything." "The Federal Budget, 1985–1988 Legislative Overview," CQ Electronic Library, CQ Public Affairs Collection, originally published in *Congress and the Nation, 1985–1988*, vol. 7 (Washington: CQ Press, 1989), http://library.cqpress.com/cqpac/catn85-0012178814 (accessed January 31, 2007).

36. White and Wildavsky, *The Deficit and the Public Interest*, p. 460.

37. The exclusions included interest on the debt, Social Security, Aid to Families with Dependent Children, child nutrition, Medicaid, veterans' pensions and compensation, food stamps, and the Earned Income Tax Credit. White and Wildavsky, *The Deficit and the Public Interest*, pp. 455–56.

38. Primo, *Rules and Restraint*, p. 112. See Figure 6.1 with targets and actual deficits under GRH.

39. Ibid., pp. 109–11. White and Wildavsky, *The Deficit and the Public Interest*, p. 460.

40. White and Wildavsky, *The Deficit and the Public Interest*, p. 4.

41. "Text of Statement on Economic Matters Adopted by House Democratic Caucus," *New York Times*, April 9, 1981.

42. Timothy J. Conlan, Margaret T. Wrightson, and David R. Beam, *Taxing Choices: The Politics of Tax Reform* (Washington: CQ Press, 1990), p. 146.

43. A caveat is in order here. Shifting the burden of taxation to those not covered by the tax preference might increase the intensity of their opposition to the policy status quo, which could equal or exceed the lowered level of resistance bought by the tax preference.

44. W. Lance Bennett and Erik Asard, "The Marketplace of Ideas: The Rhetoric and Politics of Tax Reform in Sweden and the United States," *Polity* 28 (Autumn 1995): 6.

45. Conlan, Wrightson, and Beam, *Taxing Choices*, p. 239.

46. Packwood said: "The lower we can get those rates, the better off we are going to be. And, if we can get it down to 25 percent, there will be a sea change in the debate over the political implications of deductions. . . . People will say, 'At that rate, I don't mind giving a quarter of my income to the federal government so long as I can keep the other three-quarters.' " Ibid., p. 164.

47. But tax preferences increase the ambit of the government. Tax preferences grew alongside the growth of government in the 1960s and 1970s.

48. White and Wildavsky, *The Deficit and the Public Interest*, p. 468.

49. Conlon, Wrightson, and Beam, *Taxing Choices*, p. 35.

50. Ibid., p. 95.

51. Bradley did not set out to soak the rich, largely for lack of public support. He said, "The 1981 tax law demonstrated clearly that many Americans are concerned about the tax treatment of the wealthy—probably because they hope to be wealthy themselves someday." Ibid., p. 38.

52. Ibid., p. 49.

53. "Tax Policy, 1985–1988 Legislative Overview," CQ Electronic Library, CQ Public Affairs Collection, originally published in *Congress and the Nation, 1985–1988*, vol. 7 (Washington: CQ Press, 1989), http://library.cqpress.com/cqpac/catn85-0012178862 (accessed April 24, 2007).

54. White and Wildavsky, *The Deficit and the Public Interest*, p. 476.

55. David R. Beam, Timothy J. Conlan, and Margaret Wrightson, "Solving the Riddle of Tax Reform: Party Competition and the Politics of Ideas," *Political Science Quarterly* 105 (Summer 1990): 205.

56. White and Wildavsky, *The Deficit and the Public Interest*, pp. 480–81.

57. West, *Congress and Economic Policymaking*, pp. 135–37.

58. Conlan, Wrightson, and Beam, *Taxing Choices*, p. 146.

59. Ibid., pp. 157–58.

60. Ibid., p. 166; and White and Wildavsky, *The Deficit and the Public Interest*, pp. 484–88.

61. West, *Congress and Economic Policymaking*, p. 140.

62. "Tax Law Overhaul, 1985–1986 Legislative Chronology," CQ Electronic Library, CQ Public Affairs Collection, originally published in *Congress and the Nation, 1985–1988*, vol. 7 (Washington: CQ Press, 1989), http://library.cqpress.com/cqpac/catn85-0012178867 (accessed April 24, 2007).

63. Conlan, Wrightson, and Beam, *Taxing Choices*, p. 3.

64. "Tax Law Overhaul."

65. Their effective rates were expected to rise from as low as 23 percent to as high as 41 percent. "Tax Policy, 1985–1988 Legislative Overview."

66. Beam and others, "Solving," p. 197.

67. Conlan, Wrightson, and Beam, *Taxing Choices*, p. 2.

68. "Tax Policy, 1985–1988 Legislative Overview."

69. White and Wildavsky, *The Deficit and the Public Interest*, p. 496.

70. Aaron Wildavsky, "President Reagan as Political Strategist," in *Elections in America*, ed. Kay Lehman Schlozman (Boston: Allen & Unwin, 1987), p. 227.

71. White and Wildavsky, *The Deficit and the Public Interest*, p. 503. But not everyone agreed that Reagan was essential. They argue that Reagan did not mobilize a coalition behind the reform. Many congressional Republicans did not like the reform idea and doubted it would attract new voters to the GOP. They found in their districts much doubt about the law. Beam and others, "Solving," p. 200.

72. Bennett and Asard, "The Marketplace of Ideas," p. 14.

73. Ibid., p. 7.

74. Conlan, Wrightson, and Beam, *Taxing Choices*, p. 239. Another survey indicated that tax reform changed little in partisan politics. Younger voters and those who reported improved family finances tended to support the measure; support was also correlated with increased education and income. At the same time, union members and working-class individuals did not support tax reform. The numbers were not strong enough in general to suggest the issue might move voters into the Republican column. "It may be that tax changes are simply too technical and complicated to generate the intensity that traditionally has been associated with realigning issues." Darrell M. West, "Public Assessments of Tax Reform," *Western Political Quarterly* 43 (September 1990): 653–57.

75. Gary C. Jacobson and Samuel Kernell, "National Forces in the 1986 House Elections," *Legislative Studies Quarterly* 15 (February 1990): 65–66.

76. 1986 was in many ways a typical Senate election year. In such races, the president's party generally loses eight Senate seats in the midterm election of a president's second term. Overall, the Democrats gained eight Senate seats in 1986. "Congressional Elections of 1986: Assessing Victory and Explaining the Results," CQ Electronic Library, CQ Voting and Elections Collection, originally published in Paul R. Abramson, John H. Aldrich, and David W. Rohde, *Change and Continuity in the 1984 Elections* (Washington: CQ Press, 1987), http://library.cqpress.com/elections/cc1984-124-6516-380756 (accessed March 27, 2007). See also "The Political Year, 1986," CQ Electronic Library, CQ Voting and Elections Collection, originally published in *Congress and the Nation, 1985–1988*, vol. 7 (Washington: CQ Press, 1989), http://library.cqpress.com/elections/catn85-0012178157 (accessed March 27, 2007).

77. "Congressional Elections of 1986: Outcomes," CQ Electronic Library, CQ Voting and Elections Collection, originally published in Abramson, Aldrich, and Rohde, *Change and Continuity in the 1984 Elections*, http://library.cqpress.com/elections/cc1984-124-6516-380750 (accessed March 27, 2007).

78. "The Federal Budget, 1985–1988 Legislative Overview."

79. "Although the range of contending causes for the 1987 crash differs from that for 1929, again the evidence does not point unambiguously to any simple explanation of the timing and magnitude of the price fluctuations. What is notable is that, by contrast with 1929, the crash of 1987 is not associated with a subsequent recession. The financial system continued to function—there was no collapse." Roy E. Bailey, *The Economics of Financial Markets* (New York: Cambridge University Press, 2005), p. 240.

80. "The Federal Budget, 1985–1988 Legislative Overview."

81. See Gallup Brain, "Stock Market Crash," survey dates October 22–23, 1987, *Newsweek*. Available at http://institution.gallup.com

82. "The Federal Budget, 1985–1988 Legislative Overview."

83. Ibid.

84. See "Job Performance Ratings for President Reagan," Gallup Poll, Roper Center for Public Opinion Research, http://webapps.ropercenter.uconn.edu/CFIDE/roper/presidential/webroot/presidential_rating_detail.cfm?allRate = True&president Name = Reagan.

85. Paul J. Quirk, "The Election," in *The Elections of 1988*, ed. Michael Nelson (Washington: CQ Press, 1989), p. 85.

86. Little changed in Congress. In the Senate, Democrats won 19 of the 33 races, maintaining the 55–45 majority they had seized in the 1986 elections. Bush became the first candidate since John Kennedy to win the presidency while his party lost House seats. In the House, stability reigned: 98 percent of the members seeking reelection won. Only 6 of 408 incumbents on the ballot lost, 4 Republicans and 2 Democrats. The Democrats picked up a net of 2 seats, putting the partisan lineup in the House at 260 Democrats and 175 Republicans. "Politics and Issues, 1987–1989," CQ Electronic Library, CQ Voting and Elections Collection, originally published in John L. Moore, Jon P. Preimesberger, and David R. Tarr, eds., *Guide to U.S. Elections*, vol. 1 (Washington: CQ Press, 2001), http://library.cqpress.com/elections/gusel1 152-7223-393099 (accessed March 29, 2007).

87. The same proportion of the electorate expected him to break his pledge and ask for new taxes. Gerald M. Pomper, "The Presidential Election," in *The Election of 1988: Reports and Interpretations* (Chatham, NJ: Chatham House, 1989), p. 150.

88. "The Political Year, 1988," CQ Electronic Library, CQ Voting and Elections Collection, originally published in *Congress and the Nation, 1985–1988*, vol. 7 (Washington: CQ Press, 1989), http://library.cqpress.com/elections/catn85-0012178169 (accessed March 29, 2007); and Quirk, "The Election," p. 74.

89. Jean Bethke Elshtain, "Issues and Themes in the 1988 Campaign," in *The Elections of 1988*, ed. Michael Nelson (Washington: CQ Press, 1989), p. 123.

90. Geoffrey Layman, *The Great Divide: Religious and Cultural Conflict in American Party Politics* (New York: Columbia University Press, 2001), pp. 141–43.

91. Ibid., pp. 171, 173.

92. Roger Finke and Rodney Stark, *The Churching of America, 1776–2005: Winners and Losers in Our Religious Economy* (New Brunswick, NJ: Rutgers University Press, 2005), p. 246.

93. The National Economic Commission was created as part of the deficit reduction agreement in 1987. The panel's membership was bipartisan (the cochairs were Robert S. Strauss, a former chair of the Democratic National Committee and former U.S. trade representative, and former transportation secretary Drew Lewis, a Republican) and was supposed to bridge partisan and ideological differences on the budget deficit and related issues. In the event, the meetings and reports of the commission ended up reflecting rather than reconciling those differences. Bush said the group sought to raise taxes. Democrats decried his stand but offered little in the way of alternatives. This commission was an idea whose time did not come. "The Federal Budget, 1989–1992 Legislative Overview," CQ Electronic Library, CQ Public Affairs Collection, originally published in *Congress and the Nation, 1989–1992*, vol. 8 (Washington: CQ Press, 1993), http://library.cqpress.com/cqpac/catn89-0000013470 (accessed January 31, 2007).

94. Ibid.

95. The agreement also foresaw $5.3 billion in "new revenues" whose source was not specified. Congress spent the next seven months trying to translate the agreement into a budget reconciliation bill. They failed to hit the $100 billion Gramm-Rudman target, and $16.2 billion in automatic spending cuts were triggered in mid-October. The final reconciliation bill took back part of those automatic cuts, but about one-third remained so Congress could claim budget savings of around $15 billion. Ibid.

96. Janet Hook, "President's Hill Troops Have Mutinied Whenever He's Issued Budget Orders," *CQ Weekly Online*, September 28, 1990, pp. 3096–97, http://library.cqpress.com/cqweekly/WR101401489 (accessed February 13, 2007).

97. Ibid.

98. Ibid.

99. Ibid.

100. "The Federal Budget, 1989–1992 Legislative Overview."

101. George Hager, "Outline Begins to Take Shape as Deadlines Come and Go," *CQ Weekly Online*, September 14, 1990, pp. 2895–98, http://library.cqpress.com/cqweekly/WR101401366 (accessed February 13, 2007). See also *Congressional Quarterly Almanac*, 97th Cong., 1st sess., 1989, vol. 37 (Washington: Congressional Quarterly, 1990), p. 149.

102. See Pierson, *Dismantling the Welfare State*, p. 139.

103. Janet Hook, "The Selling of a Budget Deal: Trial by Fire for Leaders," *CQ Weekly Online*, September 14, 1990, pp. 2893–94, http://library.cqpress.com/cqweekly/WR101401364 (accessed February 13, 2007).

104. George Hager, "Outline Begins to Take Shape."

105. Pamela Fessler, "Tensions Build among Rank and File as Budget Talks Go Down to the Wire," *CQ Weekly Online*, September 28, 1990, pp. 3094–95, http://library.cqpress.com/cqweekly/WR101401488 (accessed February 13, 2007).

106. Farrier, *Passing the Buck*, p. 155. OMB gained new powers related to discretionary spending caps, retained its sequestration authority, and was empowered to score congressional spending during the budget process. Ibid., p. 37. OMB was chosen over CBO, even though OMB was thought to be more partisan and less reliable. In that way, Congress delegated "enforcement provisions to outside and opposition-party agents arguably beyond the easy control of majority party leaders." Ibid., pp. 130–31.

107. Primo, *Rules and Restraint*, p. 113.

108. David Brady and Craig Volden, *Revolving Gridlock*, 2nd ed. (Boulder, CO: Westview Press, 2006), p. 103.

109. "The Federal Budget, 1989–1992 Legislative Overview."

110. Janet Hook, "The Selling of a Budget Deal: Trial by Fire for Leaders."

111. Farrier, *Passing the Buck*, p. 137.

112. Brady and Volden, *Revolving Gridlock*, pp. 103–5.

113. Ibid.

114. Adapted from "Congressional Elections of 1990: National and Local Influences," CQ Electronic Library, CQ Voting and Elections Collection, originally published in Paul R. Abramson, John H. Aldrich, and David W. Rohde, *Change and Continuity in the 1988 Elections* (Washington: CQ Press, 1991), http://library.cqpress.com/elections/cc1988-126-6534-381035 (accessed September 5, 2007).

115. I will return to ethics in the next chapter.

116. Adapted from "Congressional Elections of 1990: Assessing Victory and Explaining the Results," CQ Electronic Library, CQ Voting and Elections Collection, originally published in Abramson, Aldrich, and Rohde, *Change and Continuity in the 1988 Elections*, http://library.cqpress.com/elections/cc1988-126-6534-381030 (accessed September 5, 2007). The three big states with Republican governors where the president campaigned most intensively went badly. The GOP lost the gubernatorial election in Florida (where Bush visited three times) and in Texas (where he spent the last three days of the campaign). They retained the office in California. However, the president's efforts did not help Republicans all that much. Adapted from "Congressional Elections of 1990: National and Local Influences," CQ Electronic Library, CQ Voting and Elections Collection, originally published in Abramson, Aldrich, and Rohde, *Change and Continuity in the 1988 Elections*, http://library.cqpress.com/elections/cc1988-126-6534-381035 (accessed September 5, 2007).

117. Brady and Volden quote a Bush OMB official: "We knew if he was going to do anything for the environment and education and keep the Reaganites we would have to figure out how to do it without adding to the budget." Also, the Reaganites "never trusted us so we had to be especially careful on how we created a kinder, gentler America." Bush thus looked to do things off budget like the Clean Air Amendments and the Americans with Disabilities Act and a minimum wage increase. Brady and Volden, *Revolving Gridlock*, pp. 99–100.

118. From 1980 to 1990, the political mood of the nation shifted toward favoring more spending by government. The rise was not as steep as an earlier increase in the 1950s that peaked in 1961, but it was significant. Updated from James A. Stimson, *Public Opinion in America: Moods, Cycles, and Swings*, 2nd ed. (Boulder, CO: Westview Press, 1999).

119. Bush promised that the federal government would tighten environmental regulations, extend Medicaid coverage, subsidize child care, spend more on Head Start, subsidize the cost of college, and improve primary and secondary education. In practice, Bush signed a new civil rights bill, a new clean air bill, a disabled Americans bill, a transportation bill, and a revival of economic regulations. As Steven Skowronek observes, Bush "went out of his way to make it clear that he had commitments on all sides of the issues." Stephen Skowronek, *The Politics Presidents Make* (Cambridge, MA: Harvard University Press, 1993), pp. 434–35.

120. Walter Dean Burnham, "The Reagan Heritage," in *The Election of 1988: Reports and Interpretations* (Chatham, NJ: Chatham House, 1989), p. 1.

121. David Stockman, *The Triumph of Politics: How the Reagan Revolution Failed* (New York: Harper & Row, 1986), p. 68.

122. Eric Patashnik, "Budgets and Fiscal Policy," in *Institutions of American Democracy: The Legislative Branch*, Institutions of American Democracy Series (New York: Oxford University Press, 2005), pp. 390–91.

123. John F. Cogan and Timothy J. Muris, "Changes in Domestic Discretionary Spending during the Reagan Years," in John F. Cogan, Timothy J. Muris, and Allen Schick, *The Budget Puzzle: Understanding Federal Spending* (Stanford, CA: Stanford University Press, 1994), p. 80.

124. Ibid., pp. 96–97. Money appropriated by Congress is not the only source of budgetary resources for an agency. During the 1980s, for example, Congress switched some agencies from public revenues to users fees. The Patent and Trademark Office consumed slightly less budget authority in 1989 than in 1981. However, its actual spending was 73 percent higher in 1989. The additional money came from fees from

applications, that is, user fees. Congress directed other agencies and programs to do similar mechanisms. The Agricultural Stabilization and Conservation Service lost all its budget authority and yet experienced an 80 percent increase in its outlays during the Reagan years. The increase came from user fees and transfers from the Commodity Credit Corporation, the core of the government's farm subsidy programs. As such, the spending on the ASCS changed from the government's discretionary budget to its mandatory spending; it became an entitlement. Ibid., p. 84.

125. Ibid., p. 102.

126. Ibid., p. 100.

127. Ibid., p. 103.

128. Some of the increases reflected emerging issues of the time: immigration concerns led to the Immigration and Naturalization Service increases, drug abuse and AIDS, and the need for more revenues benefited (ironically given Reagan's hopes) the budgets of the Internal Revenue Service. Ibid., pp. 98–99.

129. Ibid., p. 80.

130. Martin Anderson, *Revolution: The Reagan Legacy* (Stanford: Hoover Press Publication, 1990), p. 178.

131. Ibid., p. 101.

132. Ibid.

133. Ibid., p. 102.

134. Ibid., pp. 80, 102.

135. Ibid., p. 178.

136. Pierson, *Dismantling the Welfare State?* pp. 137–38.

137. Cogan and Muris, "Changes in Domestic Discretionary Spending," p. 97. The "other means" mentioned in the text are "sources of budgetary resources that are not reflected in or accurately measured by appropriated budget authority." Ibid., p. 82. Examples of such funding include trust funds, proprietary receipts and transfers from other programs. For an extended discussion of such funding, see ibid., pp. 83–87.

138. Anderson, *Revolution*, p. 116.

139. The last Carter budget foresaw steady increases in government revenue culminating in taxes taking 24 percent of GNP in 1986. The Reagan people saw revenue dropping to 19.3 percent by the 1984 fiscal year. William A. Niskanen, *Reaganomics: An Insider's Account of the Policies and the People* (New York: Oxford University Press, 1988). p. 11; and Wildavsky, "President Reagan as Political Strategist," p. 225.

140. Niskanen, *Reaganomics*, p. 106.

141. Ibid., as well as Christine D. Romer and David H. Romer, "What Ends Recessions?" NBER Working Paper 4765, National Bureau of Economic Research, Cambridge, MA, June 1994.

142. Niskanen, *Reaganomics*, p. 313.

143. Thomas E. Mann, "Thinking about the Reagan Years," in *Looking Back on the Reagan Presidency*, ed. Larry Berman (Baltimore: Johns Hopkins University Press, 1990), p. 28.

144. Niskanen, *Reaganomics*, p. 71.

145. Ibid., p. 326.

146. The Economic Bill of Rights comprised constitutional limits on the income tax, a line-item presidential veto, a balanced-budget constitutional amendment, and a constitutional amendment prohibiting the federal government from imposing wage and price controls. See Anderson, *Revolution*, pp. 116–20.

147. "Line-Item Veto," CQ Press Electronic Library, *CQ Almanac* online edition, originally published in *CQ Almanac 1984* (Washington: Congressional Quarterly, 1985), http://library.cqpress.com/cqalmanac/cqal84-1152340 (accessed December 1, 2008).

148. "Line-Item Veto Fails," CQ Press Electronic Library, *CQ Almanac* online edition, originally published in *CQ Almanac 1985* (Washington: Congressional Quarterly, 1986), http://library.cqpress.com/cqalmanac/cqal85-1146881 (accessed December 1, 2008).

149. See Stimson, *Public Opinion in America*, http://www.unc.edu/~jstimson/Mood5206.xls, especially the years 1980 to 1990.

150. Christopher Ellis and James A. Stimson, "On Conservatism in America," paper prepared for the Annual Meetings of the American Political Science Association, September 2, 2007, Figure 8, p. 20.

151. "The Federal Budget, 1985–1988 Legislative Overview."

152. A word of caution should be offered here. As noted in the text, the Reagan budgets after 1981 were "dead on arrival" on Capitol Hill and thus stood no chance of actually being enacted. It is possible that if Reagan's cuts in programs were likely to be enacted and the administration thus held politically responsible for the consequences, the president would not have proposed such cuts.

153. Niskanen, *Reaganomics*, p. 27. See also Stockman: "The Republican quarrel with the American welfare state is over. . . . GOP politicians want it for their constituents no less than the Democrats do." Stockman, *Triumph of Politics*, p. 401.

154. "The Federal Budget, 1985–1988 Legislative Overview." David Stockman (and others in the White House) were interested in cutting back the welfare state but "536 politicians who had actually been elected by the voters" sought incremental constraints. See Stockman, *Triumph of Politics*, p. 277.

155. Martin Anderson remarks: "The structure of economic interest groups in this country has produced a fiscal stalemate. Our political institutions are unable to override the combined political power of Americans with special economic interests, even though taking the national point of view would benefits almost all of us. The current rules of the economic political game make it impossible." Anderson, *Revolution*, p. 184. A later analysis of social welfare programs argued that the groups that benefited from them precluded cutbacks. See Pierson, *Dismantling the Welfare State?* p. 165.

156. Stockman, *Triumph of Politics*, p. 391.

157. "President R. Reagan's Fiscal Year 1986 Budget Message," in *Historic Documents of 1985* (Washington: CQ Press, 1986), http://library.cqpress.com/cqpac/hsdc85-0001141066 (accessed April 24, 2007).

Chapter 5

1. Adapted from "Congressional Elections of 1992: Candidates' Resources and Outcomes," CQ Electronic Library, CQ Voting and Elections Collection, originally published in Paul R. Abramson, John H. Aldrich, and David W. Rohde, *Change and Continuity in the 1992 Elections* (Washington: CQ Press, 1995), http://library.cqpress.com/elections/cc1992-128-6548-381293 (accessed September 10, 2007). The average share of the vote for all incumbents was 61.7 percent in 1974; in 1980 it was 65.5 percent. The share then continued to grow, peaking at 68.2 percent in 1986 and 1988. The number of elections where congressional incumbents faced no opposition

also rose during this period. This rise in vote share thus understates the increasing success of incumbents on election day.

2. Albert D. Cover, "One Good Term Deserves Another: The Advantage of Incumbency in Congressional Elections," *American Journal of Political Science* 21 (August 1977): 523–41.

3. Adapted from "Congressional Elections of 1992: Candidates' Resources and Outcomes."

4. Ibid.

5. See the relevant years of data from the National Election Studies archive: Table 5A.1, "Trust the Federal Government"; Table 5A.2, "Is the Government Run for the Benefit of All"; Table 5A.3, "Do People in Government Waste Tax Money"; Table 5A.4, "Are Government Officials Crooked"; and Table 5A.5, "Trust in Government Index," http://www.electionstudies.org/nesguide/gd-index.htm#5.

6. Jean Bethke Elshtain, "Issues and Themes in the 1992 Presidential Election: Spiral of Delegitimation or New Social Covenant?" CQ Electronic Library, CQ Voting and Elections Collection, originally published in *The Elections of 1992*, ed. Michael Nelson (Washington: CQ Press, 1993), http://library.cqpress.com/elections/elec92-131-6643-382495 (accessed September 14, 2007).

7. "Speaker Wright's Alleged Violations," CQ Press Electronic Library, *CQ Almanac* online edition, originally published in *CQ Almanac 1989* (Washington: Congressional Quarterly, 1990), http://library.cqpress.com/cqalmanac/cqal89-851-25637-1137003 (accessed December 23, 2008). The violations included accepting improper gifts, failing to disclose income and gifts, exceeding the limit on outside earned income, and receiving favors that might influence his performance of public duties.

8. "Wright Becomes First Speaker to Resign," CQ Press Electronic Library, *CQ Almanac* online edition, originally published in *CQ Almanac 1989* (Washington: Congressional Quarterly, 1990), http://library.cqpress.com/cqalmanac/cqal89-1137757 (accessed December 23, 2008). Wright's fall reflected political as well as ethical weaknesses. He had tried to centralize authority in the Office of the Speaker, thereby alienating many committee chairs of his own party. When Wright came under attack for ethical issues, he found few defenders among his own party caucus. See Nicol C. Rae, *Conservative Reformers: The Republican Freshmen and the Lessons of the 104th Congress* (Armonk, NY: M. E. Sharpe, 1998), p. 19.

9. "Rep. Tony Coelho Quits, Leaving Whip Position," CQ Press Electronic Library, *CQ Almanac* online edition, originally published in *CQ Almanac 1989* (Washington: Congressional Quarterly, 1990), http://library.cqpress.com/cqalmanac/cqal89-1137775 (accessed December 23, 2008).

10. They earned much less from their loans than they were required to pay to attract new funding. When they failed, their customers' assets were largely backed by federal deposit insurance; by 1980, experts estimated the federal government would need to pay $60 billion to cover losses in the industry. "Aid for Savings & Loans," CQ Press Electronic Library, *CQ Almanac* online edition, originally published in *CQ Almanac 1981* (Washington: Congressional Quarterly, 1982), http://library.cqpress.com/cqalmanac/cqal81-1171947 (accessed December 23, 2008).

11. "Lincoln Savings Scandal Examined in Hearings," CQ Press Electronic Library, *CQ Almanac* online edition, originally published in *CQ Almanac 1989* (Washington: Congressional Quarterly, 1990), http://library.cqpress.com/cqalmanac/cqal89-1138250 (accessed December 23, 2008). See also "Politics and Issues, 1991–1993," CQ Electronic Library, CQ Voting and Elections Collection, originally published in *Guide*

to U.S. Elections, ed. John L. Moore, Jon P. Preimesberger, and David R. Tarr, vol. 1 (Washington: CQ Press, 2001). http://library.cqpress.com/elections/gusel1-152-7223-393108 (accessed September 11, 2007).

12. "Indictments, Convictions Plague Congress," CQ Press Electronic Library, *CQ Almanac* online edition, originally published in *CQ Almanac 1993* (Washington: Congressional Quarterly, 1994), http://library.cqpress.com/cqalmanac/cqal93-1104620 (accessed December 23, 2008).

13. Adapted from "Congressional Elections of 1992: Outcomes." CQ Electronic Library, CQ Voting and Elections Collection, originally published in Paul R. Abramson, John H. Aldrich, and David W. Rohde, *Change and Continuity in the 1992 Elections* (Washington: CQ Press, 1995). http://library.cqpress.com/elections/cc1992-128-6548-381282 (accessed September 10, 2007
One might add to this list of wrongdoing the Abscam scandal of the early 1980s. This scandal involved the exposure of bribe taking by several members of Congress that resulted in the first expulsion of a member since the Civil War. "Politics and Issues, 1989–1991," CQ Electronic Library, CQ Voting and Elections Collection, originally published in *Guide to U.S. Elections*, ed. John L. Moore, Jon P. Preimesberger, and David R. Tarr. (Washington: CQ Press, 2001), http://library.cqpress.com/elections/gusel1-152-7223-393104 (accessed September 5, 2007).

14. Ibid. Limiting how long an elected official could hold office was an idea as old as the republic. Several of the original states limited the tenure of their governors, in part because they feared a strong executive. The Articles of Confederation had limited the terms of delegates to the Continental Congress. An early version of the Constitution also limited the terms of House members. Alexander Hamilton argued at the Constitutional Convention against requiring rotation for the presidency. Anti-Federalists criticized the absence of rotation in their unsuccessful effort to prevent ratification of the Constitution.

15. Ibid.

16. See Thad Kousser, *Term Limits and the Dismantling of State Legislative Professionalism* (New York: Cambridge University Press, 2005).

17. "The Political Year, 1990," CQ Electronic Library, CQ Voting and Elections Collection, originally published in *Congress and the Nation, 1989–1992*, vol. 8 (Washington: CQ Press, 1993), http://library.cqpress.com/elections/catn89-0001359051 (accessed September 5, 2007).

18. The relevant Congresses were the 91st (1969–1971), 93rd (1973–1975), and 97th (1981–1983).

19. Douglas L. Koopman, *Hostile Takeover: The House Republican Party, 1980–1995* (Lanham, MD: Rowman & Littlefield, 1996), pp. 11–12. Gingrich also had some luck. The potential GOP leaders ahead of him in the leadership group departed for the Senate or the administration.

20. Nicol Rae, *The Decline and Fall of Liberal Republicans: 1952 to the Present* (New York: Oxford University Press, 1989), pp. 20–21; and William F. Connelly Jr. and John J. Pitney Jr., *Congress' Permanent Minority?: Republicans in the U.S. House* (Lanham, MD: Rowman & Littlefield, 1994), pp. 153–73.

21. Koopman, *Hostile Takeover*, p. 16.

22. "Presidential Elections of 1992 and 1996: Clinton's Election and Reelection," CQ Electronic Library, CQ Voting and Elections Collection, originally published in John L. Moore, Jon P. Preimesberger, and David R. Tarr, eds., *Congressional Quarterly's*

Guide to U.S. Elections, vol. 1 (Washington: CQ Press, 2001), http://library .cqpress.com/elections/gusel1-152-7225-393237 (accessed September 17, 2007).

23. "The Political Year, 1992," CQ Electronic Library, CQ Voting and Elections Collection, originally published in *Congress and the Nation, 1989–1992*, vol. 8 (Washington: CQ Press, 1993), http://library.cqpress.com/elections/catn89-0001359074 (accessed September 11, 2007).

24. Sam Riley, *Biographical Dictionary of American Newspaper Columnists* (Westport, CT: Greenwood Press, 1995), pp. 45–46.

25. R. J. Barilleaux and R. E. Adkins, "The 1992 Nominations: Process and Patterns," in *The Elections of 1992*, ed. M. Nelson (Washington: CQ Press, 1993), http:// library.cqpress.com/elections/elec92-131-6640-382404 (accessed January 5, 2009).

26. See "Dr. Whitehead and the First Amendment," *Washington Post*, December 22, 1972.

27. One example involved the recent fall of the Soviet Union and subsequent liberation of its proxy states in Eastern Europe. Buchanan also said that "the central organizing principle of this republic is freedom," which he contraposed to Al Gore's view that the organizing principle should be the environment. "Republican National Convention: Buchanan Urges His 'Brigades' to Stand beside President," *CQ Weekly Online*, August 22, 1992, pp. 2543–44, http://library.cqpress.com/cqweekly/ WR102408070 (accessed January 5, 2009). The word "freedom" appears one other time in regard to "freedom of choice for religious schools." At that time, proponents of freedom of choice in schools hoped parents could choose to send children to schools not run by the government, including secular and church-related institutions.

28. The speech also hints at protectionism as a way to say the jobs of "our people."

29. Paul J. Quirk and Jon K. Dalager, "The 1992 Presidential Election: A 'New Democrat' and a New Kind of Presidential Campaign," CQ Electronic Library, CQ Voting and Elections Collection, originally published in *The Elections of 1992*, ed. Michael Nelson (Washington: CQ Press, 1993), http://library.cqpress.com/elections/ elec92-131-6641-382464 (accessed September 17, 2007). Perot appeared to be an outsider but was not in fact. He "had made his fortune by gaining rights to a computer accounting system for government health programs, and it was only his behind-the-scenes lobbying that prompted the Nixon administration to halt a government battle for control of the computer system. "Clinton's Election and Reelection."

30. "The Political Year, 1992."

31. I. M. Destler, *American Trade Politics* (Washington: Peterson Institute, 2006), p. 200.

32. Quirk and Dalager. "The 1992 Presidential Election."

33. "The Political Year, 1992."

34. Clinton also won the eastern states and most of the Midwest except for Indiana, the home of Vice President Dan Quayle. Clinton's appeal to the middle class also yielded dividends. The Democrats in 1992 made deep inroads into the suburban vote. In 1988, Michael Dukakis had carried 6 of the 28 largest suburban counties across the country. In 1992, Clinton carried three times as many. Ibid.

35. Geoffrey Layman, *The Great Divide: Religious and Cultural Conflict in American Party Politics* (New York: Columbia University Press, 2001), p. 188.

36. Ibid., p. 190.

37. Adapted from "Congressional Elections of 1992: Candidates' Resources and Outcomes." See also Marjorie Randon Hershey, "Congressional Elections," *The Election of 1992* (Chatham, NJ: Chatham House Publishers, 1993), pp. 173–74. Other statistics

suggested continuity rather than revolt against the insiders. Only 31 of the 110 new House members had never held elective office, and several of these "inexperienced" winners had worked in government or party politics. "The Political Year, 1992."

38. David Brady and Craig Volden, *Revolving Gridlock*, 2nd ed. (Boulder, CO: Westview Press, 2006), pp. 121–22.

39. The Democrats' percentage of all votes cast fell to its lowest level since 1980 (50.8 percent), which translated into 59.3 percent of all House seats. That number, 258, however, was lower than their average number of House seats in the post-1960 period and well below their surges in seats in the elections of 1964 and 1974. Ibid.

40. Ibid., pp. 76–77, 123–26.

41. "Politics and Issues, 1993–1995," CQ Electronic Library, CQ Voting and Elections Collection, originally published in *Guide to U.S. Elections*, ed. John L. Moore, Jon P. Preimesberger, and David R. Tarr, vol. 1 (Washington: CQ Press, 2001), http://library.cqpress.com/elections/gusel1-152-7223-393112 (accessed September 24, 2007).

42. As Daniel Yankelovich noted shortly after the Clinton debacle, most people support universal coverage "if the nation can afford it and it doesn't limit choice of doctors or raise taxes or cause employers to cut jobs." Daniel Yankelovich, "The Debate That Wasn't: The Public and the Clinton Health Care Plan," in *The Problem That Won't Go Away: Reform U.S. Health Care Financing*, ed. Henry J. Aaron (Washington: Brookings Institution Press, 1996), pp. 75, 79.

43. See comments by Karlyn Bowman in ibid., p. 98.

44. Yankelovich, "The Debate That Wasn't," p. 75. Two issues undermined Clinton and the Democrats, according to the poll. The first was health care reform. Of the 54 percent of voters who said they had been disappointed by Clinton, half cited the fact that he proposed big government solutions like health care reform. See Dan Balz, "Health Plan Was Albatross for Democrats; Big Government Label Hurt Party, Poll Finds," *Washington Post*, November 18, 1994.

45. Balz, "Health Plan Was Albatross."

46. Adapted from "Congressional Elections of 1994: National and Local Influences," CQ Electronic Library, CQ Voting and Elections Collection, originally published in Abramson, Aldrich, and Rohde, *Change and Continuity in the 1992 Elections*, http://library.cqpress.com/elections/cc1992-128-6543-381177 (accessed September 24, 2007).

47. Katharine Q. Seelye, "The 1994 Campaign: Voters Disgusted with Politicians as Election Nears," *New York Times*, November 3, 1994.

48. ABC News, "Six Months In, Rising Doubts on Issues Underscore Obama's Challenges Ahead," July 20, 2009, http://abcnews.go.com/images/PollingUnit/1092a1ObamaatSixMonths.pdf.

49. See "Job Performance Ratings for President Clinton," January 23, 1993–January 18, 2001, Roper Center for Public Opinion, http://webapps.ropercenter.uconn.edu/CFIDE/roper/presidential/webroot/presidential_rating_detail.cfm?allRate = True &presidentName = Clinton.

50. Rae, *Conservative Reformers*, p. 60.

51. On election day 1994, 75 percent of those surveyed disapproved of the job Congress was doing or about the same as at the peak of the House bank scandal in July 1992. The campaign had done nothing to improve the public's mood: the number of those who disapprove of their own representatives doubled to 33 percent from September to November. When asked about Congress as a whole, only 12 percent responded that members of Congress deserved reelection, while 82 percent wanted

Congress to begin again with all new people. Yet more than half said that even if all new people were elected, the government would not work any better. Ibid.

52. For a political science treatment of the importance of constituency and locality to House members, see Richard Fenno, *Home Style: House Members in their Districts* (New York: Longman, 2002).

53. As Gary C. Jacobson points out: "All politics was not local in 1994. Republicans succeeded in framing the local choice in national terms, making taxes, social discipline, big government, and the Clinton presidency the dominant issues." Gary C. Jacobson, "The 1994 House Elections in Perspective," in *Midterm: Elections of 1994 in Context*, ed. Philip Klinkner (Boulder, CO: Westview Press, 1996), p. 3.

54. "The plan had been devised with the extensive use of polling to gauge public approval for specific proposals, and Gingrich indicated that each of the ten items had at least 60 percent support." Adapted from "Congressional Elections of 1994: National and Local Influences."

55. The text of this bill may still be found at http://www.house.gov/house/Contract/familiesd.txt. The American Dream Restoration Act also reduced the marriage penalty in the tax code. See http://www.house.gov/house/Contract/amdreamd.txt.

56. It did promise to remove earnings limits and taxes on Social Security recipients while providing incentives for long-term care insurance. Senior Citizens' Equity Act, http://www.house.gov/house/Contract/seniorsd.txt.

57. Such reforms also appealed to more moderate members of the GOP caucus, many of whom had grown tired of abuses by the majority party within the institution. Gingrich won many votes from moderates by promising to stand up to such abuses. See Koopman, *Hostile Takeover*, p. 105.

58. The eight were "require all laws that apply to the rest of the country also apply equally to the Congress; select a major, independent auditing firm to conduct a comprehensive audit of Congress for waste, fraud or abuse; cut the number of House committees, and cut committee staff by one-third; limit the terms of all committee chairs; ban the casting of proxy votes in committee; require committee meetings to be open to the public; require a three-fifths majority vote to pass a tax increase; guarantee an honest accounting of our Federal Budget by implementing zero baseline budgeting." See "Republican Contract with America," http://www.house.gov/house/Contract/CONTRACT.html.

59. See James G. Gimpel, *Legislating the Revolution: The Contract with America in Its First 100 Days* (Boston: Allyn & Bacon, 1996), p. 5.

60. Citizen Legislature Act, http://www.house.gov/house/Contract/termlimd.txt.

61. The Democrats saw the Contract with America as a continuation of Reagan's efforts. Clinton's pollster Stanley B. Greenberg claimed that "when they put the contract down, they were very clear that they wanted to go back to Reagan policies. . . . And people believe those times got the country in trouble." Adapted from "Congressional Elections of 1994: National and Local Influences."

62. David W. Brady, John F. Cogan, and Douglas Rivers, *How the Republicans Captured the House: An Assessment of the 1994 Midterm Elections* (Stanford, CA: Hoover Institution on War, Revolution and Peace, 1995), pp. 2, 13, 16–17.

63. Rae, *Conservative Reformers*, p. 59.

64. "The Sea Change," *Washington Post*, November 10, 1995.

65. Rae, *Conservative Reformers*, p. 58.

66. Richard Fenno, *Learning to Govern* (Washington: Brookings Institution Press, 1997), p. 25; and Timothy J. Barnett, *Legislative Learning: The 104th Republican Freshmen in the House* (New York: Routledge, 1999), p. 59.

67. Barnett, *Legislative Learning*, pp. 63–64.

68. Ibid., p. 65.

69. Ibid.

70. Ibid.

71. Ibid.

72. These terms are used by Koopman, *Hostile Takeover*, p. 135.

73. Ibid., p. 136. A measure of the attitudes of Democratic House members may be found in what their leaders said at various times. The majority leader: "Republicans are just going to have to get it through their heads that they are not going to write legislation." The majority whip: "What difference does it make what the Republicans think?" The Rules Committee chair: "Hey, we've got the votes. Let's vote. Screw you." A top Education Committee staffer: "We rolled the Republicans every time. We had no fairness. We *just screwed them.*" Fenno, *Learning to Govern*, p. 12.

74. " 'Contract with America' Signed by 300 Republican Candidates for the U.S. House of Representatives," CQ Electronic Library, CQ Voting and Elections Collection, originally published in *Historic Documents of 1994* (Washington: CQ Press, 1995), http://library.cqpress.com/elections/hsdc94-0000089781 (accessed September 24, 2007).

75. Adapted from "Congressional Elections of 1994: Impact on Congress," CQ Electronic Library, CQ Voting and Elections Collection, originally published in Abramson, Aldrich, and Rohde, *Change and Continuity in the 1992 Elections*, http://library.cqpress.com/elections/cc1992-128-6543-381187 (accessed September 24, 2007).

76. Charles O. Jones, *Clinton and Congress, 1993–1996: Risk, Restoration, and Reelection* (Norman: University of Oklahoma Press, 1999), pp. 125–26.

77. "Congressional Elections of 1994: Impact on Congress."

78. Fenno, *Learning to Govern*, p. 38.

79. Quoted in Michael Kelly, "You Ain't Seen Nothing Yet," *The New Yorker*, April 24, 1995, p. 41, cited in Jones, *Clinton and Congress*, p. 126.

80. The account of the struggle that follows draws on Brady and Volden, *Revolving Gridlock*, pp. 156–59.

81. "Comparing House, Senate Paths to a Balanced Budget by 2002," *CQ Weekly Online*, May 13, 1995, pp. 1300–1, http://library.cqpress.com/cqweekly/WR407816 (accessed November 13, 2007).

82. Jonathan Oberlander, *The Political Life of Medicare* (Chicago: University of Chicago Press, 2003), p. 131, Table 5.2.

83. "The Speaker has done a superb job of figuring out what was important to all of the health care groups and what it would take for them to support it, given some of the less attractive parts of the plan," noted Pam G. Bailey, president of the Healthcare Leadership Council, an organization representing the 50 largest health care companies in the nation. "Medicare Cuts Vetoed as Part of Budget Reconciliation," CQ Press Electronic Library, *CQ Almanac* online edition, originally published in *CQ Almanac 1995* (Washington: Congressional Quarterly, 1996), http://library.cqpress.com/cqalmanac/cqal95-1100565 (accessed February 10, 2009).

84. Ibid.

85. Fenno, *Learning to Govern*, p. 43.

86. See, for example, Sean Wilentz, *The Age of Reagan: A History 1974–2008* (New York: Harper, 2008), p. 262.

87. Fenno, *Learning to Govern*, pp. 39–40.

88. Ibid., pp. 39–42.

89. Ibid., p. 38.

90. For the text of the speech, see William Jefferson Clinton, State of the Union Address, January 23, 1996, http://clinton4.nara.gov/WH/New/other/sotu.html.

91. Fenno, *Learning to Govern*, p. 49.

92. "Clinton's Election and Reelection."

93. Ibid.

94. He took 49.2 percent of the popular vote and 379 electoral votes to Robert Dole's 40.7 percent and 159 electoral votes. Ross Perot ran again to declining interest: he received 8.4 percent of the vote, less than half of his 1992 total. Clinton became the first Democrat to win reelection since Franklin Roosevelt in 1936. He was also the first Democrat to be elected to the presidency along with a Republican-controlled Congress. Clinton won every state he had captured in 1992, except for Colorado, Georgia, and Montana. He also took Arizona and Florida, both of which had long been Republican. Clinton won the female vote by 16 percent, the largest margin ever. Clinton also beat Dole among every age group and won minority groups overwhelmingly. Ibid. While Republicans remained the party of the suburbs in Congress in the 1990s, they again lost that distinction leveling the presidential contest. Clinton did reasonably well in the suburbs in 1992 and even better in 1996. Of the nation's 28 largest suburban counties (those with a 1990 population of more than 500,000), Clinton carried 24 in 1996—a level of suburban success enjoyed by Republicans Eisenhower, Nixon, and Reagan. "Suburbia: A Growing Political Force," CQ Electronic Library, *CQ Almanac* online edition, originally published in *CQ Almanac 1997* (Washington: Congressional Quarterly, 1998), http://library.cqpress.com/cqalmanac/cqal97-16-24571-1089990 (accessed December 17, 2007). Before Clinton, 17 of these suburban areas had not voted for a Democratic presidential candidate since the 1960s. Seven of them were counties that Clinton had not won in 1992.

95. "Clinton's Election and Reelection."

96. Senior Republicans, in contrast, lost on average about 5 percent of their vote compared to 1994. David Brady, John F. Cogan, and Douglas Rivers, *The 1996 House Elections: Reaffirming the Conservative Trend* (Stanford, CA: Hoover Institution, 1997), p. 16.

97. In the first session of the 104th Congress, more than half the House Republicans had an Americans for Democratic Action score of zero. More than 90 percent had ADA scores of less than 20 percent. The average was 6. Ibid., p. 8.

98. Ibid., pp. 11–12.

99. Samuel Patterson and Joseph Quin Monson, "Reelecting the Republican Congress: Two More Years," in *Reelection 1996: How Americans Voted*, ed. Herbert Weisberg and Janet Box-Steffensmeier (New York: Chatham House Publishers, 1999), p. 191.

100. Layman, *The Great Divide*, p. 171.

101. Ibid., p. 188.

102. Ibid., p. 190.

103. "Reconciliation Package: An Overview," CQ Electronic Library, *CQ Almanac* online edition, originally published in *CQ Almanac 1997* (Washington: Congressional Quarterly, 1998), http://library.cqpress.com/cqalmanac/cqal97-0000181045 (accessed December 13, 2007).

104. "Tone, Tenor of First Session Seemed Like Old Times," CQ Electronic Library, *CQ Almanac* online edition, originally published in *CQ Almanac 1997* (Washington: Congressional Quarterly, 1998), http://library.cqpress.com/cqalmanac/cqal97-16-24570-1089963 (accessed December 11, 2007).

105. Ibid. See also "Reconciliation Package: Spending Cuts," CQ Electronic Library, *CQ Almanac* online edition, originally published in *CQ Almanac 1997* (Washington: Congressional Quarterly, 1998), http://library.cqpress.com/cqalmanac/cqal97-0000181054 (accessed December 13, 2007). The Senate bill proposed a substantial change in Medicare, linking the annual deductible for Medicare's Part B program to seniors' incomes. The bill also included provisions to gradually increase the eligibility age for Medicare benefits from 65 to 67 by 2027 and to require a $5 co-payment for some home health care services. The proposal was opposed by the White House and the AARP and did not survive into the final law.

106. "Reconciliation Package: Tax Cuts," CQ Electronic Library, *CQ Almanac* online edition, originally published in *CQ Almanac 1997* (Washington: Congressional Quarterly, 1998), http://library.cqpress.com/cqalmanac/cqal97-0000181033 (accessed December 13, 2007).

107. Ibid.

108. "Reconciliation Package: An Overview."

109. ""Gingrich Weakened by Ethics Case," CQ Electronic Library, *CQ Almanac* online edition, originally published in *CQ Almanac 1997* (Washington: Congressional Quarterly, 1998), http://library.cqpress.com/cqalmanac/cqal97-16-24570-1089974 (accessed December 11, 2007).

110. Ibid.

111. Brady and Volden, *Revolving Gridlock*, p. 149.

112. Ibid., p. 150. See also "Budget Amendment Sinks in Senate," CQ Electronic Library, *CQ Almanac* online edition, originally published in *CQ Almanac 1995* (Washington: Congressional Quarterly, 1996), http://library.cqpress.com/cqalmanac/cqal95-1099955 (accessed December 13, 2007).

113. Brady and Volden, *Revolving Gridlock*, pp. 151–52.

114. Clinton used the veto on 11 bills—2 budget-reconciliation measures and 9 of the 13 regular appropriations bills. He cut 82 items from the appropriations bills, totaling $1.9 billion over five years—a fraction of the $9 trillion federal budget over that period. Clinton first vetoed provisions of tax bills, which engendered some complaints from Congress. The dissent grew louder when Clinton vetoed more than three dozen projects worth $287 million from the $9.2 billion fiscal 1998 military construction spending bill. In the Senate, several Republicans disavowed the line-item veto, and Ted Stevens introduced a bill to restore all but two of the vetoes. Congress had little problem overriding Clinton's veto of the 38 military construction projects. The Senate passed the Steven's bill rejecting 36 of the 38 vetoes. The vote was 69–30, giving sponsors a 3-vote cushion over the two-thirds majority needed to override a veto. Shortly thereafter, the House overwhelmingly passed a bill disapproving of all 38 vetoes; the vote was 352–64. The Senate agreed to the House bill the next day, clearing it by voice vote. "Line-Item Veto Makes Rocky Debut," CQ Electronic Library, *CQ Almanac* online edition, originally published in *CQ Almanac 1997* (Washington: Congressional Quarterly, 1998), http://library.cqpress.com/cqalmanac/cqal97-0000181040 (accessed December 12, 2007).

Clinton vetoed these bills, but his negative was overridden in early 1998. "Members Made the Deals, But Scandal Made the News," CQ Electronic Library, *CQ Almanac* online edition, originally published in *CQ Almanac 1998* (Washington: Congressional Quarterly, 1999), http://library.cqpress.com/cqalmanac/cqal98-0000191016 (accessed December 18, 2007).

115. Dan Balz, "GOP 'Contract' Pledges 10 Tough Acts to Follow," *Washington Post* November 20, 1994.

116. The case was *U.S. Term Limits Inc. v. Thornton* and involved an Arkansas law. "Politics and Issues, 1989–1991."

117. It did not help the cause that "the effort to pass term limits was the most disorganized and halfhearted operation of the first 100 days" of the new Congress. See Gimpel, *Legislating the Revolution*, pp. 99, 102–4.

118. In 1997, Bill McCollum (R-FL), a key proponent of the main term limits proposal in the House, could not put together more than a simple majority for his plan, which left him 69 votes shy of the two-thirds majority necessary to pass a constitutional amendment. Ten alternative term limits proposals failed to get even a simple majority. "Term Limits Plan Fails in the House," CQ Electronic Library, *CQ Almanac* online edition, originally published in *CQ Almanac 1997* (Washington: Congressional Quarterly, 1998), http://library.cqpress.com/cqalmanac/cqal97-0000181052 (accessed December 11, 2007).

119. Gimpel, *Legislating the Revolution*, pp. 38–41.

120. Jones, *Clinton and Congress*, p. 124.

121. "Gingrich Address: Speaker Calls for 'Partnership' to Pass 'Major Reforms,' " *CQ Weekly Online*, January 7, 1995, pp. 118–20, http://library.cqpress.com/cqweekly/WR406877 (accessed February 9, 2009).

122. Andrew Taylor, "A Tough Task," *CQ Weekly Online*, January 7, 1995, p. 34, http://library.cqpress.com/cqweekly/WR406897 (accessed February 9, 2009).

123. "The Social Security system remains the cornerstone of personal security for millions of the elderly. In 1983, a Republican president, working with the Republican chairman of the Senate Finance Committee—Bob Dole—saved the Social Security system from fiscal disaster. "We have a legal and moral responsibility to America's seniors and will continue to do everything in our power to ensure that government honors our commitment to Social Security beneficiaries, now and in the future. We will keep it financially sound and keep politics out of its administration. We will work to ensure the integrity and solvency of the Social Security trust funds." See "Prosperity, Self-Government and 'Moral Clarity,'" CQ Press Electronic Library, *CQ Almanac* online edition, originally published in *CQ Almanac 1996* (Washington: Congressional Quarterly, 1997), http://library.cqpress.com/cqalmanac/cqal96-841-24590-1091043 (accessed February 9, 2009).

124. John F. Cogan, "The Congressional Response to Social Security Surpluses 1935–1994," Essays in Public Policy, Hoover Institution, Stanford, CA, July 20, 1998.

125. "Budget Amendment Sinks in Senate." The same problem and the same result would be repeated the next year, see "Budget Amendment Rejected Again," CQ Press Electronic Library, *CQ Almanac* online edition, originally published in *CQ Almanac 1996* (Washington: Congressional Quarterly, 1997), http://library.cqpress.com/cqalmanac/cqal96-841-24598-1091861 (accessed February 9, 2009).

126. "Budget Amendment Sinks in Senate."

127. Clinton proposed investing about 4 percent of the total equity market and less than 15 percent of the Social Security trust fund. "Congress, White House at Odds over How Best to Protect Social Security," CQ Press Electronic Library, *CQ*

Almanac online edition, originally published in *CQ Almanac 1999* (Washington: Congressional Quarterly, 2000), http://library.cqpress.com/cqalmanac/cqal99-0000201206 (accessed February 9, 2009).

128. According to Clinton's estimates, about $2.8 trillion of the projected budget surplus would be dedicated to Social Security over the next 15 years. The government would invest one-quarter of that amount in the stock market. See "Congress, White House at Odds over How Best to Protect Social Security."

129. Cogan, "The Congressional Response to Social Security Surpluses 1935–1994," passim.

130. "The State of the Union: Clinton Offers Proposals on Education, Retirement Security, Health Care, Urges Nation to 'Aim Higher,' " CQ Press Electronic Library, *CQ Almanac* online edition, originally published in *CQ Almanac 1999* (Washington: Congressional Quarterly, 2000), http://library.cqpress.com/cqalmanac/cqal99-18-4002-216066 (accessed February 9, 2009).

131. "Congress, White House at Odds over How Best to Protect Social Security."

132. Ibid.

133. In 1996, the Republicans lowered their proposed constraint on Medicare spending to $168 billion over six years; Clinton stuck with his proposed $124 billion in cuts. "Finger-Pointing, but No Deal on Medicare's Budget Woes," CQ Press Electronic Library, *CQ Almanac* online edition, originally published in *CQ Almanac 1996* (Washington: Congressional Quarterly, 1997), http://library.cqpress.com/cqalmanac/cqal96-1092546 (accessed February 10, 2009).

134. Andrew Taylor and others, "Provisions: What the Budget Bill Does," *CQ Weekly Online*, December 13, 1997, pp. 3082–91, http://library.cqpress.com/cqweekly/WR19971213-49PROVISIONSBUDGET001 (accessed February 11, 2009).

135. Mary Agnes Carey, "Medicare: Long-Term Fixes Are Delayed, but Political Logjam Broken," *CQ Weekly Online*, August 2, 1997, pp. 1843–46, http://library.cqpress.com/cqweekly/WR19970802-31MEDICARE001 (accessed February 11, 2009)

136. " 'Givebacks' to Medicare Providers Will Rise to Double Previous Year's Level," CQ Press Electronic Library, *CQ Almanac* online edition, originally published in *CQ Almanac 2000* (Washington: Congressional Quarterly, 2001), http://library.cqpress.com/cqalmanac/cqal00-834-24299-1082127 (accessed February 10, 2009); and Mary Agnes Carey and Rebecca Adams, "$35 Billion More for Medicare," *CQ Weekly Online*, December 16, 2000, p. 2861, http://library.cqpress.com/cqweekly/weeklyreport106-000000188192 (accessed February 11, 2009).

137. John D. Klemm, "Medicaid Spending: A Brief History," *Health Care Financing Review* 22 (Fall 2000): 105. See also the table "National Health Expenditures by Type of Service and Source of Funds: Calendar Years 2007–1960," http://www.cms.hhs.gov/NationalHealthExpendData/02NationalHealthAccountsHistorical.asp#TopOfPage.

138. "Average Annual Growth in Medicaid Spending, FY1990–FY2007," Statehealthfacts.org, http://www.statehealthfacts.org/comparebar.jsp?ind=181&cat=4&sub=47&yr=1&typ=2. Both spending and enrollment rose steeply from 1990 to 1995; thereafter until 2000, the number of recipients leveled off and nominal spending continued to increase at much the same pace as it had in the previous five years. Klemm, "Medicaid Spending," Table 1, p. 106.

139. Klemm, "Medicaid Spending," pp. 110–11.

140. "Big Medicare, Medicaid Changes Enacted in Budget Bills," CQ Press Electronic Library, *CQ Almanac* online edition, originally published in *CQ Almanac 1997*

(Washington: Congressional Quarterly, 1998), http://library.cqpress.com/cqalmanac/cqal97-0000181134 (accessed February 12, 2009).

141. Robert Pear, "Hatch Joins Kennedy to Back a Health Program," *New York Times*, March 14, 1997.

142. Jerry Gray, "Through Senate Alchemy, Tobacco Is Turned into Gold for Children's Health," *Washington Post*, August 11, 1997.

143. Adam Clymer, "8 G.O.P. Senators Back Bill to Aid Uninsured Youths," *New York Times*, April 8, 1997.

144. Adam Clymer, "Child Insurance Bill Opposed as Threat to Cigarette Revenue," *New York Times*, May 21, 1997.

145. Helen Dewar, "Senate Battle on Child Health Care Symbolizes Kennedy-Lott Power Struggle," *Washington Post*, May 23, 1997.

146. Clymer, "8 G.O.P. Senators."

147. Patrice Hill, "House GOP Open to Raising Cigarette Tax," *Washington Times*, June 21, 1997.

148. Gray, "Alchemy."

149. The definition comes from the U.S. Department of Health and Human Services website, http://aspe.hhs.gov/HSP/abbrev/afdc-tanf.htm.

150. "Carter, Congress and Welfare: A Long Road," CQ Press Electronic Library, *CQ Almanac* online edition, originally published in *CQ Almanac 1977* (Washington: Congressional Quarterly, 1978), http://library.cqpress.com/cqalmanac/cqal77-1203267 (accessed February 17, 2009).

151. "Welfare Reform," CQ Press Electronic Library, *CQ Almanac* online edition, originally published in *CQ Almanac 1979* (Washington: Congressional Quarterly, 1980), http://library.cqpress.com/cqalmanac/cqal79-1185852 (accessed February 17, 2009).

152. "Welfare Benefits Cut by Reconciliation," CQ Press Electronic Library, *CQ Almanac* online edition, originally published in *CQ Almanac 1981* (Washington: Congressional Quarterly, 1982), http://library.cqpress.com/cqalmanac/cqal81-1173288 (accessed February 17, 2009).

153. "After Years of Debate, Welfare Reform Clears," CQ Press Electronic Library, *CQ Almanac* online edition, originally published in *CQ Almanac 1988* (Washington: Congressional Quarterly, 1989), http://library.cqpress.com/cqalmanac/cqal88-1141998 (accessed February 17, 2009).

154. "Welfare Reform Takes a Back Seat," CQ Press Electronic Library, *CQ Almanac* online edition, originally published in *CQ Almanac 1994* (Washington: Congressional Quarterly, 1995), http://library.cqpress.com/cqalmanac/cqal94-1103655 (accessed February 18, 2009).

155. "The Personal Responsibility Act (Welfare Reform)," http://www.house.gov/house/Contract/persrespd.txt.

156. "After 60 Years, Most Control Sent to States," CQ Press Electronic Library, *CQ Almanac* online edition, originally published in *CQ Almanac 1996* (Washington: Congressional Quarterly, 1997), http://library.cqpress.com/cqalmanac/cqal96-1092425 (accessed February 9, 2009).

157. Ibid.

158. Yet the next year, Congress revisited welfare reform as part of the budget agreement. They passed a fund worth $3 billion to help states place long-term welfare recipients into the work force in fiscal years 1998 and 1999. Congress also increased spending by a total of $1.5 billion over five years for food stamps and employment

and training benefits for people who might otherwise have lost their eligibility under the welfare overhaul law. The 1997 budget also included almost $10 billion over five years to restore Social Security Income and Medicaid benefits to about two-thirds of the 500,000 legal immigrants who would otherwise lose them under the 1996 reform. "Reconciliation Package: Spending Cuts"; and "$13 Billion in Welfare Cuts Restored," CQ Press Electronic Library, *CQ Almanac* online edition, originally published in *CQ Almanac 1997* (Washington: Congressional Quarterly, 1998), http://library.cqpress.com/cqalmanac/cqal97-0000181128 (accessed February 19, 2009).

159. Jeffrey Grogger and Charles Michalopoulos, "Welfare Dynamics under Time Limits," *Journal of Political Economy* 111 (June 2003): 530–54.

160. See Vee Burke, "Welfare Reform: An Issue Overview," CRS Issues Brief for Congress, Congressional Research Service, Washington, March 11, 2004, pp. 1–2. On Temporary Assistance for Needy Families, see "Spending Bill Provisions," CQ Electronic Library, *CQ Almanac* online edition, originally published in *CQ Almanac 1997* (Washington: Congressional Quarterly, 1998), http://library.cqpress.com/cqalmanac/cqal97-0000181041 (accessed December 17, 2007).

161. Christine Scott, "The Earned Income Tax Credit (EITC): An Overview," CRS Report for Congress, Congressional Research Service, Washington, March 15, 2007.

162. Ibid., p. 28.

163. Rebecca M. Blank, "Was Welfare Reform Successful?" *The Economist's Voice*, March 2006, pp. 1–5.

164. Even many poverty experts accepted the older ideals of work and personal responsibility. See Alice O'Connor, *Poverty Knowledge: Social Science, Social Policy, and the Poor in Twentieth-Century U.S. History* (Princeton, NJ: Princeton University Press, 2001), p. 284.

165. Mickey Kaus, *The End of Equality*, 2nd ed. (New York: Basic Books, 1995), pp. xvi–xvii.

166. David M. Herszenhorn, "Farm Income Up, but Subsidies Stay," *New York Times*, April 24, 2008.

167. For a good overview of such subsidies, see Daniel A. Sumner, "Agricultural Subsidy Programs," in *The Concise Encyclopedia of Economics*, ed. David R. Henderson (Indianapolis: Liberty Fund, 2008), pp. 2–4.

168. Eric Patashnik, "After the Public Interest Prevails: The Political Sustainability of Policy Reform," *Governance* 16 (April 2003): 217–18.

169. Ibid., p. 218.

170. "Longstanding Farm Laws Rewritten," CQ Electronic Library, *CQ Almanac* online edition, originally published in *CQ Almanac 1996* (Washington: Congressional Quarterly, 1997), http://library.cqpress.com/cqalmanac/cqal96-1092001 (accessed December 18, 2007).

171. See Finn E. Kydland and Edward Prescott, "Rules Rather than Discretion: The Inconsistency of Optimal Plans," *Journal of Political Economy* 85 (1977): 473–90.

172. "Longstanding Farm Laws Rewritten."

173. Fifty-four House Democrats and 20 Democratic senators voted for it. See Adam D. Sheingate, "Agricultural Retrenchment Revisited: Issue Definition and Venue Change in the United States and European Union," *Governance* 13 (2000): 352–53. See also Patashnik, "After the Public Interest Prevails," pp. 217 ff. and sources therein.

174. Patashnik, "After the Public Interest Prevails," p. 219.

175. Sheingate, "Agricultural Retrenchment Revisited," pp. 343–44.

176. See the explanation to the relevant part of the contract, the Job Creation and Wage Enhancement Act, at http://www.house.gov/house/Contract/cre8jobsd.txt.

177. The bills that passed by wide margins required risk assessment through scientific and economic methods, cost-benefit analysis of regulations, and an easier procedure for compensating private property owners deprived of their use of their property by federal regulators. See Bob Benenson, "House Easily Passes Bills to Limit Regulations," *CQ Weekly Online*, March 4, 1995, pp. 679–82, http://library.cqpress.com/cqweekly/WR407297 (accessed February 5, 2009).

178. Bob Benenson, "GOP Sets the 104th Congress on New Regulatory Course," *CQ Weekly Online*, June 17, 1995, pp. 1693–97, http://library.cqpress.com/cqweekly/WR408077 (accessed February 5, 2009).

179. Bob Benenson, "Regulations: Senators Roll Back Restrictions Proposed by Regulatory Overhaul," *CQ Weekly Online*, July 22, 1995, pp. 2160–61, http://library.cqpress.com/cqweekly/WR408418 (accessed February 5, 2009).

180. Allan Freedman, "Republicans Concede Missteps in Effort to Rewrite Rules," *CQ Weekly Online*, December 2, 1995, pp. 3645–47, http://library.cqpress.com/cqweekly/WR409519 (accessed February 5, 2009).

181. "The FDA answered its GOP critics, unveiling four new initiatives to speed cancer treatments to market. Five days later, the agency announced another set of reforms to ease the regulatory burden on medical-device manufacturers." Jonathan Weisman, "True Impact of GOP Congress Reaches Well beyond Bills," *CQ Weekly Online*, September 7, 1996, pp. 2515–20, http://library.cqpress.com/cqweekly/WR402797 (accessed February 5, 2009).

182. Steve Langdon, "FDA Drug Approval Process May Undergo Surgery," *CQ Weekly Online*, January 27, 1996, pp. 221–24, http://library.cqpress.com/cqweekly/WR409815 (accessed February 5, 2009).

183. Weisman, "True Impact of GOP Congress," pp. 2515–20.

184. Ibid.

185. Ibid.

186. Cisneros claimed that under his direction HUD had destroyed 23,000 public housing units by the end of 1996. He also claimed that federal and local police made 6,826 arrests in public housing. HUD's FY97 budget request looked toward conflating more than 20 programs into 3. Later the agency planned to merge more than 60 programs, slowly terminate 29 inactive programs, and end 37 others. HUD would go from 11,600 employees to 10,447, with 7,500 planned by 2001. See Weisman, "True Impact of GOP Congress," pp. 2515–20.

187. "Public Housing Overhaul Bill Dies," CQ Press Electronic Library, *CQ Almanac* online edition, originally published in *CQ Almanac 1996* (Washington: Congressional Quarterly, 1997), http://library.cqpress.com/cqalmanac/cqal96-1092621 (accessed July 14, 2009).

188. "Three Years of Negotiations Yield a Housing Bill That Compromise Built," CQ Press Electronic Library, *CQ Almanac* online edition, originally published in *CQ Almanac 1998* (Washington: Congressional Quarterly, 1999), http://library.cqpress.com/cqalmanac/cqal98-0000191105 (accessed July 14, 2009).

189. Some freshman Republicans claimed the proposal was not in order. However, I have learned from staff involved at the time that members were in fact given a detailed plan for eliminating the Department of Energy, including where to place the residual agencies. It seems possible that House members decided not to go with

the detailed proposal for other reasons; the profession of incompleteness offered a plausible explanation for rejecting the detailed proposal.

190. "Energy Bill Spreads Cuts Evenly," CQ Press Electronic Library, *CQ Almanac* online edition, originally published in *CQ Almanac 1995* (Washington: Congressional Quarterly, 1996), http://library.cqpress.com/cqalmanac/cqal95-1099727 (accessed July 14, 2009).

191. Congress cut O'Leary's "technology transfer" program to $150 million. The White House got the message and asked for just $49 million for industrial partnerships in 1997, effectively ending that effort. Weisman, "True Impact of GOP Congress," pp. 2515–20.

192. Such spending rose from $3.2 billion for FY95 to $3.5 billion for FY96 to a White House request of $3.7 billion for FY97, more than the cold war average, even though the United States no longer created or tested nuclear weapons. Ibid.

193. Its defenders claimed, however, that only 14 percent, or $285 million in FY95, of that money comes from the federal government, however. Jon Healey, "Opposing Interests Brace for a Culture Clash," *CQ Weekly Online*, January 28, 1995, pp. 272–75, http://library.cqpress.com/cqweekly/WR407055 (accessed November 12, 2007).

194. Robert Marshall Wells, "House Passes Labor-HHS Bill, but Senate Outlook Unclear," *CQ Weekly Online*, August 5, 1995, pp. 2364–65, http://library.cqpress.com/cqweekly/WR408570 (accessed November 13, 2007).

195. "Appropriations: Labor-HHS-Education," *CQ Weekly Online*, August 12, 1995, p. 2447, http://library.cqpress.com/cqweekly/WR408576 (accessed November 13, 2007).

196. "Labor-HHS-Education Spending (Chart)," *CQ Weekly Online*, September 23, 1995, p. 2918, http://library.cqpress.com/cqweekly/WR408900 (accessed November 13, 2007).

197. In 1996, the Democratic platform would boast: "We are proud to have stopped the Republican attack on the Corporation for Public Broadcasting—we want our children to watch Sesame Street, not Power Rangers." "1996 Democratic Convention Guide—Text: Draft Democratic National Platform," *CQ Weekly Online*, August 17, 1996, pp. 35–52, http://library.cqpress.com/cqweekly/WR402616 (accessed November 13, 2007).

198. Dan Carney. "Public Broadcasting Develops Dialogue With House GOP," *CQ Weekly Online*, March 23, 1996: pp. 791–792, http://library.cqpress.com/cqweekly/WR401212 (accessed November 12, 2007).

199. "Fiscal 1997 Labor-HHS-Education," *CQ Weekly Online*, September 21, 1996, p. 2676, http://library.cqpress.com/cqweekly/WR402892 (accessed November 13, 2007).

200. Steven Kosiak and Elizabeth Heeter, "Post–Cold War Defense Spending Cuts: A Bipartisan Decision," Center for Strategic and Budgetary Assessments, August 31, 2000, http://www.csbaonline.org/4Publications/PubLibrary/H.20000831.Post-Cold_War_Defe/H.20000831.Post-Cold_War_Defe.php.

201. "Congress Adds Little to Defense Request Despite Criticism of Clinton Policies," CQ Press Electronic Library, *CQ Almanac* online edition, originally published in *CQ Almanac 2000* (Washington: Congressional Quarterly, 2001), http://library.cqpress.com/cqalmanac/cqal00-834-24316-1083195 (accessed February 24, 2009).

202. Katharine Q. Seelye, "Republicans Plan Ambitious Agenda in Next Congress," *New York Times*, November 15, 1994.

Chapter 6

1. Timothy J. Barnett, *Legislative Learning: The 104th Republican Freshmen in the House* (New York: Routledge, 1999), pp. 7–11.

2. Ibid., p. 13.

3. "GOP Backs Down on Disaster Aid Bill," CQ Electronic Library, *CQ Almanac* online edition, originally published in *CQ Almanac 1997* (Washington: Congressional Quarterly, 1998), http://library.cqpress.com/cqalmanac/cqal97-0000181083 (accessed December 17, 2007). See also Barnett, *Legislative Learning*, p. 17.

4. James Stimson's measurement of the public mood may be found by downloading the data file available at http://www.unc.edu/~jstimson/. The biennial data and chart may be viewed by selecting the relevant tabs on the downloaded spreadsheet. The biennial chart (but not the annual chart) shows a decided liberal shift in the public mood starting about 1997.

5. "Omnibus Spending Package Provides $20.8 Billion in 'Emergency' Funds," CQ Electronic Library, *CQ Almanac* online edition, originally published in *CQ Almanac 1998* (Washington: Congressional Quarterly, 1999), http://library.cqpress.com/cqalmanac/cqal98-0000191018 (accessed December 18, 2007).

6. "Members Made the Deals, but Scandal Made the News," CQ Electronic Library, *CQ Almanac* online edition, originally published in *CQ Almanac 1998* (Washington: Congressional Quarterly, 1999), http://library.cqpress.com/cqalmanac/cqal98-0000191016 (accessed December 18, 2007).

7. Both Clinton and Republicans supported spending on the Bosnia peacekeeping mission ($1.9 billion), year 2000 computer fixes ($3.4 billion), embassy security ($1.8 billion), and farm relief ($5.9 billion). Apart from the transportation spending, Congress added money to Head Start and other education funding. They also increased funding to the International Monetary Fund. For Republicans, the supplemental included more money for defense (especially missile defense) and intelligence. Congress also increased funding for the war on drugs, including $870 million for more radar surveillance planes, patrol boats, x-ray devices, and other equipment to detect and prevent smuggling. Overall, Congress agreed to spend $18 billion to fight drug importation and use, a sum equal to the cost of the entire Justice Department. "Omnibus Spending Package Provides $20.8 Billion in 'Emergency' Funds."

8. Jeffrey L. Katz and Andrew Taylor, "House Accuses Clinton of Perjury, Obstruction," *CQ Weekly Online*, December 19, 1998, pp. 3320–25, http://library.cqpress.com/cqweekly/WR19981219-50IMPEACH001 (accessed February 23, 2009).

9. In January, reports came to light that Clinton had had a sexual relationship with Monica Lewinsky, a White House intern in 1996. The reports seemed credible enough that several commentators, not all hostile to Clinton, thought the president would have to resign. He fought back by giving a good State of the Union speech. He also explicitly denied having sex with "that woman, Miss Lewinsky," or having lied about it. As it turned out, Clinton was lying as he admitted eight months later in a four-minute televised speech. The lying to the public was not Clinton's most significant problem.

10. Clinton denied the perjury charge. He had admitted having "inappropriate intimate physical contact" with Lewinsky and yet denied having sex with her. The president argued that the former admission did not constitute having sex as defined in the context of the case. James Bennet, "Clinton Admits Lewinsky Liaison to Jury; Tells Nation 'It Was Wrong,' but Private," *New York Times*, August 18, 1998.

11. Art. II, sect. 4.

12. "Job Performance Ratings for President Clinton," January 23, 1993–January 18, 2001, Roper Center for Public Opinion, http://webapps.ropercenter.uconn.edu/CFIDE/roper/presidential/webroot/presidential rating detail.cfm?allRate = True &presidentName = Clinton.

13. Katz and Taylor, "House Accuses Clinton of Perjury," pp. 3320–25.

14. "GDP Growth Rate," data360.org, http://www.data360.org/dsg. aspx?Data_Set_Group_Id = 354.

15. Geoffrey Layman, *The Great Divide: Religious and Cultural Conflict in American Party Politics* (New York: Columbia University Press, 2001), p. 248. The president also benefited from social changes evident at the time: the measures of crime, parenting without marriage, drug use, and welfare dependency were all dropping for the first time in while. See Molly W. Andolina and Clyde Wilcox, "Public Opinion: The Paradoxes of Clinton's Popularity," in *The Clinton Scandal and the Future of American Government* (Washington: Georgetown University Press, 2000), p. 182.

16. In September, a bipartisan poll indicated that moral issues had moved to the top of voter concerns, presumably because of Clinton's conduct. A leading GOP pollster contended that "the scandal's having an impact both in terms of the issue agenda for this fall and a tremendous dampening effect on Democratic turnout." Gingrich told House Republicans that the House in 1999 might comprise 250 GOP members (a 22-seat gain). Adapted from "Congressional Elections of 1998: Assessing Victory and Explaining the Results," CQ Press Electronic Library, CQ Voting and Elections Collection, originally published in Paul R. Abramson, John H. Aldrich, and David W. Rohde, *Change and Continuity in the 1996 and 1998 Elections* (Washington: CQ Press, 1999), http://library.cqpress.com/elections/cc1996-129-6552-381332.

17. This view was widespread: "Many politicians, as well as more neutral observers, had expected all through 1998 that the president's sex scandal would finally damage his standing with the public, and that the negative reaction would spill over to his party in the congressional elections." Adapted from "Congressional Elections of 1998: Assessing Victory and Explaining the Results."

18. Andrew Kohut, John C. Green, and Scott Keeter, *The Diminishing Divide: Religion's Changing Role in American Politics* (Washington: Brookings Institution Press, 2000), p. 93. Other Evangelical Protestants in this polling held views about Clinton closer to the norm for other groups. See ibid. A poll done at the time of the impeachment vote showed a strong partisan divide about the wisdom of the process as well as a strong majority of independents against the move. CBS News Poll, December 18, 1998 (*N* = 548 adults nationwide).

19. The Christian Coalition's "Contract with the American Family" had been taken up ambivalently by the new House majority in 1995. This contract comprised 10 planks on topics ranging from abortion and pornography to the tax relief for charities. For its text, see "Lobbying: 'Contract with the American Family,'" *CQ Weekly Online*, May 20, 1995, p. 1449, http://library.cqpress.com/cqweekly/WR407860 (accessed March 10, 2009). At the time, Republican House leaders welcomed the Christian contract and professed no enthusiasm for enacting its parts. See Annie Tin and Juliana Gruenwald, "Lobbying: 'Contract with Family' Welcomed Cautiously by House GOP," *CQ Weekly Online*, May 20, 1995, pp. 1448–50, http://library.cqpress.com/cqweekly/WR407859 (accessed March 10, 2009). None of its planks became law, and by election day a leading scholar of social conservativism could conclude, "Of all the major constituency groups that were part of the so-called Republican revolution,

the Christian right once again finished last." See Clyde Wilcox's quote in David Hosansky, "Christian Right's Electoral Clout Bore Limited Fruit in 104th," *CQ Weekly Online*, November 2, 1996, pp. 3160–62.

20. The post–World War II history of the United States indicated that a president's party in such circumstances could expect to lose on average 44 seats. A similar story could be told for Senate elections. Adapted from "Congressional Elections of 1998: Assessing Victory and Explaining the Results."

21. Turnout among secular-minded voters and African-American Protestants, both of whom tended to vote Democratic in the 1998 election, increased over 1994 levels. Turnout remained stable or declined slightly among committed Evangelicals, mainline Protestants, and Catholics. Less committed mainline Protestants went to the polls much less than in 1994. Kohut, Green, and Keeter, *Diminishing Divide*, p. 92.

22. Adapted from "Congressional Elections of 1998: Outcomes," CQ Press Electronic Library, CQ Voting and Elections Collection, originally published in Abramson, Aldrich, and Rohde, *Change and Continuity in the 1996 and 1998 Elections*, http://library.cqpress.com/elections/cc1996-129-6552-381329 (accessed March 6, 2009).

23. *Congressional Quarterly* reported: "Almost from the start of the Clinton scandal early in 1998, the whip DeLay positioned himself on the House floor and in network television talk shows as the conscience of conservatives angered by what they saw as moral decay in the White House. By year's end, DeLay was the only Republican leader willing to lead the congressional excoriation of Clinton." See "Speaker Hastert Gently Gavels in an Era of 'Order' in the House," CQ Press Electronic Library, *CQ Almanac* online edition, originally published in *CQ Almanac 1999* (Washington: Congressional Quarterly, 2000), http://library.cqpress.com/cqalmanac/cqal99-18-24528-1087258 (accessed March 9, 2009).

24. See Tom D. DeLay with Stephen Mansfield, *No Retreat, No Surrender: One American's Fight* (New York: Sentinel, 2007), pp. 99 ff.

25. "House of Representatives Casts Historic Vote to Impeach Clinton," CQ Press Electronic Library, *CQ Almanac* online edition, originally published in *CQ Almanac 1998* (Washington: Congressional Quarterly, 1999), http://library.cqpress.com/cqalmanac/cqal98-17-24538-1087774 (accessed March 9, 2009).

26. Andrew E. Busch, "On the Edge: The Electoral Career of George W. Bush," in *Considering the Bush Presidency*, ed. Gary L. Gregg and Mark J. Rozell (New York: Oxford University Press, 2004), p. 178.

27. Thomas B. Edsall, "GOP's Own Successes Weaken Its Draw, Strategists Say," *Washington Post*, November 25, 1998.

28. Dan Balz, "One Challenge for Bush: Remaking Image of Divided GOP," *Washington Post*, June 11, 1999.

29. A good brief summary of compassionate conservatism may be found in Alison Mitchell, "Bush Draws Campaign Theme from More than 'the Heart,'" *New York Times*, June 12, 2000.

30. Micky Kaus, "The Curse of 'Compassion': The Republicans Can Have It," Kausfiles.com, June 26, 1999, http://www.kausfiles.com/archive/index.06.26.99.html.

31. "The hope inside the Bush camp is that he can project a blend of conservative social values and a spirit of social justice that will define 'compassionate conservatism' as something more than a split-the-difference approach to bridging the GOP's divisions." Balz, "One Challenge for Bush."

32. George W. Bush, "Foreword," in Marvin Olasky, *Compassionate Conservatism: What It Is, What It Does, and How It Can Transform America* (New York: Free Press,

2000), pp. xi–xii. Olasky argued that American voluntary aid and charity had required some kind of work in exchange for food and shelter. Olasky also argued that what he called "the Early American Model of Compassion" relied on private, religious organizations (not government subsidies) and "the transforming power of faith." See Marvin Olasky, *The Tragedy of American Compassion* (Washington: Regnery Gateway, 1995), chap. 1; and W. W. Riggs, "Compassionate Conservatism Meets Communitarianism," in *George W. Bush: Evaluating the President at Midterm*, ed. Bryan Hilliard, Tom Lansford, and Robert P. Watson (Albany: State University of New York Press, 2004), p. 31.

33. Briggs summarizes Bush: government and charity should "become partners with government fulfilling the role of the 'subsidiarist,' whereby the state funds and monitors social policy but contracts it out to civil institutions." Riggs, "Compassionate Conservatism," p. 32.

34. Compassionate conservatism thus embraced the concept of subsidiarity, borrowed from Roman Catholic social thought. Subsidiarity stipulates that no large or more encompassing association should undertake what can be done by a smaller association. Charities should thus be the primary way of dealing with the needy rather than the federal government. A leading philosopher notes: "Subsidiarity . . . is a theory of and for civil society. It keeps alive alternatives between individualism, on the one hand, and collectivism, on the other." See Jean Bethke Elshtain, "Civil Society, Religion, and the Formation of Citizens," in *United We Serve: National Service and the Future of Citizenship*, ed. E. J. Dionne, Kayla Meltzer Drogosz, and Robert E. Litan (Washington: Brookings Institution Press, 2003), p. 220.

35. Shirley Anne Warshaw, *The Co-Presidency of Bush and Cheney* (Stanford, CA: Stanford University Press, 2009), p. 32.

36. See Ronald J. Pestritto and William J. Atto, "Introduction to American Progressivism," in *American Progressivism: A Reader*, ed. Ronald J. Pestritto and William J. Atto (Lanham, MD: Lexington Books, 2008), p. 11. The authors note the "remarkably explicit religious language employed by many progressive politicians." Ibid., p. 10.

37. Eldon J. Eisenach, *The Lost Promise of Progressivism* (Lawrence: University Press of Kansas, 1994), p. 189.

38. David M. Shribman, "George W. Bush's Main Man as Chief Strategist for the Bush Campaign, Karl Rove Tells the Candidate What to Say, When to Say It, How to Say It, and Where to Say It," *Boston Globe Magazine*, July 23, 2000, p. 10.

39. In his preface to Olasky's book, Bush mentioned "churches, synagogues, mosques, and charities" as the institutional reflection of compassionate conservatism. See Bush, "Preface," *Compassionate Conservatism*, p. xii.

40. Mitchell, "Bush Draws Campaign Theme." Traditionally Democrats had enjoyed strong support from Catholic voters. Republican presidential candidates begin to become competitive for the Catholic vote during the Reagan era. Clinton revived Democratic prospects among Catholic voters. Layman, *The Great Divide*, p. 107.

41. See Donna E. Shalala, Secretary, U.S. Department of Health and Human Services, Testimony on the President's FY 2000 Budget Request for HHS, before the Senate Appropriations Subcommittee on Labor, Health and Human Services, Education and Related Agencies, February 23, 1999, http://www.hhs.gov/asl/testify/t990223a.html.

42. "Voting Behavior in the 2000 Presidential Election: The Balance of Power in American Politics," CQ Press Electronic Library, CQ Voting and Elections Collection,

originally published in *The Elections of 2000* (Washington: CQ Press, 2001), http://library.cqpress.com/elections/elec00-134-6614-381961 (accessed March 18, 2009).

43. Barbara Burrell, *Women and Political Participation: A Reference Handbook* (Santa Barbara, CA: ABC-CLIO, 2004), p. 118.

44. The Bush team thought their candidate should in the general election "establish himself as an unconventional Republican, less bound by an unyielding conservative ideology, more open to practical solutions, sensitive to the aspects of life in America that cry out for improvement and prepared to offer fresh ideas." See Frank Bruni, "Bush Signaling a Readiness to Go His Own Way as an Unconventional Republican," *New York Times*, April 3, 2000.

45. Bush spoke of more funding for the military to keep the peace. Taxes should be cut so that Americans could keep more of their money. The speech also gave significant space to Bush's new proposal to offer personal accounts in addition to Social Security. He was quick to assure Social Security recipients that no changes would be made in their entitlement and that a new benefit for prescription drugs would be added during his presidency.

46. "Text of Bush Acceptance Speech," *USA Today*, November 4, 2000. Bush began his presidential campaign by promising not to shut down the Department of Education. See Bruni, "Bush Signaling."

47. "Text of Bush Acceptance Speech."

48. "The Political Year, 2000," CQ Press Electronic Library, CQ Voting and Elections Collection, originally published in *Congress and the Nation, 1997–2001*, vol. 10 (Washington: CQ Press, 2002), http://library.cqpress.com/elections/catn97-97-6342-324249 (accessed March 17, 2009).

49. Republicans also suffered in the struggle for voter identification, the most important factor affecting vote choice. The number of Americans identifying themselves as Republicans fell sharply between 1994 and 1998; in 2000, Republican Party identification remained where it had fallen two years earlier. Meanwhile citizens that most strongly identified with the GOP continued to fall from 1998 to 2000. The number of Americans professing a weak affiliation with either party, in contrast, rose sharply from 1998 to 2000. See American National Election Studies, *ANES Guide to Public Opinion and Electoral Behavior*, Table 2A.1, http://www.electionstudies.org/nesguide/gd-index.htm.

50. Ibid., Tables 9A.1.2 and 7A.2.

51. "Voting Behavior in the 2000 Presidential Election."

52. Gary Jacobson in 2000: "The battle for control of the House in 2002, then, is likely to be determined mainly by the Bush administration's performance in managing the economy. If the economy continues to grow and Bush maintains decent public approval ratings, redistricting may offset the usual midterm decline sustained by the president's party and the Republicans may hold on. But if history is any guide, the 2002 elections offer Democrats their best chance of retaking the Congress since they lost it in 1994." See "The Political Year, 2000," CQ Press Electronic Library, CQ Voting and Elections Collection, originally published in *Congress and the Nation, 1997–2001*, vol. 10 (Washington: CQ Press, 2002), http://library.cqpress.com/elections/catn97-97-6342-324249 (accessed March 17, 2009).

53. Andrew Rudalevige, "No Child Left Behind: Forging a Congressional Compromise," in *No Child Left Behind? The Politics and Practice of School Accountability*, ed. Paul E. Peterson and Martin R. West (Washington: Brookings Institution Press, 2003), pp. 34–35.

54. Ibid., p. 40.

55. Ibid., p. 38.

56. Ibid., pp. 41–42.

57. Ibid., pp. 42–43.

58. Congress had already approved charitable choice for four major federal programs, all with little public comment. The first charitable choice program was included in the 1996 welfare overhaul measure and allowed faith-based groups to compete for funding from the Temporary Assistance for Needy Families programs. Congress subsequently included charitable choice provisions in three other measures: the 1998 Community Services Block Grant Program (PL 105-285); the Children's Health Act (PL 106-310); and the Community Renewal Tax Relief Act of 2000 (PL 106-554). In the latter two, faith-based groups could apply for drug abuse and treatment grant programs. See "Faith-Based and Community Initiative Executive Orders, Signed by President George W. Bush," CQ Press Electronic Library, CQ Public Affairs Collection, originally published in *Historic Documents of 2001* (Washington: CQ Press, 2002), http://library.cqpress.com/cqpac/hsdc01-93-3609-181152 (accessed March 19, 2009).

59. Ibid. See also Kathryn Dunn Tenpas and Stephen Hess, "Organizing the Bush Presidency: Assessing Its Early Performance," in Gregg and Rozell, *Considering the Bush Presidency*, p. 41.

60. "GOP Resolution Squeaks By," CQ Press Electronic Library, *CQ Almanac* online edition, originally published in *CQ Almanac 2001* (Washington: Congressional Quarterly, 2002), http://library.cqpress.com/cqalmanac/cqal01-106-6386-328686 (accessed March 18, 2009).

61. See Bruce Bartlett, "The Difference between Keynesian Stimulus and Supply Side Tax Cuts," National Center for Policy Analysis, February 26, 2001.

62. See Stimson, yearly averages for 2001 and 2002 available at http://www.unc.edu/~jstimson/index.html.

63. The bill did not permit the Internal Revenue Service to disclose tax information to federal law enforcement and intelligence agents or allow information obtained by foreign government wiretaps to be used against Americans even if the wiretap was unconstitutional. The Senate bill also limited the attorney general's authority to jail noncitizens indefinitely. "Anti-Terror Bill Zooms into Law," CQ Press Electronic Library, *CQ Almanac* online edition, originally published in *CQ Almanac 2001* (Washington: Congressional Quarterly, 2002), http://library.cqpress.com/cqalmanac/cqal01-106-6376-328229 (accessed April 3, 2009).

64. Ibid.

65. For a detailed analysis of the provisions of the Patriot Act, see "Provisions of the Anti-Terrorism Law," CQ Press Electronic Library, *CQ Almanac* online edition, originally published in *CQ Almanac 2001* (Washington: Congressional Quarterly, 2002), http://library.cqpress.com/cqalmanac/cqal01-106-6376-328240 (accessed April 3, 2009).

66. "Texts of Presidential and Vice Presidential Debates, Vice President Al Gore, Texas Governor G. W. Bush, Senator J. I. Lieberman, R. B. Cheney," CQ Press Electronic Library, CQ Public Affairs Collection, originally published in *Historic Documents of 2000* (Washington: CQ Press, 2001), http://library.cqpress.com/cqpac/hsdc00-0000033488 (accessed March 20, 2009).

67. Colin Dueck, "Ideas and American Grand Strategy," *Review of International Studies* 30, no. 4 (2004): 514–15.

68. Ritchie and Rogers remark: "The Bush administration . . . came to power having articulated a worldview that had one foot in the political realist camp and the other in the primacist camp, a view that was characterised as hard-line realism or assertive nationalism." Nick Ritchie and Paul Rogers, *The Political Road to War with Iraq: Bush, 9/11 and the Drive to Overthrow Saddam* (New York: Routledge, 2007), p. 138. Up until September 11th, most of the Vulcans—a group of Bush's most crucial foreign policy advisers—reflected realism and assertive nationalism. See Ritchie and Rogers, *Political Road to War with Iraq*, p. 149. Some neoconservatives were concerned before September 11th that the new administration would act on "old world realpolitik." Richie and Rogers, *Political Road to War with Iraq*, p. 154. Michael Mazarr remarked in 2003: "It is easy to forget, now, that the early conventional wisdom held that President Bush and his foreign policy team in fact embraced realism as their guiding philosophy." Michael J. Mazarr, "George W. Bush, Idealist," *International Affairs* 79, no. 3 (2003): 504.

69. George W. Bush, "A Period of Consequences," a speech delivered at the Citadel, Charleston, SC, September 23, 1999, http://externalaffairs.citadel.edu/pres_bush.

70. John Guelke, "The Political Morality of the Neo-Conservatives: An Analysis," *International Politics* 42 (2005): 103.

71. Mazarr, "George W. Bush, Idealist," p. 506. This optimism about the potential of humans everywhere was shared by Paul Wolfowitz, a leading advocate of spreading democracy in the Middle East. Ibid.

72. "Before the 2000 election, Bush confessed to Saudi Ambassador Prince Bandar, 'I don't have the foggiest idea about what I think about foreign policy.' " Michael C. Desch. "America's Liberal Illiberalism: The Ideological Origins of Overreaction in U.S. Foreign Policy," *International Security* 32, no. 3 (Winter 2007–2008): 7–43. Ibid., p. 37. See quote to Woodward.

73. "Bush Evokes Jefferson, Calls for Tackling Society's Problems 'One Person at a Time,' " CQ Press Electronic Library, *CQ Almanac* online edition, originally published in *CQ Almanac 2000* (Washington: Congressional Quarterly, 2001), http://library.cqpress.com/cqalmanac/cqal00-834-24292-1081739 (accessed March 20, 2009).

74. See the September and October 2001 polling on presidential approval, "Job Performance Ratings for President Bush," November 8, 1990–January 15, 2009, Roper Center for Public Opinion, http://webapps.ropercenter.uconn.edu/CFIDE/roper/presidential/webroot/presidential_rating_detail.cfm?allRate = True&president Name = Bush.

75. Edward Walker, assistant secretary of state at the Bureau of Near Eastern Affairs under Clinton, wrote in March 2000: "Iraq under Saddam Hussein remains dangerous, unreconstructed and defiant. Saddam's record makes clear that he will remain a threat to regional peace and security as long as he remains in power. He will not relinquish what remains of his weapons of mass destruction arsenal. He will not live in peace with his neighbors. He will not cease the repression of the Iraqi people." Quoted in Ritchie and Rogers, *Political Road to War with Iraq*, pp. 23–24.

76. Ibid., p. 24.

77. Ibid., p. 34.

78. Ibid., p. 52

79. Ibid., p. 49.

80. William Kristol and Robert Kagan, "Toward a Neo-Reaganite Foreign Policy," *Foreign Affairs*, July–August 1996, p. 27.

81. Ibid., p. 28 (emphasis added).

82. Ibid., p. 32.

83. Stefan Halper and Jonathan Clarke, *America Alone: The Neo-Conservatives and the Global Order* (New York: Cambridge University Press, 2004), p. 161.

84. Ibid., pp. 169–70.

85. Ibid., p. 171.

86. Ibid., p. 177. Even many of the older generation of neoconservatives thought the United States fought the cold war to defend its people rather than to bring the blessings of democracy to the world. Ibid., p. 180.

87. Ibid., p. 178.

88. Irving Kristol, *Reflections of a Neoconservative: Looking Back, Looking Ahead* (New York: Basic Books, 1983), p. 117; and Michael C. Williams, "What Is the National Interest? The Neoconservative Challenge in IR Theory," *European Journal of International Relations* 11 (2005): 312.

89. Williams, "What Is the National Interest?" p. 317 and quotes therein.

90. See "President Bush's State of the Union Address to Congress and the Nation, *New York Times*, January 30, 2002, http://www.nytimes.com/2002/01/30/politics/30BTEX.html.

91. Halper and Clarke argue that Evangelicals and neoconservatives had much in common. Both opposed the 1960s counterculture as a danger to American society and morality. Both valued religion in daily life and worried about the emergence of an increasingly secular ethos in the United States. Both had similar political histories. Both groups had high hopes from Jimmy Carter and Ronald Reagan and both were disappointed. Reagan had disappointed the neoconservatives on the cold war while the Evangelicals were unhappy with abortion and social conservatism. Halper and Clarke, *America Alone*, pp. 196–97.

92. President Bush made the connection in remarks from February 2002. His administration would focus its national security effort on "countries which develop weapons of mass destruction, nations with a history of brutality. If they're ever able to mate up with terrorist organizations, the free world will be threatened." Iraq was a primary culprit in this regard along with Iran and North Korea. Quoted in Ritchie and Rogers, *Political Road to War with Iraq*, p. 87.

93. "President Bush's State of the Union Address." This passage in the speech was later incorporated in the National Security Strategy of the nation, see "The National Security Strategy of the United States," September 2002, p. 3, http://www.global security.org/military/library/policy/national/nss-020920.pdf.

94. Preface, "The National Security Strategy of the United States."

95. Ibid., p. 1.

96. See D. Andrew Austin, "Trends in Discretionary Spending," *CRS Reports to Congress*, March 26, 2008, pp. 1–2, including figures therein. The troubling question was whether 2002 would be an omen of a return to big government. That question remained unanswered at the close of the Bush administration. However, in the years after 2002, both defense and nondefense discretionary spending at first rose rapidly and then leveled off. Ibid.

97. See my account of the origins of McCain-Feingold in John Samples, *The Fallacy of Campaign Finance Reform* (Chicago: University of Chicago Press, 2006), chap. 8.

98. The new law included countercyclical payments based on crop prices. Bush had spoken in favor of the 1996 effort to liberalize agriculture markets in the 2000 campaign, but in the end, he did not want to risk a veto given that the partisan control of Congress was at stake in the 2002 elections. Experts estimated that the 2002 farm bill would cost $190 billion over its decade or $83 billion more than

the cost would have been of continuing the estimated status quo before the 1996 liberalization. Grain and cotton payments rose by 66 percent, price supports for wool and mohair returned, and new subsidies for some dairy farmers appeared in the law. Charles Stenholm, the ranking minority member of the House Agriculture Committee remarked: "The 1996 farm bill was a philosophical document written by the House committee leadership. It was an utter failure. It failed our farmers." See Eric Patashnik, "After the Public Interest Prevails: The Political Sustainability of Policy Reform," *Governance* 16 (April 2003): 219–20.

99. "Analysis of the Elections of 2002," CQ Press Electronic Library, CQ Voting and Elections Collection, originally published in Richard M. Scammon, Alice V. McGillivray, and Rhodes Cook, *America Votes 25* (Washington: CQ Press, 2003), http://library.cqpress.com/elections/amvt25-181-9622-602649 (accessed April 7, 2009).

100. This similarity of the election to previous midterms was noted by James E. Campbell, "The 2002 Midterm Election: A Typical or an Atypical Midterm?" *PS: Political Science and Politics* 36, no. 2 (April 2003): 203–7.

101. Gary C. Jacobson, "Terror, Terrain, and Turnout: Explaining the 2002 Midterm Elections," *Political Science Quarterly* 118 (Spring 2003): 9.

102. "Analysis of the Elections of 2002."

103. James Campbell estimates that the 2000 redistricting created more Republican-leaning districts. Campbell, "The 2002 Midterm Elections," p. 205. See also Jacobson, "Terror, Terrain, and Turnout," pp. 10–11.

104. Bureau of Economic Analysis, National Income and Product Accounts Table, Table 1.1.1. Percent Change from Preceding Period in Real Gross Domestic Product, http://www.bea.gov/national/nipaweb/TableView.asp?SelectedTable=1&FirstYear =2007&LastYear=2008&Freq=Qtr. The public's view of the economy was also negative and pessimistic. About one in four Gallup Poll respondents rated the economy "excellent" or "good," while three out of four saw it as "fair" or "poor," the worst assessment of the economy since 1994. People who thought the economy was getting worse outnumbered those who thought it was improving, 54 percent to 34 percent. Consumer confidence in the future of the economy was also quite low. See Jacobson, "Terror, Terrain, and Turnout," p. 8.

105. Campbell, "The 2002 Midterm Elections," p. 206.

106. For the results of a number of different surveys from that era, see "Job Performance Ratings for President Bush," November 8, 1990–January 15, 2009, Roper Center for Public Opinion, http://webapps.ropercenter.uconn.edu/CFIDE/roper/presidential/webroot/presidential_rating_detail.cfm?allRate=True&presidentName= Bush. Bush sought to exploit his popularity late both in fundraising and in campaign appearances for GOP candidates, the latter at a furious pace in the weeks just before election day. At the time, his campaigning for Republican candidates appeared to matter, but later analysis raised doubts on that score. Luke J. Keele, Brian J. Fogarty, and James A. Stimson, "Presidential Campaigning in the 2002 Congressional Elections," *PS: Political Science and Politics* 37, no. 4 (October 2004): 827–32.

107. Jacobson, "Terror, Terrain, and Turnout," p. 7, fn. 18.

108. Ibid., p. 4.

109. Ibid., p. 6.

110. Ibid. In October 2002, almost half of *Democrats* thought the Republican Party was more likely to "make the right decisions when it comes to dealing with terrorism." See ibid., question 4b, p. 14.

111. Ibid., p. 15.

112. Philip Everts and Pierangelo Isernia, "The War in Iraq and US Public Opinion," *Public Opinion Quarterly* 69, no. 2 (2005): 264–323; and Table 7, p. 279.

113. Ibid., Table 8, p. 280.

114. Ibid., pp. 264–323; and Table 10, p. 281.

115. Ibid., Table 16, p. 284.

116. Ibid., Table 27, p. 292.

117. Ibid., Table 31, pp. 297–98.

118. Ibid., Table 17, p. 285.

119. Ibid., pp. 264–323; and Table 20, p. 286.

120. Such evidence can be found later. Survey researcher Daniel Yankelovich would find in 2006 that only 20 percent of respondents ranked promoting democracy as a "very important goal" for American foreign policy. See Christopher A. Preble, *The Power Problem: How American Military Dominance Makes Us Less Safe, Less Prosperous, and Less Free* (Ithaca, NY: Cornell University Press, 2009), fn. 7, p. 204.

121. Everts and Isernia, "The War in Iraq," Table 10, p. 281.

122. Ibid., Table 16, p. 284.

123. Ibid., Table 17, p. 285.

124. Ibid., Table 18, p. 285.

125. Ibid., Table 31, p. 287. The question generally queries whether Bush had "presented enough evidence" to justify war. Notice, however, the drop in support for Bush in mid-February and early March on this question. In both cases, the sample sizes are unusually small.

126. Ibid., Table 27, p. 293.

127. Ibid., Table 30, p. 298. See also Christopher Gelpi, Peter D. Feaver, and Jason Reifler, *Paying the Human Costs of War: American Public Opinion and Casualties in Military Conflicts* (Princeton, NJ: Princeton University Press, 2009), pp. 128–29.

128. Thomas R. Oliver, Philip R. Lee, and Helene L. Lipton, "A Political History of Medicare and Prescription Drug Coverage," *Milbank Quarterly* 82 (2004): 307.

129. Ibid., p. 327.

130. Greg M. Shaw and Sarah E. Mysiewicz, "Social Security and Medicare," *Public Opinion Quarterly* 68 (2004): 403.

131. Jonathan Oberlander, "Through the Looking Glass: The Politics of the Medicare Prescription Drug Improvement and Modernization Act," *Journal of Health Politics, Policy and Law* 32 (2007): 191–92. The $400 billion estimate for the program may turn out to be low; others argued it would cost as much as $534 billion over the ensuing decade. Oliver, Lee, and Lipton, "A Political History of Medicare," p. 284.

132. Oberlander, "Through the Looking Glass," p. 190.

133. "The Bush administration believed that passing a Medicare drug benefit represented an important political opportunity for Republicans to take ownership of a Democratic issue and to make headway with elderly voters (whose considerable electoral presence will only grow as population ages). Medicare's expansion was instrumental to Bush adviser Karl Rove's 'grand design' of adding constituency groups to the Republicans' electoral coalition." Oberlander, "Through the Looking Glass," p. 190. "Republicans believed it allowed them to go into the 2004 elections having co-opted one of the Democrats' signature issues." See "Medicare Revamp Cuts It Close," CQ Press Electronic Library, *CQ Almanac* online edition, originally published in *CQ Almanac 2003* (Washington: Congressional Quarterly, 2004), http://library.cqpress.com/cqalmanac/cqal03-835-24327-1083636 (accessed April 9, 2009).

On the connection to "compassionate government," see Dana Milbank and Claudia Deane, "President Signs Medicare Drug Bill," *Washington Post*, December 9, 2003.

134. Oberlander, "Through the Looking Glass," pp. 195–96.

135. Eighty-nine percent of House and 83 percent of Senate Republicans voted in favor, while 92 percent of House and 76 percent of Senate Democrats voted against the bill. Ibid., p. 191.

136. Ibid., p. 190.

137. Oliver, Lee, and Lipton, "A Political History of Medicare," p. 329. Congress was wary about imposing costs because of the voter response to a 1988 effort to shift the costs of Medicare onto wealthier recipients. See ibid., p. 338.

138. For example, in separate polls from the 1999 to 2001 period, respondents supported increased Medicare spending and opposed higher payroll taxes to pay for the program by more than 60 percent. See Shaw and Mysiewicz, "Social Security and Medicare," pp. 401–2.

139. Oberlander, "Through the Looking Glass," p. 202.

140. Oliver, Lee, and Lipton, "A Political History of Medicare," p. 334.

141. David E. Campbell and J. Quin Monson, "The Religion Card, Gay Marriage and the 2004 Presidential Election," *Public Opinion Quarterly* 72 (Fall 2008): 403.

142. Ibid., pp. 403–4.

143. Ibid., p. 405.

144. Ibid., p. 406.

145. The effect of moral traditionalism on the 2004 contest has been examined by Kenneth Mulligan, "The 'Myth' of Moral Values Voting in the 2004 Presidential Election," *PS: Political Science and Politics* 41 (January 2008): 109–14.

146. See the table "GDP Percent Change from Previous Quarter," Bureau of Economic Analysis, National Economic Accounts, http://www.bea.gov/national/xls/gdpchg.xls.

147. See Fair's prediction from October 29, 2004, at http://fairmodel.econ.yale.edu/vote2004/vot1004.htm.

148. Author's calculations based on data available at http://www.uselectionatlas.org/RESULTS/.

149. Richard C. Eichenberg and Richard J. Stoll, *The Political Fortunes of War: Iraq and the Domestic Standing of President George W. Bush* (London: Foreign Policy Centre, July 2004), pp. 1–3. See "Job Performance Ratings for President Bush," for all approval ratings from the period, http://webapps.ropercenter.uconn.edu/CFIDE/roper/presidential/webroot/presidential_rating_detail.cfm?allRate=True&presidentName=Bush.

150. See the charts in Eichenberg and Stoll, *Political Fortunes of War*, pp. 7–10.

151. Ibid., p. 8.

152. See Eichenberg and Stoll's update of their study at http://www.ruf.rice.edu/~stoll/bushpop/.

153. Gary C. Jacobson, "The Effects of the George W. Bush Presidency on Partisan Attitudes," *Presidential Studies Quarterly* 39 (June 2009): 177.

154. See Gelpi, Feaver, and Reifler, *Paying the Human Costs of War*, chap. 6.

155. The authors report that Gallup Polls found that almost as many respondents reported that international concerns were the nation's "most important problem" as did economic concerns. Ibid., p. 172. However, in their survey, 60 percent of the respondents thought the economy was the top concern guiding vote choice while 30 percent assigned foreign policy the same status. Ibid., pp. 183–84. In the Gallup data,

it may be that the decline significance of economic concerns would be correlated with a rise in the importance of such issues to Bush's reelection. A strong economy might make a vote for the incumbent more likely.

156. The authors do indicate that believing the war was the right thing to do and would be successful predicts a vote for Bush even after controlling for a prospective evaluation of how well a candidate would handle social and economic issues. See ibid., p. 182, fn. 7. However, short-term retrospective evaluations of the economy have been found to strongly influence vote choices. See Larry M. Bartels, "Constituency Opinion and Congressional Policy Making: The Reagan Defense Build Up," *American Political Science Review* 85 (June 1991): 457–74.

157. See the charts at http://www.pollster.com/polls/us/issue-iraq-rightormistake.php.

158. Oliver, Lee, and Lipton, "A Political History of Medicare," pp. 284–85.

159. Shaw and Mysiewicz, "Social Security and Medicare," p. 404.

160. See Gallup Brain, Question: qn5N FormB: Do you think the Republicans in Congress or the Democrats in Congress would do a better job of dealing with each of the following issues and problems? How about — Health care costs? survey dates January 3, 2003–January 5, 2003

161. See Fox News/Opinion Dynamics poll, February 18–19, 2004 available at www.opiniondynamics.com.

162. In states with a gay marriage ban (GMB) on the ballot, "Bush turned out more evangelicals, thus adding to his share of the vote. Conversely, in those same states, secularists were more likely to abstain. Importantly, we find no evidence that Kerry picked up votes among secularists in GMB states. . . . Republican-leaning evangelicals increased their probability of voting for Bush from .49 in a non-GMB state to .64 in a state with a GMB on the ballot. Secularist GOP leaners, meanwhile, went from a probability of voting for Bush of .63 in a state without a GMB, to only .27 in a GMB state. . . . Bush's evangelical gains and the secularist losses came at the expense of abstainers, with Kerry's vote total unaffected. . . . The probability that a Republican-leaning evangelical abstained was .13 in a non-GMB state, dropping to .04 where gay marriage was on the ballot. On the other hand, abstention among GOP-leaning secularists rose from .06 in a non-GMB state to .39 in states with a GMB." Campbell and Monson, "The Religion Card," p. 413.

163. http://www.presidency.ucsb.edu/ws/index.php?pid=58745

164. See the charts at http://www.pollster.com/polls/us/issue-iraq-rightormistake.php.

165. See the trends reported on the chart in Charles Franklin, "Three Elements of Iraq War Opinion," Pollster.com, September 10, 2007, http://www.pollster.com/blogs/three_elements_of_iraq_war_opi.php.

166. See the trends reported in "National Job Approval: President George W. Bush," November 10, 2008, http://www.pollster.com/polls/us/jobapproval-bush.php.

167. Shortly after winning reelection, Bush remarked: "Let me put it to you this way. I earned capital in the campaign, political capital, and now I intend to spend it." See "President Bush on Social Security," CQ Press Electronic Library, CQ Public Affairs Collection, originally published in *Historic Documents of 2005* (Washington: CQ Press, 2006), http://library.cqpress.com/cqpac/hsdc05-429-18655-1003703 (accessed April 23, 2009). Like Bill Clinton before him, George W. Bush overestimated his political capital after an election victory. See Terry Weiner, "Touching the Third

Rail: Explaining the Failure of Bush's Social Security Initiative," *Politics & Policy* 35 (2007): 893.

168. Jacobson, "Effects of the Bush Presidency," p. 175.

169. "Bush Renews Effort to Create Tax-Free Savings Accounts," *CQ Weekly*, January 31, 2004, p. 280, http://library.cqpress.com/cqpac/weeklyreport108-000000989552 (accessed April 23, 2009).

170. "President Bush on Social Security," CQ Press Electronic Library, CQ Public Affairs Collection, originally published in *Historic Documents of 2005* (Washington: CQ Press, 2006), http://library.cqpress.com/cqpac/hsdc05-429-18655-1003703 (accessed April 23, 2009).

171. I write "perceived" because Bush's actual proposal did not change the program for current recipients or those near retirement.

172. "That Social Security's crisis . . . was set to occur at some distant future date . . . makes success unlikely." Weiner, "Touching the Third Rail," p. 894.

173. "President Bush on Social Security."

174. Weiner, "Touching the Third Rail," p. 888.

175. Philip Sherwell, "Christians Give Bush Ultimatum to Ban Gay Marriage," *Sunday Telegraph* (UK), January 30, 2005.

176. "President Bush on Social Security."

177. See the remarks of Republican Senator Lindsey Graham, quoted in Weiner, "Touching the Third Rail," p. 891.

178. Ibid., p. 889.

179. "President Bush on Social Security."

180. Jacobson, "Effects of the Bush Presidency," p. 178.

181. Matthew Eshbaugh-Soha and Jeffrey S. Peake, "The Contemporary Presidency: 'Going Local' to Reform Social Security," *Presidential Studies Quarterly* 36 (November 2006): 700.

182. "President Bush on Social Security."

183. Martha Derthick remarked in 1994, "A public that has become generally distrustful of government is likely to be skeptical of changes that are hard to comprehend and easy to criticize, as virtually any conceivable change will be." See Martha Derthick, "Reflections on 'Policymaking for Social Security,' " *PS: Political Science and Politics* 37 (July 2004): 444.

184. See "Three Elements of Iraq War Opinion" chart, http://www.pollster.com/blogs/1ReviewofWarOpinionlarge.php.

185. Keep in mind that Bush's approval rating declined steadily from January to November 2005. If we extrapolate the trend in Bush's approval rating from January to mid-August 2005 (Hurricane Katrina struck in late August), we would expect the president to have a 40 percent approval rating by mid-November. The trend in polling on presidential approval ended up just above 38 percent by November. Thereafter, Bush's approval rating began to climb. Bush's decline in support after Katrina seems consistent with the trend before the storm. Author's calculations based on data at Roper Center for Public Opinion, http://webapps.ropercenter.uconn.edu/CFIDE/roper/presidential/webroot/presidential_rating.cfm. See also the trend charted at Pollster.com, http://www.pollster.com/polls/us/jobapproval-bush.php. That trend closely follows declining public approval of Bush's handling of the war in Iraq; that measure of the president's popularity went into free fall from mid-August to early October 2005. The uptick in Bush's approval rating follows a rise in public approval of

his handling of Iraq beginning in mid-November. See the data charted at Pollster.com, http://www.pollster.com/blogs/three_elements_of_iraq_war_opi.php.

186. Her husband's efforts to discontinue her feeding were opposed by her parents over a seven-year period. In March 2005, Congress tried to transfer the case to the federal courts to overturn state court rulings that permitted removing Schiavo's feeding tube. Congressional Republicans acted at the behest of pro-life Christians and believed the case offered potential political benefits. A memo to GOP Senator Mel Martinez (R-FL) argued that intervening in the Schiavo case offered several potential political benefits, including an appeal to pro-life groups: "This is an important moral issue and the pro-life base will be excited that the Senate is debating this important issue." See Mike Allen, "Counsel to GOP Senator Wrote Memo on Schiavo; Martinez Aide Who Cited Upside for Party Resigns," *Washington Post*, April 7, 2005; and *Washington Post*, "GOP Memo Says Issue Offers Political Rewards," *Seattle Times*, April 4, 2005.

187. Rep. Randy Cunningham (R-CA) had pleaded guilty in 2005 to accepting millions in bribes related to defense contracts. A former lobbyist associated with the GOP, Jack Abramoff, was convicted of conspiracy, mail fraud, and tax evasion. He agreed to testify for prosecutors. Eventually, two former aides to Tom DeLay, the House majority leader, were convicted of federal charges related to bribery in the Abramoff case. Bob Ney (R-OH), a former chair of the House Administration Committee, pleaded guilty to accepting bribes from Abramoff. His plea came two weeks before the 2006 election. A Democratic prosecutor in Austin, Texas, had brought charges against DeLay for violating Texas campaign finance law. DeLay resigned from his seat in Congress in June 2006. Later as the election drew closer, a scandal emerged involving alleged solicitation of House pages by Rep. Mark Foley (R-FL). See Susan Ferrechio, "2006 Legislative Summary: Ethics Investigations," *CQ Weekly*, December 18, 2006, p. 3339, http://library.cqpress.com/cqpac/weeklyreport109-000002418334 (accessed April 28, 2009). On Ney, see Susan Schmidt and James V. Grimaldi, "Ney Pleads Guilty to Corruption Charges; Lawmaker's Conviction is 8th in Abramoff Probe," *Washington Post*, October 14, 2006.

188. Robert J. Blendon and Drew Altman, "Voters and Health Care in the 2006 Election," *New England Journal of Medicine* 355 (2006): 1931.

189. Sixty-one percent of respondents believed that the Democratic Party was more likely to make prescription drugs for the elderly affordable, while only 18 percent felt that the Republican Party would.

190. Forty-eight percent answered "not working." See Gallup Survey, Questionnaire: April Wave 2, April 28, 2006–April 30, 2006, question 34, http://institution.gallup.com.

191. See the chart reporting support from surveys conducted by the Kaiser Family Foundation, Kaiser Health Poll Report, "The Public on Prescription Drugs for Seniors," March–April 2005, p. 3, http://www.kff.org/healthpollreport/apr_2005/1.cfm. Note that public support for adding the entitlement was higher at several points during the 1990s.

192. Kaiser, *Public Opinion Spotlight*, p. 7 available at http://www.kff.org/spotlight/.

193. Patel Kant and Mark Rushefsky, *Health Care Politics and Policy in America* (Armonk, NY: M. E. Sharpe, 2006), p. 168.

194. Charles Franklin, "Iraq Opinion Review," Pollster.com, January 10, 2007, http://www.pollster.com/blogs/iraq_opinion_review.php.

195. http://www.cnn.com/ELECTION/2006/pages/results/states/US/H/00/epolls.0.html.

196. The human costs of the Iraq War appear to have had a decisive effect on key Senate races. See Scott Sigmund Gartner and Gary M. Segura, "All Politics Are Still Local: The Iraq War and the 2006 Midterm Elections," *PS: Political Science and Politics* 41 (January 2008): 95–100.

197. "Voter Discontent Fuels Democrats' Day," *CQ Weekly* 64, no. 44 (November 13, 2006): 2983, http://library.cqpress.com/cqpac/weeklyreport109-000002401371 (accessed April 28, 2009).

198. Political scientist Gary Jacobson remarks: "In 2006, with Bush's pre-election approval rating at 38%, Republicans lost 31 House seats and control of Congress." Gary C. Jacobson, "The War, the President, and the 2006 Midterm Congressional Elections," paper presented at the Annual Meeting of the Midwest Political Science Association, the Palmer House Hilton, Chicago, Illinois, April 12–15, 2007, pp. 1–2. And in 2008, with only 25 percent approving, Republicans lost another 21 House seats, leaving the Democrats with a 257–178 majority. "A conventional regression model of House seat swings as a function of presidential approval, real income change, and seat exposure predicts Republicans to lose 37 seats in 2006 and 20 seats in 2008." Gary C. Jacobson, "Effects of the Bush Presidency," *Presidential Studies Quarterly* 39 (June 2009): 201.

199. Jacobson, "Effects of the Bush Presidency," pp. 178–82.

200. Ibid., p. 191.

201. David W. Brady, Douglas Rivers, and Laurel Harbridge, "The 2008 Democratic Shift," *Policy Review*, no. 152 (December 2008–January 2009), http://www.hoover.org/publications/policyreview/35560574.html.

Chapter 7

1. I cannot exclude the possibility that had Carter won in 1980 and later Democrats succeeded him, the same relative constraint in spending would have happened. The Clinton experience of 1993–94 and the Obama experience in 2009 suggest this counterfactual is unlikely, but it cannot be excluded.

2. Ross Douthat and Reihan Salam, *Grand New Party: How Republicans Can Win the Working Class and Save the American Dream* (New York: Doubleday, 2008). The authors note that Nixon offered a "positive program" that would build a new majority by reconciling ideological conservatism with operational liberalism. Electronic book reader, Loc. 952.

3. Ibid., loc. 111.

4. Ibid., loc. 117.

5. David Frum, *Comeback: Conservatism That Can Win Again* (New York: Broadway Books, 2008, with an afterword, 2009), p. 3.

6. Ibid., p. 5.

7. Ibid., p. 13.

8. Ibid., pp. 29, 179.

9. Ibid., p. 29.

10. Frum argues for developing a permanent capacity to "nation-build" that suggests a future need in failed states. See ibid., p. 160.

11. David Brady, Douglas Rivers, and Laurel Harbridge, "The 2008 Democratic Shift," *Policy Review*, no. 152 (December 2008–January 2009), http://www.hoover.org/publications/policyreview/35560574.html.

12. Gerald F. Seib, "Health Care Debate Isn't about Health," *Wall Street Journal*, August 11, 2009.

13. See the trend reported by James Stimson in the table titled "Public Policy Mood: 1952 to 2008," http://www.unc.edu/~jstimson/.

14. After 1985, defense spending relative to national wealth declined. See "Budget of the United States Government, Fiscal Year 2009, Historical Tables," White House, Washington, 2008, Table 5.1, p. 87, http://www.whitehouse.gov/omb/budget/fy2009/pdf/hist.pdf.

15. See the *Washington Post*-ABC News poll, March 29, 2009, http://www.washingtonpost.com/wp-srv/politics/polls/postpoll_072009.html, which found 62 percent of respondents view Obama in this way.

16. James A. Stimson, *Tides of Consent: How Public Opinion Shapes American Politics* (New York: Cambridge University Press, 2004), p. 63. The New Deal promised "that government will be used to intervene in the economy to promote the welfare of those who might be harmed by the excesses of laissez-faire."

17. William E. Leuchtenburg, "Progressivism and Imperialism: The Progressive Movement and American Foreign Policy 1989–1916," *Mississippi Valley Historical Review* 39 (December 1952): 483–504.

18. Just fewer than 40 percent of House Democrats voted for the Iraq war resolution; 55 percent of Senate Democrats voted yes on the measure. On the other hand, 1 Republican in the Senate and 6 House GOP members voted against the war. For the votes, follow the links available at http://thomas.loc.gov/cgi-bin/bdquery/z?d107:HJ00114:@@@R.

19. Democrats, like Republicans, appear devoted to criminalizing drug use by consenting adults. The question between the parties seems to be whether people's conduct should be overseen for religious or Progressive reasons. Neither party believes virtue and vice remain the responsibility of the individual. Of course, the parties do disagree about whose conduct should be controlled by public officials.

20. See the three-question measure of libertarianism based on American National Election Studies data in David Boaz and David Kirby, "The Libertarian Vote 2009," unpublished manuscript, Cato Institute, 2009.

21. I assume that the debt is not inflated away or renounced. The latter is not likely; the former may be.

22. Such programs are not realistic absent large productivity gains for what government offers, an unlikely scenario. Defense spending may be an exception. Apart from nuclear weapons, American defense forces are surely capable of killing more people and destroying more property per dollar expended than they were in earlier years. But, of course, it is not legitimate to exclude nuclear weapons from this calculation.

23. Christina D. Romer and David H. Romer, "Do Tax Cuts Starve the Beast? The Effect of Tax Changes on Government Spending," *Brookings Papers on Economic Activity* (Spring 2009): 139–214.

24. See William A. Niskanen, *Reaganomics: An Insider's Account of the Policies and the People* (New York: Oxford University Press, 1988), p. 313.

25. Internal Revenue Service, Individual Income Tax Rates and Tax Shares, Table 5, http://www.irs.gov/taxstats/indtaxstats/article/0,,id = 133521,00.html#_grp2.

26. Scott A. Hodge, "Number of Americans Paying Zero Federal Income Tax Grows to 43.4 Million," *Fiscal Facts*, March 30, 2006, http://www.taxfoundation.org/files/ff54.pdf.

27. A good and accessible introduction to consumption taxes is Al Ehrbar, "Consumption Tax," in *The Concise Encyclopedia of Economics*, ed. David R. Henderson (Indianapolis: Liberty Fund, 2008), pp. 83–86. I put aside the question of whether a majority would enact a consumption tax if a progressive income tax were an alternative.

28. Perhaps a small degree of progressivity in a consumption tax would be compatible with an improved matching of the costs and benefits of government.

29. European nations rely heavily on a consumption tax on value added to a product at each stage of production, the value-added tax, or VAT. The VAT obscures the cost of government, thereby making it harder to overcome the fiscal illusion that marginal public spending has not marginal costs. For evidence that a VAT does facilitate larger government, see Michael Keen and Ben Lockwood, "Is the VAT a Money Machine?" *National Tax Journal* 59 (December 2006): 905.

30. Here, I understand the Constitution of 1789 to include its first 12 amendments.

31. The first year of the Obama administration ended with a similar low level of trust of the government. "Only 23 percent say they trust government 'just about always' or 'most of the time,' which is the lowest number on this question since 1997." See Mark Murray, "Support for Afghanistan Troop Surge Rises," October 28, 2009, http://www.msnbc.msn.com/id/33495798/.

32. Congressional Budget Office, *The Budget and Economic Outlook: An Update* (Washington: Congress of the United States, August 2009), Table 1-1, p. 2.

33. Estimates of the costs of health care spending are available. It seems likely that they underestimate the costs significantly. See Donald Marron, "Yes, the House Health Bill Costs More than $1.2 Trillion," November 2, 2009, http://dmarron.com/2009/11/02/yes-the-house-health-bill-costs-more-than-1-2-trillion/.

34. In 2008, "Last year, outlays for those three programs combined (not including offsetting receipts) accounted for about 9 percent of GDP. Spending for those programs is expected to rise rapidly over the next 10 years, outstripping the growth of GDP. By 2019, such spending is projected to total nearly 12 percent of GDP. Under long-term projections recently published by CBO, spending for those programs would continue to rise and could total almost 17 percent of GDP by 2035 if no changes are made to current law." Congressional Budget Office, *The Budget and Economic Outlook*, p. 26. In the longer run, these commitments would lead to a doubling of the federal share of GDP by 2080. By 2050, the government would have increased by 50 percent relative to national wealth. See Keith Hennessey, "America's Long Run Fiscal Problem Is Spending Growth, Not Taxes," April 16, 2009, http://keithhennessey.com/2009/04/16/americas-long-run-fiscal-problem-is-spending-growth-not-taxes/. Hennessey reports here projections of spending prepared by the Office of Management and Budget.

35. See Congressional Budget Office, *The Long-Term Budget Outlook* (Washington: Congress of the United States, June 2009), Table 1-2, p. 6.

36. Thomas J. Sargent and François R. Velde, "Macroeconomic Features of the French Revolution," *Journal of Political Economy* 103 (June 1995): 476.

37. The late 1990s would appear to be an exception to this expectation. As we saw, however, that short period of balanced budgets quickly came undone through spending increases. The balance of the time also depended on a rate of economic growth that proved unsustainable.

Index

Page references followed by t or f denote tables or figures, respectively.

About the Author

John Samples directs the Center for Representative Government at the Cato Institute. His book *The Fallacy of Campaign Finance Reform* was published by the University of Chicago Press in the fall of 2006. He has edited three books for the Cato Institute, including *Welfare for Politicians: Taxpayer Financing of Campaigns* (2005). Samples co-directed the Brookings-Cato project on the decline of electoral competition that led to the volume he co-edited entitled *The Marketplace of Democracy* (2006). Samples previously served as director of the Georgetown University Press and vice president of The Twentieth Century Fund. He received a Ph.D. in political science from Rutgers University.

Cato Institute

Founded in 1977, the Cato Institute is a public policy research foundation dedicated to broadening the parameters of policy debate to allow consideration of more options that are consistent with the traditional American principles of limited government, individual liberty, and peace. To that end, the Institute strives to achieve greater involvement of the intelligent, concerned lay public in questions of policy and the proper role of government.

The Institute is named for *Cato's Letters*, libertarian pamphlets that were widely read in the American Colonies in the early 18th century and played a major role in laying the philosophical foundation for the American Revolution.

Despite the achievement of the nation's Founders, today virtually no aspect of life is free from government encroachment. A pervasive intolerance for individual rights is shown by government's arbitrary intrusions into private economic transactions and its disregard for civil liberties.

To counter that trend, the Cato Institute undertakes an extensive publications program that addresses the complete spectrum of policy issues. Books, monographs, and shorter studies are commissioned to examine the federal budget, Social Security, regulation, military spending, international trade, and myriad other issues. Major policy conferences are held throughout the year, from which papers are published thrice yearly in the *Cato Journal*. The Institute also publishes the quarterly magazine *Regulation*.

In order to maintain its independence, the Cato Institute accepts no government funding. Contributions are received from foundations, corporations, and individuals, and other revenue is generated from the sale of publications. The Institute is a nonprofit, tax-exempt, educational foundation under Section 501(c)3 of the Internal Revenue Code.

CATO INSTITUTE
1000 Massachusetts Ave., N.W.
Washington, D.C. 20001
www.cato.org